THE LADY
AND THE
PRESIDENT

The Life and Loss of the *S.S. President Coolidge*

Front Cover: *The Lady*, a wall ornament in the First Class Smoking Room of the *SS President Coolidge*. Troops abandon ship as the *President Coolidge* lists to port on the reef at Espiritu Santo.

A PROUDLY AUSTRALIAN BOOK

UFELA OLGETA OLSEM FIS SUPOS YU KAM LONG VANUATU,
ME MAEKEM BLONG SPEL YU HAPI TO MUS.

First printing 1997.
Second printing 1999.
Third printing 2006.

THE LADY AND THE PRESIDENT
The Life and Loss of the *S.S. President Coolidge*.

Published by Oceans Enterprises
303-305 Commercial Road, Yarram, Victoria 3971, Australia

National library of Australia Cataloguing-in-Publication entry:

Stone, Peter, 1943-
The lady and the president.
Bibliography.
Includes index.
ISBN 0 9586657 2 9

1. President Coolidge (Troopship).
2. World War, 1939-1945 - Pacific Area.
3. Scuba diving - Vanuatu - Esp*iritu Santo Island.
4. Esp*iritu Santo (Vanuatu) - Description. And travel.
I. Title.

359.985830973

THE LADY

AND THE

PRESIDENT

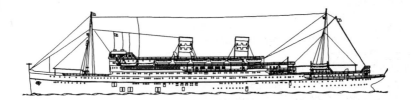

The Life and Loss of the
S.S. President Coolidge

Peter Stone
with Allan Power and Reece Discombe

Geographical names:

Names vary between military and general reports. To maintain a standard, geographical names have been standardised from the Admiralty Chart, Espiritu Santo #179. If a geographical name varies, it is usually by one or two characters, and is easily recognisable, however should there be a possibility of confusion, alternative names are indicated in the text. If name is not on the Admiralty Chart, the text used for spelling has been the Lonely Planet Publications book on Vanuatu. This may not necessarily be the definitive word - but it is a popular book. Of note: Bogacio Island was later reamed Bokissa Island. Aesi Island protecting Palikulo Bay on the east coast has various spellings, but all are recognisable; but not to be confused with Aore Island south of Segond Channel. Palikulo is also spelt in various ways.

Units

Both the imperial and metric system are used by divers to the *SS President Coolidge*, hence both units have been used throughout the book.

1 mile = 1.6 kilometre = 1609 metres = 1760 yards
1 kilometre =- 0.621 miles
1 knot = 1 nautical mile per hour = 30.85 metres per minute
1 nautical mile = 1852 metres
1 ft = .305 metres = 30.5 centimetres
1 metre = 3.28 ft

Deck levels.

The engineering plans for the President Coolidge differ from that referred to as Cabin Plans, the latter being used by passengers to select a suitable cabin and to navigate the ship. It is not known why this has occurred. The Cabin Plan designation has been used throughout the book. The following chart shows the comparison.

Accommodation plans:	Engineering drawings:
Sun Deck (Navigation Deck)	Sun Deck (Navigation Bridge)
Boat Deck	Boat Deck
Promenade Deck	Promenade Deck (A - Deck)
A - Deck	Bridge Deck (B - Deck)
B - Deck	C - Deck (Shelter Deck)
C - Deck	D - Deck (Upper Deck)
D - Deck	E - Deck (Main Deck)
E - Deck	F - Deck (Lower Deck)

Greenwich Mean Time is 11 hours behind Vanuatu. Hence 9.00 am on 26 October is 10.00 pm GMT. This is perhaps why some reports show the *President Coolidge* as having sunk on 25 October. GCT is Greenwich Civil Time and is the US Military nomenclature for 'local time'. All times referred to in this publication are local time. If referring to military time, the 24 hour clock is used, ie 1300 hours is 1.00 pm.

CHAPTERS

FOREWORD

When I arrived in the New Hebrides fifty years ago, in 1947, World War 2 had been over for not quite two years, the military installations in Santo were as the US forces had left them. Santo consisted of five stores, no Chinese and not one house on the eastern side of the Sarakata River. Not even a place to stay. Quonset huts and warehouses were full of war material. No one was game to touch this material, as we always thought that the Americans would come back and remove it all. However, this never eventuated. Very few New Hebrideans could be seen in the area. Some of the planters who lived on adjacent islands visited Santo occasionally. The only white people around in these early post-war years were men like Tom Harris, Mat Wells, Pascal Michelle, Robby Robinson, Lenis Harvery, Jean Simmonson, Robert De Plonque, La Borde, the Gardels, Leon Wright, Charles Grazianni. They have all passed on, but it was through these people that I gathered much information on the establishment of the base at Santo.

In 1942 the Japanese had already landed in the Solomon islands. With the Japanese heading south, the Americans were on their way north from New Caledonia. The rapid Japanese advance was halted during the Battle of Santa Cruz, a small group of islands halfway between the New Hebrides and the Solomon Islands. This marked the turning point of the war.

Before a foothold was established in the Solomon Islands, every sortie had to be carried out from Santo or Vila. Bombers would drops their bombs and return, whilst the fighters would fly to the war zone, have a shoot out or strafe with their machine guns and return, a distance of around 650 miles one way. Many planes were lost or ran out of fuel and crashed in the sea or in the dense jungles of Espiritu Santo. Many still remain unaccounted for and are being found in the jungles after fifty years.

Santo was the largest U.S. military base in the south-west Pacific, with warehouses for supplies, docking and repair facilities, engine and aircraft maintenance. There is still much evidence of this on the island. Fifty years ago the planters would talk about a huge ship lying on the seabed in the Segond Channel. I was determined to locate the wreck and dive on it. One must remember that fifty years ago the Aqualung had not reached Australia nor the United States. Most of our diving was done with home-made equipment using high altitude oxygen cylinders used in aircraft. Even the regulators had aluminium parts and these did not last long in the salt water.

I had two very good French friends who like myself were very ardent divers and between us we spent many long hours in the sea, looking for American equipment, and fish. Of course, a dive on the *President Coolidge* was foremost in our lives. Robert Charles, Jean Desplat and myself made a very good team, and we dived the destroyer *USS Tucker*, Million Dollar Point, Aisse Island where the giant floating dock was located - and the *President Coolidge*. To locate the wreck we dragged a grapple off the bottom until we caught on something. On our first dive, the grapple had caught on the railing around the bridge.

We needed many many dives to have a good close look at this giant of a wreck. I had the first Cousteau-Gagnan double-hose regulator that came into the Pacific; Robert Charles and I used these with four oxygen cylinders (filled with air at 1800 psi). This we called 'Cousteau's Monster'. Jean managed to purchase a complete Cousteau-Gagnan rig from France.

Many stories have been written in various magazines and books as to what went on at the base at Santo. Some information has been incorrect, and in order to bolster the sensational, it has been quoted that over a half a million men were stationed at Santo. In actual fact, there was only a maximum 47,000 stationed there, although some 500,000 could have passed through during the period of the war. To add to the romanticism of the place, it was said that Dorothy Lamour swam at the famous Blue Hole. She was never there. And how many people did die in the mining of the *President Coolidge*?. Certainly not five as indicated in some publications.

Over the past few years I had given much thought to correcting some of these fables. With my knowledge of the military base at Santo, and Allan Power's knowledge of the *President Coolidge*, there was sufficient first-hand information to put together a book on Santo. Allan, being the uncrowned 'captain' of the *President Coolidge* (Mr. President as he is sometimes called), has an intimate knowledge of the wreck; I on the other hand have a wealth of information on the New Hebrides, and also re-located the wreck at the end of the war.

Allan said he couldn't write well enough for such a venture, and as for myself, the first thing I do when I buy a typewriter is to file off the commas. We can both talk about our adventures, but not write about them. So enter, Peter Stone. I had known Peter for some fifteen years, introduced by that remarkable diver and gentleman, and fellow countryman, the late Kelly Tarlton. Peter has had a long standing interest in the *President Coolidge* and helped to promote tourism to the wreck in the early 1980s. His writing style and practical experience could not be surpassed, so vast that Peter was the obvious choice for such a story, aided by his great knowledge and the many stories he has written over the years. To add to this choice was Peter's knowledge of modern day computers, the Internet, e-mail and his ability to use the media for research. He has found material that we never new existed, and located people who had a direct influence on events in Santo and the sinking of the *President Coolidge*.

This is therefore a book based on first hand observations and experiences, and far surpasses the impersonal war history texts that abound. It is a book that records the life and loss of the *President Coolidge* and equally important, makes for most interesting reading. Peter has done an excellent job and I for one am proud to have been associated with *The Lady and the President*.

Reece Discombe
Port Vila, Vanuatu.
August 1997.

Often I have divers ask, 'Is there a book on the *President Coolidge* that I can buy?'. Well, here it is. For the first time the correct information on her loss, and the dives available on the wreck appear together in this long awaited book.

Thousands of divers have dived on the wreck of the *President Coolidge* since I first dived it in 1969. Like myself, many have become Coolidge addicts. Once a diver has been bitten by the Coolidge bug he or she is done for. The wreck has a fascination for many divers like no other wreck in the world. Its sheer enormity, its accessibility and the intact artifacts and fittings that are still there for all to see bring divers back again and again.

The *President Coolidge* is a huge time capsule with not only the interest of the 1930s fittings and furnishings but also the added attraction of its wartime armament, military cargo and personal possessions of the troops that it carried.

I have often been asked, 'Is the *President Coolidge* a safe wreck to dive?' I would say there is no such thing as a safe wreck, only a safe diver. Due to its size and stable condition, the *President Coolidge* is a comfortable wreck to dive and will still be an interesting dive a hundred years from now.

Peter Stone has done meticulous research to bring all the true facts together in this book. Right from the start we said, 'Let's get it right'.

The book is not intended as a do-it-yourself guide to the *President Coolidge*. The wreck is very much a site where the services of an experienced dive guide are needed. With this book, you will now have a greater appreciation of the ship and what she has to offer.

Allan Power
Espiritu Santo, Vanuatu.
August 1997.

PREFACE

The first time I was introduced to the Lady was in 1982. It was my second dive on the *President Coolidge*, Allan Power having first checked me out on the bridge and forward holds. At the time I was a partner in a travel company specialising in diving tours, and we were planning to promote Vanuatu. I had no idea at the time how magnificent the President was, and how beautiful the Lady would appear in the gloom of the First Class Smoking Room. Both Allan Power and Reece Discombe speak of their apprehension on diving the ship for the first time. Her size is awesome, and she rightly deserved the title of the world's largest accessible shipwreck. I was also to marvel at how easy that accessibility was - a short walk off shore, a swim of fifty metres and there she was.

Our travel company enthusiastically promoted Espiritu Santo and I would like to think that we did much to bring the ship to the notice of divers worldwide. I was writing and photographing for dive, travel and airline magazines at the time, so an appropriate medium was available for such promotion. A friendship and respect developed with Allan and I have dived The Lady on many occasions, although on my last visit in 1996 I simply had no time as I was deep into research interviewing Allan and making use of his wealth of verbal and written information. Reece I had met in New Zealand a few years prior to my first visit to Vanuatu, introduced by the remarkable diver and entrepreneur Kelly Tarlton who had a shipwreck museum at Pahia. Reece had arrived in the New Hebrides in 1947; Allan arrived twenty-two years later. Reece was one of the first post-war divers on the *President Coolidge*; Allan came with a salvage team and never left.

With my writing interests it was not long before I realised that divers and maritime enthusiasts should have further knowledge on the life and loss of the *President Coolidge*. I was about to write this book many years ago, but a documentary film producer said he was going to do one, so I backed off. Ten years was long enough to wait, and so I started research again in 1992. I soon realised the wealth of knowledge that Allan and Reece had, and it was not difficult to get their support. They had already discussed the possibility of a book, and my interest boosted their enthusiasm. Reece gained the support of the government of the Republic of Vanuatu through their airlines, Air Vanuatu and Vanair, the government being well aware of the importance of the ship to tourism. With Allan and Reece providing the foundation material for the book, I was able to add a considerable amount of material through further research which brought me in contact with men who had been on the ship at the time she was lost, and even those who had laid the mines that led to her demise. My knowledge of the wreck through diving, although not as intimate as that of Allan, held me in good stead to write the story of The Lady and the President.

Although appropriately acknowledged elsewhere in the book, I must emphasise that *The Lady and the President* could not have been produced without the support of Reece Discombe and Allan Power. With their input I was able to produce a book that leant heavily on personal experiences and anecdotes, combined with the required measure of historic fact. Add a little supposition, suspense and intrigue, and the book is made. Chapters on the development of the base at Espiritu Santo, Million Dollar Point, and the loss of the *USS Tucker*, have been added as they complement the story of the loss of the *President Coolidge*, and would be of interest to anyone visiting Espiritu Santo.

I can only hope that *The Lady and the President* adds to the reader's appreciation of the loss of this beautiful liner and provides some understanding of the futility of war, doing so in a manner that is readable and entertaining. If I have succeeded I would be delighted to share any accolades with Allan and Reece, however any errors or omissions I accept full responsibility for the words are my own.

Peter Stone, Yarram, Australia
September 1997.

CHAPTER ONE

A DOLLAR FOR THE AMERICAN PRESIDENT

The great liners of the century have all but gone to the shipbreaking yards, the speed of air travel usurping the opportunity for a casual cruise across the great oceans due to the demands of international business. Yet the American President Lines Ltd. remains as one of the largest shipping companies in the world despite its demoralising war-time casualties and post war rise in a precarious industry. Gone are the luxury liners that crossed the Pacific between San Francisco and Yokohama in less than ten days. In their place are the super-efficient bulk tankers and containerships that still provide cost-effective competition for air carriers. Yet, the mere fact that the APL line exists at all is a credit to the foresight, patience and strength of its early and current management.

As John Niven states in his excellent company profile *The American President Lines and its Forebears 1848-1984*: 'This company has evolved to its present status over a century and a half of dramatic development, beginning with its predecessor the Pacific Mail Steamship Company, which ran the first shipping line between Panama and California in 1849. It has seen profits and losses; mergers and acquisitions; and leaders who were merchants, railroad tycoons, speculators, lumber magnates, oilmen, and management experts. Fortunes have been made and lost in its varied history, which began with coal-burning paddlewheel steamers of 2,500 gross tons and now features modern diesel-powered containerships of 40,600 gross tons.'

Timber merchant Robert Dollar commenced his shipping interests with the establishment of a fleet of U.S. west coast schooners, and in 1902 expanded his interests to include a chartered voyage to Yokohama and the Philippines.

A new government agency, the U.S. Shipping Board, was established in 1916, and was to play a significant role in the continuance and eventual demise of many of the 'President' ships. The Shipping Board formed the Emergency Fleet Corporation a year later to build and operate ships for the Allied war effort. While Robert Dollar maintained a close personal relationship with members of the board, he refused to involve his shipping line with government charters, which would require American registry and the employment of

American crews. The Dollar organization was a small, tightly controlled family business. Government involvement would require a rapid expansion of personnel and facilities that Robert Dollar was not prepared to undertake, and temporary profits from government charters spelled a disruption of traditional practices and a considerable investment of capital funds.

The entry of the United States into World War I stimulated the American economy and especially enhanced the demand for shipping. Though the United States Shipping Board requisitioned all of Pacific Mail's vessels for war service, the line continued to operated all but two of its ships on its established routes, and in 1917, it added another service between San Francisco, Manila, Calcutta, and Colombo with two chartered vessel and opened a service to the U.S. east coast through the Panama Canal.

Immediately after the end of the war, various shipping lines were operating Shipping Board vessels on a bareboat charter basis or as managing operators. But there had been no definite policy. Finally in 1920 Congress passed into law a comprehensive Merchant Marine Act that established a permanent Shipping Board, The act also presaged the sale of the government's huge fleet to private interests. It was so broad in scope that it gave the board a virtual carte blanche over what was to be done with several billion dollars worth of public property.

By 1920 the company had reached its pinnacle with forty-six steamers under its house flag, but the following year traffic began to slacken as a postwar recession set in. Despite the downturn, the company added a fleet of fine 14,000 ton passenger ships that were to honour past U.S. presidents: *President Cleveland, President Lincoln, President Pierce, President Taft,* and *President Wilson,* names that were to be carried on by the successors of the Pacific Mail down to the present day. The first of these ships, owned by the Shipping Board but managed by Pacific Mail, sailed from San Francisco in March 1921, and now the Pacific Mail could offer fortnightly service between San Francisco and the Orient "in ships admirably suited to the trade".

Bad times were ahead however, and in the following years the company was forced to cut back. Niven writes: 'It continued to make reasonable profits on its curtailed service, but the management and board of directors seemed to have lost the aggressive leadership that had characterized its past policies, even when it was the victim of Wall Street speculators.'

When the Shipping Board offered for sale the five 'President' ships that Pacific Mail had been operating on the trans-Pacific run, built at a cost of some $30 million, both the fledgling Dollar Steamship Lines and Pacific Mail made a bid. The Dollar bid was $5,625,000 cash, but Pacific Mail offered one million more, in cash and stock. The Shipping Board decided that the Pacific Mail's higher bid did not meet the terms set in its advertisement for the ships and in April 1925 they were sold to the Dollar Steamship Lines, which continued to operate them in the trans-Pacific trade.

The astute Robert Dollar and his son R. Stanley Dollar had thus acquired millions of tons of government-built ships, a modern 'President' fleet from the United States government, at a bargain price. Pacific Mail, and also the Admiral Oriental Line, were soon out of business, and their corporate structures were eventually taken over by the Dollar company.

Robert Dollar was born in Dalkirk, Scotland, in 1844, and died in May 1932, at the age of eighty-eight. Son Stanley was born in the USA and was devoutly patriotic. Somewhat less than a zealous student, he left school at

Founder of the Dollar
Steamship Line,
Robert Dollar, circa
1920. Robert Dollar
was born in Dalkirk,
Scotland, in 1844,
and died in May
1932, at the age of
eighty-eight. It is said
that he lived by four
rules: Fear God, Be
Honest, Work Hard,
Be Thrifty.

thirteen to work in his father's lumber office. Shortly afterwards, in 1895, the
Dollar Steamship Company was founded, and Stanley, displaying innate
business acumen, flourished along with the company.

For a brief period, the Dollar Steamship Line was one of the most profitable
shipping companies in the USA. But the Dollar enterprises became over-
extended, and when the depression struck in 1929, the newly formed Dollar
Steamship Line, Inc. Ltd. was seriously weakened. By now however arrangements were well underway to construct the shipping line's two flagships.

Robert Dollar's attitude toward government charters had, by necessity, now
changed. The Dollar Line was lent over five million dollars by the Government
for the construction of the two major liners, which were to be subsidised at the
rate of ten dollars per mile for their voyages between the Orient and the U.S.

On 6 December 1930, at the Newport News Ship Building and Dry Dock Company slip, Mrs. Herbert Hoover smashed a bottle of water across the bow of the first of the two fleet-ships, *President Hoover,* prior to the hull sliding down the ways at Newport News. A little over a year later, Mrs. Calvin Coolidge christened her sister ship, the *President Coolidge.* The *President Coolidge* and the *President Hoover* were regarded as the American answer to the new Japanese motor liners of the Asama class. But they were hardly up to the standard of the most magnificent ship ever built for the Pacific, the *Empress of Japan*, built a year previously.

With these two fine ships, the Dollar Line now had the largest fleet of passenger and cargo liners under the U.S. flag.

John Niven writes: 'When the flag-bedecked new liner *President Hoover* arrived in her home port of San Francisco on 26 August 1931, the city turned out to welcome her. A splendid ship, the largest passenger liner ever built in American yards, she represented the nation's technological achievements in naval architecture and marine engineering and its continuing belief in the importance of the Pacific traffic for passengers and for freight. To the San Francisco Chamber of Commerce, the *President Hoover* and her sister ship the *President Coolidge,* guaranteed a prosperous future for the port and all those industries dependent on its economic well-being.'

Neither the crash of Wall Street nor the next year of rapid decline in the economy seemed to unduly concern the company. The Depression put an end to the passenger boom, but government financing continued until the completion of the *President Coolidge* in 1931, and R. Stanley Dollar managed to secure yet another loan from the Shipping Board 'at most favourable terms' to outfit the two liners. However, extravagant plans for two or three additional liners were wisely shelved.

With steeply declining world trade, the company's round-the-world service was forced to cut rates across the board on passengers and freight, but profits continued to be made, due in no small part to a rise in the mail subsidy, which reached $8 million a year after the *President Hoover* and *President Coolidge* went into service. Despite the reduction in luxury passenger traffic, it appeared that the two new liners could meet expenses and turn in a modest profit.

Until 1930, Dollar Steamship and associated company American Mail had managed to keep up interest and principal payments to the Anglo-California Bank and the United States government. The following year however the companies requested a two-year moratorium on payments to the government, and in 1932 Dollar Steamship Line Inc. had a net loss of $1 million. Unable to meet its obligations, the Comptroller General of the United States stepped in and insisted that the delinquencies be made up either from the mail subsidy or from tighter financial control over the company's management. Facing bankruptcy due to what could only be described as misappropriation of funds by senior management, the Dollar lines came under a Shipping Board resolution that effectively placed financial management in the hands of the Shipping Board, ie the US government.

It would appear that the Dollar family made a concerted effort to look after its own. Niven writes: 'From various sources the comptroller general had learned that Dollar management had been diverting large sums from the working capital of the lines through the seventeen service companies it controlled. In 1932, for example, one of these subsidiaries, the Robert Dollar Company - which acted as managing agent for all the lines - reported a profit of $60,000 and an outlay for executive salaries of $135,000. Yet that year, the Dollar Steamship Company reported a loss of $1 million and in 1931, when it received a two-year extension for payments on its government debts, R. Stanley Dollar received $216,447 in salaries alone from Dollar Steamship, American Mail, and Tacoma Oriental. His brother J. Harold Dollar, H. M. Lorber, and Herbert Fleishhacker of the Anglo-California Bank divided an additional $202,759. Altogether, from 1923 when the Dollars first began acquiring ships from the government, these four individuals were paid almost $5 million, with the lion's share of over two and-one-half million dollars going to R. Stanley Dollar. Considering the deteriorating condition of the Dollar-controlled fleet and the failure to modernize, it seemed the height of poor administration and personal irresponsibility, if not unethical behaviour on the part of the managers, to divert ten percent of the mail subsidy to their own pockets through the Robert Dollar agency. This particular charge on working capital, of course, was only a part of the systematic draining of company assets that had been going on for ten years before it became evident to Washington.'

Dollar Steamship Lines management resisted efforts to make changes in disbursements of funds, nor would Stanley Dollar permit the U.S. Shipping Board to examine the books of the subsidiary companies. Only after the government auditors reported their concerns to Washington were the books released. An accident that claimed two lives and caused damages of about $500,000 to the *President Madison* on 24 March 1933 eased the pressure. The liner was undergoing repairs at her pier in Seattle when she capsized in sixty feet of water. Stanley Dollar accepted the $1 million insurance payout and paid off much of the companies' debt, whilst making no effort to repair the stricken vessel. There was no formal investigation into the loss of the *President Madison*.

The *President Madison* settlement bought only temporary relief. Stanley Dollar continued to draw generous funds for his personal account, facts that were drawn out in an investigation of mail subsidies in 1933 which uncovered wholesale diversions of mail funds to the personal accounts of shipping executives. Also, the Dollars had agreed to construct four new vessels but had built only two, the *President Hoover* and the *President Coolidge*. Other shipping lines were, however, if anything, more delinquent than the Dollar Steamship Line. President Roosevelt directed Postmaster General James Farley to make a further investigation of the mail contracts; the subsequent report was a severe indictment of the shipping industry's policies on mail subsidies. [NI]

Then came the maritime strikes of 1934 and 1936. The seafaring unions were successful in their demands, placing a greater financial burden on the shipping companies. The Dollar Steamship lines came close to bankruptcy; by October 1935, the companies were $3 million in arrears to the government on a debt of $15 million. Some $3 million was owed the Anglo-California Bank and $2.5 million to other creditors, primarily suppliers.

Although there was none of the violence that characterized the strike in 1934, the consequences of the 1936 strike for the Dollar lines were much more serious. Their ships were tied up for over three months, and, as Dollar had predicted, the settlement that in almost every respect met the unions' demands increased operating costs significantly at a time when freight and passenger traffic on their Pacific routes was still far below pre-depression levels. Furthermore, all the shipping lines had to refund or honour passenger tickers. Considering events that were only five years hence, it must have hurt the Dollar

Carl Petersen, of
Newsport News
Shipbuilding and Dry
Dock Company,
designer of the
President Hoover and
the *President Coolidge*.
(Love those spats!)

Line to pay the Japanese shipping company Nippon Yusen Kaisha to transport
stranded passengers.

On 18 November 1936, the first of the Dollar lines filed for bankruptcy.
Early the following year the assets of subsidiary Tacoma Oriental were
disbursed to satisfy creditors and the company was dissolved. The slide of the
Dollar empire had commenced. Loss of Tacoma Oriental did not so much
impair the financial situation of the Dollar companies as it injured their credit
status among banks and created further doubts about their management in
Washington.

In 1936 US Congress passed the Maritime Act which put the entire American merchant marine on a new footing as it resulted in the abolishment of the Shipping Board. The domestic condition of the industry and the rise of hostile, totalitarian states in Europe and in the Far East prompted the Roosevelt administration to establish a subsidy policy and a large shipbuilding program to strengthen the merchant navy. A new government agency, the Maritime Commission, took over all the powers of the previous maritime agencies and was assigned additional powers to regulate the industry. Joseph P. Kennedy, as first chairman of the agency, began a thorough investigation of the by-now crippled Dollar lines. [N2]

By now, the Sino-Japanese war had escalated with Japanese armies occupying Peking, Tientsin, Shanghai, and Nanking. Not only had freight and passenger traffic from Chinese ports declined and insurance rates risen sharply, but with the major port of Shanghai closed, Dollar vessels had to be re-routed. This, perhaps not so indirectly, led to the loss of the *President Hoover* off Formosa (Taiwan) in December 1937.

As the *President Hoover* and the *President Coolidge* were the most profitable ships of the line, the loss of the *President Hoover* meant a reduction of a quarter of the Dollar lines' revenue. Most of the insurance money would go for the reduction of indebtedness and since Dollar Steamship and American Mail were on the brink of bankruptcy, the loss of the *President Hoover* seemed likely to take them both under. The Maritime Commission was faced with the gravest crisis yet in the tangled affairs of the Dollar companies.

John Niven writes: 'As the government began to phase out of the mail subsidy program and prepared to institute a direct subsidy, it became apparent that unless quick action were taken to supply funds, Dollar Steamship and American Mail would follow Tacoma Oriental and Pacific Steam's Admiral Line into receivership. But the Maritime Commission was unwilling to grant a long-term subsidy until it was satisfied that Dollar management was sound and that Dollar resources were sufficient to meet long-deferred repairs, not to mention new construction that was required under the terms of the 1936 act.'

Such was the magnitude of the financial problems of the Dollar line that, on 3 June 1938, the *President Coolidge* was 'attached' by four creditors, that is, the ship was in effect arrested and prevented from leaving San Francisco harbour. The claims, amounting to a total of $35,000 were for general engineering work. A bond of twice that amount had to posted before the ship could leave on its scheduled passage east.

The result of the Kennedy investigation was that the commission forced the Dollars to transfer most of their stock to the government, relieving them of liability for the huge mortgage debt the company has incurred. On 15 August 1938, in return for release of all liability, the Dollar family assigned their voting stock to the commission. Dollar insisted that his employees be retained, and that whatever organization succeeded Dollar Steamship it would not use the Dollar name, as the integrity of the family name was to be protected and 'I didn't know what kind of management was going in'. The commission was happy to comply with these requests. As far as the Dollar name, goodwill, and house flag were concerned, the commissioners felt that the past several years of neglect and mismanagement had, if anything, produced a negative image. It had already decided that the Dollar organization below the top executive level must be kept intact at all costs. After 3 June 1938, operations of the Dollar Steamship Line Inc. and American Mail were suspended.

Included in the government 'takeover' was, of course, the Dollar Line's flagship, *S.S. President Coolidge*. The United States of America Certificate of Registry, Official Number 231219, shows that the ownership of the *President Coolidge* was surrendered by the owners, Dollar Steamship Lines, Inc., in favour of the United States Department of Commerce on 20 July 1938.

The Maritime Commission assigned a private company to manage the company. William Gibbs McAdoo replaced Robert Dollar as chairman of the board and Joseph Sheehan, now executive director of the Maritime Commission, became president of the corporation. At its first meeting in San Francisco on 1 November 1938, the new management voted to change the name of the company to American President Lines, Ltd. A white eagle would replace the white dollar sign that had for the past thirty-four years marked the stacks and the house flag of a merchant fleet that had fallen victim to economic depression and mismanagement. Dollar Steamship Line Inc., so long a potent force in American shipping, was relegated to a role in American maritime history. [N3]

The new management had a hard and thorough look at its inherited fleet, and directed many of its ships to the docks for refit or laid up. Being in prime condition, the *President Coolidge* continued to be used in the trans Pacific run, visiting Hawaii, Hong Kong, China and Japan under her new flag.

While efforts to rejuvenate the line were underway, management became increasingly concerned about the threatening situation in Europe during the summer of 1939. Problems had already arisen in the Far East as the Sino-Japanese War flared up in 1938, and as mentioned previously, resulted in some re-routing of their ships. An additional problem had risen during early 1939 when the Japanese government refused to repatriate yen surpluses that stood at the company's credit. It took determined U.S. State Department intervention before the money, the equivalent of some $250,000, was released in 1939. By then Europe had been plunged into war and the round-the-world vessels were being held up in Suez by British inspection for contraband. By the summer of 1940, when Italy came into the war and France collapsed, the round-the-world vessels had to be rerouted around the Cape of Good Hope.

Operating costs began to escalate sharply because of war bonuses for ship's companies and war risk insurance. Both categories of expenditure were covered by US government subsidies, but there was always a delay which threatened adequate cash flow. Other increases in overhead were not balanced by subsidy however, with fuel oil doubling in cost during the short time between the Allied declaration of war in September 1939 and the end of the year. But the uncertainties of the new war situation were more than compensated by a sharp rise in passenger and freight traffic. Even the trans-Pacific vessels were operating well with freight and passenger business. In response to U.S. State Department warnings, the families of American businessmen, missionaries, and army and navy dependents crowded into ships for passage back to the United States. The *President Coolidge* sailed from Manila in September 1939 with the largest number of passengers ever carried from that port. Freight traffic also responded to the stimulus of war.

The situation in Europe also directly affected the operations of the American President Line. Italy's entry into the war placed sailing the Mediterranean Sea a major hazard, until finally it became necessary to abandon the regular course and route its vessels from the Far East around the Cape of Good Hope (South Africa), a deviation of more than 3,000 miles which lengthened the voyage by some ten days additional steaming, a serious matter when speed was vital in

Honolulu Harbour was at peace on 1 September 1932 when these four major liners lay at their berths. From left, *SS Mariposa, SS Aoragi, SS President Coolidge*, and *SS Empress of India*.

building up the nation's stock pile of strategic material. An example of how American imports of important materials jumped during 1941 is offered in the statistics of crude rubber. Prior to 1940, America imported an average of 400,000 tons of rubber per annum. In 1941, rubber imports exceeded one million tons, a substantial portion of which was carried in ships owned or operated by American President Lines. Comparable increases were also reflected in the figures for tin and other war-making commodities.

After the Neutrality Act was repealed, American President Lines, along with many other American steamship companies, diverted much of its tonnage to carrying Lend-Lease cargoes to the Red Sea, and to Murmansk and Archangel. With America's formal entry into the war, the APL's trans-Pacific service was completely disrupted, and all APL tonnage then became consolidated in the newly formed War Shipping Administration pool.

American exports to the Allies in Europe and to Southeast Asia were exceptionally strong and the United States government and American industry increased purchase of commodities like tin and rubber that might be cut off or in short supply due to wartime conditions. Despite the war, indeed because of it, APL was not only meeting its obligation to its creditors but was also earning a profit. Allied purchases of commodities and finished goods in the United States, the stockpiling of strategic resources by the Allies and the United States, and the flight of British, French, and American nationals from the Far East were all combining to push up revenues.

As a result of the war in Europe, regular trades and services of many Allied Nations in competition with American President Lines were either disrupted or completely suspended. In order to offset this serious loss of ship tonnage and at the same time cope with the abnormally heavy movement of critical strategic materials and the general cargo movement, American President Lines, through various charter and agency agreements, supplemented its own ship tonnage with vessels of other American flag owners. This supplemental tonnage was placed on the American President Lines' vital routes between the USA and China, Philippines, Netherlands Indies, Malaya, Burma, India and Ceylon. Thus prior to Pearl Harbor, American President Lines, in addition to their own vessels, were operating agents for ships owned or controlled by a number of other shipping companies. [N4]

While the majority of these ships were freighters, which during 1940 and eleven months of 1941 were pouring essential raw materials into the United States, the big passenger carriers, such as the *President Coolidge, President Pierce*, and *President Taft* were sailing back and forth across the Pacific, bringing home capacity loads of evacuees and refugees. On their outward voyages these same vessels were carrying Army and Navy personnel and needed supplies to US overseas bases. It was on one of these voyages, on the *President Coolidge*, that General Douglas MacArthur arrived in Manila.

IMMEDIATE PRE-WAR YEARS

After the Japanese bombing of Shanghai many Americans besieged the office of the American President Lines for passage home. One of the Company's two capital ships, the luxury liner *President Hoover*, dispatched on an errand of mercy to pick up these passengers, was bombed and severely damaged when off Woosung on 30 August 1937. The aggressors however were not the Japanese, but the Chinese, in an accidental daylight attack made by four aircraft. The *President Hoover* was not armed, but her commander, Captain George Yardley, and other deck officers, seized the ship's side arms, stood upon the bridge and fired away at the dive-bombing planes. One bomb struck the sun deck on the port side of the after funnel and penetrated to the A-deck staterooms. Fortunately the staterooms were unoccupied at the time. One crew member was killed and five others, plus three passengers, were injured in the attack. The ship was holed in several places above the water line, but the damage, to the extent of half a million dollars, did not impair her operating efficiency. Later it was reported that the Chinese believed the ship to be a Japanese vessel.

A few months later, the *President Cleveland*, on a similar errand of mercy, was fired upon from shore and strafed from the air while in the Yangtze River, but no casualties resulted.

Following the *President Hoover's* return to San Francisco where the bomb damage was repaired, the American President Line, on advice from the U.S. State Department, charted a new course for her which would bypass the turbulent China Sea. Hereafter, she would take the 'outside' passage, sailing south to Manila in the open sea east of Formosa. On her first voyage over this new course however, the 22,000-ton liner, with 600 passengers on board, ran aground on a tiny rocky island off Formosa and became a total loss. This was on 10 December 1937. Eugene Hoffman, Vice President Public Relations, states in his pamphlet *American President Lines' Role in World War 2*, published in 1957, that: 'The seamanship of the officers and crew was so expert that not a life was lost, and many not even had wet feet.' The loss of the *President Hoover* was almost four years before the Japanese attack on Pearl Harbor, bringing the United States of America into World War 2.

Salvage proved not to be feasible after several days of heavy seas broke the ship's back, and the *President Hoover* was adjudged a total loss. The Japanese salvaged the vessel and took some 14,000 tons of scrap metal from the hulk, after eventually paying the insurance underwriters $50,000. No doubt the scrap metal was eventually put to good use against the original owners.

The day after the loss of the *President Hoover*, the U.S. gunboat *Panay* was bombed and sunk near Nanking by Japanese planes. Despite these grave losses, it would take till July 26 1939 before the United States government notified the Japanese Government of its decision to abrogate the American Treaty of Commerce and Navigation. With Wang Ching Wei's puppet government in control over most of southern China from 30 March 1940, under Japanese directives of course, the US government was forced to look at the seriousness of the situation in South-east Asia, and consider its options. To provoke Japan into war would not be an acceptable situation, yet Japan seemed to be on a direct course of aggression which the U.S. Congress had to, inevitably, accept. By 29 July 1941, Japan had occupied all of Indo-China.

On 16 October, 1940, the United States government placed an embargo on scrap iron and steel exports to Japan, and concurrently urged all non-essential men and all women and children to leave the Far Eastern danger zones.

By the end of 1940, France had fallen, and with Hitler seemingly assured of victory, it appeared that War Minister Hideki Tojo might lead Japan into active military alliance with Germany and Italy, against Britain and America. The advent of a war involving America created a sellers' market for ships, with several laid-up *President* ships becoming valuable assets and were thus sold. Such was the confidence of American President Line's management that in 1939 the line entered into an agreement with the Baltimore Mail Steamship Company for the charter of four vessels for scheduled service between New York and the Malaysian Straits, ostensibly for the freight of rubber and tin.

With thousands of United States citizens scattered throughout the Orient, the U.S. State Department arranged for their return by the earliest possible date. During the first week in October, 1940, fourteen months before the surprise bombing of Pearl Harbor, the *SS President Pierce* sailed from San Francisco on her regular schedule to the Orient with instructions to bring home the first evacuees, wives and children of Americans stationed in the Far East. The *President Pierce* arrived in San Francisco in late November 1940 with the first trickle of what later was to become a heavy stream of evacuees from the Orient, most of whom were brought home in vessels of the American President Lines. The *President Coolidge* arrived in San Francisco on January 16, 1941 with a total of 832 evacuee passengers aboard to set an all-time record for number of passengers carried by a merchant vessel in regular trans-Pacific service. [N5]

AT WAR

Having, on 5 September 1939, declared the U.S. a state of neutrality in the war raging in Europe, President Franklin D. Roosevelt proclaimed a state of national emergency on 27 May 1941. Both the army and navy began purchasing or chartering American President Lines' major ships as the round-the-world and trans-Pacific services were curtailed by increasing wartime disruption of normal trade routes and American economic sanctions against

THE LOSS OF THE PRESIDENT HOOVER

Dollar Steamships' *SS President Hoover*, aground off Hoishoto Island 12 December 1937. The ship is so close to shore that passengers hardly got their feet wet.

The *President Hoover*, the first of the two 'flagships' built for the Dollar Steamship Line, was launched on 9 December 1930 and completed the following 16 June at the yards of the Newport News Shipbuilding and Dry Dock Company in yard number 339.

She was similar in nearly every respect to her sister ship *President Coolidge*, with the prime exception being that her turbo-electric propulsion was powered by General Electric Company, whereas Westinghouse provided the power for the *President Coolidge*.

After being delivered to her owners on 11 July 1931, she left New York on 13 August 1931 on her maiden voyage to San Francisco via the Panama Canal and on to the Far East.

It was said that even old and fastidious Captain Robert Dollar, who was far from well at the time, was quite overwhelmed by the *President Hoover*. After saying a few words to the hundreds of visitors who crowded the liner's main lounge, an effort that caused him considerable pain, he wrote in his diary, "The ship is a wonder".

The *President Hoover* was in Kobe when her captain, George W. Yardley, received a wireless message from the home office that the fighting between Japanese and Chinese forces around Shanghai had brought all operations in that busy port to a complete halt. He was instructed to sail directly to Manila, omitting Shanghai. Yardley decided to cut time and distance by sailing east of Formosa (Taiwan) rather than following the traditional course south through the Formosa Strait. The new course involved some risk because of shoal waters and dozens of small islands off the coast. But Yardley had good charts, from which he concluded that the Japanese government had marked the sea routes off the eastern coast of Taiwan with ample navigational aids.

The *President Hoover* left Kobe on a stormy morning and as she steamed south encountered rain squalls and low visibility. When she arrived in the vicinity of Taiwan's northeast coast, Yardley discovered that the Japanese had extinguished most of the lights and removed many of the other navigational aids on the mainland of Taiwan and the islands offshore.

Despite these hindrances to a safe passage and the fact that because of weather conditions the *President Hoover* was proceeding on dead reckoning in shallow waters with tricky currents, Captain Yardley maintained his cruising speed of twenty knots.

At midnight on 11 December 1937 Eugene Lukes, an assistant purser on the vessel at the time, recalled that he was awakened by a heavy jarring and bumping. 'If you had that feeling once,' said Lukes, 'you would recognize it. We had come to a halt. Even with flood lights we could not see anything. Apparently we were in the middle of the ocean, but we could hear surf'.

Captain Yardley immediately ordered soundings at number three hatch forward under the bridge. Soundings revealed twenty feet of water in the hold and the same depth of water surrounding the vessel from the bow to amidships. The President Hoover was not only hard aground on Hoishoto Island but had lost her bottom plates almost to her firerooms, approximately half of the ship.

Since no immediate damage was posed to crew and passengers, Captain Yardley waited until there was enough light to disembark without unnecessary hazard. He ordered oil spread on the lee of the huge ship, which smoothed out the choppy waves. He then had several lines taken ashore so that the lifeboats could make their way through the surf. In about two hours, all of the passengers and most of the crew were landed safely.

Yardley himself and a skeleton force remained aboard. He hoped to get the President Hoover off and radioed to Kobe for divers and a salvage tug.

Salvage proved not to be feasible and the President Hoover was adjudged a total loss. The Japanese salvagers, who recovered an estimated 14,000 tons of scrap metal from the hulk, eventually paid the insurance underwriters $50,000.

It was thought that the Japanese had always maintained a light on rocky Hoishoto Island, but on the night the President Hoover went aground the light was out. Speculation credited Japanese wreckers with responsibility for the accident, it being claimed that they had removed well-known lights on shore to lead the ship to disaster. This rumour has never been substantiated, but in light of future events it is quite reasonable to assume that the Japanese could have done this.

The loss of the President Hoover was a considerable blow to her owners. At one stroke revenues for Dollar Steamship were cut by about one-fourth. The President Hoover and the President Coolidge were the most profitable ships of the line. Most of the insurance money would go for the reduction of indebtedness and since Dollar Steamship and American Mail were on the brink of bankruptcy, the loss of the President Hoover seemed likely to take them both under. [N8]

Japan. By mid-year of 1941 American President Lines suspended all trans-Pacific schedules, a move that American Mail quickly followed. After the Japanese attack on Pearl Harbor, 7 December 1941, the U.S armed forces took over all ships that still remained in private hands, some outright, the remainder on a bareboat charter basis.

In mid-1941, due to mounting tension and repeated hostile actions of Japanese toward American and British nationals in China, American President Lines moved its Far Eastern headquarters from Shanghai to Manila. Already the Company had discontinued steamer calls at Japanese ports, first curtailing them and finally bypassing Japan entirely.

Headquarters staff, then under the direction of Vice President Oscar G. Steen, arrived in Manila in late August 1941. Japan made her move on 7 December 1941 with the bombing of Pearl Harbour in the Hawaiian islands, commencing a full scale war in the South-Pacific between the main antagonists, Japan and the U.S.A. Despite intelligence on Japanese military intentions, Japan had a jump start and within two months Malaya, Singapore, Hong Kong and Manila had fallen. On 2 January 1942 when Japan took Manila, all staff members of the American President Line, except four who had previously joined the U.S. Armed Forces, were captured by the Japanese and interned at

Santo Tomas prison in Manila. The Company's Singapore staff escaped by plane to Java, and eventually made their way to Australia.

Although the headquarters office had been removed from Shanghai, a skeleton crew had been retained there to look after the Company's interest. This staff was not immediately imprisoned, but was confined to a restricted area in the International Settlement. However, in February 1943, the Shanghai staff members were interned in various Japanese prison camps. In September, 1943, three of them were repatriated to the U.S. Three others remained in internment. In September, 1943, three of the staff at Manila were also repatriated, leaving fourteen still interned there.

Having anticipating the impending conflict with Japan, the US government had already sent the *President Harrison*, and the *President Madison* to the Philippines loaded with United States Marines. The ships left San Francisco on 27 and 28 November 1941 respectively, the the first ships of the American President Line to be used as specific troop transports.

Thus for many months before the United States formally entered the war, the entire merchant fleet of the American President Lines was already engaged in war work, or more appropriately as it was known at that time, 'defense work'. Not only were her trans-Pacific transport ships bringing home American repatriates and evacuees of other nationalities, but they and other passenger liners were returning to the United States with their holds laden with essential raw materials needed for the national defense of an inevitable war.

On 21 February 1942, President Roosevelt proclaimed the War Shipping Administration, which assumed the duties of the Maritime Commission in building, organizing, and coordinating the shipbuilding and shipping industries. All US shipping was now under government control. Until this time, all APL-owned vessels were bareboat chartered to the government but now the shipping companies, such as APL, operated their own ships under the direction of the US government. In addition, key staff members of APL were made available to the War Shipping Administration for important overseas assignment. Some APL staff members were already on loan to the Government in such positions as administrator for China Defense Supplies Corporation and Lend-Lease assignments in India and Burma. The American President Lines, her staff and ships, were now well entrenched in the Pacific War. Vice-President Eugene Hoffman wrote, 'After the die was cast at Pearl Harbor, the entire physical resources and facilities of the American President Lines, plus the experience and energy of the management and personnel, were placed at the disposal of the United States Government and consecrated to the task of winning the war at the earliest possible moment.'

The day after the attack on Pearl Harbor, with Japan formally at war with the United States and Great Britain, the steamer *President Harrison* which had previously delivered a complement of United States Marines at Manila, was on her way back to Chinwangtao, North China to evacuate additional Marines from Peking. The *President Harrison* was overhauled by Japanese naval units off Woosung and seized as a prize of war. When the Captain and crew saw that capture was inevitable, they risked their lives by running the ship hard aground on a rocky island in the East China Sea, deliberately wrecking the vessel in order to render her useless to the Japanese. Her crew were interned and all officers and passengers aboard with naval or military ratings were transferred to prison camps. Thus, the *President Harrison* became the first gold star in American President Lines service flag for floating equipment lost.

When the Philippines was bombed on 8 December 1941, three APL vessels were in or near Manila: *Ruth Alexander, President Grant* and *President Madison*. The *Ruth Alexander* and the *President Grant* were in port in Manila when the shooting started, and became a major target for aerial bombardment. The Navy notified Company officials that they would not be able to give protection to ships in Manila Harbor and suggested that it would be safer for the vessels to 'make a run for it'. After consultation with the Masters it was decided to sail and both ships departed under cover of darkness.

The *President Grant*, under Command of Captain W. S. Tyrrell, made good her escape and after an exciting and eventful voyage made safe port in Australia. The *Ruth Alexander*, under Command of Captain F. P. Willarts, was not so fortunate. She escaped at night some time after the *President Grant* had left but was caught by Japanese bombers in the Celebes Sea off Balikpapan. Defenceless against the merciless bombing, the 'gallant little steamer was blasted to the bottom of the sea', and so became gold star No. 2 in the Company service flag. One member of her crew was killed and a half dozen others were wounded.

After tossing about in open boats for many hours, survivors were sighted and picked up by a Dutch Dornier flying boat and taken to Balikpapan. The rescue was heroic. The Dutch pilot of the Dornier ordered all his bombs and supplies jettisoned to make room for the 46-man crew of the sunken vessel. The only way this number could be accommodated was to have them stand upright packed close together. Even the wounded had to stand straight up. The plane's load was so heavy the pilot had to taxi five miles before he could get his ship into the air.

The *President Madison*, commanded by Captain Vaidemar Nielsen, was south of the Philippines when the war broke out. This vessel played hide and seek, through the Dutch East Indies, sailing mostly at night, and eventually made home port safety.

When the *President Taylor* sailed from San Francisco January 5, 1941, it marked the 17th anniversary of the inauguration of the APL's famous 'Round-World' service. In seventeen years 'President' liners, sailing every two weeks west-ward from San Francisco, had completed more than 350 circumnavigations totalling ten million miles. This record had been achieved without loss of a single passenger's life as a result of accident.

The *President Taylor* with 1334 souls aboard, became the American President Line's fourth vessel casualty on 'Friday, the 13th' of February, 1942, off Canton Island in the South Pacific. No lives were lost. The *President Grant*, mentioned earlier as having escaped from Manila after the Japanese attacked the Philippines, became the Company's fifth war casualty, also in the South Pacific. It was loaded with troops and a full crew, but all hands were saved.

Several other distinguished 'President' liners, which had been taken over on requisition by the Armed Forces early in the war, also became casualties of battle. These included *President Cleveland* and *President Pierce*, both troop carriers, which were lost in the North African invasion; and another smaller 'President' taken over by the Navy and used as a supply ship. This latter vessel was grounded in the Eastern Mediterranean and became a total loss.

Not all American President Line ships were lost due to direct enemy action. As mentioned, the *President Hoover* lay abandoned off Taiwan, and on 26 October 1942, the APL lost its other beloved flagship. With over 5,000 troops and crew on board, the *President Coolidge* struck two American mines at the entrance to the Segond Channel in Espiritu Santo, one of the major islands of New Hebrides. She too was a total loss, and it is on her demise that this book is based.

Eugene Hoffman wrote of the loss of the *President Coolidge* in the New Hebrides: 'Due to the expert seamanship and the high morale of the troops, all hands were saved except one crew member and one soldier, who were reported missing. The tragic loss of this big troop carrier was a severe blow to the Army transport service.' [N6]

During the Pacific war that was to rage till August 1945, American President Lines lost no less than nine of her own vessels, precisely one-third of its pre-war fleet. Administrative pressure was enormous. In pre-war peaceful times, APL controlled less than twenty ships. However, from 7 December 1941, cargo operations on various other vessels assigned to Army, Navy and Lend-Lease, for which American President Lines also acted as agent on behalf of the War Shipping Administration, ran well into the hundreds of ships. Many of these were the famous Liberty vessels, ships built to a standard blueprint in double-quick time, that served so well as transports in every theatre of the Pacific war.

In addition to eleven Liberty ships and other agency-operated vessels, American President Lines lost as casualties of war a total of five of its own former peacetime fleet of vessels: *President Harrison*, captured in the China Sea; the *Ruth Alexander*, bombed off Borneo; the trans-Pacific liner *President Coolidge* in the New Hebrides; *President Taylor* and *President Grant*. These were under APL control at the time. Prior to the attack on Pearl Harbor, American President Lines had twenty owned vessels. All twenty went to war, under APL control or requisitioned by the Army ... only three remained at the end of hostilities on 15 August 1945.

POSTWAR YEARS

From 1938 until 1952, including the important war years, the American President Lines was operated by the United States government, through the Maritime Commission and War Shipping Administration. The Dollar family however were determined to recover their lost line, and from 1946, for six years, the Dollars entered litigation that saw one of the longest law suits in American maritime history. A compromise was finally reached whereby the line would be put up for bid and the proceeds divided between the Dollar family and the government.

Of the twenty vessels owned by the American President Lines immediately pre-war, only the old *President Johnson* (which had advanced in age to 42 years), *President Polk* and *President Monroe* were returned to the Company. Eugene Hoffman, Vice President Public Relations wrote in 1957, 'It is a stirring testimonial to the American Way that within a period of little more than a decade this humble fleet of three war-weary ships could evolve into the mighty merchant armada that now fans out over four major world trade routes under the American President Lines' flag. Like the winning of the war itself, this notable achievement of building a peace-time merchant fleet would not be possible without the three-way partnership of Government, Private Industry and Labor - all working together for the common good'.

After the war, government-owned stock in American President Lines was bought by a group of venture capitalists headed by Ralph Davies who formed APL Associates. Davies became the principle management force behind the line until his death in 1971, during which time he acquired several other shipping lines under the control of APL Associates. [N7]

The American President Lines managed to successfully recover from its devastating war-time loses, and with the injection of much needed captain from war-time insurance claims, went on to become one of the largest shipping lines in the world. In 1951, the line pioneered the concept of containerization, with 1000 containers in use in its trans-Pacific service. In 1973 it introduced its first fully containerized ship, and six years later pioneered the first full dedicated containerised railway across the United States. In 1982, APL introduced larger containers up to 53 ft and refrigerated containers. It has grown in strength to its current position as a leader in containerised transportation. And yes, there is another *President Coolidge* - but she carries cargo, not passengers.

American President Lines remains as a leader in the U.S. shipping industry, with a global network of containerized transport. At the time of writing (1997), Nepture Orient Lines Ltd. were looking at making a bid to acquire APL Ltd. Perhaps, by the time this book is published, American President Lines will have run its full term.

On 21 February 1931, seconds after Mrs. Grace Goodhue Coolidge smashed a bottle of Vermont river water on her bow, the *President Coolidge* glided down the slipway into the James River at the Newport News Shipbuilding and Dry Company's yards. Eight months later, the ship was on her maiden voyage.

CHAPTER TWO

BIRTH
OF A
PRESIDENT

The two Dollar liners, *President Hoover* and *President Coolidge,* were products of the Depression of 1930-31. Perhaps there is irony in the fact that such a massive project during a time of financial instability would have the almighty "$" sign emblazoned on its funnels, but this was only a product of coincidence. The contract for the two ships was signed on 26 October, 1929. The first keel plate, for Hull No.339, was laid on 24 March 1930, and for Hull No. 340 on 21 April 1930. It was quite a remarkable feat of engineering and construction that the two vessels were both launched within ten months of the laying of their keels.

The contract price for each ship was $7,050,000, and the Newport News Shipbuilding and Dry Dock Company, of Newport News, Virginia, USA, "made a good profit at that figure". It also provided much needed employment for this well respected shipbuilding company that was later to build the huge *SS United States* in 1952, seven battleships and several aircraft carriers including the worlds first nuclear-powered aircraft carrier, *Enterprise.*

The two President ships were to be the pride of the Dollar Steamship Company. Each vessel - they were identical twins - was 654 feet 3 inches long, 81 feet in beam, depth 34 feet and 21,936 tons gross, and were the largest merchant ships built in the United States up to that time. There was cargo space of 633,000 cubit feet of which ten percent was refrigerated. The ships could also carry one hundred automobiles. Her turbo electric engines were rated at 32,000 shaft horsepower and drove twin screws at a cruising speed of 21 knots.

J.H. Isherwood in *Steamer of the Past,* writes, 'The *President Coolidge* was certainly a very fine-looking ship, with nice proportions, pleasing lines and a graceful counter stern which was bossed out below the water line to cover the rudder. She looked very smart in her Dollar Line colours, with a thin yellow line just below the white strake round the hull and black funnels with a broad red band and, on it, the white Dollar sign'.

S.S.PRESIDENT COOLIDGE

Fastest Service between
San Francisco and the Orient
via Honolulu and the
Sunshine Route.

SPECIAL FEATURES

The number of private baths and toilets available in proportion to passengers carried is greater than in many vessels. 112 first class staterooms have a private bath or are directly connected to one.

IMPRESSIVE PUBLIC ROOMS - because of their extent and wide use of woods in the interior designing. Among the woods are many so rare and costly they are seldom heard of: Avodire, Framire, Bubinga, Eroka, African Mahogany, Padouk and Teak from Burma, Satinwood from India, Harewood from England, Prima Vera from Central America, Mahogany from the Philippine Islands, Circassian Walnut from Russia, Zebrawood from Brazil and many of our American woods such as Oak, Walnut, Cherry and Maple.

SPACIOUSNESS - is indicated by the following dimensions: the Lounge 51 by 48 feet clear of any obstructions, Smoking Room 48 by 48 feet, Tea Garden 29 by 78 feet. All of these have a deck height of 13 feet 6 inches.

GYMNASIUM - large and equipped with the latest mechanical exercising machines and devices. Children's Playroom, a joy to young travellers ... a fairyland.

EXCEPTIONALLY LARGE STATEROOMS - some 10 feet by 15 feet, with additional space of 8 feet by 13 feet for bath, wardrobe, passage way, etc., others 9 feet by 23 feet, with additional space for bath, -etc.

THE TOP DECK- or Sun Deck, is practically without obstructions; here the many deck games are played, walks, sun baths and a place for observation and rest.

The two Dollar liners were the only sister ships known to have been christened by wives of Presidents of the United States. The *President Hoover* was christened on 9 December 1930 by Mrs. Herbert Hoover with 'waters from the seven seas'. Bottles of sea water were procured by vessels of the Dollar Line from the Pacific, Atlantic and Indian Oceans, the Inland (Japan) Sea, the Mediterranean and Caribbean Seas and the Panama Canal. The waters were 'blended' by Mrs. Hoover on the launching stand shortly before the christening. A writer at the launching commented, 'To many it seemed a particularly happy thought, and we are now sufficiently accustomed to the occasional abandonment of the traditional champagne to view the situation with equanimity.' There was no choice of course in abandoning champagne for these were the days of the notorious prohibition. [N1]

Mrs Grace Goodhue Coolidge christened the *President Coolidge* with a somewhat less complicated concoction than that for her sister ship - with a bottle of water taken from the Black River, which ran through the former president's Vermont farm. [N2]

Just fifteen seconds before the appointed hour of eleven thirty, on the morning of Saturday, 21 February 1931, the *President Coolidge* started down the launching ways. About a minute later, the 13,000 ton hull was floating comfortably on the James River. The *Shipyard Bulletin* of the Newport News Shipbuilding and Dry Dock Company reported, 'Everyone characterized it as a mighty fine launching. The Dollar Line people are to be congratulated in securing sponsors who not only give distinction to the occasion because of their high position, but who are just naturally good sponsors. Mrs. Coolidge's enthusiasm was infectious both on the launching stand and at the luncheon which followed. It is easy to believe that vessels so auspiciously started on their careers will be fortunate and popular.' [N3]

Those fortunate to attended the prestigious luncheon had an excellent view of the two sister ships from the windows of the Tidewater Club, overlooking the James River at Newport News, Virginia. The newly launched hull of the *President Coolidge* was brought in to the fitting dock near where the *President Hoover* was berthed. It was reported that: 'The two vessels will be, to all appearances, exact duplicates, but the electric propelling machinery and all the principal auxiliaries, while of the same type and power, are the products of two different companies, the General Electric Company on the *President Hoover* and the Westinghouse Electric and Manufacturing Company in the case of the *President Coolidge*. In a healthy rivalry, each of these two great concerns is endeavouring to turn out the best machinery possible, while the Shipyard is impartially bending its energies to make both installations eminently successful. It is a very interesting situation and one which promises much from an engineering standpoint.'

The *President Coolidge* was, indeed, exactly the same as the *President Hoover* in regard to tonnage, dimensions, and cargo and passenger carrying capacity. The only difference of any consequence between the two vessels was, as mentioned, in the propulsion machinery. A minor difference occurred in the First Class Smoking Room, but more of that later. The propelling machinery for the *President Coolidge* consisted of twelve high pressure, superheated steam boilers and turbo electric machinery by the Westinghouse Electric and Manufacturing Company, to develop the 26,500 shaft horsepower. The speed of the vessel in service was expected to exceed twenty and a half knots, which it did.

Mrs Grace Goodhue Coolidge, second lady from left, wife of President Calvin Coolidge, prepares to break a bottle of water taken from a river running through their Vermont property over the bow of the *President Coolidge* at the launching of the ship on 21 February 1931. The ladies, from left, are Mrs. R. Stanley Dollar, Mrs. Coolidge, her daughter-in-law Mrs John Coolidge, and Miss Diana Dollar.

The use of electricity on ships was hardly in its infancy, however the use of turbine-electric propulsion machinery on such a large vessel was a fine engineering achievement, and one in which the shipbuilders took pride. 'It is doubtful if on any vessel electricity has played a more prominent part than on these, the greatest American built merchant ships. Not only does it, in the 26,500 horsepower propelling machinery, furnish the smoothest, most flexible and satisfactory form of gearing between the turbines and the propellers, but practically every operation on the vessel is performed by its aid. It warms you in the cheerful glow of luminous radiators and cools you by motor-driven fans. In the galley it cooks appetizing dishes and, if these tempt you to the extent of excessive avoirdupois, just go to the gymnasium and have it taken off with the electric vibrator. Radio, that lusty infant in the electrical field, is much in evidence. If figureheads had not gone out of fashion on ocean liners we might suggest, for a ship like the *President Coolidge*, Benjamin Franklin with his kite string and key.'

The Dollar Line's *S.S. President Coolidge*, recently launched.

The *President Coolidge* had accommodations for 988 and her crew numbered 324 to 385. Passengers who strolled her broad decks and through her spacious public rooms were impressed by her two outdoor swimming pools and the fully equipped gymnasium, as well as the tasteful furniture and fabrics in her staterooms and lounges in first and special classes. No money had been spared in making her art deco furnishings the equivalent of the best hotels of the day. Every room had its own telephone. All first-class and many special-class quarters had private or connecting baths. The first-class dining saloon was two decks high with a balcony for the musicians, and seated 272 persons. Adjoining it was a private dining room seating eighteen. The special-class dining room seated 120, at small tables. Special attention had been paid to forced ventilation in all public spaces as well as in passenger staterooms although this was before the era of air conditioning. Nor had the safety of the passengers been neglected. A flip of a switch on the bridge closed all watertight doors in thirty seconds. Each of the twenty lifeboats was equipped with a special shortwave magneto-powered radio that could transmit messages over one thousand miles. [N4]

No expense was spared to ensure the comfort and entertainment of the passengers, particularly those travelling in the upper classes. An article printed on 21 October 1931 in the New York Times, reported with some astonishment: 'The air in the living quarters is conditioned by an electrical device maintaining an even temperature.' No less remarkable was the complete installation of a theatre for sound pictures. (The first 'sound' movie, the Al Jolson Story, was released in 1929, only two years previously). Fifty-one radio loud speakers were placed at strategic places around the ship, in the public living spaces and the first-class staterooms, to give passengers and crew at all times entertainment 'captured from the air in mid-ocean'. Three electric lifts (elevators), two for passengers and one for the engineering crew, were also installed in the ship 'to facilitate communication between the nine decks'.

When launched, the two 'President' ships were in the first-class category of international passenger ships, and proved very popular. The Dollar Line promoted the opportunity that passengers could relax in one of two saltwater swimming pools, one with an area of sand to form an artificial beach for bathers, or enjoy music from the musicians gallery in the First Class Dining Room. There was also a library and writing room decorated with a large mural of deep sea marine life.

One of the largest and most impressive public spaces on the ship was the First Class Smoking Room. It is here, above an electric fake fireplace, that The Lady gazed down upon the priviledged passengers. The *President Hoover* had a similar decorative panel, of the same size, depicting a rampant horse.

There was even a shipboard stock exchange, a gymnasium, children's playroom, shopping arcade, soda fountain, beauty salon, barber shop as well as a marine tea-garden and a play-deck for golf, tennis, handball, squash and quoits.

As those who have travelled on the ship, and indeed those who have dived on the *President Coolidge*, have noticed, there is an extraordinary amount of ornamental glass work on the ships. Before the contracts for the President liners were received, all shipboard glass preparation was contracted with outside companies. This system involved many hazards of transportation and delays in meeting production schedules, hence the shipbuilding company decided to establish an 'art glass shop' in the grounds of the works. Intricate ornamental glass designs were built for ship domes, skylights and windows. The huge dome of the main lounge in the ships contained over three thousand separate pieces of glass.

The contract dates for delivery of the completely fitted-out ships were 26 October 1931 for the *President Hoover* and 26 February 1932 for *President Coolidge*. 'It is now anticipated that the first vessel will be delivered more than three months ahead of contract and the second one even further in advance of the contract date', reported the shipbuilders. And so they did. The *SS President Coolidge*, completed on 10 September 1931, was given a magnificent welcome as she steamed into San Francisco Bay on her maiden voyage in October. As the vessel moved up the bay to her home port she was surrounded by hundreds of smaller craft all sounding a welcome, as had been done for her sister ship *President Hoover* two months earlier. A public reception was held for Captain Karl A. Ahlin and his senior officers after the ship docked at the Dollar Line's pier, No. 42.

Within six months, the *President Coolidge* had set the record for an east-west passage across the Pacific between Yokohama and San Francisco, wresting the award from the Japan Mail liner *Asama Maru*. The trip took just over twelve days, clipping four hours and four minutes off the previous record. This translates to an average speed of 19.5 knots. The west-bound trip had been even faster, at 11 days, 4 hours and 22 minutes, averaging 20.78 knots. Four years later, in 1937 (after having collided with the tanker *Frank H. Buck* in San Francisco Bay), the *President Coolidge* broke the westbound record again with a voyage of nine days, nine hours and fifty-one minutes.

The *President Coolidge* and the *Asama Maru* may have held the official record, but the actual record for a westbound passage had stood for no less than

The S.S. *President Coolidge* set several records for crossing the Pacific between Japan and San Francisco.

thirty-five years, until finally broken by the *President Coolidge* in 1937. The Pacific Mail Line steamship *Korea* made the passage in 1902 in a remarkable ten days and fifteen hours.

In January 1933, the *President Coolidge* established a new record for the Honolulu - San Francisco run of four days, two hours and fifty-eight minutes, clipping fourteen hours off the record held by her sister ship.

The 1930's saw the era of shipboard travel at its romantic zenith and it was while en route from San Francisco to Manila aboard the *President Harding* in 1935 that General Douglas Macarthur met his future wife, Jean Faircloth. (Also aboard that cruise was another name destined for the annals of history, Major Dwight Eisenhower). Following their subsequent wedding in New York, the Macarthurs returned to Manila from San Francisco aboard *President Coolidge,* departing 10 May 1937.

Mrs. Cathy Jaquith, wife of the present owner of the wreck of the *President Coolidge*, had taken passage on the ship and recalls, 'The *President Coolidge* was a beautiful ship, large but not too large. One had the opportunity of meeting most of the passengers with the true feeling of being on board a ship. Food and accommodation were super - an experience unduplicated in the day of the monster ships which resemble a city more than a ship. A voyage on the *President Coolidge* is one of my many cherished memories'.

The fate of the two President ships was sealed with the growing tensions in Europe and Asia, but a domestic mishap was to literally hit the *President Coolidge* before any international aggression directed her fate.

On 6 March 1937, the *President Coolidge* left San Francisco with a full load of passengers for Yokohama via Honolulu. Whilst near the Golden Gate Bridge, a heavy fog set in. Although it was the policy of the Dollar Steamship Line to proceed only with the utmost caution during a fog, Captain K.A. Ahlin U.S.N.R. did not, apparently, reduce speed. Entering San Francisco Bay was the Associated Oil tanker *Frank H. Buck.*

Julius Larsen, a marine lookout for the San Francisco Chamber of Commerce, based at Lands End, reported: 'I heard the fog horns of both vessels for some minutes. The fog was too thick to see anything, but I listened hard as the sound of their fog horns easily distinguished them from the regular fog warnings along the shore, grew closer together. Then, all of a sudden, came the crash. Through the heavy fog it sounded like a big, muffled boom of a Presidio gun. At once the Coolidge - I knew it was her for I was waiting for her to pass through - sent up three short whistle blasts and I knew right away something went wrong, for that was a distress signal. After that there was an awful silence, broken only by buoy horns. I knew by that they had stuck together by the impact, so I telephoned for help.'

Mr. J.K. Caldwell, returning to his post as United States consul-general at Tientsin, said: 'I was standing on the upper deck within earshot of the bridge. The fog was thick enough to slice. The Coolidge's whistle was sounding every few minutes. Then we heard a blast from the other ship. In less time than it takes to tell, the tanker's masts loomed up dead ahead. I heard Captain Ahlin shout an order to reverse the engines. The ship shuddered, but almost immediately we crashed. There was only a slight shock, but I could see the tanker was badly hurt. Captain Ahlin and his officers worked very quickly and efficiently in getting a boat over the side to help the tanker's crew.'

Blaming the fog for the collision, Captain Ahlin, who took his first command out of San Francisco Bay in 1894, said: 'There was no time to do anything between the time when we saw the Buck and the time we collided. I ordered the Coolidge engines put to emergency full speed astern, and that cushioned the shock. After we hit, I shouted to the Buck to stand where she was, to keep her nose up. Our engines were full astern at the time we hit. We could not see the tanker until she was almost on us. As soon as she hit I yelled to the skipper of the tanker that we would hold our bow into the hole until he could get his men off. I sounded general alarm and ordered all the water-tight

The S.S. *President Coolidge* limps back to San Francisco after crashing into the tanker *Frank H. Buck* near the Golden Gate bridge.

bulkheads closed. As a precautionary measure, although it was not necessary, I had all life boats cleared and swung out under the command of the first officer. We lowered boats, of course, for any assistance we might give the crew of the tanker.'

This action allowed time for swinging life boats from both vessels into effective position, and may have averted loss of life. When the ships parted, the *Frank H. Buck* immediately went down by the bow, but the crew members were safely in boats. In giving evidence at a later inquiry, *President Coolidge* engineers Dougan and Patton, said that for ten to fifteen minutes before the collision the *President Coolidge* was under slow bell, barely moving. Chief Engineer Peltret of the *Frank H. Buck* testified that his engines were at full speed astern at the moment of impact.

The *San Francisco Call-Bulletin* reported: 'The tanker, spouting black oil from a gaping hole in her bow, took on a sharp forward list, as if poised for a plunge to the channels bottom. Through the gloom had come the frantic calls for help of the tanker's whistle. At once, before the straining eyes of passengers lining the deck rails, a dramatic rescue of the tanker's crew of forty was effected as the vessel reportedly began to sink.'

Although there was not a fast tide running, heavy swells hampered boatmen and made rescue work perilous. The majority of the crew were taken aboard the *President Coolidge*; eight men and a dog, the ship's mascot, were taken to shore by a motor lifeboat from the Point Bonita Coast Guard station.

The damaged *President Coolidge*, with its compliment of 678 passengers and 350 crew, and the rescued sailors from *Frank H. Buck* started back to port under her own power. A yawning hole twenty feet wide pierced the thick steel plates of her forward starboard side. Her prow, bearing the full brunt of the crushing impact, was bent and twisted into a grotesque question mark. It was soon determined however that the liner was not in grave danger. Although there was some confusion aboard as the two vessels collided with a screeching impact, there was no panic. Newspaper's reported that the 'Cool alertness of ship's officers quickly restored order. Passengers, in pleasure mood, had less than an hour before leaned over the liner's rails shouting and throwing spiralled serpentine to a crowded dock in a gay bon voyage party at Pier 42.' No lives were lost in the incident.

The *Frank S. Buck* was badly damaged 'with her bow down and stern up', but did not sink immediately and drifted, crewless, before going on to rocks at Lands End. A salvage effort removed the 67,000 barrels of oil she was carrying, and the ship was refloated.

The *President Coolidge* was taken to Bethlehem Shipbuilding Corporation's drydock at Hunters Point for repair, expected to take ten days. The estimated cost of the accident to the Dollar Line ship was $250,000 which included repairs, loss of passage fares and cargo charges. The ship finally sailed for Yokohama on 25 March 1937, having eliminating Honolulu from her schedule. Meanwhile, first and special class passengers to the Hawaiian Islands were turned over to other American lines. After re-crossing the Pacific, the *President Coolidge* was scheduled to again sail from San Francisco on 10 May, and was back on its regular Pacific schedule by June.

Two years later, in July 1939, the *President Coolidge* collided with the Japanese freighter *Nissan Maru* in China's Whangpoo River. Side plates on the liner were bent but it did not prevent the ship from continuing its passage. Again, no one was hurt in the incident. In January the following year however,

The S.S. *President Coolidge* sails under the colours of her new owners, the American President Line.

a sailor from the *President Coolidge* was believed drowned in the Whangpoo River when a launch returning him to his ship collided with a tug and capsized. Two Chinese from the launch were also lost. [N5]

On this same outward journey the *President Coolidge* was to figure in a remarkable encounter in the Pacific Ocean. Bobbing on the high seas 700 miles from Yokohama, five men and a woman in a small craft were found hungry and in need of assistance. The 'vagabond mariners' as the press reported, accepted food, water and medicines, but declined to be rescued and continued on their journey from Shanghai to San Francisco. The sextet were reported to be 'white and English speaking' and could well have been fleeing the Sino-Japan war.

The *President Coolidge* received some early indications of the impending war with Japan when, in October 1938, the Japanese refused to clear the ship for a return trip to San Francisco from Japanese-occupied Shanghai. The ship was to sail with more than $4,000,000 worth of silver which the Japanese-controlled government claimed to be their own. Chinese customs officials had approved of the export of the silver prior to the Japanese intervention 'with the co-operation of Japanese military and naval authorities'. The Dollar Line agreed to unload the silver which had been consigned to the Chase National Bank of New York, thus allowing the *President Coolidge* to sail. Although in no way related to the incident, the following month the Dollar Steamship Line would no longer exist, and the *President Coolidge* came under the new flag of the American President Line. [N6]

In October 1940, the *President Coolidge* participated in the evacuation of Americans from Hong Kong when Japanese-British relations became strained, and again in early 1941 when she brought many refugees from the Orient. As mentioned in the preceding chapter, the *SS President Coolidge*, under Captain Henry Nelson whom we shall hear of more later, carried the largest number of passengers to cross the Pacific on a merchant vessel in regular service. And when again she docked in San Francisco on 30 May 1940, she carried over a thousand passengers, many escaping the Japanese aggression in Asia.

In November 1940, wives and children from American consulate officials and businessmen arrived in the USA, several for the first time in their young lives. On this voyage, there were over 800 passengers. It was perhaps after this voyage that America, and the world, received the first eye-witness news of the horror being perpetrated by the Nazis in Europe. 'From the hesitant lips of a Polish refugee came a story of the horror of modern warfare. Still afraid to reveal his identity, though safe in America, he told of the seventeen day siege of Warsaw; of women, weaponless, tearing at Nazi tanks with their fists, while the dead lay piled high in the streets.'

It was on the outbound voyage to Yokohama in October 1940 that the *President Coolidge* ran into a typhoon. Five passengers were seriously hurt when wind velocities of 100 miles per hour whipped up high seas to batter the ship. But she came through with only superficial damage.

In March 1941, the First Secretary of the American Embassy in Tokyo, Edward S. Crocker, returned on the *President Coolidge* to the United States on leave, and reported, with some concern no doubt, the situation in Japan: 'Life in Tokyo has been very interesting the last six months. There is still a police guard around the embassy but it is there as a precautionary measure. Only a handful of American women are now left in Japan and virtually all businessmen have discovered it advisable to leave. At present a larger percentage of missionaries than any other group are still there.'

The Nanking Massacre of December 1937 is well documented, but the personal tragedy was graphically realised by eye-witness accounts. In January 1941, thirteen year old Esther Bernhelm arrived in San Francisco on the *President Coolidge*, lucky to be alive, yet having the terrible image of seeing her parents die at the hands of bandits 'We were too frightened to cry,' she said. 'They looked like devils. There must have been forty or more of them. Before they shot my papa they asked for money.'

Meanwhile, the situation in China was growing worse. In June 1941 the *President Coolidge* reported seeing some one hundred Japanese battleships, cruisers, aircraft carriers, destroyers, submarines and supply ships moving slowly southward in the Formosan Straits off Amoy.

On 2 June 1941, with the possibility of war becoming ever more a certainty, the *President Coolidge* went into service with the American Army as a transport ship for the reinforcing of garrisons in the Pacific. On 15 July she began her initial voyage for the United States Army departing San Francisco. The ship was required to make a fast voyage to Honolulu and the Philippines. From Manila, the ship evacuated 250 Americans who had been stranded due to the inability of obtaining passage elsewhere.

In August 1941, the Japanese denied permission for the *President Coolidge* to enter Yokohama to collect one hundred Americans waiting for evacuation. A formal U.S. State department announcement said the Japanese government refused to permit the Americans to board the ship. The Japanese foreign office was willing to permit the *President Coolidge* to enter a Japanese port to take aboard approximately twenty American officials who wished to return home, but not the private citizens. The U.S. State Department said that, 'under these circumstances the vessel, which was at Shanghai, would proceed directly to San Francisco without calling at a Japanese port'. The Department announced that it, 'continued to give its close and serious attention to the question of providing transportation for American citizens desiring to return to the United States from Japan'. In the meantime, the Japanese N.Y.K. Line's *Asama Maru* had free entry into San Francisco and was embarking Japanese nationals at will.

The American press reported its belief that the Japanese government had decided to hold the American citizens in Japan pending completion of arrangements to transport Japanese nationals in the United States who may wish to return to their native land. It was clearly stated that the American citizens were hostages of the Japanese. On 26 August 1941, Japanese officials in Tokyo permitted twenty-six United States embassy and consular officials to board the N.Y.K. Line's *Tatuta Maru* for passage to Shanghai, where they could be expected to obtain trans-Pacific passage.

When the *President Coolidge* entered Shanghai in October 1941 for the last time, it was reported by passengers that a cruiser and several PT boats had escorted her on the Honolulu-Manila run, one of the first cases on record of an official Pacific convoy.

On 1 November 1941, the *President Coolidge* sailed from San Francisco for Honolulu and Manila. The day the Japanese attacked Pearl Harbor, 7 December 1941, the *President Coolidge* was outward bound from Manila under escort by the heavy cruiser *Louisville* about halfway to a scheduled landfall at Honolulu. She reached San Francisco Christmas Day, 25 December 1941. [N7]

With war officially declared, the *President Coolidge* was soon to be stripped of her finery and painted in the drab grey 'colours' of a warship. It is interesting to note that records show that the *President Hoover* and the *President Coolidge* were both designed with 'several features suggested by the U.S. Navy', so that the vessels could be easily converted as transports if the need should arise. One of the major suggestions was the provision for the mounting of guns on her bow and stern. These are clearly seen in the plans of the ship.

Within two months she had undergone hasty but extensive remodelling to convert her from the epitome of trans-Pacific luxury to the far less fastidious but infinitely more crucial task of carrying troops and military supplies into Pacific battle zones. Her compliment of 290 officers and men were still familiar faces, taken from American President Lines crew lists. Although seconded to the US Navy, they remained essentially merchant navy men and continued receiving their pay from the shipping company rather than the government. The vessel itself, however, was under charter to the War Department. Instead of the 845 fare-paying passengers seeking sun and fun in the Pacific and Far East, lounging by the pool or strolling the broad promenade decks, there were thousands of freshly trained troops crammed into in the same accommodation area. Many of those who travelled on in the *President Coolidge* during her supply runs across in the Pacific would later participate in some of in the fiercest battles in in the Pacific war.

When fully converted early in 1942 she was able to carry over 5000 troops. Gutted of most of her luxurious fittings, the *President Coolidge* was modified to carry 5000 troops where previously less than a thousand civilians were accommodated. The tourist class swimming pool, which was probably made of canvas, was removed completely to give access to in the hold beneath. This was not difficult, as the removal of in the pool was normal practice, to provide access to cargo hatch number six. Most of the luxurious furniture was removed and replaced by rows of bunks. Extra toilets were constructed. All the permanent fixtures remained, and where possible, boarded up for protection. Such, it is assumed, was the fate of The Lady.

The *President Coolidge* first 'went to war' on 12 January 1942, carrying a full compliment of troop reinforcements, plus their supplies, to in the South-West Pacific region. During this voyage she called at Melbourne and Wellington. President Manuel Quezon of in the Philippines came aboard at Melbourne on 15 February 1942, and with General Douglas MacArthur and his staff, sailed for in the United States.

She was back in San Francisco by 7 March and left again on 19 March 1942 with Melbourne once more on her itinerary, and Bora Bora in French Polynesia, returning 8 May. Another voyage, her second last, began from San Francisco on 26 May and took her to in the Fiji capital of Suva and in the northern New Zealand port city of Auckland, returning 29 August. [N8]

On 6 October 1942, the *President Coolidge* sailed from San Francisco on her final voyage.

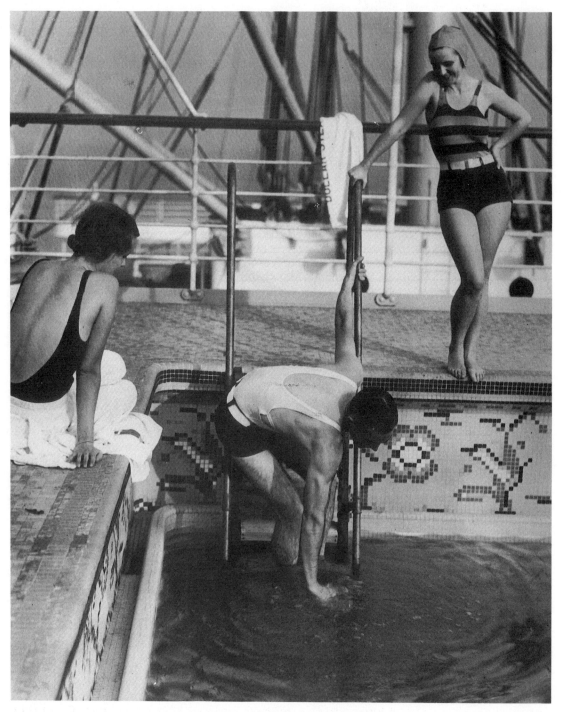

Modestly dressed first-class passengers test the sea-water in the swimming pool on the boat deck of the *S.S. President Coolidge*. The view is looking aft.

CHAPTER THREE

STATEROOMS AND STEERAGE

The *President Coolidge* could not be regarded as a luxury liner in the same breath as the famous Queens, the speedy *United States*, nor the lesser-known yet opulent *Conte di Savoia*. She was however well fitted for first class travel and her design included the latest innovations in contemporary technology.

The interior architecture of the *President Hoover* and *President Coolidge* was the responsibility of the A.F. Martin Company of San Francisco. Besides planning and designing the interiors the company produced in its workshops most of the furniture and furnishings and supervised their installation. Their aim was to 'combine the decorative possibilities of this modern machine age with the highest quality and type of creative handwork'. *Marine Engineering and Shipping Age* stated: 'The result of the efforts in interior design on these vessels is splendid. While the illustrations indicate in a measure the general scheme of treatment, the very beautiful colour effects in all of the spaces is missing. In every respect the *President Hoover* and *President Coolidge* from the standpoint of interior architecture represent the highest development of any American ship so far built.'

The following detailed descriptions of the ship are taken predominantly from *Marine Engineering and Shipping Age*, published at the time of the launching of the *President Coolidge* in 1931. I shall retain the verbosity and elequence of the descriptions as it reflects the view at the time.

At the forward end of the promenade deck is located the First-class Library and Writing room, impressively finished in a contemporary design, with special hardwood panelling and trim. With its increased deck height, this room has an extremely lofty effect, which is emphasized by the absence of pillars. The walls are flush panelled, full height, in mottled African mahogany, and the wide panels have their side margins decorated with vertical inlays in colour.

A large decorative mural by A. F. Marten, of deep sea marine life, is framed in all African mahogany moulding, at the centre of the after end of the room, and an extensive library for passengers use is installed in a recessed bookcase,

inlaid in rare woods, at each side of it. A flush ceiling is fitted overhead, of painted Vehisote divided into panels by strips of carved composition.

The Library is furnished with overstuffed sofas and arm chairs and upholstered chairs with mahogany frames. The writing tables are of mahogany. Ample light is provided by chandeliers, wall bracket lights and reading lamps. The draperies are of heavy silk brocade and the floor is covered with high pile Saxony wool carpet.

The design of the first-class lounge lobby on the promenade deck, like that of the lounge itself, is distinctly marked by a contemporary feeling, but the architectural effect is obtained by the use of special hardwood panelling and trim. The walls are finished throughout in West African avodire, a pale yellow wood with a diagonal rippling grain, in full height flush panels bordered by sunken panel bands of satinwood trimmed with yellow poplar mouldings. In the centre of the forward side of the lobby there is a clock with dial inlaid in the panelled balustrade of the stair to the boat deck lobby, and below it is a fountain of running fresh water in a recess finished in mosaic tiling. (See page 205). At the top of the light well over the centre of the lobby there is a shallow dome with a flat skylight of cathedral glass set in a polished brass frame. Special light fixtures of tubular design are fitted between panels in the sides and ends of the well.

One of the largest and most impressive public spaces on the ship is the first-class smoking room, which is finished in a modern style of architecture, and completely panelled, at the sides and overhead, in West African bubinga, with a rich dark red mottled grain. At the after end of the room there is a verde antique marble fireplace, equipped with a realistic electric Magicole grate, and ornamented with a smoke hood of dull hammered stainless steel, edges with cast brass. Above the mantle there is a decorative panel of majolica set in a dull stainless steel frame with moulded iron. (This is The Lady and the Unicorn).

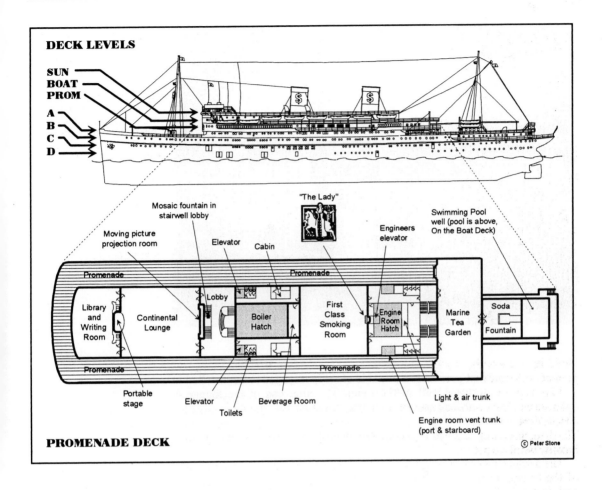

DECK LEVELS

SUN
BOAT
PROM
A
B
C
D

Moving picture
projection room

Mosaic fountain in
stairwell lobby

"The Lady"

Engineers
elevator

Swimming Pool
well (pool is above,
On the Boat Deck)

Elevator   Cabin

Promenade   Promenade

Lobby

Library
and
Writing
Room

Continental
Lounge

Boiler
Hatch

First
Class
Smoking
Room

Engine
Room
Hatch

Marine
Tea
Garden

Soda

Fountain

Promenade   Promenade

Portable
stage

Elevator

Toilets

Beverage Room

Light & air trunk

Engine room vent trunk
(port & starboard)

PROMENADE DECK

© Peter Stone

The forward end of the first-class smoking room is decorated with an
Aubusson tapestry panel, depicting the story of Rip Van Winkle, especially
woven for the purpose. The smoking room is comfortably fitted out with
overstuffed chairs and settees, walnut armchairs upholstered in green leathery
large baize-covered game tables and round card tables, all of walnut; and glass
topped smoking stands. The floor is in shadings of green and vermilion rubber
tile. The lighting system of this room is an entirely new approach to the question of illumination. Every second beam space carries a 12-foot trough light by
which the entire beam space is flooded with light.

Forward of the promenade deck lobby is the first-class lounge [Continental
Lounge], about which the social life of the ship revolves. In keeping with the
architectural treatment of the other public spaces, the design of the lounge
reflects a contemporary influence throughout, the effect being obtained by the
use of a pale greenish yellow enamel finish with gold-leafed ornament and
special hardwood trim. The walls are full panelled throughout in enamelled
plywood, set off by gold-leafed applied mouldings, with baseboard of prima
vera and narrow carved cornice of the same material, faced with satinwood at
the top and crowned by a deep composition moulding.

The Continental Lounge, the main lounge for first-class passengers only on board the *SS President Coolidge* at the Promenade Deck level. Note the high ceiling which extended through the Boat Deck above and was capped by a skylight of round 'portholes' at the Sun Deck level.

For entertainment purposes, a portable stage is arranged to be installed in a recess in the forward wall of the room. The after end of the lounge is decorated with an authentic antique Sumatran mural on silk, dating from about the fifteenth century.

A flush ceiling is fitted overhead, divided off by narrow moulded panel strips and decorated in gold-leafed composition around the indirect lighting fixtures, which are of sunburst design with finish of dull and polished gold and dull chromium plate. A light trough for indirect lighting of the tile dome is formed by a flaring cornice around the opening, with composition decoration and turned cap moulding. A parquet dance floor is laid in the centre of the lounge.

The lounge is luxuriously furnished with large overstuffed sofas upholstered in modern fabrics and with numerous occasional tables of various designs, all inlaid in rare woods.

The marine tea garden at the after end of the promenade deck is enclosed at the sides and most of the after end with sliding frameless plate-glass storm windows, which when opened in favourable weather make it practically an open-air space. The finish of this space as well as the furnishings are in keeping with the outdoor character of the space. A calked teak deck is fitted over the entire floor and is finished for dancing.

The soda fountain room adjoining the marine tea garden is invitingly finished in colour. The soda fountain, which is located in the centre of the room and has three service sides, is finished in African walnut, with yellow Siena marble top.

Located on the upper deck amidships just aft of the first-class foyer, is the first-class dining room of contemporary design with pinkish gray panel work and trim. The walls are flush panelled for their full height with applied mouldings finished in gold leaf. The airports are arranged in groups of four in

The grand stairwell leading down to the First Class Dining Saloon on C Deck of the *S.S. President Coolidge*. To the right is a doorway to a smaller private dining room.

one recess. In the lower part of the recess, a ventilation duct enclosure is fitted, with painted panelling and walnut top.

Over the centre of the room there is a large well extending to the bridge deck with sides decorated by full height cut-glass mirrors, ornamented in gold leaf and separated by wide concave painted pilasters.

A musicians' gallery is provided at the forward end of the well. The ceiling over the entire space, including the well, is of painted Vehisote with mullions of white pine, and is fitted below the beams. Above the entrance stairway landing there is a large mural by Frank Bergman, representing the various countries visited by ships of this line in round-the-world service. The dining room has a total seating capacity of 272 persons.

A private dining room accommodating eighteen persons is provided aft of the first-class dining saloon, on the port side of the ship.

The first-class main entrance lobby or foyer, on the upper deck just forward of the main dining room, is entered through a vestibule at each side of the vessel in way of the entrance ports in the hull. The main passenger stairway leads up from the after end of the lobby, at the centre of the ship, and at each side of the stair there is an electric passenger elevator serving the various accommodations on the decks above. Like most of the public spaces, the foyer is finished in modern style, and the walls and ceiling are panelled in framing throughout, with white birch panel strips and African mahogany trim.

The forward stair lobby on the bridge deck is featured by an up-to-the-minute novelty shop, with curved plate-glass front, African mahogany counter and outside trim, and glass-shelved show-cases lined with silvery gray hardwood.

A children's play room is provided, opening off the after boat deck lobby. This room is attractively furnished with small wicker armchairs, settees, and tables, and quaint painted settees with high backs, and is equipped with sandbox, merry-g-round, slide and toys.

A fully appointed barber shop and a beauty parlour are available to first-class passengers.

A completely equipped gymnasium for first-class passengers is located on the port side of the after boat deck lobby, provided with adjoining toilet and showers and connected with a therapeutic room with electric bath, ultraviolet ray and massage facilities.

The special-class public spaces, though less elaborate than those for first-class passengers, are exceptionally attractive and roomy. The lounge and smoking room are both situated in special houses on the sheltered weather deck aft of the bridge enclosure, thus securing the maximum of light and air, and are reached by spacious stairways from the lobbies below, as well as by entrances from the deck. The design of the lounge is marked by a French influence, with walls flush panelled in eroke or African teak, and the furniture is in antique French style of the period of Louis XV.

The special-class smoking room follows a modern design, and the walls are finished in raised panels of dark Philippine mahogany, with cornice and trim of the same material. The room is furnished with walnut topped tables on metal pedestals, walnut cabinets with carved fronts, overstuffed settees, walnut chairs up bolstered in leather, and marble top smoking stands.

The special-class dining room extends over the full width of the ship, forward of the special-class entrance lobby and is panelled full height, with old ivory enamel finish. The furniture is of walnut.

In practically all of the public rooms and in the promenade spaces special window equipment has been mentioned. These windows were in general supplied by the Kearfott Engineering Company, Inc., New York, including 100 shelter windows for the promenade deck, 30 inches by 48 inches, mechanically operated and equipped with 3/4-inch frameless plate glass. This same type mechanically operated window in which 1-inch glass is used and which also has a fixed transom above is applied across the front enclosures of the promenade. This window, 30 inches wide and 20 inches high, is of the all-metal type, no wood trim being required.

This company supplied 132 water tight windows for the deck house. These are equipped with 1/2-inch and 1-inch thick frameless lights, the windows. including a bronze frame for the opening in the steel plate. These frames are arched top and bottom with an opening 20 riches by 36 inches. Weathering is effected by hand tighteners on either side of the window which weather. the glass against a rubber gasket.

Opening onto the veranda are six inside windows of the frameless glass type, the openings being operated from either side.

Children's Play-room at the starboard side, aft, of the Boat Deck on the *S.S. President Coolidge*. This view is toward the bow, with the lobby through the doors on the left.

In addition to this equipment the Kearfott Company also supplied sixty-one bronze casement windows for the public spaces. All of these casements are arched top and bottom, about one half the number having double hinged sash, while the remainder are single-hinged.

The airports throughout the accommodations are of the Utley pivoted type manufactured under license at the shipyard.

Hotel equipment in general was supplied by the Dohrmann, Hotel Supply Company, San Francisco.

Accommodation for a total of 988 passengers are provided on each of the steamships, *President Hoover* and *President Coolidge,* of which over 30 percent are regular first-class. The number of staterooms and passengers of each class are as follows:

	Staterooms	Passengers
First-class	112	214 or 307
Special-class	39	133
Third-class	23	170
Steerage	0	378
Totals	174	988 (max)

It is interesting to note that steerage accommodation was allowed for. Had the *President Coolidge* been designed for the Atlantic run, any space allowed for steerage would have by now been upgraded to a third class level. Steerage is, as the name suggests, accommodation at the stern of the ship, usually in large dormitories with the barest of facilities. The objective of course was to pack as many people into the ship. It became prevalent post World War 1, when the United States was going though a massive immagration phase from

THE POWER WITHIN

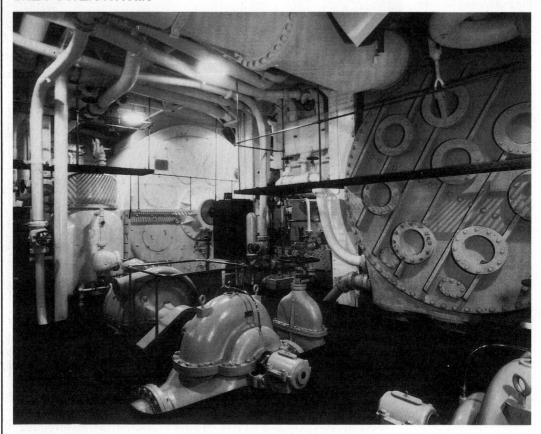

One of the turbines in the engine room of the *S.S. President Coolidge*.

The turbine-electric propulsion machinery on the President Coolidge includes two 13,250-horsepower, 4000W-volt, 3-phase, 44-cycle, 40-pole, 133 revolutions per minute propelling motors of the synchronous type. These motors are self-contained units, the rotors being carried in sleeve-type bearings supported by heavy end brackets secured to the motor frame. The motors are separately ventilated, the cooling air being taken out of the engine room, drawn through the motor, and passed out of a duct in the after stack. This ventilation is obtained by means of a motor-driven propeller-type blower mounted in the duct above each main motor.

For supplying power to these motors there are two main turbine-generator sets, each consisting of a 14,000 brake-horsepower turbine and a 10,200-kilowatt generator. The turbines are of the Westinghouse combination impulse and reaction type. These units operate at 2660 revolutions per minute for full-power conditions. They are designed for use with steam at 275 pounds per square inch gage pressure at the throttle, 200 degrees F. superheat and 28 1/2 inches vacuum.

Each main turbine is fitted with a full oil-operated governor. This governor depends for its operation on the variation in oil pressure produced by changes in speed of an impeller which is mounted on the turbine rotor. Since the speed of the propelling motor with this system of propulsion is controlled by varying the speed of the turbine, an adjustable-speed mechanism is provided in connection with the turbine governor. This consists of a simple relief valve which is located on the main control board and is operated by a lever. Thus, the only connection between the control board and the main turbine required for speed control is a small pipe to carry the oil from the governor and a drain pipe to sump the oil.

The turbine is also provided with an automatic stop governor and an oil-operated throttle valve. Lubricating oil for the bearings of the main units and oil for operation of the governor systems is furnished by either of two small turbine-driven lubricating oil pumps which provide oil for these services at required pressures. The lubricating oil is pumped through coolers to a gravity tank and from this point it is led to the bearings.

The main generators are of the 2-pole type, somewhat similar to generators for central-station use, except that they are of different proportions. This is necessary in order to provide machines which will have their first critical speed above the maximum operating speed. These machines have closed ventilating systems with air coolers mounted beneath the generators and supplied with cooling water from the main condenser circulating pumps. This arrangement of the ventilating system serves to reduce to a minimum the noise which would otherwise be caused in connection with a highspeed unit. It also makes unnecessary the construction of long air ducts from the machine to the deck.

The main control equipment is arranged in two unit groups, each self-contained and supported in angle-iron framework. One unit contains all of the high-voltage control devices including the main motor reversing switches, changeover and tie switches for making connections for operating both main motors from either main generator, and motor field switches and other low voltage apparatus. The high-voltage section cannot be entered except through a door placed between the two groups and arranged so that it cannot be opened without interrupting the excitation circuit to the main generators. This makes it impossible for an operator to enter this compartment with the high-voltage circuits energized.

The low-voltage unit, located immediately forward of the high-voltage compartment, carries the main generator and motor field switches and all of the low voltage auxiliary

control devices incident to the propulsion equipment.

Directly in front of the low-voltage units is placed the instrument panel. This panel carries all of the necessary electrical instruments for the complete propelling plant as well as steam and vacuum gages for the turbines. At the centre of this panel an operating deck is provided with the necessary control levers for complete operation of the control units including the levers which control the speed of the turbines.

For supplying power for excitation of the main generator and motor fields as well as for all ship auxiliaries there are four 500-kilowatt, 240/120-volt auxiliary turbine-generator sets. The turbines for these sets operate at 6000 revolutions per minute, driving the generators through gears at 1200 revolutions per minute. The generators are of the 3-wire-type so as to provide a normal voltage of 120, when operating on the excitation bus, for the main generator fields and 240 volts for generator excitation during manoeuvring. These auxiliary sets are of the new high-efficiency type.

There are two balancer sets which are used to supply 115-volt power for lights and other ship circuits from the 240-volt auxiliary power bus. Each balancer set has a capacity of 300 amperes unbalance.

To move the considerable amount of cargo that she ship could carry, the two ships were fitted with 24 motor-driven cargo winches, operated by marine water-proof motors. Two 15-horsepower capstans were used to assist the storing of automobiles in the 'tween deck garage aboard this ship.

The steering gear, 'the most vital auxiliary equipment for the operation of the vessel and its safety', is driven by either of two 75 horsepower marine self-ventilated motors. A similar type of motor is used for driving practically all of the under-deck auxiliaries including pumps for ice-water circulation, ballast, main condensate and auxiliary condensate service, fuel-oil service, fire and sanitary purposes, main circulating and sewage disposal. The total number of motors used for such auxiliaries is 126 with a total capacity of over 2900 horsepower.

Europe. This diminished greatly in the early 1930s, and ships constructed after this time considered Third-Class as the basic accommodation. Gone were the dormitories, but cabins of six and eight, in bunk-beds, were not uncommon. It is conceivable that the designers of the *President Coolidge* retained the concept of the steerage class because of the passenger movement of 'orientals'. It would not do to have 'orientals' travel in the upper classes, even if they had the wealth to do so. Steerage on the *President Coolidge* was predominantly on the stern of D-Deck, and would have been dark and noisy, with the propellers only a matter of a few feet away. Bunks were removable so the steerage area could be used for cargo if so required. That alone gives some indocations of the lack of refinery for these 'lower-class' passengers.

The designation of 'First-Class' passengers is retained to this day in all forms of transport, but it was soon realised that 'Second-Class' was not an appropriatee term, and various classifiactions were introduced to define the next level of accomoodation and services. Special-class was popular in the 1930s, but later gave way to Tourist Class. First Class and Tourist Class remain the only classification on many trans-oceanic liners even to the present day, but the Third-Class was retained on some of the larger ships, or where there was an opportunity for further fares to be gained from those less financially fortunate - from immigrants for example.

Returning to the descriptions provided by *Marine Engineering and Shipping Age*: Four *de luxe* suites are located on the bridge deck just aft of the main entrance lobby, two on each side of the vessel, adjoining each other. Each suite contains a private veranda, sitting room, bedroom and bathroom; and for each pair of suites there is a large trunk room directly across the passage, in which lockers are fitted for the occupants of each suite. One suite on each side is modern in design and the other French.

Each bedroom is furnished with two single beds, two night tables, a dressing table, chest of drawers, etc., in designs conforming with the character of the suite. The furniture in the sitting room and veranda is also of attractive period design.

The regular staterooms may be roughly divided into four types: (1)) Those with exclusive private baths; (2) those with a connected bath between two staterooms; (3) one-person rooms with toilet and shower; and (4) two-person rooms with either private or connecting toilet and shower. All staterooms are fitted with single metal-framed beds; there are no upper berths in any first-class rooms. Two rooms on the promenade deck are for one person only; all others have two beds. In all the large rooms there is also a settee or day-bed, which may be used for a third person when desired.

It was one of these single-bed cabins, on the starboard side of the promenade deck, that was removed to make way for the three-rows of toilets installed early 1942 when the ship was converted to military use.

The Westinghouse Company developed a special stateroom heater designed to suit all of the special marine requirements, such as method of mounting, type of enclosure, switch arrangement and various features to provide safety from fire hazard and at the same time present an artistic appearance. There are 292 of these heaters on the *President Coolidge*.

All regular first-class rooms have panelled overhead ceilings and panelled plywood walls, the latter painted a light salmon in some cases and cream in others. The floors are all carpeted, and all beds and the furniture in-general are the same in all rooms; the only marked difference is in the colour of the

A 'Suite Modern'
stateroom on the *S.S.
President Coolidge*.
There were four Suites,
located on A deck. Two
were made up in a
'French' style, the others
'modern' in what we
would now call *art-deco*.
Each Suite had a private
sitting room, and a
'verandah'.

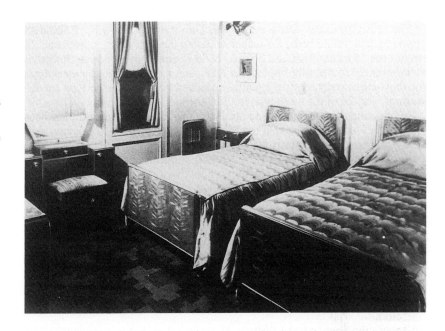

upholstery on the daybeds. All rooms have bed lights, mechanical ventilation and electric heating.

The special-class staterooms are all located on the shelter deck adjoining the first-class staterooms on that deck and are so arranged that they may be used for first-class passengers when desired. Of the 39 staterooms in this class, 23 are arranged for three passengers each and the remainder for four. Each stateroom is fitted with two single beds, exactly the same as those in the regular first-class rooms, and folding metal Pullman berths are fitted over one of the beds in the three-passenger rooms and over both beds in the four-passenger rooms.

All of the rooms have natural light and air through Utley pivoted airports. A number of the rooms are arranged on the Bibby principle with alcoves in which a chest of drawers is fitted. Built-in wardrobes like those in the first-class rooms are provided in each room.

All third-class staterooms are located at the after end of the upper deck; the majority of them are arranged to accommodate six or eight persons each. All rooms are fitted with metal berths of fixed lower and upper type furnished by The Rome Company, and a lavatory with running hot and cold water supply. Each room is provided with steam heat and mechanical ventilation and has asbestolith floor covering.

As mentioned, accommodations for steerage passengers are located on the main deck aft. At the extreme after end of this deck there are fitted six compartments in which permanent berths are provided for 60 persons. The remainder of the steerage berths are portable and are located in compartments which are also available for general cargo. All steerage berths are of metal, of the standee type.

For the passenger accommodations The Rome Company, Baltimore, supplied 224 single beds, 36 inches wide for the first-class staterooms; 24 single beds 36 inches wide, and 55 double deck, with folding upper, 36 inches wide lower, 33 inches wide upper for special-class rooms; 85 double-deck beds for third-class staterooms; 67 white-enamelled berths, standee type for the steerage, and 20 of the same type for the hospital.

In finishing the staterooms and public rooms in general, mention has been made of the Vehisote ceilings. In this connection the Pantasote Company, Inc., New York, supplied 83,500 square feet of this material on each vessel. Some Pantasote also was used in upholstering certain furniture. For built-in furniture, mahogany panels were supplied by the Roddis Plywood Company, New York. The United States Plywood Company, Inc., New York, supplied Plycozite which was used exclusively for all panel work, including stateroom panelling in each vessel. This company also supplied metal-covered plywood known as Armorply, for the doors of the smoking-rooms; this is a special construction, consisting of plywood , faced on two sides with a satin-finish Allegheny metal. Allegheny metal, supplied by the Allegheny Steel Company, Brakenridge, Pa., also was used for the trim and decorations in the barber shop and beauty. parlour, for the strap work decorations above the fireplace in the first-class smoking rooms, as well as towel racks for toilet cabinets in tourist-class stateroom.

Among the many special features of the vessel probably none will appeal more to the first-class passenger than the unusual bath and toilet facilities which have been provided for their comfort. These are particularly noticeable in the elaborately tiled and equipped private bathrooms with which the ship abounds. Both in colour schemes and fixtures these spaces are as modern and complete as have ever been installed on a ship anywhere and they will stand favourable comparison with those in the finest hotels.

Exclusive of the four suites, each of which has of course, its own private bathrooms there are 39 staterooms with private bathrooms. There are also 32 staterooms in which a private bathroom is fitted between each pair of rooms, 26 bathrooms thus connected. Besides these there are six staterooms, each of which has a private toilet and shower bath, and ten staterooms in which a similar private toilet and shower bath is fitted between each pair of rooms.

The bathrooms for the suites are tiled the full height of the room all around; all other private bathrooms and showers are tiled full height in way of the tub and shower and have a 4-foot tile wainscot elsewhere. In all these spaces grab rods, soap dishes, toilet paper holders, etc., are of vitreous ware the same colour as the tiling in which they are set, all supplied by The Fairfacts Company, New York. Towel baskets and towel shelves are enamelled to match the plumbing fixtures.

All bathtubs are fitted with a wall shower with hot and cold salt water to the tubs and hot and cold fresh water to the showers. All separate showers, except in the steerage, and all lavatories throughout have hot and cold fresh water supply.

CHAPTER FOUR

PEKOA, PALIKULO and PALMS.

After Pearl Harbour, and the subsequent declaration of war against the Japanese, the U.S. military moved quickly into the Pacific, but not fast enough to prevent the capture of Hong Kong on 25 December 1941, Singapore on 15 February 1942, and the fall of the Philippines in May 1942.

The Japanese rapidly extended their sphere of influence west across the Pacific as far south as New Guinea and Dutch East Indies. The Australian garrison of some 1500 at Rabaul fell on 23 January 1942, just six weeks after the attack on Pearl Harbor. From Rabaul the Japanese were able to direct their objectives further south into the Pacific and into Papua and Australia. By mid 1942, Japan had conquered a massive land and sea area west to Burma and the Andaman Islands, south to Timor, Papua, New Guinea and the Solomons, and west to the Gilbert islands.

The occupation of Australia and the remainder of the Pacific islands seemed only a matter of time, as Japan won victory after victory in the first six months of the war. Japanese intentions were quite clear - they intended to move further into the south Pacific and destroy any possible communication lines between the United States and Australia. Once this was achieved, Australia would be thus isolated and clearly left to its own defences.

Although American and Japanese losses were similar, the Battle of the Coral Sea south of the Solomon Islands in May 1942 was a moral victory for the allies, as it prevented, or should we say discouraged, the Japanese from moving further south. The Solomon Islands were quickly captured by the Japanese in May 1942, only to lose control after the American invasion of Guadalcanal three months later on 7 August. The ensuing land and sea battles claimed many lives on both sides, but Japanese moves south-west into the Pacific had been halted. The Battle of Santa Cruz in October 1942 virtually sealed Japan's fate and ensured no further penetration into the Pacific. The Solomons remained an active war zone for the remainder of the war. A safe harbour for allied warships was required in the eastern Pacific from which to launch further defensive action, and later offensive campaigns. The islands of the New Hebrides were selected.

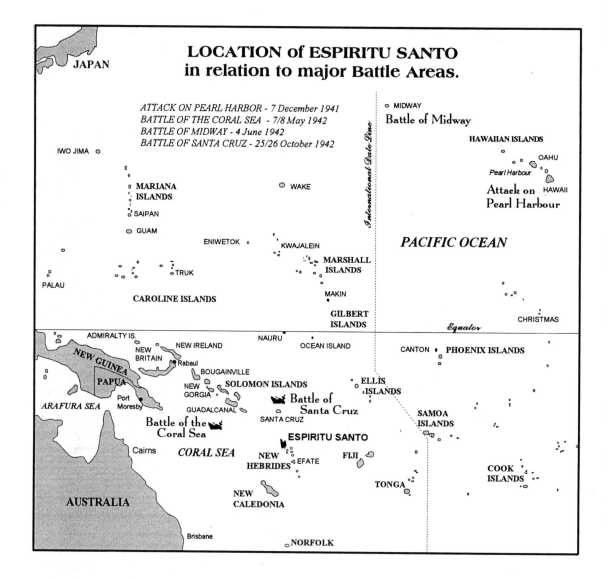

LOCATION of ESPIRITU SANTO in relation to major Battle Areas.

ATTACK ON PEARL HARBOR - 7 December 1941
BATTLE OF THE CORAL SEA - 7/8 May 1942
BATTLE OF MIDWAY - 4 June 1942
BATTLE OF SANTA CRUZ - 25/26 October 1942

The specific directive to Admiral Chester W. Nimitz, Commander in Chief of the Pacific Area, and General Douglas Macarthur was (a) to hold the lines of communication between the United States and Australia, (b) to contain the enemy in the western Pacific, and (c) to prepare for any major amphibious offensives that may be required. Nimitz was supported by Vice Admiral Robert L. Ghormley to command the South Pacific Area.

Few Americans would have known of the New Hebrides. Located 2000 kilometres east from the Australian mainland on approximately the some latitude as Cairns, the seventy-three islands that make up the nation have had a tumultuous history. Their early reputation for inter-tribal violence and cannibalism is well documented, heralding a tormented history of political handball at the expense of the local population. The remote islands were ideal for the objectives of the ruthless blackbirders, who, through coercion and downright slavery, 'captured' young men to work the canefields of Australia's Queensland and other islands, including Hawaii.

As the settlers arrived with weapons and promises to stake claim to land that was clearly not their own the indigenous population commenced a slide into becoming second-class citizens on their own land. Political possession was desperately disputed between France, England and Germany with no better objective than to lay claim to the islands just in case they could be useful to their needs, without knowing just what use that may be. Finally it was agreed that both France and England would administer the islands. Of course the local natives had no choice in the matter, and to the people of the New Hebrides, political confusion was added to repression for seventy-four years Those early settlers who managed to overcome the rain, malaria, earthquakes, the environment, and the hostility of some island peoples gradually introduced commerce and trade, benefiting themselves predominantly, but inevitably drawing the islands into the western world. During this period, World War 2 came to the New Hebrides, with huge American bases on the islands of Efate and Espiritu Santo. Fortunately there was no military conflict other than the occasional shelling of the base at Espiritu Santo by Japanese submarines, but the presence of the Americans and their wealth presented another aspect to the native's frustrations. The people of New Hebrides gained independence on 30 July 1980 and the Republic of Vanuatu was formed.

After the surprise attack on Pearl Harbor on 7 December 1941 which commenced the Pacific War, and the subsequent Japanese thrust toward Australia and into the Pacific, the first significant American defence was established on the French island of New Caledonia on 12 March 1942. Two months later the United States Navy beat back the Japanese in the Battle of the Coral Sea, northeast of Australia, south-west of the Solomons, and west of New Caledonia. This allowed the rapid development of a base of operations. From the headquarters in Noumea advance bases were set up in the archipelago of the New Hebrides. On August 7,1942, the United States made its first landing on Japanese-held territory, Guadalcanal in the Solomon Islands.

Apart from occasional aerial bombing of Espiritu Santo in 1942, the closest the Japanese came to the New Hebrides was during the Battle of Santa Cruz, a small group of islands between the Solomons and the New Hebrides. During the battle on 26 October 1942, U.S. fliers damaged three enemy aircraft carriers, one battleship and five cruisers. The Japanese sank the U.S. aircraft carrier *Hornet* and the destroyer *Porter*. The aircraft carrier *Enterprise* and the battleship *Dakota* were damaged in the engagement. This date was also to be of significance as the date of the loss of the *S.S. President Coolidge*.

Almost all new troops and supplies from the United States, Australia and New Zealand meant for the forward bases in New Hebrides and thence to the actual fighting on Guadalcanal came through New Caledonia. Similarly the sick and wounded were returned to New Caledonia for hospitalization, treatment and then evacuation to Australia or the United States.

Author, explorer, engineer and later citizen of New Hebrides, Reece Discombe writes, 'It was most unexpected that the New Hebrides was to play an important role in the Pacific War; for when the Japanese bombed Pearl Harbour in 1941 nobody realised that their strength was such that they would have entered the South Pacific, let alone the Solomon Islands just to the north of the New Hebrides.'

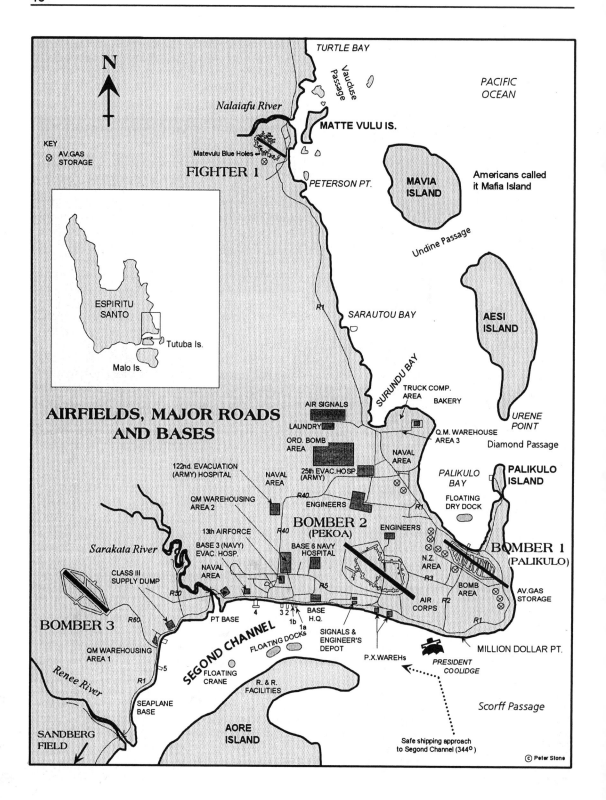

N

FIGHTER 1

TURTLE BAY

Vaucluse Passage

PACIFIC OCEAN

Nalaiafu River

MATTE VULU IS.

Matevulu Blue Holes

KEY
⊗ AV.GAS STORAGE

ESPIRITU SANTO

Tutuba Is.

Malo Is.

PETERSON PT.

MAVIA ISLAND

Americans called it Mafia Island

Undine Passage

R1

SARAUTOU BAY

AESI ISLAND

AIRFIELDS, MAJOR ROADS AND BASES

SURUNDU BAY

TRUCK COMP. AREA

BAKERY

URENE POINT

Diamond Passage

AIR SIGNALS

LAUNDRY

ORD. BOMB AREA

Q.M. WAREHOUSE AREA 3

NAVAL AREA

PALIKULO ISLAND

122nd. EVACUATION (ARMY) HOSPITAL

NAVAL AREA

25th EVAC. HOSP. (ARMY)

PALIKULO BAY

FLOATING DRY DOCK

QM WAREHOUSING AREA 2

R40

ENGINEERS

R1

13th AIRFORCE

R40

BOMBER 2 (PEKOA)

ENGINEERS

ENGINEERS

BASE 3 (NAVY) EVAC. HOSP.

BASE 6 NAVY HOSPITAL

N.Z. AREA

BOMBER 1 (PALIKULO)

Sarakata River

CLASS III SUPPLY DUMP

NAVAL AREA

R50

R5

BOMB AREA

R3

AV.GAS STORAGE

BOMBER 3

R60

PT BASE

4

3 2

1b

1a

BASE H.Q.

AIR CORPS

R2

R1

QM WAREHOUSING AREA 1

5

SEGOND CHANNEL

FLOATING DOCKS

SIGNALS & ENGINEER'S DEPOT

P.X.WAREHs

MILLION DOLLAR PT.

PRESIDENT COOLIDGE

Renee River

R1

FLOATING CRANE

SEAPLANE BASE

R. & R. FACILITIES

Scorff Passage

SANDBERG FIELD

AORE ISLAND

Safe shipping approach to Segond Channel (344°)

© Peter Stone

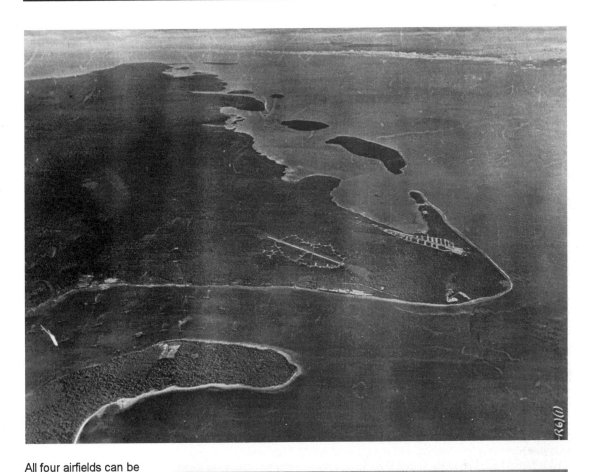

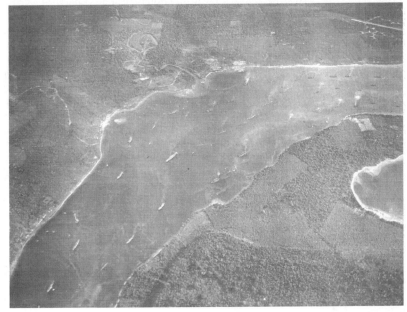

All four airfields can be seen in these two photographs. Fighter One is toward the top of the above photograph, to the west of Mavia Island. Bomber One near Palikulo Bay, is on the far right corner of the island, and Bomber Two is clearly seen in the centre. The eastern entrance to the Segond Channel is boarded on the south by Aore island. The cleared patch on Aore is the Rest and Recreation area, now the site of a modern tourist resort. The wreck of the *President Coolidge* lies just to the left of the clearing (white patch) below the eastern end of Bomber One. Bomber Three can be seen in the lower photograph.

A small contingent of American infantry and engineers landed on Efate (island) in the New Hebrides on 18 March 1942, initially setting up headquarters in Port Vila. One report suggests that U.S. military intelligence at the time was not up to its usual high standard, and that U.S. Task Force 9156 under the command of Brigadier General William Rose was fully prepared to fight its way ashore at Efate. 'However this force was pleasantly surprised to be welcomed by the local inhabitants.'

They established what is now Bauerfield Airport, the current international airport at Port Vila, together with two other airfields on north Efate. They also constructed roads around the coast of Efate, in particular the road over Khlem's Hill, linking Port Vila with Havannah Harbour and North Efate. The first airborne unit to be established in the New Hebrides was the VS-55 Squadron who used Kingfisher seaplanes. They later established a base at Espiritu Santo, and were the first to fly to the island in preparation for the development of the major naval and military base.

Havannah Harbour, nestled between Leleppa and Moso Islands, offered shelter to a large number of warships as they made their way north to the combat zone. The initial group were joined on 8 April 1942 by a marine defence battalion. Engineers and marines with the assistance of some 200 natives had soon cleared 2,000 feet for a fighter strip on Efate and had began the arduous task of providing a road system to support the new base. Most of the island was jungle wilderness, with only fifteen miles of 'track' near the town of Port Vila, the capital of New Hebrides, on Efate.

The main Efate task force arrived from the United States on 1 May 1942, at the time the Japanese were occupying Tulagi in the Solomon Islands. Included were Company B of the 116th Engineer Combat Battalion and two companies of 'Seabees' (civil construction battalions). The new arrivals set to extending the airstrip to 6,000 feet. With the Japanese less than 800 miles to the north-west, pressure for completion of the runway was intense, but the strip was completed within four weeks, and operational on 28 May 1942.

In April 1942, Brigadier General Rose and an Australian Squadron Leader flew to Espiritu Santo from Efate to pick out a suitable site for the construction of an airfield. Plantation operator Pascal Michel and Burns-Philp manager Tom Harris took the General over the areas most suitable for the construction of an airfield. The following month, on 28 May 1942, Brigadier General Rose returned to Espiritu Santo on the New Zealand cruiser *Leander*, escorted by two American destroyers. With him were four hundred American troops to establish a base at Espiritu Santo, 200 miles north of Efate. After General Rose appealed to the planters for native help, four hundred natives were recruited (among them some eighty cannibals from Malekula). Such was the potential of Espiritu Santo that Admiral R.E.Byrd expressed amazement that Efate had even been considered as a base in the first place, although Havannah Harbour was an excellent refuge, and advised Brigadier General Rose that 'we will soon be neighbours', suggesting that the base at the township of Luganville on Espiritu Santo was much more suitable than Efate for the Navy's needs. [N1]

A small reconnaissance party of three men left Efate on 28 June 1942 to find a suitable airfield site, the requirement being to position an airstrip closer to Henderson Field in the Solomons. On 8 July 1942 another small group of Seebees from the Efate detachment arrived on Espiritu Santo with a Marine anti-aircraft battery and 'a company of coloured infantrymen' to begin work on the Turtle Bay area airfield.

Ships in the Segond Channel, looking south-west from Espiritu Santo, with Aore Island to the left.

In its earliest beginnings the base at Espiritu Santo was hastily set up to serve as a protective unit for the earlier established base at Efate and to support operations during the Solomons Campaign. However, the strategic military importance and ultimate development of Button, as the base on Espiritu Santo was called, into one of the greatest advanced bases in the Pacific was soon appreciated. Espiritu Santo is approximately half way between Noumea (where the first US base was established in the Pacific), and Guadalcanal, and was thus the most advanced island at which a large base could be established short of the Solomons. [N2]

Espiritu Santo is the largest island in the New Hebrides archipelago, with an area of 1,500 square miles and a population of approximately 16,242 (1979), some 180 miles north of Efate. It was named by the explorer de Quiros in 1606. Prior to the arrival of the American troops in 1942, there were very few buildings, mainly stores, a hospital, and a school run by the Catholic Mission. The European population of the southern region where the base was to be established was 242 in 1938, with 22 British and 220 French citizens.

Luganville was the main town on Espiritu Santo, on the shore of the Segond Channel dividing the main island from Aore Island. Named after the captain of the first missionaries ship to arrive at Espiritu Santo in the 1880s, it progressed slowly and perhaps did not deserve the title of town. Prior to the U.S. forces arriving, there were no buildings at all to the east of the Sarakata River where the main township now stands, except for a single French-owned store.

Several small business houses were located on the west side of the Sarakata, including Burns Philp, a French store (C.F.N.H.), and Tom Harris' store. The land that is now the main town of Luganville was predominantly swamp.

One of the few available accounts of the early war days on Espiritu Santo appeared in an issue of the *Santonian*, a weekly Navy publication 'in the interest of Base Personnel'. An interview with Tom Harris, local resident, was recorded as follows: 'On May 12th Mr. Harris celebrated his 20th year on the island. The last time he was in "civilization" which was New Caledonia, was some time in 1925. He stayed here in the dark days of early 1942 when the planters momentarily expected to find a Jap task force anchored off any of their doorsteps. He stayed on knowing that if the Japanese did come his only choice was to follow the example of many of his colleagues, take to the bush and become one of that little known, un-medalled band who operate within the enemy's lines - the Coastal Watchers.'

Harris was a quiet, reserved, New Zealander, an agent for the Australian firm of Burns-Philp, and an island planter. Queried about what was it like before the military occupation and before the war, Mr. Harris spoke of the days when all transportation was by boat. 'There was only one road worthy of the name on the entire island - it ran from the French Delegation to the Sarakata River. And that road was built only about a year before the first United States troops moved in. Boats were used to call on a neighbour, four hundred yards down the beach. In those days there was no electric lights on the island. The planters did not have their own small light plants until just before the Army came in. Transportation inland and on the plantations was by bullock cart. Indeed, many of the planters are still using this primitive conveyance. Entertainment? Amusement? Well, you didn't wonder what was playing at NAB, or 1007. You might go visit a neighbour, but that was pretty awkward too. Before 1927, the planter did not dare get sick.

Over twenty ships are shown anchored in this section of the Segond Channel. The entrance to the Sarakata river is seen to the left, whilst Bomber Two, now the commercial airport, Pekoa, is to the right.

Quonset huts consititute the greater part of the huge naval base near Pier Four, bottom right, which could handle several ships and was the main unloading dock.

Doctors would call sometimes, but a man couldn't depend on that. Then in 1927 the island got its first doctor in residence, but before he could get a hospital built, there was an epidemic of dysentery which played havoc among the planters. Still, there were compensations - everyone had gardens; the Pacific was bountiful with its fish; 'pigs was pigs', and plentiful - and the wild pigeons found on the island made excellent eating.'

It was Harris that Brigadier General W.R. Rose consulted when on 27 April 1942 he landed by seaplane in the Segond Channel to inspect the area for a military base. Harris continued to assist the military in the establishment of Espiritu Santo as a base, and provided the 'local' knowledge.

The impact on the environment of the island, and the indigenous people was enormous. Before the arrival of the Americans, roads were almost non-existent, as already mentioned, most travelling being done by boat, or on horseback. The Americans landed ships at the edge of the jungle. Within two months a flourishing base was established east of the Sarakata River in what was previously a muddy swamp, and soon 'Santo' had a population of over 40,000 troops, in addition to the 15,000 or so New Hebridean inhabitants.

The trading centre of Santo on the southern shores of this vast heavily wooded island was chosen as the advance base as it was the most suitable site, offering a large stretch of water capable of accommodating the entire US fleet, the Segond Channel, protected on the south by Malo and Aore islands. This area of water stretches for 15 miles, its average width about two miles.

As mentioned, the occupation of Espiritu Santo by United States Army Forces occurred on 28 May 1942, when a landing was made by Force 'A' of Task Force 9156, predominantly 'M' Company of the 182nd Infantry, and a small Engineer Platoon. Brigadier General Rose assumed command and made the island a sub-base of Efate.

This huge floating dry dock off Aesi island was capable of accommodating a battleship.

On 28 September 1942, the designation of the base was changed from task Force 'A' to Provisional Base Command, Base Button. In October 1942, General Rose moved his headquarters from Efate to Espiritu Santo. It became, in the early stages of the war, the largest base in the south-west Pacific. And it was from here that the allied forces headed north to the Solomons to recapture Henderson Field.

Four major airfields and a number of smaller strips were built on Santo. The speed of construction was nothing short of amazing. The first of these was constructed at Palikulo, chosen because it was flat land under cultivation and hence little earthmoving was required. Army Seebee units and the 7th Naval Construction Battalion constructed the field at Palikulo Bay, near the south-eastern tip of the island, on the plantation 'Bencula', operated by Pascal Michel. The property comprised one 1,700 hectares including, 85 hectares of coconut grove and 67 hectares of cocoa trees, the rest being undeveloped jungle for the most part. On 7 July 1942 boundary limits were marked out by Army and Navy officers with Pascal Michel's assistance, and on the following day 'one big ship come Palikulo Bay' and unloaded dozers and other equipment.

About four hundred natives were recruited to assist the Army in building the strip under direction of Navy Lieutenant Sam Mathis, who had experience building airfields at Efate. The actual building of the strip took about two weeks, bad weather causing some delay plus 'the fact that the native labour was not very efficient'.

Palikulo airfield, later known as Bomber One, was operational on 28 July 1942, just two weeks after the felling of the first coconut tree. On 30 July, Major Allen J. Stewart of the 11th Bomb Group 26th Bomb Squadron set down the first B-17E on the new strip, followed by five others. B-17s headed for Guadalcanal were able to take on full bomb loads on Efate Island, and refuel at Espiritu Santo Island on the return leg. Tulagi and Guadalcanal in the Solomons were thus bombed on 5 August 1942.

The original foundation of Bomber One was coral, but in October 1942 a Marston matting cover was placed on the field. The overall length of the landing strip was approximately four thousand five hundred feet, but later an additional one thousand five hundred feet were added giving its present length of six thousand feet. The airstrip eventually comprised taxiways and parking bays, workshops, and camps. Initially however it was described as: 'A narrow strip cut partly from a coconut grove, partly from the encroaching jungle; revetments barely deep enough to keep a B-17's nose off the runway and so narrow a man had to stand at each wing tip to guide the pilots out to the short taxiway. There were no lights. Bottles of oil with paper wicks flickered along the runway and jeep headlights marked its end as the early morning missions took off.'

Among the first Air Groups operating from the field were the 98th Bomb Group (Heavy) of the Army who employed B-17s. Navy Kingfishers of VS-55 had been flying in the area as early as May 1942 on general reconnaissance patrol, being stationed at Segond Channel near Alhena Landing. Navy Squadrons comprising TBMS, F4Fs and a few SCDs also operated from Palikulo Field, and by September 1942, the #38A Squadron of the Royal New Zealand Air Force had moved in with Hudsons.

On 24 August 1942 at 1215 hours, Colonel Laverne 'Blondy' Saunders was advised of a contact with an enemy carrier force 720 miles (1,333 km) from Espiritu Santo Island. The risk of night landings on return was accepted and seven B-17s were dispatched in two flights. At 1745 hours three aircraft attacked a Japanese carrier, dead in the water and under tow by a cruiser. On the first run the bombs overshot and the B-17s banked for another try. Four direct hits were claimed. (Whether this vessel was HIJMS Ryujo, blasted more than an hour before by *USS Saratoga's* aircraft, or another small carrier is unknown.) When the flight returned to Espiritu Santo Island the night landing took its toll. As described, the field at this stage was just a wide slash through the jungle, with low hills close in. As the planes approached, a tropical rainstorm drenched the field and the darkness was complete. Lieutenant Robert E. Guenther's plane, the No. 4 engine failing, went into a steep bank and crashed into the hillside. The pilot and four of the crew were lost.

While Palikulo was under construction, work had already begun on a second bomber airfield at Pekoa, eventually to become the main commercial airfield of Santo, Pekoa. The 7th Naval Construction Battalion, and engineers from the 810 Army Engineers cleared the tangled growth of teak and banyan trees which covered the Pekoa site, itself a major undertaking, 'made still more difficult by the occasional enemy bombings'. With the jungle growth and palm trees cleared, the relatively flat ground was graded and surfaced with coral. By early December 1942 a coral runway 5,500 ft long, two miles of taxiways, and 75 hardstands had been constructed. This was completed by the 15th Battalion, and became Bomber Two. The strip was used for heavier aircraft as it offered better approaches than Bomber One and had a longer runway. It was started in November 1942 and was officially opened on 6 January 1943. It had the longest runway of any of the local fields, and grew to seven thousand one hundred feet of Marston matting over coral. Its thirty nine coral hardstands were able to accommodated seventy eight heavy bombers normally and one thousand nine hundred forty three (1943) in an emergency. All through its existence Pekoa was an Army installation with comparatively little Navy activity, although the Navy assisted in its construction with the 15th Naval Construction Battalion.

ESPIRITU SANTO AIRFIELDS

Above:
Bomber One was located along the shore of Palikulo Bay. This was the first airstrip built, with aircraft landing within two weeks of beginning construction.

Left:
Bomber Two remains the domestic airport, Pekoa. Bomber One can be seen to the top-left. The island to the right is Tutuba, across Scorff Passage. It is through here that the *President Coolidge* passed. The mines were located in the section of the passage shown in the photograph.

Above:
Bomber 3 was used
after the war as the
commercial airstrip for
Luganville, but being on
high ground it was often
clouded in. The
preference was then
made for Pekoa.
Right:
The seaplane base was
located between he
Renee and Sarakata
rivers, and was manned
by US and New Zealand
units.

From 13 January 1942 to 20 January 1944 the 13th Army Air Force operated from Pekoa. The field was also the headquarters of the South Pacific Combat Air Transport of the Army, Navy and Marine detachments. Later it was also used by Army Transport Command and Naval Air Transport land planes. [N3]

On 23 November 1942 the 822nd Engineer Aviation Battalion landed and immediately went to work. Part of the unit went to Palikulo to build hardstands, taxiways, a pier, and a control tower, whilst another unit went to Pekoa to help the engineers there. Most of the battalion however was put to building roads, camps and a hospital. Although the facilities were limited and crude, they played an important role in backing up the forces in the Solomons.

The 7th and 15th Naval Construction Battalions were also engaged in providing other necessary facilities for the base as a whole. The 7th erected sixty Quonset huts to be used as galleys, wards, operating rooms, dispensaries, and the like for Cub One Hospital, and forty Quonset huts and warehouses for Base Hospital Three. Another hospital of 100-beds, including quarters, wards, mess hall, operating building, and other structures, was established by the 15th battalion for Acorn 2 Hospital.

Many Quonset and Nissen huts, made of steel and iron sheeting, still remain on the island, and are clearly recognisable by their characteristic dome shape. The large Quonset huts were some 100 ft long by 40 ft wide, many with concrete floors. They are characterised by their half dome shape of corrugated iron, over a steel frame, and were mainly used for storage and workshops. A smaller 'version' of a similar dome shape was called a Nissen hut. These were only about forty feet long by fifteen feet, and used for offices and sleeping quarters. They were generally built on wooden piles (mainly coco-nut), had a wooden floor, and were insulation lined. Many of these were dismantled after the war and shipped to other islands, and even down to New Zealand. Another type of building, the Dallas hut, was of a totally different construction - usually square, made of plywood with a hipped or peaked roof. These did not survive the war as they soon rotted in the tropical climate.

For a seaplane base the 7th Battalion constructed a parking area and hangers with two ramps into the Segond Channel, and also established a PT-boat base with extensive facilities on the Sarakata River.

When the first troops landed on unknown Espiritu Santo they lacked adequate equipment, and depended on the local civilians Small boats were commandeered, and plantations combed for tools, particularly axes and machetes. Roads were mere ruts between the countless palm trees, there were no harbour facilities for the incoming ships to discharge cargo, the danger of malaria was ever present, the extreme heat together with the heavy rainfall were ever recurrent, there were no facilities for stowage or communications. Nearly all handling of cargo had to be done by hand. Very little of the cargo was palletised and mobile and cargo handling equipment was very scarce. These were but a few of the many problems facing the men constructing a base of supply at this site.

Initially, the unloading facilities at Espiritu Santo were described as 'one barge, a sandy beach and a prayer.' Heavy equipment was slung over the side of cargo vessels into a lighter. Ashore there were no cranes and the small, finger piers made of coconut logs salted down with coral washed out and disappeared after 2 or 3 weeks' use. Since the supply officer seldom was informed of arrival dates, boxes and crates accumulated in the coconut groves.

Electricity was supplied to the bases on Espiritu Santo. Each unit took pride in their base, with neat roads and pathways adding to the attractiveness of the area.

There was no question of living off the land; each item of food, clothing, and housing had to be brought in. The mud was there in abundance, the island having 'a foot-thick covering of soft black dirt, a quagmire after the tropical rains'.

Matt Wells, a plantation owner from Malo Island provides a contemporary report on events in Santo: 'The first task force of the American Invasion commandeered all the available barges and punts belonging to the French trading companies and plantation owners residing along the Segond Canal. It was indeed a jury rush up job to land all the troops with their gear, arms, rations, trucks and machinery etc. before the Japanese were aware of what was happening at the south end of Santo. The Americans worked night and day to accomplish this herculean task, and they had to land everything on punts and barges which were loaded alongside the ships anchored off shore, towed ashore and beached, and unloaded by man power only. At that time there were no piers or cranes to assist in the unloading of the punts, and as the rain pelted down on the Americans they just had to keep going to accomplish the job in time. When this was over the Americans had to erect their tents and build roads and attend to sanitary conditions and prepare drums to receive water for the troops, besides placing outposts equipped with radio and dozens of other things to attend to. As time went on the big Liberty cargo ships began to arrive bringing with them the heavy machinery for road making and draining the swampy land adjacent to the camping grounds. The Naval Construction Battalions kept coming in thousands and when they got going, good roads took shape quickly, and piers were built to accommodate the large steamers, and where it took a couple of weeks to discharge the ships by punts landing cargo ashore, the piers

Quonset huts served a number of useful purposes and were the most common of all the buildings erected by the U.S. navy and army on Espiritu Santo. Used as accommodation, they were set beneath palm trees on plantations, their trunks painted white to assist location at night, and to define wide access roads. Below: Some units however had to make do with tents, still laid out with a measure of pride.

facilitated matters quickly, until today the big ships were emptied in three or four days, and were ready to return to other ports. From 1942 to 1944, the Americans worked ceaselessly around the clock seven days a week to build up Santo from practically virgin brush, until today it resembles a small city with modern equipment, roads, drains, electric light, sanitary arrangements, hospitals, radio stations, recreation grounds, huge refrigerators, store houses, machine shops of various kinds, and everything that is wanted to run such a glib outfit.' [N4]

Wells continues: 'Too much praise cannot be given to the American Navy and Air Force. They had a very hard, monotonous, trying, dirty job guarding the approaches to harbors, keeping tho sea lanes open, sweeping of Japanese mines, destroying submarines, and escorting troops etc. in all sorts of weather. During the hurricane season it can be miserable, muggy and hot with pouring rains for days and nights on end. Sometimes the visibility is restricted to a few hundred yards away from a ship, and the flying men simply fly in heavy soaking mists and rain blind, taking numerous chances of not making it daily. The Americans on the whole have behaved splendidly indeed.'

During the early months of the struggle, the engineers did their chief work on Espiritu Santo. Since the unfinished Japanese airstrip on Guadalcanal had been damaged in the pre-invasion bombardment, Espiritu Santo was for a time the most advanced place from which land-based planes could operate. Even after the runway on Guadalcanal, Henderson Field, became usable late in August 1942, Espiritu Santo continued to serve as a major base for bombers and reconnaissance planes and as a staging point for transports. Barely finished on 7 August, the Espiritu runway had almost no facilities. Supplies were stored under coconut trees, pilots slept on the ground and under their planes, and bombers were fuelled by 'bucket brigades', emptying fuel from 44-gallon drums using hand pumps. With the arrival of additional construction units, conditions began to improve.

The initial services at the base were indeed primitive, with no cranes, little earthmoving equipment and few transport vehicles. Getting the fuel out of the drums and into the tanks of the B-17's was one of those impossible jobs which somehow got done. Gasoline trucks and trailers did not exist; the steel drums were dumped over the ship's side, floated ashore in nets, hand-rolled up under the trees, and dispersed in dumps of 20 to 30. From these they were loaded on trucks, rolled up on stands, and emptied into the tank wagons which serviced the aircraft. On 6 August, all available hands, including Colonel Saunders and Brigadier General William C. Rose who commanded ground forces on Espiritu Santo and Efate Islands, worked a bucket line for twenty hours in a driving storm to put 25,000 gallons of gasoline aboard the bombers. But such labours were not always enough, and many strike missions were delayed for lack of service facilities.

Santo boasted more services during the war than many American cities, including a telephone system with seven exchanges and 570 distinct distribution boards. Santo also rejoiced in having a superb interlocking teletype network, a radio station, miles of fine roads, 43 cinemas, a PX department store, industrial shops of all descriptions, an optical laboratory, four large hospitals, a mammoth steam laundry, and to cap it all there was a fully fledged Masonic Temple. One mess hall could seat and feed a thousand men in the one sitting. [N5]

There were five military hospitals on Espiritu Santo - two Navy, three Army with 'an appreciable percentage of female nurses'. A fully operational carbon dioxide plant existed near the Sarakata River, and the oxygen plant produced more than 300 cylinders a day. The water system was chlorinated and pumped to the various units.

At one end of this vast installation there were a few homes occupied by Frenchmen and a few grubby tropical stores. Farther out were the hovels in which indentured Tonkinese slept after working the plantations. And beyond them, in the bush, lived some of the world's most primitive people.

Snafu Weekly, a 15th CB Publication, interestingly tells of the units first year on Espiritu Santo. The 15th Naval Construction Battalion arrived on 6 October 1942 to find that numerous challenging conditions had to be overcome and many problems had to be solved in common with other units that arrived in the early stages of the base's development. 'Since the *Island Mail* first dropped anchor in Palikulo Bay with the 15th aboard, and the first details came ashore to a strange tropical island, a year has lapsed... a year which has seen our camp grow from a temporary makeshift abode to one of permanence, comfort, and security. At this time it is felt that we may say, without fear of contradiction, that we inhabit the most liveable camp on the island. Let us stop for a moment to take stock. For those early details, the island was not an especially friendly place. To be sure the lizards were a curiosity, the coconuts tasty, and the flies a pestilence; but there was something else ... we wish that a canteen held more water, that we had some ammunition, that we had something to eat, and that we could be sure that those were our planes up there. The days which ensued weren't pleasant ones. Tents were pitched while supplies continued to stream ashore. All hands were plagued with severe cases of diarrhea and the sick bay did a land office business in aspirin and paregoric until their temporary supplies were depleted. Speculation ran high as to the causes of the universal ailment....among the most popular theories recalled were .... the flies, the water, the coconuts, the heat etc. But the plague continued until we were acclimated [*sic*]. Weeks march on.....men continued to join their mates ashore.. company offices and a battalion office were established .... a twelve hour work day was established ... a central watering place was created where you could fill your canteen with a hot mixture of gasoline, redwood sap, chlorine and water. Then we saw our first payday since leaving the states, and practically everyone drew some money although there was nothing to buy. Cigarettes were fairly scarce, and matches rare. Later candy was sold and that which was left after the rats and ants had been satisfied was used to fill up after a delicious meal of spam or canned hash. In the period that followed, the chaos subsided and a certain regularity and efficiency prevailed. Two mess halls and galleys were built which at that time were considered the acme of perfection. Officers quarters were constructed and office buildings were erected. The water distillation began functioning and slightly later the ice machine which were the envy of the entire island, were set up.' [N6]

Captain (Ret'd) William Paull, who later arrived as a Private First Class with an infantry division from the Solomons on the *President Jackson* on 12 August 1942 has a more idyllic recollection: 'Santo was as close to the romantic Hollywood version of the South Pacific as I ever came. There were no enticing, bare-breasted, nubile maidens with swaying hips, warm kisses, fragrant flower leis .... but there were swaying palms, warm surf, a sweet fragrant scent in the air. At night the stars seemed so much closer. The sweet redolence was somewhat counter-balanced by the reek from the copra sheds where coconut meat was spread out to dry and cure. We made sure our camp was located up-wind and far away from these native enterprises. I'm now certain that my fondness for this island was a strongly influenced by what it didn't have, as by what charms it did have. It didn't have Japs.'

The units were eventually served with electric power, and in many instances tents were replaced with ingenious buildings made from any material, particularly dressed timber, that could be bartered, bought, scrounged or simply 'borrowed'. The ingenuity of man is not to be taken lightly, and chairs, tables

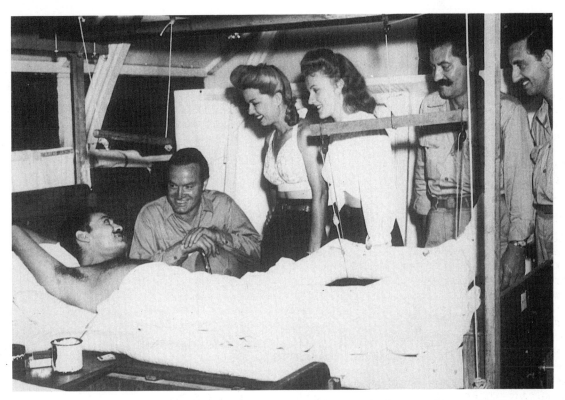

Cooped up in a Quonset hut evacuation hospital is no fun, but at least for Sergeant Norman Weintraub, the monotony of his day was diminished with a visit by actor/comedian Bob Hope, actress Francis Langford, dancer Patty Thomas, actor Jerry Colona, and guitarist Tony Romano.

and wardrobes, and even beds with innerspring mattresses were constructed. The objective of the men, accepting their fate of a permanent assignment on the island, was to make life as comfortable as possible.

Snafu Weekly wrote: 'And speaking of recreation, we can also proudly display a fine [base]ball diamond, tennis courts, a basketball court, movie theatre, and a beach complete with raft and diving board. The officers and chiefs are aptly proud of their clubs which are undoubtedly the best on the island. In the centre of camp we have a fine barber shop, a tailor shop, and even a cobbler shop. I almost forgot the laundry, a service which has been faithfully rendered for many months.'

With thousands of troops with nowhere to go and money to spare it was natural that they would wish to venture forth and try something other than camp cooking. In a very short time, numerous restaurants sprang up around Santo and steak was the most popular dish, making a change from the routine camp meals. Charles Grazziani, who had property at beautiful Champagne Beach to the north of the island, set up a steak restaurant that did exceptionally well. For every 'stroke of the knife I earnt a dollar' he told Reece Discombe. Laundries sprang up overnight as the Tonkinese were very quick to capitalise on this profitable business. By 1944 there were more than 40,000 men stationed permanently there, as well as the constant coming and going of troops

Clarinetist Artie Shaw and his band entertain military personnel at an outdoor concert on Espiritu Santo.

in transit. There would have been more than 500,000 men who passed through 'Santo' during the course of the war.

A man will do what he can to find a drink in the harsh climate of the islands. Although the penalties were severe for the sale of hard liquor, it did little to deter the black market, and indeed encouraged a few entrepreneurs to try their own brew. Liquor was the premium currency, unofficial of course, and if for example somebody wished to purchase truck tyres or engine parts, these could be readily exchanged for a bottle of gin, brandy, whisky or whatever. And 'whatever' was the operative word. When liquor supplies, illegally brought up from Port Vila, dried out, it was time for the special brew. Some marines were known to take the alcohol from compasses and torpedoes, and to mix it with fruit juice, making a potent cocktail called the infamous 'torpedo juice'. The Air Force had a similar brew, made from the glycol from the radiators of their aircraft mixed with coconut milk. This made an extremely potent concoction. It is not recorded how many lost their lives through drinking these lethal brews.

William Paull recalls: 'The natives loved those awful C-Rations whilst we craved the fresh fruit. They were reputed to be cannibals and head-hunters. Maybe so, but they were the most courteous people I've ever met. Also, the blackest. They wore little G-strings made from woven leaves and most were adorned with shell necklaces and bracelets. They were short, muscular, bandy-legged, and shiny coal-black. None of them displayed the runny sores that we saw on the natives of many of the other islands we visited. The natives we encountered near the beach were accustomed to seeing white men but those we met in the interior were very curious about us. They always indicated that they wanted us to undress so that they could see if we were white all over. The first few times this happened I was uncomfortable being surrounded by a crowd of grinning natives. They would point and touch and then jabber something to the rest of their group. These unintelligible comments always seemed to provoke great laughter and glee. At first, this was disconcerting but we got used to shedding our clothes and running around like the natives.'

By 1943 it was found that because of increased war activity, the two existing strips were insufficient, hence a third airfield was constructed, on the plateau above the then existing Burns Philp store. This strip became Bomber Three, the most modern and largest of all the airfields constructed in the New Hebrides. It was completed by the 5th Naval Construction Regiment in July 1943, and serviced a Carrier Aircraft Service Unit and a Field Overhaul Unit based on the field .

Bomber Three continued to be used as a civilian airstrip right up until the 1970s by both domestic and international airlines. Bomber Three lost its commercial status to Bomber Two, which is now the commercial airport, Pekoa, at the south-east corner of the island. Bomber Three was a ideal in many respects as it has a huge strip, but as it was on high ground, it was often clouded in, blocking out effective use of the airport. After many landing delays it was decided to open up Bomber Two. Meanwhile, both Bomber One and Bomber Three have defied the encroaching jungle, but are totally inoperable. Visitors to Espiritu Santo travel along the overgrown, but clearly discernable Fighter One when they visit the famous Blue Holes. (See Chapter 13).

Besides the many land based Army, Navy and Marine squadrons, several Air Groups from carriers at anchor in the Espiritu Santo harbors were flown onto the field for repairs, testing and training. During the summer of 1944, the field reached its top capacity of approximately six hundred fifty planes, five hundred officers and three thousand enlisted personnel. Mobile Training Unit One was based at the field for about fifteen months and during this period, trained hundreds of enlisted air crewmen in aerial gunnery. The South Pacific Aircraft Training Unit was aboard for twelve months, training squadrons in Anti-Submarine Warfare and Rockets.

Fighter One, on the east coast near Turtle Bay, was completed 18 November 1942 on a coconut plantation, eight miles north-west of Pekoa field. Marine Aircraft Group Eleven (MAG11) occupied the field and employed it for rehabilitation of pilots and enlisted men after they had spent a tour of combat duty, operational and tactical training of pilots, receiving all new TBFs and F4Fs allocated to the Marines in the South Pacific in order to place them in combat commission and to have them ferried north, and for maintenance of squadron planes in operating condition. The strip itself was four thousand four hundred feet long and three hundred feet wide, with an elaborate system of taxiways and revetments, all of coral surface and considered an all-weather field. It could handle eight operating squadrons and three hundred carrier type planes. The maximum number of personnel was attained in November 1943 when there were 432 officers and 4678 enlisted men quartered at the field. A large number of aircraft were delivered directly to the field from CVEs that were anchored in Turtle Bay. It was necessary to lighter the aircraft ashore through a narrow and winding channel to a pier, which was about one hundred yards from the strip. Fighter One officially shut down on 2 January 1945.

Note also that a fifth field was constructed at Espiritu Santo. The 27th Division built a small air-strip on the water's edge about three miles southwest of the Renee River, near Brigstocke Point, in late 1944. This was known as Sandburg Field, and was used for smaller aircraft used to spot artillery fire. [N7]

By the end of 1943, Army construction activity on the island had ground to a standstill, however Navy construction units were kept busy. Army buildings were being dismantled and transported north to the Solomons. The Navy appeared to be settling in permanently. Lieutenant A.E. Gordon, RANVR (Special Branch) reported: 'The Naval area is very compact and all offices, storehouses, ammunition dumps, installations etc are clustered around the pier areas, from Pier 1 to Pier 5. They are arranged in an orderly manner with well made roads, fairly wide, running between each row of buildings. There is very little dispersal of buildings or installations and the whole set-up is being modelled on peace time, not war time, lines. The airfields also appear to be maintaining their organisation and personnel at full strength.'

There were also three floating docks at Espiritu Santo, one large enough to accommodate a battleship. The large dock was constructed from four independent sections towed out from the USA. During assembly, one section sank in 300 ft of water and could not be raised. A replacement was towed out from the USA. [N8]

Shipping was also received at Palikulo Bay which proved to a favourite anchorage for large ship, particularly aircraft carriers. Merchant ships also unload here, at the dock on the southern side of the bay, generally for the Army supply depot at Surundu Bay, just to the north.

A seaplane base was established near the western end of Segond Channel, used by the US Navy and the Royal New Zealand Air Force, the latter with a fleet of sixteen aircraft.

Despite the strong Naval presence, or permanence as it may have appeared, the Navy gradually came to prefer the use of Port Purvis in the Florida group of the Solomon islands as their forward base, being closer to the (now) combat areas. The largest number of ships of over 1,000 tons to be assembled in the Segond Channel at the one time had been no less than ninety-seven.

As the Allies gained the ascendency against the Japanese during the latter years of the war, there was little cause for all the fields to remain open and all air traffic for Pekoa was routed to Palikulo Airfield effective from 8 February 1945. This was in line with the general roll-up plan for the island in concentrating air activity on one field adequate to handle all the traffic likely to come to Espiritu Santo in the future. With the Navy planning to remove all its air facilities from the island, Palikulo Airfield was turned over to the United States Army Air force on 16 February 1945, and remained the major airstrip. Pekoa however was highly thought of and many Army officers believed that it, rather than Palikulo, was the field that should have been maintained.

In hindsight, this was to prove true. Bomber One was used immediately after the war for commercial flights, and then Bomber Three, but eventually Pekoa was re-opened and remains today as the commercial airport for Espiritu Santo.

Although no allied infantry other than the Americans were based on Espiritu Santo, the New Zealand Air Force No 5 & 6 squadrons had their base at the western end of Segond Channel, initially established by the U.S. These New Zealand squadrons used Catalinas (PBY flying boats), whilst other New Zealand squadrons were based at Palikulo (Bomber One). Their job was to assemble Corsair aircraft for the U.S. Marines and service their own and U.S.

PBY Catalina aircraft of
No. 5 New Zealand
Squadron at their base
on the Segond Channel
near the Renee River.

planes, and do operational duties flying to the Solomons. They also flew
Dauntless SBD bombers.

Although no land combat took place in the New Hebrides, the Japanese did
shell Espiritu Santo on several occasions. A direct enemy attack was experienced on 15 October 1942, when a Japanese submarine shelled Bomber One
for about five minutes but inflicted no damage to either personnel or equipment. Bomber One was again shelled by a submarine, from a position about
five miles east of the east entrance to Segond Channel, on 23 October, without
damage. On 18 November 1942, a U.S. Patrol Boat attacked and damaged a
Japanese submarine at the west entrance to Segond Channel.

Another attack took place over several nights between 21 and 30 January
1943. These five bombing raids caused very little damage. The first of these
spate of bombings occurred on the night of 21-22 January 1943 when four
Japanese planes dropped between eleven and eighteen Type 98 General
Purpose Bombs in the jungle about a mile southeast of Bomber Two (Pekoa)
without doing any damage. The following night, just past midnight, one or two
enemy bombers came over and dropped fourteen bombs which straddled
Bomber One. None landed directly on the strip. Three men were wounded, but
no damage was done to the strip nor equipment. On the night of 27-28 January
1943, again just past midnight, one enemy bomber came over Espiritu Santo.
The weather, however, was bad and after circling the island, the plane dropped
fifteen bombs in the jungle about four miles from the west end of Aore Island
without damage to either personnel or equipment.

On the night of 21-22 February 1943, one enemy bomber came over and
dropped six bombs. The target on this raid was Bomber Two and two of the
bombs landed in a bunker damaging one of the bombers. These bombs were
of the five hundred pound type making craters of ten to twelve feet deep and
fifteen to eighteen feet wide. Three of these bombs failed to explode.

On the night of 23-24 May 1943, an enemy bomber approached Espiritu Santo and dropped five or six bombs in Segond Channel with no damage to personnel or equipment. These bombs fell through the berth occupied by a US aircraft carrier which had left the previous morning. On the night of 10 August 1943, a small reconnaissance plane flew over Palikulo Bay, Segond Channel and Bomber Strip One. It was assumed that this plane came from a submarine. Again on the morning of 24 August 1943, another reconnaissance plane flew over the bomber strips and Segond Channel. On 31 August 1943 the tanker *William S. Rheem* was torpedoed off Espiritu Santo but did not sink and with assistance made the Segond Channel.

A bombing attempt on 9 September 1943 again caused little damage but did take one life. A sad occasion, the attack caused the sudden demise of one, Bossy, a cow. A monument was erected to her parting: 'Here lies Bossy, 11.00pm 9/9/43 because she was walking around during a blackout'.

On the night of 14-15 September 1943, one enemy bomber came over, dropped flares over Palikulo Bay and Bomber Strip One and unloaded fourteen bombs in the jungle adjacent to the 350th Engineer Regiment Area, and not far from the Army 25th Evacuation Hospital. There was no damage to personnel or equipment. Notes taken at the Captain's Saturday Morning Conference suggest clearly that these enemy nuisance raids served very beneficially in keeping personnel in readiness and on the alert. The last air raid experienced by the base took place on the night of 14 October 1943. A Japanese reconnaissance plane appeared over Bomber One and Two and dropped flares over Bomber One and Palikulo Bay. No bombs fell in the raid.

At no time was an attacked regarded as being major and relatively insignificant damage was caused. Nevertheless, during the early days of the New Hebrides Military Bases at Efate and Espiritu Santo, there was constant peril of enemy action until the Solomons Islands were firmly under Allied Control.

The loss of the *SS President Coolidge* on 26 October 1942 was of course a major disaster, and is covered in detail in the next chapter. This was an 'own goal' as the soccer fans would suggest, and resulted in the loss of equipment badly needed by the Espiritu Santo base, as well as all the arms for the troops on board. It could be said that the loss of the *President Coolidge* was simply just one of those things that happens in war, but the loss of any ship cannot be taken that lightly. Human mistakes will always occur, particularly in the confusion and haste of war.

When enthusiasm is added to a lack of communication, anything can happen. Such it was on 16 August 1944. Two SBD aircraft of the South Pacific Air Training Unit were conducting anti-submarine warfare exercises with submarine *USS S-38* off Espiritu Santo. The carrier, *USS White Plains* which had just arrived at Espiritu Santo that morning, had one of its TBF planes on anti-submarine patrol. The pilot of the TBF saw the two SBDs approach the surfaced submarine and make what appeared to be an attack. The submarine immediately started a crash dive as would be expected. The TBF flashed a 'continuous recognition signal' to the submarine but the sun obscured the signal, and no positive response was received by the TBF in return. The carrier's planes were thereby scambled and went in for an attack, dropping two 300 lb. depth bombs, one exploding close by the submarine. Fortunately, the bombs exploded at a distance not to inflict injury on the submarine personnel and only caused hull and internal damage to the craft itself. *S-38* was able to resurface and return to port safely. No doubt words were exchanged when the submarine made dock. It could well have been that Espiritu Santo could claim a submarine to its diver attractions, but fortunately it was not to be.

The military activity in the New Hebrides was on such a scale that it is hard to credit today, with more than half a million military personnel, mainly U.S., but also Kiwis and Australians, passing through on their way to the various fronts in the Solomons, active in aerial combat, or on naval and army ships. When the fighting ended on Guadalcanal, Espiritu Santo boasted five airfields, a seaplane base, three hospitals, ten small camps and thirty-two miles of roads. Its role in the defeat of the Japanese in the Pacific War is significant, and it continues to have an effect on the people of Vanuatu, and the economy of the nation.

SETTING THE MINES

Minefields were laid across the entrances to the Segond Channel in order to prevent enemy surface and underwater craft from entering the harbour, thus causing mischief amongst the ships at anchor.

At four minutes past midnight on Monday 3 August 1942, *USS Gamble*, in company with *USS Tracy* and *USS Breese*, cruised out of the Segond Channel at 8 knots heading west and then south-west to exit the entrance. At 9.30 am the ships commencing mining at the western entrance to the Segond Channel, dropping forty-five No. 6 mines. The operation was over in eight minutes. Minefield 1 running north-south from Brigstocke Point on Espiritu Santo to the northwest tip Malo Island closed the western entrance to Bruat Channel.

This was followed by a drop of sixty three mines, extended generally east-west between Espiritu Santo and the northeast tip of Aore Island. Minefield Two closed the western entrance to the Segond Channel. The ships then proceeded east through Bruat Channel between Aore and Malo Island, and north between Bogacio and Tutuba Islands toward the eastern entrance of the Segond Channel. At 1.00 pm, the three ships commenced laying the first of two lines of mines roughly north-south between Bogacio and Espiritu Santo, leaving an entrance into the Segond Channel at the northern end close to Espiritu Santo. A second line between Espiritu Santo and Tutuba Island effectively blocked the Segond Channel to vessels attempting to enter from due east. Minefield Three consisted of sixty-three mines blocking off the eastern entrance to the Segond Channel except for a narrow passage through the mines and a gap to the west. Thus a total of 171 mines were laid by *Gamble*, *Breese*, and *Tracy*.

Later, in 1943, Minefield Four was planted across the seaward of Undine Passage. Minefield Five was the last to be laid, on 10 February 1944, extending across the seaward entrance to Scorff Passage, from what we now know as Million Dollar Point to the north-western tip of Tutuba.

During 1942, Ensign Richard J. 'Pete' Peterson was aboard the *USS Gamble*, one of the three ships which laid mines across the Segond Channel. 'When we arrived at Espiritu Santo to lay the mines only a few French copra plantation owners, a Catholic Church and a few Army personnel were there. I doubt if such a place as 'Luganville' existed at the time.' He recalls that it was 3 August 1942 when the south-west and north-east entrances to Segond Channel at Espiritu Santo were mined, 'making it a safe harbour and staging area for the invasion of Guadalcanal'.

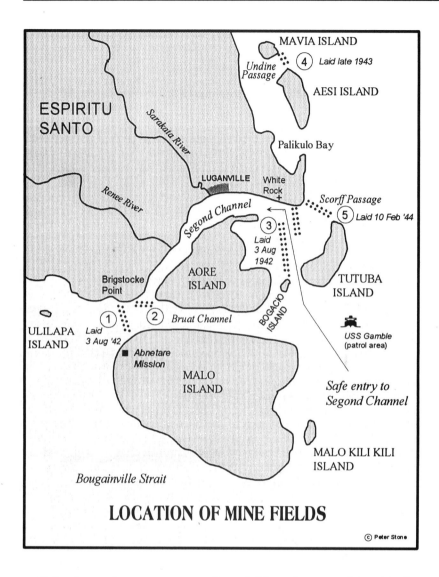

LOCATION OF MINE FIELDS

© Peter Stone

Only the north-east entrance to Segond Channel was used by shipping. Luganville did exist, and was known as such, but was developed more to the east of the Sarakata River, and was a mere shadow of what is now the town of Luganville. The mine depot was on the island of Aore, across the Segond channel from Luganville. [N9]

The Mark VI mine used was a round ball of about 3-ft diameter containing 1600 pounds of TNT. Each mine was carried mounted on its own dolly which had four wheels, capable of locking into a 'U' shaped mine track on the minelayer. The tracks on the minelayer lay on both the port and starboard sides of the ship from about midships to the stern. Laying of the mines consisted of manually pushing the armed mine off the stern at timed intervals. The entire mine unit had positive buoyancy and floated while a weight on a cable slipped to the seabed and measured the depth. This set the mechanism so that as the

U.S.S. Gamble was initially a 4-stack destroyer, DD-123, launched in May 1918. She was converted to a minelayer, DM-15, on 13 June 1930 and during her active duty in the Pacific was awarded no less than ten battle stars. This historic photograph show her before conversion.

dolly flooded and sank, the correct amount of cable was released between the dolly and the mine. The dolly became the mine's anchor and the mine then floated at the required distance beneath the surface. A small float, attached to the mine, was also released which floated just beneath the surface. When armed, contact by a ship with the mine itself, or the float and its cable, would set off the mine. The distance between mines in line resulted from the ship's speed, and the predetermined dropping interval. [N10]

The Santo field received a further plant on December 21, 1942, when Gamble dropped 42 mines, and a third on May 17, 1942, when Preble, Gamble, and Breese planted 140 more, brought to Espiritu Santo from Pearl Harbor by *SS James McPherson*. The first three mine fields were removed by sweeping between 2 and 23 January 1944, and replaced February 10, 1944, by

Gamble, Sicard, and *Monadnock*. Field 4 was disposed of by sweeping operations conducted from 13 to 19 October 1944. Field 5 was swept in three days from 28 through 31 March 1945. [N11]

Dick Hansen was also aboard *USS Gamble*. 'We laid the naval mines at both ends of Segond Channel that sank the *USS Tucker* and the *President Coolidge*,' he comments with what could be mistaken for a sense of pride. 'We had hauled the mines down from Pearl Harbor beginning in late July, 1942 and we stopped at Palmyra Island, and Suva in the Fiji Islands before proceeding to Espiritu Santo. I remember we painted a rock white to guide the ships into the channel. Later we went to Noumea to pick up mines to patch the mine field in December 1942. They swept the mines in 1944 and I believe replanted. They were Mark VI mines with a plumb bob and a K-device.'

The 'white rock' is of course still there, and may be seen a short walk along the shore from the President Coolidge site, west toward Luganville. It is actually marked on Admiralty Chart 179.

The *President Coolidge* was the second ship to have been sunk by the minefields at Espiritu Santo. Lt. Kralovec in his *The Naval History of Espiritu Santo* simply states: 'Two very unfortunate incidents occurred during the life of these fields'. Indeed. Immediately after Field 1 was laid, 3 August 1942, the new destroyer, *USS Tucker*, "not having notice of its existence", ran into the field and was sunk. The second instance occurred on 26 October 1942, when the heavily laden troop ship, *USS President Coolidge*, steamed into Field 3, and was sunk'. Minefield 5 also claimed a victim, although, fortunately, only superficially. On 19 March 1944, shortly after the laying of the field, the *SS Oriental* passed through it striking one mine and suffering considerable hull damage. Only a moment earlier, a patrol boat began sending *Oriental* a blinker signal which reached her master too late to be helpful: KEEP CLEAR OF MINE FIELDS. The patrol craft had watched *Oriental* for 30 minutes before it began signalling. The edge of a minefield is no place to procrastinate. Fortunately the ship did not sink and was able to make port under her own power. Well, two out of three ain't bad!

During the life of all five mine fields at Espiritu Santo, no enemy craft were known to have been damaged or destroyed by entering the mined areas. Kralovec states, 'Of course, we must not lose sight of the fact that knowledge by the enemy that the waters at Santo were defensively mined, may well have kept his submarines from attempting entrance to our harbors. This, if it be a fact, is alone enough to justify the existence of the fields.'

CHAPTER FIVE

NO TUCKER
FOR TERRELL

If indeed the justification for mining the entrances to the Segond Channel was to keep out inquisitive Japanese submarines, then it came at a cost. On the very same day that the western entrance to the channel was mined, the U.S. Navy lost a destroyer that blundered into the mines. Like the circumstances of the loss of the *President Coolidge* thirteen weeks later, *USS Tucker* (DD 374) had been warned of the minefield. The U.S. Navy didn't make a fuss of her loss, not in the public press anyway, as there was no other but themselves to blame. Interest in the wreck of the *President Coolidge* tends to overshadow that of the *Tucker*, both in its controversy, and its persona as a pleasure dive. And after all, who would want to dive a demolished destroyer when an intact liner twice her size lies nearby?

The destroyer, authorized under the National Industrial Recovery Act of 16 June 1933, was built by the Norfolk Navy Yard, Norfolk, Virginia. Her keel was laid there on 15 August 1934 and she was launched on 26 February 1936. The new ship was named in honour of Commodore Samuel Tucker, USN. Commodore Tucker commanded the privateers *Franklin, Boston, Beane* , and *Thorn* during the Revolutionary War, and was commissioned captain by General George Washington on 20 February 1776. Mrs. Leonard Thorner, a third cousin four times removed from her namesake, christened the vessel, which was placed in commission on 23 July 1936. The destroyer was one of the first ships to use stainless steel extensively throughout the ship.

Tucker arrived at Pearl Harbor on 14 February 1941, from San Diego, and then proceeded to New Zealand arriving at Auckland on 17 March 'to show the flag' demonstrating U.S. support for New Zealand. Returning to Pearl Harbor she took part in routine exercises at sea before sailing to her home port of San Diego on 19 September 1941. After a short stay she returned to Hawaii and as part of Task Force 19 she began operations anew in the Hawaiian islands in November 1941. After one month of manoeuvres she returned to Pearl Harbor for a tender overhaul.

Tucker was lying in berth X-8, East Loch, part of a nest of five destroyers (with *Selfridge, Case, Reid* and *Conyngham*) alongside the tender *USS Whitney*, undergoing a tender overhaul when the Japanese launched their raid on Pearl Harbor on 7 December 1941. Lieutenant Commander W. R. Terrell was in command. 'Suddenly the drone of airplane engines and the roar of exploding bombs and torpedoes shattered the Sunday morning calm. Japanese planes swept over the harbor and wheeled above like hawks.' [N1]

On board *Tucker*, GM2c W. E. Bowe observed the unfolding attack and promptly manned a machine gun on the ship's after superstructure, commencing to fire even before the general quarters alarm sounded. Within two minutes the aft 5-inch guns came into action, joining the concentrated gunfire emanating from the nest of ships in which *Tucker* lay. This veritable storm of shells and bullets produced hits on three enemy aircraft, two of which spun into the hills behind Pearl Harbor and exploded, whilst the third disappeared over a low ridge, in flames and smoking. Meanwhile the engineering crew of *Tucker* worked feverishly to reassemble machinery torn down for the tender overhaul.

Neither Tucker nor the other destroyers in the nest were significantly damaged, and Tucker immediately commenced patrolling off Pearl Harbor before spending the next five months escorting convoys between San Francisco and Hawaii. Early in April 1942, *Tucker* was ordered to the South Pacific, and spent the next four months on escort duty to Fiji, Australia and New Zealand. At Suva, she received orders to escort the *SS Nira Luckenbach* to Espiritu Santo, and on 1 August 1942 the two ships departed by way of a route north of Efate Island and west of the Malekula islands.

On arrival at Espiritu Santo, *Tucker* planned to enter via the western entrance to the Segond Channel. She had just transited Bruat Channel between Aore and Malo islands and was swinging north to enter Segond Channel, Espiritu Santo late in the evening of 3 August when she struck an American mine, planted only that morning. A 'Q message', a radio warning of the recently mined field, was not received by *Tucker*, whose Captain, like that of the *President Coolidge*, was totally unaware of the danger ahead. [N2]

The mine struck the destroyer amidships at 2145 hrs on 3 August 1942, lifting her high out of the water. Captain Terrell thought his ship had been torpedoed as he had no cause for concern about a minefield. As *Tucker* slowed to a halt, it soon became apparent that it was a mortal hit. The ship's back was broken and she 'began folding up like a jacknife', with the main deck amidships buckled and submerged under six feet of water. The explosion instantly killed three men. *Nira Luckenbach's* skipper, rightfully worried about the safety of his own ship in an uncharted minefield, quickly sent boats to aid in rescuing the destroyer's crew as they abandoned their sinking ship, but declined an attempt to tow the stricken destroyer.

By early the next morning, a local district patrol boat, *YP-346*, (called a 'yippie boat') had arrived on the scene and attempted to tow the stricken destroyer into shallower water to facilitate salvage operations. When the *YP-346* had gone as close to the beach as she dared, the tow line was cut and *Tucker* left to her own fate.

With all power lost, the destroyer drifted helplessly and was slowly settling, the rate increasing as the water rose toward the bridge. The ship took a sudden list to port and Commander Terrell had fears that the ship was about to sink and ordered abandon ship. A few men were instructed to remain on the forecastle and told to be prepared to let go the anchor if ordered, but these instructions were misunderstood, and the anchor was let go.

Commander Terrell was the last to leave his ship and was picked up by a missionary in a small boat. He lay alongside the ship and as soon as he became aware that the ship was not settling further, returned aboard with several men and cut the anchor with a hack saw.

Destroyer, *USS Tucker* had dimensions of overall length 341 ft (104 m), beam 35 ft (10.7 m), and a displacement of 1500 tons, with a speed of 35 knots.

A motor launch then took the ship in tow, but after some two hours the destroyer, now significantly jacknifed into a 'V' shape, grounded in ten fathoms of water not far off the village of Abnetare, on Malo Island at 0445 hours on 4 August 1942. [N3]

Minelayers *Breese, Tracey* and *Gamble* were at anchor in the Segond Channel at the time of the loss of *Tucker*. Ships logs indicate that at 0803 hrs, Tuesday 4 August, *Breese* and *Tracey* up-anchored and were underway. *Breese* went west through the Segond Channel and thus was able to later assist *Tucker*. *Gamble* and *Tracey* went east. *Gamble* reports passing White Rock, and then turned on a course of 180°, through the recently laid minefield and out between Bogacio and Tutuba Islands to their patrol area in open sea.

Lieutenant Commander Arnold S. Lott in his book *Most Dangerous Sea*, writes: '*Breese*, one of whose mines might have sunk *Tucker*, was patrolling off Espiritu Santo that morning. About 1115, an approaching plane sent all hands scurrying to battle stations. It was soon identified as a friendly Marine fighter, trying to drop a message. As it crossed *Breese's* bow in a second attempt it got too low and smacked in.'

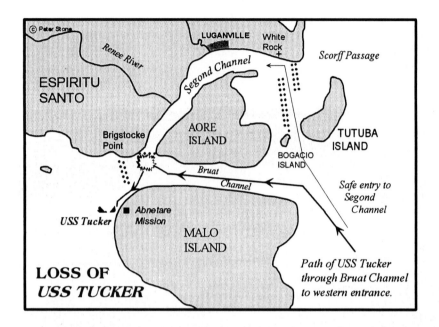

© Peter Stone

ESPIRITU SANTO

Renee River

Segond Channel

LUGANVILLE

White Rock

Scorff Passage

AORE ISLAND

Brigstocke Point

Bruat Channel

BOGACIO ISLAND

TUTUBA ISLAND

Safe entry to Segond Channel

USS Tucker

Abnetare Mission

MALO ISLAND

Path of USS Tucker through Bruat Channel to western entrance.

LOSS OF USS TUCKER

'*Breese* lowered a rescue boat and her Executive Officer, Lieutenant Commander H. F. Stout, dived to recover 2nd Lieutenant Frank C. Drury, USMCR, who was unconscious and being dragged down by his parachute. At that point, no one yet knew what urgent news Drury carried, but a few minutes later the message was recovered - a destroyer had blown up in the new mine field. *Breese* took off for a reckless 30-knot run through a channel for which she had no detailed chart, her dauntless Exec. conning the ship from the foretop to avoid shoals'.

Alongside *Tucker* at 1235, she took off thirty-eight men and three officers. Three days later she was ordered to transfer *Tucker* survivors to *USS Curtiss* - 'but only after breakfast'. (There must have been a long chow line on *Curtiss*.)

The question could be asked as to why *Breese* did not see *Tucker* when the minelayer exited the western entrance of Segond Channel. By then however the destroyer would have drifted off the western end of Malo Island and may not have been visible. After hitting one of the mines in minefield 2, the destroyer then drifted back toward minefield 1 between Brigstocke Point and Malo Island and was in danger of sustaining further damage as there is no indication that Commander Terrell had suddenly become aware of this minefield. Perhaps because *Tucker* drifted so close to shore she managed to avoid a second explosion. It also begs the question as to how *Nira Luckenbach* managed to get through. Perhaps she fortuitously remained between the two minefields and was later escorted into the Segond Channel.

Except for the first few seconds after the hit there was no great settling of the ship from the time the captain ordered all hands to abandon ship until the ship was grounded. The bow was at all times was more buoyant than the stern and was bent upward at a greater angle. That part of the ship abaft of the point where her back was broken gradually settled, and at about 2100 on 4 August 1942, sank. By then, all hands had been taken off the stricken destroyer. [N4]

In this dramatic photograph, the *USS Tucker* lies broken off the north-western tip of Malo Island. The bow rides high in the water whilst her stern is about to sink in sixty feet. Minelayer *USS Breese* stands by. A huge oil slick spread out from the wreck.

The Navy laid no blame on the commander of *USS Tucker* for running into the minefield. Lieutenant Commander W. R. Terrell, was exonerated when an investigation showed that *Tucker* had never been informed of the minefield.

The loss of *Tucker* claimed six lives in all - the three men killed instantly by the mine explosion, and three later reported missing, and assumed lost in the sinking. The bodies of James R. Clark, Chief Water Tender; Raymond H. Ross, Boiler Maker, first class, and Charles W. Simpson, Fireman, second class, were never recovered. New graves on Espiritu Santo were prepared for Edward F. Hewitt, Water Tender, first class, Ray J. Stanbaugh, Fireman, first class, and Glen R. Steinow, Fireman, second class.

Long after *Tucker* had gone her broken hull, visible in the clear water, was bombed by wary but uninformed aviators who suspected that they had got themselves a Japanese submarine.

The written report of *Tucker's* loss, for which only lack of information and delayed communications could be blamed, began its slow journey through official channels to Washington. Secretary of the Navy Frank Knox scribbled his name across it on 21 November 1942, and by that time the minefield at Espiritu Santo had claimed another unnecessary victim. *Tucker's* loss was not announced until 10 August 1945 'for reasons of national security'.

American accounts of the Guadalcanal campaign have normally omitted *Tucker* from loss figures, as her demise came three days before the official start of the campaign. However, more than a few military historians believe that the transit time of the assault force should be considered as part of the campaign, and Tuckers loss came during this period and occurred at a principal base in the theatre.

USS Tucker was struck off the Navy list on 2 December 1944. The destroyer had earned one Battle Star on her Asiatic-Pacific Area Service Medal for the Pearl Harbor Raid, 7 December 1941. R129

SALVAGE

USS Navajo arrived on 7 August 1942 to undertake salvage operations. The bow of the destroyer was settling very slowly and was thus unstable. In order to undertake any salvage operations on the forward section, it was necessary for the *Navajo* to sink the forward section. This was done the following day, separating the bow and stern sections by a reported twenty feet. The official report suggested that the stern was upright on an even keel, the bow on her port side. [N5]

The US Navy used the ship for diver training during their occupation of Espiritu Santo, but did no further salvage after the war. Material was taken from the ship, but whether this material was of actual use, or it was removed purely as a salvage exercise is not known. The guns were reported as having been removed, and the turbines were salvaged. So too were the anchors and chain.

It remained for private operators to remove what they could from the lost destroyer. Non-ferrous material was always the prize, and the ship being in only sixty feet (18 m) on a sandy bottom made the task relatively easy.

Reece Discombe first worked on the destroyer in 1954. 'I got two of the condensers out of it - quite big, all tobin-bronze - about eight foot high and six foot long and about a metre wide. And dozen and dozens of three inch shell casings. It is interesting to note that the shell casings were all loaded with cordite but they never had their projectiles in them - they were in another part of the ship. I took two or three ton of these casings - got them up and brought all the cordite back topside. I tried to get it to burn - dried it and lit it - woosh - it certainly went off. Once the natives got onto this cordite stuff they used it for lighting their fires.'

Reece recovered the stainless steel ladders of ship. He recalls that the reduction boxes were still there, but the props were taken off. He also entered the engine rooms and took out a boiler feed pumps - 'huge things they were - and plenty of brass pipes'.

The wreck of the destroyer *USS Tucker* is spread over some 500 ft, and resembles an underwater junk-yard. The propeller shaft and engine sections may be seen on the seabed.

As mentioned, the *Tucker* sits in about sixty feet of water. Her original length of 341 ft (104m) has been stretched out to 500 ft (150 m), with boilers, condensers and reduction gearboxes paving the way over the sandy bottom between the two sections. The gap between the bow and stern sections is thus about 160 ft (50m). The steam turbine engines have been removed, as have the guns and most of the shells from the aft hold. The stern section is sitting on her keel, the bow section is on her port side. Reece Discombe comments, 'I used to maintain it was one of the best diving sites there was - all the colour, corals and sponges. You could see the shining stainless steel from the surface until the marine growth started.' Much of the super structure of the *Tucker* was made of stainless steel so she will be around for a long time.

Australian salvage diver Barry May worked on the *Tucker* after he completed removal of the props from the *President Coolidge*. 'Officially nothing was taken - the US Navy said they retained ownership and salvage from warships was a no-no at that time. Coolidge was a merchant ship and considered differently.'

Allan Power worked with Barry May on the *Tucker*. 'There was brass on the *Tucker*, but the main thing was the condensers - copra-nickel - thick end plates an inch or more - long tubes. Copra nickel was bringing a dollar a pound. We brought up two large sections - only about seventy feet. The US Navy had stripped it after it sank - turrets - bridge gone - no portholes - no name. A wreck site and yet not a wreck. Its like that now - collapsing on itself - only a small section of the stern resembles any recognisable part of the ship. Quite a bit of the ship was stainless steel - all doors, portions of the deck, some parts of the bridge.'

New Zealand diver Peter Spurdle visited the *Tucker* soon after the props had been removed from the *President Coolidge*. 'We cruised up to where [Barry May's] *Seal* was working on the wreck of the *USS Tucker*. There she was, spread out over the bottom in tangled masses of twisted metal. Stainless steel

bulkhead doors lay about and the big turbines were split open like melons with the blades clustered like seeds around the rusting cores. This time we dived using the *Seal's* hookah units - hoses coupled to a large compressor. It was a new experience for some of our chaps. The *Tucker* lay on an almost clear patch of sand. A strong current flowed along and the descent was made hand over hand down a buoy rope and then over the corroded decks and through gaping steel caves. Small dead fish lay scattered in the chambers of the ruptured hull - casualties of the blasting for copper and bronze.'

Today the hull sections of the destroyer may be bare of equipment and stripped of power, but she is still an excellent dive, albeit overshadowed by the wreck of the *President Coolidge*. And being in only 60 ft, it is an ideal depth for scuba diving, allowing a good fifty minutes to explore both sections of the hull. Port Vila-based diver and photographer Sandra Middleton comments, 'Half as long and one twentieth the bulk of the *President Coolidge* it is easy enough to explore all of her in one dive, even though her bow and stern are in two separate halves. One of the joys of swimming below decks and through the cabins is the knowledge that it can be done so without fear of stirring sediment. Plenty of portholes and open bulkheads prevent claustrophobia and interesting finds are hidden everywhere. Gun turrets and mounts are covered in colourful corals and sponges. Elsewhere gorgonia fans grow across open doorways. Coral trout, cod, sweetlip, anglefish, batfish are found on the wreck, with an average visibility of 20 metres.'

On the last occasion that I dived the *Tucker*, in 1992, there was not a great deal of gorgonia and coral growth on the wreck, although fish life was abundant. There are still several interesting, and safe, swim-throughs but overall, the wreck site resembles an underwater junk yard. Still, this was once a proud destroyer, and it deserves some attention. Because of its shallow depth amd the surrounding white sand, the wreck is well lit for underwater photographers who may choose to use some creativity with natural light shots.

The *USS Tucker* was one of the first military ships to use stainless steel extensively for its superstrucccture. Although flattened, this section clearly shows a doorway and ladders which will remain on the seabed perhaps for many centuries.

A small quantity of ammunition may be found on wreck; this has usually been placed in some obvious position for photographic purposes. If given the opportunity to dive the *Tucker*, do so as you will not regret it. The boat trip down the Segond Channel and on to Malo is worth the time particularly on a fine sunny day, and after a dive on the destroyer, continue through to Bokissa Island for lunch, and perhaps a local dive on a reef or the scuttled local trader *Henry Bonneaud*. [N6]

ACTION REPORT: ESPIRITU SANTO, NEW HEBRIDES.

SINKING OF *USS TUCKER*.

Prepared by W.R. Terrell, Commanding Officer.
To: Secretary of the Navy.
August 12, 1942.

On 3 August 1942 while escorting *SS Nira Luckenbach* from Suva to Espiritu Santo by a route north of Efate and west of Malekula Islands, while in Bruat Channel, the *USS Tucker* struck a mine and on 4 August was beached in sinking condition in ten fathoms of water near Malo Island.

1. The *USS Tucker* in compliance with orders from Commander South Pacific was on 3 August (GCT [Greenwich Civil Time, ie local time]) 1942 escorting the *SS Nira Luckenbach* from Suva to Espiritu Santo by a route north of Efate and west of Malekula Islands. At about 2145 (GCT) 3 August 1942 while in Bruat Channel, and swinging to a course to enter Segond Channel , Espiritu Santo, New Hebrides Islands, the *Tucker* struck a mine. The ship was beached in a sinking condition at about 0445 (GCT) 4 August 1942 in ten fathoms of water on the northwest corner of Malo Island.

2. The mine apparently struck the ship near the keel under the after part of the forward boiler room which was in use at the time. The entire force of the explosion came up through the ship. No spray was noticed on the outside but oil, steam and soot came out of the forward stack. The ship's back was broken by the explosion. The main deck amidships buckled at about frame number 80 and immediately submerged with water six feet above the main deck at that point, the stem and stern rising out of water. The forward boiler room was flooded immediately. All power on the ship was lost. Orders were given to light off the boilers in the after boiler room. Personnel went down into it approximately three minutes after the explosion. They found it then half flooded and rapidly filling. The forward smoke stack and various structures amidships were broken loose and distorted due to the buckling. The water-tight enclosure to the ventilator to the wardroom pantry was broken off and lost due to the explosion. No watertight enclosures are fitted to engine room ventilators. Canvas and other cloth material were stuffed into the above ventilator ducts to slow down the entry of water into the compartments.

3. The ship was in Material Readiness Condition 3. The armament was in Condition of Readiness 3. The special sea and anchoring details had been called away about five minutes beforehand and were partially manned. The Commanding Officer, the Executive Officer and Officer-of-the-Deck were on the bridge. The Torpedo officer was on the main deck amidships, the Assistant Gunnery Officer was on watch at the gun director.

4. All watertight fittings which could be reached and which were undamaged were immediately closed as for material Readiness Condition A. This settling was thoroughly checked by the First Lieutenant forward and the Executive Officer aft. The FS generator was the first piece of gear jettisoned to remove top side weight. Subsequently all six hundred pound depth charges in racks were jettisoned with pistols and boosters removed, as were all three hundred pound depth charges with davits and gear for handling. All five inch ready ammunition, all twenty millimetre guns, magazines and ready ammunition and all other top-side loose gear which could be spared was jettisoned. Only three torpedoes could be jettisoned and were fired with propeller locks on. They sank in about one hundred fathoms of water.

5. After the explosion the Tucker turned and drifted in such a way that she was in water through which she had already passed. The SS Nira Luckenbach was the only ship or assistance in sight. Her captain was requested to tow the Tucker toward the beach to beach her when it felt she would otherwise sink. He declined to do so for fear of mines. However, no criticism whatever is made of his decision or judgement. He quickly sent two boats to rescue any personnel. With difficulty the port motor whaleboat was swung out and lowered. The First Lieutenant was sent to the Naval Air Station, Segond Channel to request assistance. The ship lay helpless until about an hour and a half later when the USS YP346 came to the western end of Bruat Channel from the south and was requested to tow the Tucker to the beach. Her Commanding Officer subsequently took a tow line from the Tucker's stern and towed her southward to a point near the north-west corner of Malo Island. The tow line was cut by orders of the Commanding Officer YP346. He declined to tow the ship further. It is believed, however, that he could have again taken the tow line and could have towed the ship into the beach without danger of grounding the YP346. The ship would then have been grounded in more shallower water than that in which she eventually was grounded.

6. As the *Tucker* gradually sank amidships, the Commanding Officer directed various men at different times to abandon ship. All were wearing life jackets. There were several small boats as well as own ship life rafts nearby. None of these men were lost. Just before the water reached a height to the top of the bridge, the rate of sinking increased materially and the ship took a sudden list to port. It was believed the ship would quickly sink. All hands were directed to abandon ship. The last few men left on the forecastle were told that they were being kept to let go the anchor if ordered. These instructions were misunderstood and they let the anchor go when all hands were ordered to abandon ship. The chain was run out to the bitter end. When all officers and men were off the ship the Commanding Officer left. He was picked up by a missionary in a small boat. He lay alongside close aboard the Tucker. In about ten minutes the ship apparently stopped settling and at about the same time stopped drifting. The Commanding Officer went back on board at once and found the anchor had caught hold. The ship was anchored in about seventy-five to one hundred fathoms of water. A few men were ordered back on board. The anchor chain was cut with a hack saw and the anchor and chain jettisoned. A motor launch from the Naval Air Station took the stern tow line. After about two hours it managed to tow the *Tucker* an additional three or four hundred yards until she grounded amidships in ten fathoms of water (some seven hours after the explosion).

7. From the time of the explosion until the ship was abandoned, the ward room and engine room were slowly flooded through the canvas stuffed ventilators. There was a continuing gradual sinking amidships with the bow and stern rising to a greater and greater angle. Just before she was abandoned there was a marked increase in both the above. It is difficult to estimate the angle subtended by the bow and the stern at time of grounding but it is believed it was less than ninety degrees. Except for the first few seconds there was no great settling of the ship from the time the Commanding Officer ordered all hands to abandon ship until the ship was grounded. The bow at all times was more buoyant than the stern and was bend upward at a greater angle. That part of the ship abaft of the point where her back was broken, gradually settled, and at about 2100 (GCT) 4 August 1942, sank. The *USS Navajo* arrived 7 August to undertake salvage operations. The bow was gradually sinking. In order to undertake any salvage operations on the forward section, it was necessary for the Navajo to sink the forward section and she did so on 8 August. The forward and after sections are now entirely separated by a space of about twenty feet. Both lie on the bottom in ten fathoms of water. The stern is upright on an even keel, the bow on her port side.

8. Three enlisted men are missing and three were killed. All are believed to have been in the forward boiler room on watch at the time of the explosion. No other officers or enlisted members off the crew were killed or are missing nor were any other seriously wounded. The names of the missing men are:

Jack M. Clark, 267 79 42, CWT, USN.
Raymond H. Ross, 368 14 67, Bmkrlc, USN.
Charles W. Simpson, 274 50 96, F2c, USN.

The names of the men killed whose bodies have been recovered and have been buried locally are:

Edward F. Hewett, 236 36 34, Wtlc, USN
Ray J. Stanbaugh, 258 26 02, Flc, USN
Glen R. Steinow, 382 25 50, F2c, USN

The next of kin of the above six named men have not been notified. The bodies of the three missing men, if recovered, will be buried locally for the duration of the war.

9. The following ships rendered valuable assistance in rescuing the crew as it was necessary for them at various times to abandon ship: *USS Breese, USS YP346*, and *SS Nira Luckenbach.*

10. The *Tucker* unquestionably ran into a mine field, the laying of which had been completed the day before by our own forces. The Tucker knew nothing of its existence. No notification had been received addressed directly to the Tucker informing her of its existence nor had the Tucker been included in a collective call notifying all ships of its existence. A continuous and thorough watch was always kept on the NPM Fox radio circuit. In order to quickly detect messages addressed to the *Tucker*, three Chief Petty Officers (ie CphM, CGM and CTM) stood a continuous watch breaking down the headings of all NPM Fox messages. During this trip from Suva to Espiritu Santo the Communications Officer was not detailed to stand any other watches so that he could devote his entire time to decoding messages addressed to the *Tucker*.

11. All officers and enlisted men on board reacted to the emergency and carried out their duties in a commendable manner and in the best keeping of the Naval Service.

12. Steps are being taken with the assistance of the *USS Curtiss* and *USS Navajo* to salvage all gear and records possible in addition to that already salvaged.

W.R. Terrell.

CHAPTER SIX

FOR WANT OF A STAPLE!

The *President Coolidge* slipped quietly under the huge steel suspension of the Golden Gate Bridge outward bound from San Francisco on her final fateful voyage. It had just passed midnight on 7 October 1942, a calm clear night, and there was no *Frank H. Buck* to impede her progress. Gone were the excited crowds on Pier 42 clasping coloured streamers as a final link to friends and relatives voyaging across peaceful seas for business or pleasure. In their place a few hours earlier were military police surrounding the docks and five thousand anxious passengers, with no idea of their destination or destiny.

Captain Henry Nelson had the 'con' as she proceeded out into the Pacific Ocean. Trained in the traditions of the American merchant navy, the skills and aptitude of this well-respected mariner throughout his career were rewarded by his appointment as master with the Dollar Steamship Line by early middle age - no mean feat for a merchant mariner of the 1930s. Serving as commander of glamour passenger vessels on the trans-Pacific trade, undoubtedly the most exotic route then operating anywhere in the world, Captain Nelson's reputation for respected authority matched with skilled seamanship soon became legendary in shipping circles.

At the age of sixty-three, he could have retired and been at ease at his San Francisco home surrounded by family. That he should have been assigned command of the *President Coolidge* at this time for the ship's vital and dangerous wartime supply role in the south-west Pacific was considered a wise decision by executives of the American President Line. Captain Nelson had no hesitation in accepting the assignment. In a statement made after the loss of his beloved *President Coolidge*, Captain Nelson said 'My patriotism and love of country has never been questioned. I am not a young man, having reached the age of retirement even for Naval Officers. It was because of my feeling that my country needed me in its time of crises that I continued at sea rather than to seek retirement to enjoy with my family the few remaining years of my life'.

Although still owned by the American President Line, the *President Coolidge* was under bareboat charter to the U.S. Army as a troop carrier, with the charter controlled by War Shipping Administration, and was always regarded as being a 'public' vessel (ie merchant), as distinct from a military vessel, and operated by a civilian merchant marine crew. It was not, as sometimes thought, under the control of the Navy.

Captain Nelson and his officers were in overall charge of the vessel, however Colonel Dinsmore Alter, US Coast Artillery, US Army, assumed control of the passengers - the 4,800-strong troop contingent that had embarked in San Francisco. Highly classified at the time, a breakdown of the contingent, which was destined to disembark at Espiritu Santo, gives a good insight into allied military planning then.

The US Army had assigned two main units to be transferred to the southwest Pacific on this voyage, part of the 43rd Infantry Division. Those aboard the *President Coolidge* were the 172nd Combat Team which comprised the bulk of the contingent, under the command of Colonel James A. Lewis. This was composed of the 172nd Infantry Regiment, a battalion from the 103rd Field Artillery, a platoon of engineers, and a medical company. The 172nd Infantry had been based at Fort Ord, California, about two hours from San Francisco, where they practised beach landings. [N1]

The second unit was a battalion of the 54th Coast Artillery. This was a harbour defence unit and comprised the battalion headquarters and batteries C and D. Clearly, the intention was to employ the 54th Coast Artillery in a defensive role at Espiritu Santo and introduce the 172nd into the campaign at Guadalcanal to push back the Japanese occupation in the Western Pacific islands to the north.

Second Lieutenant James Renton recalls the events that led up to his embarkation on the *President Coolidge*. 'At 0630 on 6 October 1942, we were ordered to report with all our gear to Regimental Headquarters. There were forty enlisted men, all of which, had just recently completed their 26-week Basic Infantry Training Course, an experienced sergeant, and myself. We were escorted to a railroad car which was sealed, and attached to the Daylight Limited train that ran between Los Angeles and Seattle. There were a few stops along the way but the car was finally detached in San Francisco, and moved, still in the sealed car, right out onto the dock, unlocked, and we were ordered out with all our gear. Believe it or not, there was a cordon of Military Police from the door of the railroad car to the foot of the gang plank of the SS *President Coolidge*. Our Class B duffel bags (i.e. winter overcoat, heavy jacket and pants, long johns, wool socks, winter gloves, wool stocking caps, etc.) and my foot locker and bed roll were placed in a cargo net, and each of us were checked off the ship's manifest as we boarded. The Coolidge departed under the cover of darkness as we went under Golden Gate Bridge, and onto the broad Pacific. All lights were extinguished - alone and unescorted, once well out to sea, we picked up speed and commenced to zig and zag. The ocean is frequently rough in this area and this didn't help. Many were soon to learn what it's like to be sea sick.'

With the troops cramped in every imaginable space in the ship, the holds were likewise packed to capacity with an enormous amount of military ordnance and other material, currency and much-needed medical supplies, including 519lbs of quinine, the entire reserve supply of the South Pacific Area. [N2]

Renton continues, 'Woke up the next morning with the sun at our backs just where it ought to be. We were headed west and since we had all been issued winter gear, we would be turning north in a few days. No question about it, Alaska was our destination. We zig-zagged but still the heading was generally west. It was getting on to mid-October - we'd be just in time for a real cold Alaska winter. A few more days go by - something must be wrong - we're going almost due south. Rumours were flying and wild. Getting downright hot, too.'

It is not recorded how many of the men, like Renton, had been issued with winter dress, leading quite understandably to the confusion of the ultimate destination of the *President Coolidge*. It would appear that at least a considerable number of the troops came aboard with heavy winter clothing. 'Now hear this! Now hear this!' the shipboard radio screamed. All personnel were instructed to gather all their winter gear out and parade on one of the upper decks. Renton recalls, 'Each cabin door had a sign on it, Small Woollen Gloves, Overcoat 32 Long, Heavy Jacket 28 Short, etc. We were instructed to throw the appropriate garment into the titled room. What on earth was going on? We'd surely need these unless we weren't going to Alaska.'

Infantryman Henry Schumacher recalls, 'Varied indeed were the preferred opinions as to the ultimate point of debarkation, for we were not advised as to our destination. Foremost among the possibilities were the New Hebrides islands. The description of these islands, by some self-appointed geographers, were predominantly gloomy. Furthermore, the ships radio news had twice mentioned an American base in these islands as being the site shelled by a Jap submarine.' With little else to do on board, the perpetuation and embellishment of rumour seemed a reasonable pastime.

Second Lieutenant Charles H. Schubert, Headquarters Battery, 103rd Field Artillery Battalion, 172nd Infantry Regimental Combat Team, learnt of the destination, but could not understand it. 'We knew we were heading south immediately we left the Golden Gate, and were eventually told it was to a destination called White Poppy. Nobody had ever heard of White Poppy, and we later found out it was the codename for Noumea. Before that however we had stopped at Canton Island with some engine trouble, and cruised around the island for a few days before heading south-west again.' [N3]

U.S. Infantry Staff Sergeant Stephen Parisi, was on board and recalls: 'We left unescorted and zig zagged our way across the Pacific, because I understand the belief was that the ships speed (over 20 knots) was fast enough to outrun a submarine of that era. Our final destination was to have been Guadalcanal to relieve, or support the First Marine Division that had been in combat there since August 1942. They were slowly bringing the Japanese southern thrust to a halt, and helping to turn the Pacific war around. The voyage was uneventful but a bit crowded as tiers of bunks were added to the staterooms to accommodate the 5440 servicemen. The showers were of salt water only, which made it practically impossible to lather or shampoo the hair. Also gang toilets were installed with wooden partitions four feet high between toilets. The dining hall was not large enough to seat all at one time, so the meals were divided into three sittings for the first few days.

'The weather was balmy and beautiful and the sea calm with huge swells which made the voyage seem like a pleasure cruise. Most of the men spent their time on the top deck walking, exercising, sunning and discussing the war. We had abandon ship drill three or four times during the trip which may have helped avoid panic when it became a reality. Some of the men became sea sick the first few days even though the sea was calm most of the time. Three men in my section became sick and spent most of the days lying on the hatch cover eating only fruit that was brought from the dining hall. One of the men used to crawl into one of the lifeboats to sleep at night because he felt worse below decks.'

Renton adds, 'Unless you've lived through it, life aboard a combat loaded Army Transport is impossible to describe. Aboard is the 172nd Regimental Combat Team (RCT), of the 43d Division. It had trained and staged at Ft. Ord, California which is located on the coast near Monterey from which it is about a two hour drive north to San Francisco. In addition to three battalions of infantry, were a battalion of artillery, and units of engineers, medics (including thirteen nurses), a full compliment of vehicles of all sizes including a few light tanks and some tracked reconnaissance cars, the works together with their supplies, equipment, food, and ammunition. Plus or minus 5,140 men and officers. The bunks were canvas strapped to a steel frame, I believe four or six high. Your pack was your pillow, your rifle your bunk mate, and duffel bags stowed along the bulkhead, with, at most, two feet between bunks. The floors were steel plate - can you imagine what it's like when your buddy in the top bunk gets seasick? Many did - the first night out was quite rough. Officers fared a little better. I was in what was formerly a small, inside cabin with double bunks. Now it accommodated six junior officers with their gear. Fresh water was for drinking and cooking only (cold salt water showers for all hands). The galley operated on a 20-hour schedule. Time on deck, four hours rain or shine on a rotating schedule with absolutely no lights, matches, cigarettes, etc. Blackout? You better believe it because our lives depended on it. We were without escort and relied on speed and evasive tactics to avoid submarines.'

Infantryman Arthur Allard adds, slightly contradicting Renton, 'The men slept in canvas bunks four high. Showers were cold salt water. There were two meals a day.' The galley was kept busy twenty fours hours of the day.

Parisi again: 'We were split into groups and assigned lifeboat stations with two crew members assigned to each station to guide the servicemen into the lifeboat and to lower them to the water. The crew members seemed to be Asians or Orientals. Our station was located at the stern of the ship on the port side, directly above our living quarters.

'Also mounted on the stern deck was a three inch gun which was used one day for target practice, firing on a target towed by the Coolidge. It didn't seem to me that the deck had been adequately reinforced to withstand constant firing, but the sight of a weapon on board may have given us all a feeling of security. We were ordered below deck when the practice was about to begin. It was a deafening sound that echoed throughout the ship each time they fired. It seemed that the steel deck was about to buckle.' [N4]

Second Lieutenant Schubert slept in a stateroom on B-Deck, shared with another officer, and recalls the excellent food that they were served, three meals a day, by the civilian stewards. His men were in cabins on A-Deck. 'This was incongruous luxury when we were supposed to be facing the hardships of war.'

Traditional initiations associated with crossing the equator and thus entering King Neptune's court helped relive shipboard boredom. Renton recalls, 'Because there were so many, a select few were chosen to represent the whole group. Since there were so many observers, two initiations were held. It was decided that the most representative group would be second lieutenants, one from each company or unit - including a nurse from the Medical Unit - she was a good sport and I was in the same ritual as she was. About two feet of salt water was pumped into the swimming pool. Into this was placed all the clean garbage from the kitchen. The lieutenants in their shorts, and the nurse in a bathing suit, were all blind-folded, lead to the edge of the pool, pushed in - they called it 'walking the plank' - and prodded the length of the pool where King Neptune and his Court awaited the initiates. We were fished out of the pool, greeted by King Neptune and his "Queen" - the Regimental Sergeant Major and I'll leave it to your imagination as to how he (?) was dressed - and given five lashes (with a broom). I won't say that a good time was had by all but it was great for the troops' morale. We all (the initiates) had dinner that evening with the ship's captain (there was a bottle of bourbon on the sideboard) and the Commanding General and Sergeant Major came by and thanked us for our cooperation.'

As the days passed it was quite obvious that the *President Coolidge* was heading to the south-west Pacific, and on 20 October 1942 arrived at Noumea in the French territory of New Caledonia. Renton recalls, 'Finally, Land ho!. The Captain is surely lost! The winter gear so carefully gathered together is now in cargo nets, and left ashore. A small unit of a Navy Construction Battalion with their equipment were landed as well'.

The four-day layover in Noumea was no doubt appreciated by the troops, particularly those who had not found their sea-legs, but there was no time for sightseeing. It was a welcome opportunity however to leave the cramped quarters and enjoy the clean tropical air. Renton recalls, 'It was getting unbelievably hot and humid - almost impossible below decks. Unfortunately, time on deck was still limited.'

On the 23 October, the Navy's Noumea Port Director, Lt. Commander John D. Andrews, sat in his office preparing the sailing instructions for the next stage of the journey for the *President Coolidge*. All details were completed except for the time of sailing, which was to be the following afternoon. It is from this moment that the fate of the *President Coolidge* was set.

During World War II, it was standard procedure for all vessels (Navy and merchant) to be given complete routing instructions before sailing from or to any port in the combat area. These routing instructions were the responsibility of the Naval Control of Shipping Officer or Port Directors under their respective Area Commanders. Routing instructions were supposed to keep all allied vessels on specific routes where the greatest protection from enemy action could be provided. Routing instructions, if clearly defined, and if strictly obeyed by commanding officers, were also supposed to keep all allied vessels in channels not obstructed by friendly mines. According to the transcript of the Navy Court of Inquiry, sailing orders for Captain Nelson were contained in a packet of nine pages, some of them routine and some specific as to the exact course to set from Noumea to a point in the New Hebrides, designated as 'Hypo', off Espiritu Santo.

It is these very documents, the 'sailing instructions', that are so much in contention. Did they contain clear instructions as to how the *President Coolidge* was to proceed beyond point Hypo? And indeed, were they received by Captain Nelson. This is discussed in detail in the following chapter. We can however surmise what happened.

The youthful US Navy ensign glanced at his watch as he slipped the file marked 'top secret' into the special delivery pouch. It had just gone 1300 hrs, the early afternoon of 24 October 1942. He knew that the documents were to be delivered to Captain Nelson aboard *President Coolidge*, and that the troopship was to sail that afternoon. He would have to hurry. Since his assignment to the Noumea wartime naval station Ensign John DeNovo had made several trips to deliver highly classified routing instructions that sent both fighting and merchant ships on missions into the South-West Pacific theatre. He knew the drill. It would take him at least half an hour by one of the harbour patrol picket boats to reach the position in Dumbea Bay where the *President Coolidge* lay awaiting orders to move on north at 1500 hrs. But no order to weigh anchors could be given until the sheath of papers that Ensign DeNovo carried were handed personally to the *President Coolidge*'s skipper.

In the Captain office on the starboard side of the Boat Deck, the ensign and commanding officer went through the instructions. At some time during or after the delivery, DeNovo marked each document off on a check-list. That completed, Captain Nelson signed the original and two copies of the routing instructions, acknowledged the younger man's salute and expressions for a safe passage, and saw his visitor to the door. As Ensign DeNovo reboarded the picket boat for the run back to shore, the skipper took his first detailed look at the set of sailing orders that would haunt him for the rest of his life.

Once in possession of the classified sailing instructions delivered by DeNovo, Captain Nelson made ready for a 1500 hours departure. The *President Coolidge* sailed from Noumea on 24 October 1942 and with a cargo of ammunition, war equipment, 5050 Army troops, 50 U.S. Navy Armed Guard and Signal personnel, plus 340 ships crew, and proceeded from the Port of Noumea past Amadee Lighthouse on the reef at the entrance to Boulari Passage, and out into the Pacific Ocean. A course was set for the first of the designated positions - 'Queen' due north of New Caledonia.

The possibility of Japanese submarines lurking in Pacific waters was considered minor by the higher echelon, and the *President Coolidge* travelled alone, unescorted, with her valuable cargo and passengers. Henry Nelson was not so sure however, and he slept uneasy, perhaps dreaming of a torpedo that would put his beloved ship on the bottom. The designated route was quite straightforward. Nelson was required to take his ship to a secret American military base situated at Luganville, Espiritu Santo, via several designated open ocean positions. The last of these was point Hypo, approximately 5.6 miles due east of the centre of Tutuba Island, south of the main island of Espiritu Santo. [N5]

Captain Nelson was joined on the bridge by his First Officer, Kilton I. Davis, designated the ship's navigator. With the quartermaster at the wheel, steering the proscribed departure course, and the bridge settling down to its accepted sailing routine, Captain Nelson and his navigator withdrew to the adjoining chartroom for important discussions. With several navigational charts open for reference on the table before them, the two men reviewed the secret routing that would take them to the sea approaches of Luganville, the newly established base given the military codename Button. This was the destination at which the *President Coolidge* was scheduled to off-load her important cargo of fighting men and war supplies.

Nelson handed Mr. Davis that section of the overall sailing orders package he had received two hours earlier from Ensign DeNovo dealing with the course

Destroyer *Sterett* (DD 407), on submarine patrol duty, signalled *President Coolidge* when approaching Espiritu Santo but did not warn the ship of any danger, nor was she required to.

to be plotted through various positions, terminating at a point designated by the codename Hypo. Once at Hypo, the *President Coolidge* would be only a few miles from the eastern entrance of the Segond Channel, with 'Button', a short distance further down the northern shoreline. The two officers together checked course coordinates against chart positions, discussed the requirements laid down in the instructions and monitored latest weather forecasts. Satisfied he could now leave the bridge to the charge of his subordinate, Captain Nelson retired to his cabin. There appears to have been no discussion as to the procedure and route to be taken once the *President Coolidge* passed through point Hypo and was on an approach to the Segond Channel into Luganville.

The next thirty-six hours aboard the *President Coolidge* were largely uneventful, the troops, on roster, relaxing in the warm Pacific sun as they anticipated their next landfall. Throughout the cramped accommodation sections there was a decided air of relief among the troops that the long voyage from San Francisco was finally coming to an end. Underlying the relief was a perceptible tinge of excitement mingled with curiosity as to what this dot of land so far from home would be like. Although it may not have been announced officially, it was obvious to any with a basic appreciation of Pacific islands geography, that the next destination was to be the New Hebrides. Very few had heard of the place, other than the fact that a base had been established for their advance preparation to move further north to the conflict in the Solomon islands. Now doubt a few bets were called in by now.

As the blacked-out ship sliced quietly through the pre-dawn darkness at 20 knots towards point Hypo in the early hours of Monday 26 October 1942, the primary threat in the minds of Captain Nelson and his officers was the possible attack from a Japanese submarine. It had been thus all the way across the Pacific and blackout conditions for night lighting had been strictly imposed throughout the voyage. Pointedly, watch keeping officers on the run to Espiritu Santo had noted a 14 to 25 fathom sandbank out from Tutuba Island and there was a general uneasiness among them that this would be an ideal spot for an enemy submarine to lie in wait on the bottom for the approach of just such a supply vessel as the *President Coolidge*. This was a most reasonable assumption as a Japanese submarine had shelled the island only a few days previously. Captain Nelson may not however have been aware of this, such was the poor communication between the military and a civilian vessel.

APPROACH TO DISASTER

When First Officer Davis came to the bridge to begin his 0400 to 0800 hours watch-keeping stint the sea was mirror calm with not a hint of a breeze. A glance at the chart showed that the ship would be nearing point Hypo towards the end at his watch. Somehow he felt uneasy about the routing orders. There seemed to be something missing. Up to point Hypo they were very explicit. Beyond that, though, they appeared incomplete with no details for entering port. But he consoled himself with the thought that the authorities at Luganville would surely send a destroyer or a pilot boat to assist with the civilian liner's entrance to the unknown Segond Channel.

As is customary when entering a strange port, Captain Nelson took control of the navigation. In Navy parlance he 'had the con', with first officer, Kilton Davis, also on the bridge. As mentioned, the possibility of Japanese submarines was of prime concern, yet the question of mines, enemy or otherwise, was not raised although Davis had 'heard unofficially' that not long before a destroyer had been sunk while negotiating the western entrance to the Segond Channel. (This was *USS Tucker*).

Mr Davis drew his captain's attention to the imprecise routing instructions and had asked, 'Are you going to lay off Hypo and wait for a pilot or a guide?' The captain paused for a while, mulling over the implication at his navigator's remarks. Perhaps Davis was concerned about the phrase that formed part of the general routing instructions to Hypo - 'Thence to Button noting attached instructions for entering Segond Channel, Espiritu Santo.' There didn't seem to be any more pertinent instructions.

'No,' said Captain Nelson finally. 'No, it's too dangerous to be playing around outside with the probability of submarines in the area.' If there were no last minute instructions, or if pilot assistance was not forthcoming one way or another, Captain Nelson would head straight into the Channel by the most direct route.

It is interesting to pause for a moment and contemplate what must have gone through the captain's mind at this critical stage of the voyage. Clearly the threat of a Japanese submarine attack was of paramount concern and, despite the professed doubts of US senior naval officers connected with the drama at the time, the existence of mines in the area was not appreciated by the merchant navy officers aboard the *President Coolidge*. Certainly there was nothing in the official orders, even in the vital missing document, to suggest the presence of a mined area blocking the obvious approaches to Button.

As the watch wore on First Officer Davis ordered lookouts, and the duty Signals Officer, Ensign Doran S. Weinstein, to keep a keen eye during the *President Coolidge's* final run to Button from Point Hypo. At 7.30 am what appeared to be a destroyer was sighted some eight miles. Almost immediately the still unidentified naval vessel began flashing its signal light at the *President Coolidge*. At first the flashing light format beamed at the larger vessel puzzled Ensign Weinstein. Whoever was behind the light was challenging with an outdated recognition procedure scrapped by the navy three months earlier. Although suspicious, Ensign Wainstein chose to reply with the old procedure and soon had the destroyer identified as DD-407 (*USS Sterett*), on anti-submarine patrol around the approaches to the eastern entrance of the

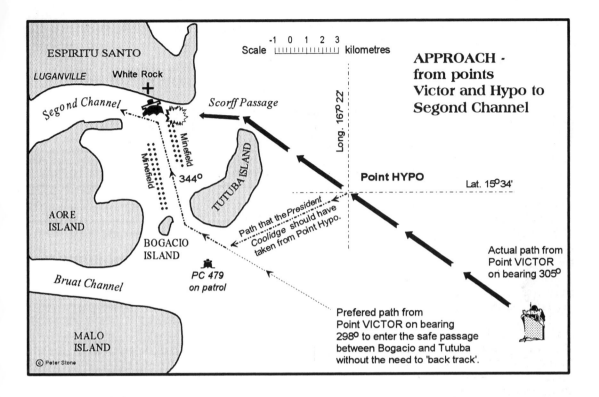

APPROACH -
from points
Victor and Hypo to
Segond Channel

ESPIRITU SANTO

LUGANVILLE   White Rock

Segond Channel

Scorff Passage

Long. 167° 22'

Minefield

Minefield

344°

Point HYPO

Lat. 15°34'

TUTUBA ISLAND

AORE
ISLAND

Path that the President
Coolidge should have
taken from Point Hypo.

BOGACIO
ISLAND

Actual path from
Point VICTOR
on bearing 305°

PC 479
on patrol

Bruat Channel

Prefered path from
Point VICTOR on bearing
298° to enter the safe passage
between Bogacio and Tutuba
without the need to 'back track'.

MALO
ISLAND

© Peter Stone

Scale   -1 0 1 2 3   kilometres

Segond Channel. The signals officer was then instructed to enquire whether the destroyer had orders for the *President Coolidge* which was clearly flying its identification flags. Back came the quick reply: 'negative'.

To the deck officers on the bridge of the *President Coolidge* at the time, the presence of the destroyer and the sequence of flashing light communications only served to underline the need for proceeding into the Segond Channel with haste. What the bridge of the *President Coolidge* could not appreciate was that *Sterett* was on submarine patrol duty and totally incidental to the arrival of the troopship. [N6]

The *President Coolidge* approached Espiritu Santo from the south-east toward the eastern entrance of the Segond Channel. Captain Nelson had the choice of three deepwater channels to enter: between Bogacio and Tutuba Islands, between Aore and Bogacio Islands, and north of Tutuba Island. Considering the location of point Hypo, the decision taken to continue north-west and proceed directly to harbour by the quickest and most direct route available, round the northern end of Tutuba Island, was reasonable and calculated at the time to minimise the risk to the vessel. Unbeknown to Captain Nelson, the safe war-time entrance to Segond Channel was on a course of 344° (true) between the islands of Tutuba and Bogacio. The channel between these two islands is narrow and difficult for a large vessel to enter, but had the advantage of being narrow enough at the entrance to permit a patrol craft to adequately patrol against submarines. The *President Coolidge*, however, was instructed to procede to point Hypo which is north-east of the safe entrance and would require the ship to turn nearly ninety degrees port from point Hypo. This would not make sense, as the objective was to reach port in the shortest possible time. In hindsight, it would have been better for Captain Nelson to have been instructed to procede at a reading of 298° from point Victor which would have placed the ship at the correct entrance. (See map). As it was, Captain Nelson was given a bearing (of 305°) from point Victor that would pass through point Hypo as required by the instructions, and straight through to the eastern entrance of the Segond Channel at Scorff Passage. From here, Captain Nelson could navigate the harbour by sight, approaching from the east, on a course of approximately 270 degrees (due west), which took the ship between the northern tip of Tutuba Island and the island of Espiritu Santo.

When still six miles from point Hypo, the *President Coolidge* was spotted at a distance of ten miles by patrol craft *PC479*, patrolling south-east of Bogacio. The PC boat had shortly before arrived at its patrolling position to the south of Tutuba and Bogacio islands, the safe entrance through the minefield toward Segond Channel. It had replaced *USS Gamble* which had requested permission from the Port Director to refuel and was at its station near Luganville when the *President Coolidge* was approaching the eastern channel. It was *Gamble*, in consort with *USS Tracey* and *USS Breese*, that laid the mines at the west and east of the Segond Channel two months previous. *PC479* patrolled 'one mile or one mile and a half off Bogacio Island steering successively 160, 70, 340, 250, each leg 30 minutes, covering square of 3 miles each'.

Richard 'Pete' Peterson was Ensign on board *USS Gamble* (and later took command of the ship). He recalls, 'In October 1942 *Gamble* was temporarily assigned to the Port Director and we were placed outside the south-east entrance patrolling back and forth at 8 knots on anti-submarine patrol. Our other function was to intercept all ships approaching the entrance and to provide a pilot for those ships which needed safe guidance through the minefield. This was very boring and exhausting work. Being continually underway meant we stood sea watches and went to General Quarters at both dawn and dusk. After many days of this duty we needed to refuel, so early on the morning of 26 October we requested permission of the Port Director to come to the harbour to fuel. Permission was given and a PC boat was sent out to relieve us, but with no instructions other than to patrol outside the entrance.'

By the time First Officer Kilton Davis returned to the bridge after taking breakfast, signals were being exchanged with the patrol boat. Within minutes, these were interrupted when the line of sight between the two ships was interrupted by Tutuba island. Unbeknown to Captain Nelson and his officers, a pilot officer was aboard the patrol boat to ensure safe passage of any ships entering the Segond Channel through the minefields. In preparing for her approach between Tutuba and Espiritu Santo islands, the *President Coolidge* had completed her turn to port and was now on a westerly heading calculated to take her down the centre of the Segond Channel. With visual contact lost, the patrol boat hastened in a desperate chase but left its run far too late and could not match the larger vessel's speed at the time off of 17.5 knots. The time was 0919 hours.

Henry Schumacher, on board the *President Coolidge*, recalls, 'The ship was steered through the channel, relatively narrow, and a closer view was possible of the islands. They were to all appearances the typical Pacific islands, so often portrayed in movies and magazines. There were noticeable changes however -

The *President Coolidge* lies hard up on the reef edge minutes after Captain Nelson cried 'hard right rudder', and rammed the ship on shore in an effort to save his passengers and his ship. Under the stern however is 240ft of water and the ship has started to list to port. Note how close the ship is to the shore, also made apparent in the following photographs. This is perhaps the first photograph of the stricken liner as boats rush to the rescue from the naval base in Segond Channel.

no natives were about in canoes ready to dive after coins; no beautiful native girls to place flowery laces around an eager doughboy's neck or dance a torrid native number, as so often exhibited in many American Hotels Tropical Room. But the palm trees were on the islands, the calm Pacific waters with hardly a ripple, lapped gently on the coral shores, while the sun's warm rays beat down on this clear October morning.'

Captain Nelson and his First Officer moved to the starboard wing of the bridge for a better view of Luganville Harbour which by now was clearly in sight across the ship's bows. At signal stations adjacent to the bridge, communications officer Doran Weinstein scanned the harbour ahead through binoculars. He noted several ships of various sizes resting at anchor and one, a US warship, challenging the approaching *President Coolidge* with its Aldis lamp. The signal officer flashed back the correct response which was duly acknowledged. Ensign Weinstein returned to scanning the shoreline in expectation of anchoring instructions. Suddenly a naval shore station close to Luganville began urgently flashing the approaching vessel. Immediately the duty signalman acknowledged and readied to note down the message to follow. Across the still, harbour waters, in faultless, rapid morse code flickered the word: S-T-O-P.

Ensign Weinstein and his signalman didn't wait for the rest of the message. Instinctively the two men leaped to the rail and bellowed down to the bridge: 'Stop..stop ..stop ...' As the bridge telegraph rang down the orders 'STOP ENGINES - FULL ASTERN' to the engine room, the two signallers grabbed pad and pencils and began taking down the message in full: 'STOP YOU ARE STANDING INTO MINES'. Scarcely had the warning been completed when a massive underwater explosion sent a shuddering lurch through the hull of the ship. [N7]

The time - 0935 hours. The ship retained forward momentum and less than thirty seconds later a second mine ripped a hole in the hull amidships. The ship heaved like a mortally wounded whale. At that moment Captain Nelson demonstrated superb seamanship which undoubtedly saved hundreds of lives. On the bridge, Nelson made rapid assessments from initial sketchy damage reports and correctly concluded that his ship had been severely holed by mines which had struck the hull, one on the port side directly beneath the engine room. The second mine had blasted the starboard bottom plates also near the engine room. He ordered that all watertight doors be closed followed by, 'hard right rudder' so as take advantage of the headway to turn the ship directly into shore, and thus to beach her in shallow water.

At 0938 the ship struck the coral ledge some fifty metres from the shore. Henry Nelson immediately called Abandon Ship. [N8]

ABANDON SHIP

Ira Wolfert, North American Newspaper Alliance correspondent and (later) author of *Battle of the Solomons*, was flying over the Segond Channel when the ship was hit. 'The slate-grey liner was slowly making its way through a slate-gray morning. Then it seemed to lurch like a man hit heavily, and a big, gaseous-looking bubble welled up on its starboard side just about midships and hung swollen on the surface of the sea for a moment before bursting.' [N9]

James Renton recalls, 'It was a beautiful, calm, and clear Monday morning, shattered by the explosions, and the Klaxton's call for all personnel to 'Boat Stations'. Ours is well forward and on the top deck. I count noses - we're all here. The ship is beginning to roll counter clockwise, is picking up speed, and headed for land. The Captain is trying to run the ship aground to save the crew, passengers, and cargo. Still rolling to the left - it hits the reef and is hard aground - both anchors are let go. Abandon ship sounds - cargo nets and rafts over the side. Our station, being starboard side, top deck, made for problems - the nets wouldn't roll down because more and more of the starboard side was being exposed due to the roll. We had more trouble. Fortunately the sides were clean - no barnacles. Over the side - no panic very orderly - all in life jackets, helmet liners, and web belt with canteen - into the warm Pacific.'

Opposite page: Troops climb down ropes hung from the bow of the *President Coolidge* as the ship takes a 35° list to port. This would put the time at about 10.00 am, just over twenty minutes after the ship hit the reef. The list increased at a rate of approximately one degree per minute, before lying on her beam ends and slipping under. Some men climbed down the anchor rope and after a short swim, waded to shore. There seems to be a particularly inefficient use of life rafts, but perhaps they returned to assist.

Sergeant Parisi recalls, 'When the ship struck the mines I was below deck and having been topside earlier and noting that we were close to land I thought the explosions could be from coastal guns. Then I thought, maybe torpedoes. I went to the top deck, and then realized what had happened. I saw the rescue boats coming to the ship to help survivors. The ship was still moving ahead when I heard Captain Nelson over the loudspeaker give the command 'hard right rudder, hard right rudder', and the ship made a sharp turn toward shore.'

Bill Bradley, Senior Assistant Purser, was on the lower bridge as they approached the harbor. 'I remember seeing round dark shapes in the water. I thought they were large turtles. The Coolidge eased through the narrow channel and was heading for the sheltered water of the harbor when there was an explosion on the port side. The dark shapes were mines. There was no panic at all. On the trip over, Captain Nelson had those troops doing fire and boat drill until they were going nuts. When it happened, they knew exactly what to do.'

Henry Schumacher vividly remembers the explosions. 'It was still breakfast time on the transport as the largest island of the group made its appearance on the starboard side, less than 1000 yards away. In contrast to our entrance at the harbor of New Caledonia, we were moving along at a fair rate of speed for being close to shore. Now, as for the past few minutes, a destroyer [*sic* -it was *PC479*] about two miles distant was signalling continuously. Even as we were thus either all absorbed with the scene about us, or breakfast below, there was a sickening explosion on the port side, amidship, which seemed to jolt every bolt and plate on the liner. While not yet recovered from the first blow, a second blast followed in a matter of seconds. Tortured thoughts ran through the minds of all aboard. The ship was mortally crippled, steered toward the shore, its momentum pushing her bow upon a ledge of coral. The reassuring sight of land, but a few hundred yards away, was a valuable contribution to the state of calmness which prevailed aboard. Troops as ordered stayed in their quarters as the boats and rafts were lowered over the sides. At last the huge operation of moving four thousand men from the stricken vessel began. By this time much of the water was thickly covered with oil and it was towards this that the escape nets led. When no boats happened to be at the bottom of the net where a man descended, he dropped into the sea, less he hold up the line above him and wasted precious time. The list of the ship grew more perilous by the minute and the men continued their descent in unending columns. The picture presented was a stirring spectacle. The sight of four thousand men scrambling down the side of this sinking ship will live in memory of all that saw it.'

Sergeant Stephen Parisi again: 'I felt the ship shudder as the keel hit bottom and dug into the coral, and I assumed, as did many of the men, that the ship was sitting on the bottom and would go no further. I suppose that thought helped to calm things. The only hint of panic that I observed was on the part of the civilian crew. When the Captain gave the order to abandon ship, the crew, instead of manning their respective stations as we practised during the trip, climbed into our assigned lifeboat and lowered themselves to the water with the boatload of crew members only. When this happened some of the men went to the next station to try boarding, but they were rebuffed and told that it was the Captain's boat. I was on deck and watched as the crew lowered themselves to the water in what was supposedly the lifeboat assigned to our group. The incidence could have been quite serious if the captain had not grounded the boat. I then proceeded to release all the life rafts in the stern for the servicemen who had already jumped into the water.

There seems to be just as much water in the raft as there is outside! If these men did not manage to keep their feet dry, at least they seem quite calm about the whole situation. The shore is only a hundred yards distant.

'I then went below and started to place clothing and equipment on the top bunks to keep them dry, because I still believed that even though the ship was listing badly to port it would go no further. Then Sergeant Thomas our mess sergeant, who had been working in the galley when the explosion occurred, came to our area with a beef roast and a loaf of rye bread he had salvaged so we sat on the deck and had a breakfast of roast beef and rye. Luckily the ship stayed afloat for over an hour after the explosions, allowing ample time for us to debark before it sank. The men on the port side were able to make use of lifeboats and life rafts to leave the ship but because of the list to port those on the starboard side were forced to use cargo nets to lower themselves to the water. The nets did not reach the surface of the water so the men had to drop several feet to the oil covered surface, then make the swim to shore.'

Charles Schubert adds: 'I was on the port side near the bow of the ship looking at the land as we entered the harbour. I thought that we were coming into the port at too high a speed. I happened to look into the water and saw a mine. I said, "My God, there is a mine and it's going to hit us". The Port Authority was frantically signalling, then the first mine struck. And I said, "There'll be a second one", and of course there was a few moments later.

The stern of the *President Coolidge* is crowded with troops waiting their opportunity to disembark by way of cargo nets and ropes. The main thought in each man's mind would have been how to keep dry. Some succeeded, although it appears touch and go for the men in the raft. As noted in the text, there was no panic, but one wonders what the reaction may have been if these men had realised that within an hour, the stern would be resting in 240 ft of water. Note the 3-inch gun on the starboard stern on A-Deck, and the lifeboats that could not be launched because of the list. The open seadoor on the right is the entry to the Tourist Class vestibule on C-Deck.

'As we had practised abandoning ship many times during our voyage, there was no panic whatsoever. The Captain tried to beach the ship - unfortunately there was no sloping sandy beach, only a coral reef. The abandon ship drill was for the lower decks to be abandoned first. My troops were on the starboard side of A-deck and more to the rear of the ship than mid-ship. By the time all troops from C-deck and B-deck had set off and my troops could abandon ship, the ship was nearly completely on its port side and water was coming in port holes of A-deck portside. My duty as an officer was to check that all of my men were safely off the ship. To do this, I had to check each stateroom to see that it was empty. I had to lean against the passage wall and push the stateroom doors open with my feet. By the time I completed the task there was no one else in sight. When I did emerge from the ship on the starboard side, I was the last man to get off the after end of the ship - the third last man altogether to get off the ship. Two fellow officers and my outfit were up toward the bow trying to rescue another officer who was on B deck and had been helping troops to set off. Sadly, the ship slipped off the reef before the officer could be saved. I watched this happening from a rescue boat. The officer was Captain Euart.'

Schubert was the last off the stern of the ship, and was taken aboard a boat. 'I didn't even get my feet wet'.

Within ten minutes of hitting the reef the list was about ten degrees and any thoughts that the ship would remain safely on the reef were abandoned. It was now a matter of time, and any leisurely disembarkation was soon forgotten. Speed was essential, and although there was much apprehension, the disembarkation was orderly under the circumstances. Within thirty minutes however the escape nets over the starboard side were crammed with soldiers like flies trapped in a web. There were insufficient boats to quickly take them off, and they were ordered to jump into the sea and make their way to a boat, or to swim to shore. Many could not swim. U.S. Congressman Craig Hosmer, who was then Commander in charge of the naval gun crews, recalls in his log, '10.16 am - Moving aft along boat deck ordering men to jump. Water is oily. Nets about ten feet or more above water. Many seem afraid to jump. Keep exhorting them to kick men in face to get them off. List about 18 degrees.'

Captain Nelson later reported that there were problems in using the cargo nets over the side of the ship. As the ship was listing, the nets clung to the side of the ship like a vine on a brick wall, making it difficult for the escaping personnel to get their hands around the rope for a positive grip. Single life-lines made of a knotted rope were extremely useful, particularly in conjunction with the escape net. This gave the men a positive grip on the knotted life-line whilst their feet could be steadied on the net.

With the ship mortally wounded and filling at a fast rate, the *President Coolidge* continued its list to port. Some of the port side lifeboats were lowered but disembarkation was mainly from the starboard side, down escape nets and into the waiting lifeboats and surface craft from the harbour. Many swam ashore, although the spreading oil soon led to a swift exit from the sea by whatever means possible. Of course, the starboard side lifeboats could not be lowered because of the list of the ship.

The immediate reaction for some of the troops was to take their rifles and whatever military and personal gear they could carry, but with rifles being caught in the escape nets, and helmets plummeting down on those below, orders were soon given to leave everything behind. A thick layer of oil soon covered the sea, and those in the water were stung whilst no doubt praying that no fire would start. It was imperative of course to get the men out of the water as quickly as possible, both from the risk of fire, and later, from the suction of the ship as she went down. And no doubt many of the men would have been thinking of what lurked below the waters of Segond Channel.

Infantryman Arthur Allard recalls, 'We took our helmets, canteens and belts'. But all equipment had to remain behind. 'I was pretty angry as I had just cleaned and polished my rifle'. Allard went down the anchor chain.

Because of Captain Nelson's prompt orders leading to abandoning the ship all but one man escaped safely, itself a tribute to his splendid leadership. The ship was close enough for most of those aboard, all wearing life jackets, to swim to shore or to get there in the ship's small boats or those hastily dispatched from Luganville. Some of the soldiers feared to jump into the water and as mentioned, had to be pushed or kicked in, but in general the discipline was described by all at the subsequent Inquiry witnesses as excellent. There were many episodes of heroism, some men with injuries being helped into the boats by men already safe who climbed back on the sloping hull to help their comrades.

BELOW DECKS

In the oily, choking heat below decks, frightened engine room crew, stunned by the immediate impact of the blast so close, came to their senses when torrents of salt water gushed over the machinery through ruptured double bottom plates beneath their feet. Generators were awash. Cascades of sparks from shorting lines and acrid smoke from fusing metal connections quickly signalled the enormity of the damage. With the power out, their situation was precarious as the engine room crew groped their way out of the dark bowls of the ship. Although the main engines struggled on, it was clear to the men in the lower sections of the ship that the vessel was in her final death throws. All but one managed to escape unharmed. Fireman Robert Reid lay dead, killed by one of the explosions. [N10]

Charles Ross (right) fireman aboard the *President Coolidge*, thanks John Patton, First Assistant Engineer, for saving his life when the ship was about to sink.

Jack Patton, who had been on the *President Coolidge* from her first voyage, was serving as first assistant engineer and remembers that first shattering moment well. 'We heard the blast and the lights went out,' he recalls. 'We reset the circuit breakers to get the lights back on, and then the second explosion hit.' Realizing that the engine room was filling with water, his first instinct was to get above as quickly as possible. 'But then I thought, maybe I'd better check to make sure there isn't someone down there.'

In his search he found one of his firemen trapped below. 'He was stuck in a ventilator, but I was able to get him out.' This simple statement disguises the heroic efforts of the engineer. Charles Ross was on duty in the wire room when the explosion tore through the ship. 'All I remember is a blast, and then everything went black,' Ross recalled. 'When I came to, everything was dark and I was alone on the floor with the water rising rapidly. I hollered for help, then I decided I had better get out of the water as quickly as I could. I climbed to the grating but the water got there almost as soon as I did. Then I climbed to the top of the boilers. The water was rising rapidly and I expected the boilers to let go any minute.'

Still dazed, Ross saw light coming down from a ventilator but he was too weak to pull himself through. Patton heard his cries, and with the thought that the ship could roll over any minute, or the boilers could explode, climbed down into the ventilator, tied a rope about Ross and pulled him out, with the help of Chief Engineer Quinn. By the time Patton reached topside, the ship was laying on her side. 'I just walked along the hull, which was above water, until I got to one of the power launches.' As the three pulled away from the ship in the last boat to get away they saw the *President Coolidge* settle by the stern, then quietly slide out of sight. 'I was working on the launch engine, and I just looked up and she was gone.' Patton was awarded the Distinguished Service Award for heroism by the War Shipping Administration for saving Charles Ross.

MILITARY CASUALTY

The one military casualty was Captain Elwood J. Euart, of the 103rd Field Artillery, attached to the 172nd Infantry Regiment aboard. As the ship listed badly, Euart thought that some of his men may have been trapped below, possibly in the galley. Although there are many versions of events, there is no doubt that his actions were heroic. [N11]

One of the brave officers who attempted to rescue Euart was Warrant Officer Robert H. Moshimer. He well remembers the day when he lost a fellow officer and a friend. 'I happened to be alone on deck at the very bow of the ship and perhaps feeling like a tourist was taking in the sights of green jungle on both sides. I glanced down into the water and actually saw a mine below the surface. A second or two later we struck it. The entire ship shuddered and shook. As we made the turn another mine was detonated on our port side. We continued on to what we desperately hoped would be a gradually sloping beach. I knew the location of our Service Battery personnel and although I had no direct responsibility for them, I went below to their area on C deck forward hatch. By the time I made my way through well packed corridors I found that my friends had just been given instructions to leave the ship by another passage way. Just about everyone aboard, knowing that the ship was beached, felt that they might be able to return another day and could pick up personal items left behind. Therefore, panic fortunately was not a problem.'

Captain Euart located his men and with great concern, supervised their escape. Moshimer again: 'I returned to the C Deck foyer [the entry for First Class passengers in front of the First Class Dining Saloon], and found myself close to a doorway into a vestibule leading to an open exterior door in the ship's starboard hull. Between these doors I found a rope and was able to toss it down across the slippery foyer thereby giving the soldiers some support on their way to the open door. When they reached my position, many of them would hesitate at the sight of water below. I then gave them verbal encouragement plus some persuasion by giving them a mighty push! Everyone wore a life preserver.'

With the assistance of Warrant Officer Moshimer, Captain Warren K. Covill, and Lt. Ward D. MacDonald, all men were removed to safety, with great difficulty as the ship was listing badly. Moshimer recalls, 'The floors were becoming more slippery by the minute as toilet bowls overflowed and sent water over the hallway floors. The angle of the sloping foyer floor was rapidly increasing and we still had soldiers aboard. When we had cleared the area, Captain Euart tied the rope I had thrown down around his waist. Captain Warren Covill of our battalion climbed up the remaining few feet from where he had stationed himself, and was beside me standing on the ship's side. In a matter of a few moments the ship had completely rolled over on its port side. What had been a flat horizontal foyer was now a vertical shaft. Captain Covill and I tried to raise Captain Euart with all the strength we could command, but we were physically exhausted. The ship by this time had keeled over on the port side until the decks were vertical and at the same instant the ship's bow slide off the edge of the reef and sank stem first into the channel.'

ELWOOD J. EUART

Elwood J. Euart, Captain, Field Artillery, United States Army, "....for extraordinary heroism, on the occasion of the sinking of the United States Army Transport *President Coolidge* at sea, on October 26, 1942. Captain Euart, Troop Mess officer on duty in the enlisted men's mess hall, personally checked the clearing of that area upon the alarm. Having safely reached his abandon-ship station, he learned of men trapped in the hold and went there. By lashing himself to the low end of the rope he was able to hold it tight enough for men to climb up it to safety, even though the ship was badly listing. Finally as he attempted to climb up, almost vertically by that moment, with the help of a few men at the other end of the line, the ship careened and sank very quickly. Captain Euart exhausted himself assisting many others, whose lives were thus undoubtedly spared at the expense of his own. By his unselfish, heroic action, and with utter disregard of his own safety, Captain Euart conducted himself far above and beyond the call of duty, saved countless lives and gave his life that many others might live."

'Then the rescue boat, realizing that it would be sucked down with the suction of the ship, gave a last despairing. warning. The three men did not even turn around. Captain Covill said he heard all the warnings clearly - that they all heard all the warnings - but felt abandoning this captain was more than they could do. The rescue boat pulled away hastily with a clanging of the coxswain's bell and a churning and putt-putt of the exhaust, and from where I was I could see the three small, dark figures turn for a moment to watch it go off and then turn back to the hold. Hundreds of men were watching the scene in silence from safe vantage points, and it filled their eyes and filled their hearts breaking.' (Ira Wolfert)

Some men made it to the lifeboats and rafts, others swam for shore or were picked up by local craft from the base at Luganville. No matter how they arrived on shore, all they had were the clothes they were wearing, and in many instances, even these were useless due to the oil spill. It appears that few boats made any haste to shore in order to off load and return to rescue further men.

'I will never forget the dirt and dust that was blown in our faces as a result of the stem filling with water and compressing the air in the corridors. Only seconds later the water came rushing over us and in an instant we were carried down and down as the ship sank. I cannot guess the length of time we were under but I do recall the difficulty removing my steel helmet and other gear from around my waist. Both Covill and I rose to the surface not more than an arm's length apart, but there was no sign of Euart.

'Immediately there was another crisis, and we both owe our lives to a fast thinking coxswain of a Higgins landing craft. A large pontoon barge that was still under power but unmanned was about to run over us and would have but for this coxswain. He lowered the ramp of his boat into the water and proceeded to scoop us up as you might a shovel full of coal. We actually looked like coal because of the heavy black bunker oil that covered us. The moving barge struck the Higgins boat just a moment or two after we were safely on the ramp, and although there was damage to the side of the craft, it could still operate. Later we attempted to find the coxswain who saved us, but were unsuccessful.'

Captain Elwood Euart was posthumously awarded the Distinguished Service Cross. Captain Warren K. Covill, Lt. Ward D. MacDonald, and Warrant Officer Robert H. Moshimer were awarded the Soldier's Medal. Technical Sergeant John S. Flanagan, Jr. was recommended for citation for courageous action above and beyond the call of duty. [N12]

TO THE DEPTHS

With the ship on her beam ends, her stern well under and the forward starboard hull and bow plates exposed, the *President Coolidge* slid off the ledge. At 1052 hours, with a great convulsive motion and turmoil of water, she disappeared from sight. Within minutes, only two small round cauldrons of white water marked her grave as she gave up her last breath of air through her funnels. The once proud flagship of the Dollar Steamship Line and the American President Line lay finally at rest, in 70 to 270 ft of water on a steep slope.

Henry Schumacher recalls: 'As the *President Coolidge* slid to her watery grave men were still racing along her hull. Before the eyes of all was the terrifying sight of a ship sinking completely from view. A ship which had brought us across thousands of miles of a war torn ocean; a ship which we had ate, worked, slept and dreamed for over three weeks; a ship that now held all our possessions to our last bullet, rifle, toothbrush, etc. Every man, though stripped of all belongings, felt thankful to be alive as he stumbled ashore, not knowing for how many the former Queen of the Pacific had become a watery tomb. Almost all were aware that the disaster was the result of a mine, whether ours or the enemy's, was for others to decide.'

Bad lucked dogged the ship even in these last minutes of her life. Although I have not personally dived off the shore-line immediately to the east and west of the ship, it has been shown that fifty yards down the beach from where she struck, in either direction, the bottom shoals off gradually and thus may have allowed the stricken ship to come to rest with some chance for salvage. The *President Coolidge* struck at a point where the bottom dropped off abruptly from the shoreline to a depth of over a hundred feet and then down to 240 feet - the only place on the entire shoreline that the bottom didn't shoal off gradually. When beached, only her bow rested on the sharp coral ledge, with her hull suspended like a huge cantilever over deep water. As the ship gradually filled, her stern submerged and she was dragged off the ledge to her final resting place hard up against the coral ledge that had given temporary respite to enable the passengers and crew to disembark.

The sinking of the *President Coolidge* made United States headlines on 12 December 1942. Nine days later *Newsweek* printed an eye-witness account by Ira Wolfert, *North American Newspaper Alliance* correspondent: 'One of the most surprising features of the tragedy was the great number of men who did not know how to swim. These men clambered obediently down the cargo nets, but when it came to letting go and dropping into the water, their minds just froze up and they could not release their holds, despite the fact that they wore life belts. Officers climbed down the cargo nets after them and walked on their fingers to break their holds. While this was going on the scene took on a nightmare quality. The silent, tense men, eyes closed ... clung desperately to the cargo nets. Equally desperate officers shouted at them and trod on and kicked their fingers . . .'

Wolfert, in *Battle for the Solomons*, writes, '..... and while this was going on, the scene took on a nightmare quality - the silent, tense men, eyes closed, faces all locked up, clinging desperately to the cargo nets, while equally desperate officers shouted at them, and walked on their fingers, and kicked at their fingers in an effort to save them, all this to an accompaniment from the interior of the ship of youthful voices lifted in ribald songs, and twanging guitars and a bedlam of phonograph records.'

With a distinct thirty degree list to port, the *President Coolidge* has less than an hour before she disappears beneath the waters of Segond Channel.

Wolfert returned to *terra firma* from his aerial observation and assisted in the rescue. He later mentions that the cargo nets were fifteen feet short of the water, which may explain the hesitation of some to hurtle down into the channel. Wolfert recalls a young soldier who hesitated, and told the boat crew that he couldn't swim. He finally jumped, missed the rescue boat, and plummeted down toward the seabed - with a fully loaded cartridge-belt around his waist. He finally struggled to the surface and gasped, 'See - I told you fellows I couldn't swim'.

Despite the tragedy of the loss of such a valuable ship, and the landing of five thousand men with nothing but the clothes on their oil soaked bodies, the officers managed to retain a sense of humour. Anxiously waiting on shore for his officers and men to escape, Brigadier General William Rose scanned the ship as she finally rolled over. Finally, a weary Colonel Lewis arrived and with all the formality that is expected in the higher echelon, presented himself to his commanding officer.

"Sir," Colonel Lewis said, pulling himself straight and offering a formal salute, "Colonel Lewis, commanding, reports for duty".

Giving the dishevelled Colonel the 'once over', the General returned the salute, and with a deliberate hesitation and a half-smile said, 'Go back and do it again'.

Colonel James A. Lewis thought his men did pretty well in abandoning ship within an hour. In a commendation of his men, he wrote: 'Without discipline of a superior kind the feat of abandoning ship by some 4,000 men in less than one hour could never have been accomplished. Coolness which forestalled panic, trust in your leaders, consideration for the safety of others, ability in scrambling down nets and ropes, all combined to prevent a terrible disaster and weld together a Combat team with mutual confidence between officers and men. To wait quietly in a dark and crowded cabin, breathing pungent fumes while the oily water rose from shoetops to knee, to hip, to count the minutes and feel the ever increasing list of the cabin until it grew so steep you plied mattresses on the floor to keep your footing; to move without stampeding when the order finally came to go; to drop from the dangling net into the green water although you may never have been out over your knees before; to wait for the soldier near you who couldn't swim although you knew you both might be engulfed at any - time by whirlpools when the ship rolled over; to lose no time ashore in building with makeshift tools so you might be dependent on nobody ... all revealed something soldiers call "what it takes". Thus, proud of our first test, every man can look forward with confidence to the future, whatever it may bring, and ask only that the Providence which has once tried our mettle keep us steadfast when our next turn comes.'

Makes ya kinda proud doesn't it? It is true that there was no panic. Severe apprehension may be the better description, for as I have stated, some men could not swim and more than a few were kicked off the nets into the water. But no man lost his life once in the water.

OBSERVATIONS - FROM A DISTANCE

Richard 'Pete' Peterson, Ensign on board *USS Gamble*, knew that it was one of his mines that put the liner on the bottom of Segond Passage. He was not pleased. 'October 26 was just another routine time for us. I don't believe that the specific information as to how to enter [the channel through the minefield] was sent out and certainly any information was sent only to Navy vessels concerning the minefields being there. We had just tied up alongside a fuelling ship in the harbour when, looking back up toward the NE entrance we could see the Coolidge standing in the wrong entrance and heading directly into the minefield. We tried to warn her as I am sure did the Port Director and other vessels in the harbour, by signal light, but to no avail. If we had waited till later in the day to refuel we'd still have been patrolling when she arrived and would certainly have placed a pilot aboard and taken her in through the proper channel. The PC boat merely greeted her and watched her steam in the wrong entrance, probably not even aware that it was a wrong entrance. Certainly the Port Director should have given proper instructions.!! I recall that 'the word' was that [the President Coolidge] came directly from Noumea unescorted because of a breakdown in communications and an argument with those in command of the area. This is all heresay, but she did arrive unescorted not knowing of how to properly enter the harbour. The merchant crew of the Coolidge certainly wasn't responsible for they were under the orders and control of the US Army. If we hadn't picked that morning to ask the Port Director to let us refuel, the event would never have happened. If the Port Director had given proper instructions to the PC boat who relieved, it wouldn't have happened, and if the Coolidge had been under escort of a Naval ship, I doubt if it would have been allowed to enter without a pilot to guide it.'

Frank Cameron was on board another ship in the harbour unloading cargo when the *President Coolidge* went down. 'The first I knew anything was wrong was via the usual alarm of loud excited talk and people running. Silhouetted against the horizon of the channel between Espiritu Santo and Tutuba islands was a large two-funnelled transport. At first I thought it was headed outward until I realized that it hadn't yet been in the harbor and that she was coming in at a good speed. By this time I gathered from the talk that she had been hit by mines. Someone said twice, and someone else said three times.

How close the *President Coolidge* was to the shore can be seen in this rare photograph taken by a B-17 bomber navigator as he returned to Bomber Two airstrip after a sortie to the Solomons. It has never been published before. Note the oil slick. The angle of view would be similar to that now seen from the left hand side of a commercial aircraft coming in to land at Pekoa airport.

'I hadn't heard the explosions but she was listing even then quite noticeably. It was perhaps a minute or two after I arrived on the bridge that she turned broadside to us and the channel, and headed directly for the shore of Espiritu Santo island. She still kept a fairly good speed. She hit the beach head on, about a mile up the channel from where we lay. The chart shows forty fathoms there with plenty of coral heads. No one, I think, had any full comprehension of the impending disaster, since it appeared as though she might be far enough up on the shelf to rest safely while her stern might settle somewhat. It was then 9:45 am.

'I watched through the glasses the boats and nets being lowered and roughly calculated about a twenty degree port list which she had assumed. It didn't seem possible that she had troops on board at the time, since there appeared to be little confusion about the decks. I didn't realize till after that there were troops.'[They would have been disembarking on the starboard side of the ship which was out of sight of Cameron who could see only the port side.]

'Although there were perhaps fifteen ships in the harbor, they sat placidly in the mid-morning calm, and there seemed no sense of anything unusual apparent. It was perhaps five minutes, although it is hard to judge the time element in these things, before I saw the first small motor boats put out.

Again we can see how close the *President Coolidge* came in to shore. It could be suggested that if all the men had been evacuated from the bow, none would have even got their feet wet. Note the men standing in the reef shallows near the bow.

' Then one after another, ships lowered their power boats, Higgins boats put off from shore, the tug *Navajo* headed up the channel, and the whole scene became a series of converging wakes from perhaps fifty boats heading toward the now badly listing Coolidge.

'On our own ship there was as yet little feeling of emergency. Various groups clustered at the rails, watching intently as one would watch a newsreel. On number-two hatch, two disinterested soldiers played ping-pong. At number-five hatch, we still continued to discharge cargo. The steward, who had once sailed on board the Coolidge, said he knew most of the personnel and that we could get all the stores we wanted from her (our food problems was getting urgent at the time). This sounded like a good possibility. It seemed that she was permanently beached, that her crew could be gotten off easily for she was only fifty or more yards from shore, and that, in all probability, the damage was repairable.

'We became aware that she was gradually listing, however, a full realization of the awful possibilities of what we were actually watching came over us. The mate had come forward from number-five hatch and in a voice that contained something of a sob swore, "What a goddamn thing to happen." Tag, our signalman, in a frustrated tone now began to explain how he had seen her heading in the channel, had seen the mines explode, had wanted to send, uninstructed, U-U-U even at the risk of a court-martial, but that our sending apparatus was pitifully inadequate at that distance in daylight. Since we had no power boat, it seemed useless to lower one of our push-pull lifeboats in the face of so much potent naval strength around us, but nevertheless, our Captain ordered it manned and lowered. It was about 10:10. At the moment the Coolidge seemed to be resting steadily on the reef, with all but two of her

The Sun Deck and the funnels are about to go under - there is only a few minutes left before the *President Coolidge* is on the seabed.

lifeboats successfully launched. But now we could make out the troops that had not at first been evident. They were strung out in continuous lines from the bow of the ship to the beach, and the first returnin motor boats were jammed to the gunwales. There seemed to be thousands, some of whom were coloured. Between 10:15 and 10:30 her increasing list to port became noticeable and alarming. I tried to picture what it must be like, disembarking so many men under such circumstances. I couldn't picture it. It was far enough away so that there was no sound. just a huge helpless ship, around which hovered a swarm of small boats, slowly tipping to an angle where her entire decks were visible and her poop slightly awash. It was quiet and it was happening, but it was unreal. I could see men high up on her superstructure silhouetted between her stacks. They just seemed to stand there and do nothing. I wondered why they made no move to safety. From her bow the long lines of troops still kept floundering shoreward. By 10:30 it became evident that she was a doomed ship. It is very hard to watch such a thing and do nothing. I tried to sit still and watch, but couldn't. I had to talk about it. Everyone else watching seemed to be under the same compulsion. Nobody said anything informative. You said it was a shame, a goddamn shame, or that it made you sick to your stomach to watch. Later the carpenter said it was like watching somebody die.

'From 10:30 on I kept watching a point on her foredeck at the break of her superstructure. Inch by inch her freeboard there lessened and the angle of her stacks became crazier. Her stern was settling and her poop deck was well under. Things were happening fast now. A huge geyser appeared by her stern bubbling furiously and she seemed to surround herself with a thin film of smoke as if to curtain the final shame of her death throes. Soon there was no freeboard left. More geysers appeared along her side. Her stacks at last touched the water and then with a tragic gracefulness, her bow rose as her stern settled more deeply and she slid off the coral ledge and disappeared from sight. It was 10:45. (Actually ten minutes later but that is of little consequence.)

'The small boats stayed around the vicinity picking up survivors amidst a mass of floating wreckage. I don't know how many men were lost, but I think not many. Shortly after noon I looked up the channel and at the point where she had first beached herself. There were the usual big white tropical clouds. A light breeze no more than ruffled the surface of the harbour. Against the sandy shore-line, the inevitable green palms were serene and colourful as always. It didn't seem as though anything had happened. I knew it would seem that way until the tide changed and the wreckage, embedded in an oil slick, would come slowly eddying past us.'

Edward F. Oliver was on board one of the fifty or so 'rusty merchant ships' in the harbour. 'This particular morning I took my after-breakfast coffee out to a chair on the boat deck, hoping to drink it in comfort away from the sweltering heat of the saloon. There was little traffic in the harbor. A few landing craft could be seen here and there leaving long white wakes on the otherwise smooth surface of the water. From my vantage point I could look directly out toward the three channels which connect the sea with the eastern part of the harbor. Shortly after I seated myself with my coffee on the boat deck, a large vessel hove into view from over the horizon. As she drew nearer I could see what appeared to be an escort off her port side. I idly watched her for several minutes as she approached the harbor; then, in horrified surprise, I noticed that she had not changed course and was proceeding directly toward the large mined entrance. From that moment on it was like watching a tragedy portrayed on the stage, knowing beforehand what the end will be. The minor character in the act, the escort, appeared to take position on the port quarter, as if not wishing to detract from the main character's entrance, and thus permitted the tragedienne to proceed majestically to the center of the stage and her execution. The minutes ticked on and I sat transfixed, telling myself that it couldn't be happening, that somehow, sometime, the minefield had been cleared away. Then the execution began! A tremendous blast sent a towering geyser of spray and water into the air, all but blocking my view.'

Oliver continues, 'The first blast shattered the early morning quiet of this South Pacific island harbor. Simultaneously with the second explosion, pandemonium broke out ashore and afloat. Signal lights from all floating naval units and shore establishments, and some signal lights which probably hadn't been used for weeks, commenced blinking as one as a multitude of orders, counter orders and questions were transmitted back and forth. Whether because of these signals or in spite of them, the men attached to every small craft afloat went into action. Fortunately, all the cargo in this small harbor was lightered by LCVPs, LCTs and self-propelled barges. Hundreds of these craft were available almost immediately. Even before the *President Coolidge* hit the beach, the smooth surface of the harbor was crisscrossed with hundreds of wakes as the little craft sped to the rescue. They surrounded the huge ship like so many water beetles, took off the survivors as fast as they came down the abandon-ship net, and picked up the men who jumped into the water.'

Stephen Parisi managed to get all his unit off safely. 'We were taken to a small salvage ship in the harbor before making the final trip to shore. From the salvage ship we watched the *President Coolidge* roll over on its port side and disappear into the channel. As I watched that beautiful ship go out of sight I could not help thinking of all the arms, ammunition, vehicles, and much more equipment and other materials crucial to the war effort. I wondered then if anything could be salvaged, or if it was possible to raise the ship.'

A Navy tug *USS Navajo* stands by to assist but by now most of the men are ashore. The *President Coolidge* came in from the left of the photograph. She should have come through the passage between Tutuba Island (left) and Bogacio (centre). Aore Island is to the right. The minefield, not visible of course, lies in two parallel lines between the main island (bottom), and Tutuba and Bogacio.

REPORTS AND RUMOURS IN THE U.S.A.

With the Battle of Santa Cruz raging on the same day as the *President Coolidge* was sunk, it is understandable that the U.S. Navy had much on their mind. Extracts from official Navy Department Communiques are somewhat sparse in their mention of events on Espiritu Santo, and in fact there is no indication of the loss of the *President Coolidge*. Little wonder that the press and hence the public were not fully aware of the situation. Obviously, it would have been quite a blow to the Navy's ego to have released the news that a ocean-going liner was on the bottom of the sea due to negligence on the part of the Navy, it having been blasted by not one, but two of their own mines. But in time the rumours would spread, the press insisting on further details. [N13]

U.S. Secretary of the Navy Frank Knox was reluctant to entertain any idea that a popular passenger liner had been sunk by a U.S. mine, but through persistent questioning by the press, the loss of the ship was gradually brought out into the open - but no mention was made that it was an American mine - better let the press assume that it was Japanese. It is quite understandable that rumours would persist. It took till 12 December 1942, some seven weeks after the *President Coolidge* sank, before the U.S. Navy officially announced the loss of the ship, saying only that 'The vessel, operating as a transport, was fully loaded with troops and equipment when it struck a mine and sank. Through prompt and efficient rescue efforts, casualties were limited to four men.' This had occurred 'in recent weeks in the South Pacific.' One newspaper reported that the US Navy had stated that the ship had hit a Japanese mine.

On questioning during a press conference, Secretary of the Navy Knox admitted to 'a question of possible fault' but pointed out that a Japanese submarine could plant mines in the same waters where American missiles were sown. He stated that he 'had no proof that the liner was lost as a result of striking an American mine somewhere in the Solomons area'. Knox said that an investigation would be held and confirmed that the ship had been sunk in the Solomons area. Perhaps the Secretary of the Navy was not informed of the correct details, that the ship had been sunk in Espiritu Santo, and that an inquiry had already been held the previous week in Noumea.

Local San Francisco newspapers expressed the sadness of 'thousands of San Franciscans as they recalled the appearance of the proud vessel plying in and out of the bay is less turbulent days'. The newspapers reminded its readers that the Yokohama to San Francisco run of 9 days, 9 hours and 51 minutes, set in 1937, was still held by the lost ship, and she also held the record for the number of passengers brought back from the orient in one trip.

The Dean of Stanford University, J. Hugh Jackson, also a director of the American President Line, disclosed in a speech to a local service club that the ship was actually sunk by two American mines, and stated that the ship 'was lost as a result of a blunder by the American Navy'. Eventually a newspaper report in the *San Francisco Call-Bulletin* on 15 December 1942 indicated, 'Word from Washington today that Secretary of the Navy Knox was investigating the cause of the sinking by a mine of the *President Coolidge* in the Solomons bore out officially word that had seeped through to San Francisco weeks ago. Sources here insist that the Coolidge struck our own, not Japanese mines, and that "someone had blundered" in ordering the great transport into the mined area. Local sources say that the investigation is actually in progress now in the Southwest Pacific.' [N14]

President Roosevelt declined to make specific comment except to question the accuracy of Mr Jackson's charge and asked reporters how an official of the shipping line could know what type of mine sank the transport. As by now however many survivors had returned to the United States, it seemed strange to some that the government was trying to keep the circumstances of the loss of the ship a secret. Within days, newspapers were reporting the eyewitness accounts of survivors who did not hesitate to provide their names. Four men who were on board, Jack Barlow, Rafael Cooper, Jack Vanderboom and William Sheesley made it quite clear that the *President Coolidge* had hit two mines 'at the entrance to a South Pacific harbour'. 'Three quarters of the way in many of the men and officers knew they were in a minefield because they could see the mines.' The location was still not mentioned, obviously for security reasons, but the newspapers were not reticent in reporting that the ship had hit American mines. It was eighteen months later, in April 1944 that the newspapers printed where the ship was sunk.

Captain Henry Nelson set the record straight for the public in an interview revealed in the *San Francisco Call-Bulletin* on 29 January 1943. 'No information was given to us and no challenge was made by either of the two ships. Just as we entered the real harbour, a blinker message broadcast the one word Stop! But it was too late. Before we could get our engines going full astern, we struck a mine and then another one.' [N15]

It was as simple as that.

CHAPTER SEVEN

FINAL MOMENTS
Pictorial Essay

With the *President Coolidge* having only a slight list to port, 172nd Infantry Combat Team scrable down the knotted ropes and cargo nets into the Segond Channel. Some swim ashore; others are more fortunate and have use of a raft. The doorway shown is the entrance into the Tourist Class lobby on C Deck.

Troops of the 172nd Infantry Combat Team climb down ropes and cargo nets to escape the sinking *President Coolidge* as the ship lists to port at a rate of about one degree per minute. Some are fortunate to be taken to shore by lifeboat or raft; others must swim. Note what has come to be known as Euart's Door, in the photographs this page. This is the entrance for First Class paassengers into the lobby next to the First Class dining room. It was here that Captain Elwood Euart entered to rescue his men, and subsequently lot his life (see page 103). In the photograph below, Euart's men may still be aboard, even though the ship has a 45° list.

It does seem rather odd that so many men climbed down from the higher starboard side, rather than take the short descent on the port side as the ship gradually listed, but each unit was allocated to a lifeboat station. There is no panic, and one man even waves to the camera. Note the three-inch guns, and the five-inch gun on the stern.

The 5-inch gun hangs over the stern of the *President Coolidge* as troops disembark from the stern of the ship. The photograph below gives a good indication of the layout of the stern of the ship.
Note the guns on A-Deck and B-Deck, the Tourist Lounge under the mast, and the First Class Swimming Pool at top, left.

120

In this dramatic photograph, the American 'Stars and Stripes' flag dips its leading edge into the sea and is about to go down with the *President Coolidge*. Debris floats off the ship as she turns on her beam ends. Her bow rises slightly (bottom photograph) as she slips beneath the oily waters of the Segond Channel, taking with her Fireman Reid and Captain Euart.

This is a sad moment for all who knew the *President Coolidge* when she travelled the Pacific as a luxury liner, and in her final days as a troopship. Air escapes from the bowels of the ship through her two funnels, marking her final resting place on the bottom of Segond Channel. Note how close she was to the shore, a significant factor in her resurrection as a wonderful recreational dive.

The Lady and the President have gone to their grave. Only foaming white water remains to indicate that once a great liner stood hard up on the reef. Thousands of men are scattered along the shore. Others are packed into lifeboats, soon to add to the chaos on shore. If panic did not arise on the *President Coolidge* then certainly confusion raged on shore. What to do with five thousand men with no shelter, no food, and little clothing, let along their personal effects and arms? Espiritu Santo was not geared up to accept these additional mouths to feed and bodies to rest. But the U.S. Army and Navy bases on shore offered their hospitality, and after some initial hardships, the 'Coolidge men' were billeted and put to work.

CHAPTER EIGHT

CHAOS RULED SUPREME

If the debarkation was orderly, then all was chaos ashore. There arose the immediate problem of feeding, clothing and housing over a regiment of men, stripped of all equipment, clothing and personal effects. Henry Schumacher comments, 'To the Navy must go the credit, albeit grudgingly on the part of many an Army man, for effectively meeting this problem on a malarial, fly infested island. A straw thatched chapel is one instance, a partially constructed mess hall in the another, would be the difference between shelter or a night out in the torrential rain. Navy and Marine uniforms clothed a large amount of this now unarmed combat team. Beards were grown and became the norm in this clean shaven U.S. Army.'

Navy personnel of the armed guard on board the *President Coolidge*, and the ships officers and crew, were quartered and subsisted by the Navy units ashore. About half the army personnel were also being quartered and subsisted by Navy units ashore with several army units ashore taking care of the other half. Eventually some of the stranded troops were issued with tents and made their own base after 'cutting out a hole in the jungle'.

James Renton offers his word of appreciation to the Army, and adds, 'I saw my group over the side (we were one of the first because we were by the railing) - struck out for shore - once there it was up a slight bank and into a coconut plantation. A dirt road parallelled the shore line. I was dirty and streaked with oil and only a pair of green shorts on. Every officer was telling everyone where to go. Where was a forty-man replacement unit to go? I told my guys to stay put as they came ashore - counted noses and all were present. There was a typical square plantation house with a screened porch all around down the road a bit. I thought I might be able to get some help. The screen was half rusted through - no problem to get in. Surely there must be some clothes around here someplace. Opened a door - it was a bedroom. A large bed with mosquito netting over it occupied most of the room. I lifted the net and pulled on the sheet. A young girl started pulling on the sheet as well and screaming for all she was worth. She was yelling in French (I understood but a word or two) and I was replying in English.

' I can well imagine what she thought. I finally found a towel on a nearby chair and beat a hasty retreat to the beach area. Chaos still ruled supreme ashore. Men were still floating in and there seemed to be no organization to speak of. I'm sure you can imagine the situation. Here were some fifty-two hundred officers and men, dirty, streaked with oil, and dressed at best in a pair of shorts. No clothing, shoes, tents, food or the stoves and utensils to prepare it. This would be just the beginning of the list because it excluded all the regiment's vehicles, arms, artillery, etc. It was also reported that all the available quinine in the United States was aboard. This was a terrible loss and caused an early shift to atabrine, the then only known alternative.' [N1]

'Mention should also be made that the officers and men of the 172nd Regimental Combat Team soon became more than adequate unloading ships and planes and refuelling aircraft. Though untrained in the use of fork lifts and tractors, they soon became experts. Instead of landing in Guadalcanal in late October, they didn't arrive until February 1943, after the Island had been declared 'secured'. For at least the next four weeks all manner of supplies flooded in from all over the Pacific. There seemed to be little we could do at the time except just stay out of the way, so I got my bunch together and headed for a small town (which turned out to be Luganville) a couple of miles down the road. It wasn't easy walking because the surface of the road was a combination of dirt and coral.

'Here we were. Welcome to Luganville, Espiritu Santo, home of the Pacific Naval Command. Hot, humid, malaria infested, and torrential rains. Probably one of the poorest destinations in the whole Pacific. I felt we would have more luck with the Army than with the Navy. We were most fortunate to blunder into a rear echelon Supply Depot of the 164th Infantry Regiment, American Division (it was a National Guard Regiment from North and South Dakota and western Wisconsin). The rest of the outfit had gone on to Guadalcanal two weeks earlier but this small group had been returned to Espiritu Santo because all the regiment's supplies were not landed due to air raids. It was a match made in heaven - the Captain had surplus equipment which we needed and he was desperate for some bodies to process incoming supplies which were shortly to arrive by air from all over the Pacific to re-outfit the 172nd - no easy task since there were some 5,400 of them who needed everything. The Captain (I'm ashamed of myself because I can't remember his name) was really good to us, clothed us, gave us three squad tents, and arranged for us to be set-up with an Army Air Force tower and flight control unit stationed, of all places, back down the road we had come down, but further east and very near the eastern coast line at what was a bomber strip but now was to handle cargo planes exclusively. It was a tough job and really more than we could handle since this was an Army problem, the Navy wasn't much help - we finally got a few Seebees to give us a hand.

'I especially appreciate two things the Captain did for us. First, he managed to supply us with three BARs (Browning Automatic Rifles) and thirty-seven M-1 Rifles (these were very new in the Pacific - the American Division had them but the Marines on Guadalcanal did not) for my men and a Carbine and side arm for me together with spare parts and ammunition. He also permitted us to have some field exercises when circumstances permitted. He and I knew that this was to be a brief interlude at best and that it wouldn't be too long before we would both be in Guadalcanal. When that day came, we'd better be conditioned, equipped, and trained.

Troops landed ashore with nothing more than the clothes on their bodies, and even these were next to useless, covered in oil as they were. Navy and Army units already established on Espiritu Santo billeted the men, placing a strain on existing supplies.

'We ran every day before breakfast - we zeroed in our new M-ls and became familiar with them - I tried to make time every day for at least a brief field exercise. I temporarily organized the men into four units of ten men each and allowed each unit to select a "leader" subject to my approval. I also think we "did the job" for the Captain because he forwarded a most flattering recommendation to the 103rd.

'We would have liked a little more time but orders came down the pike - the balance of the 164th and supplies were to report to the regiment on Guadalcanal. Exact dates are hard to pin down but we tagged along with them and arrived on Guadalcanal on or about the 12th of November. I'm reasonably sure of this date because we arrived the day prior to the naval battle of Friday, the 13th (of November, 1942).'

Arthur Allard confirmed the problems on shore. 'The disembarkation was quiet and orderly, but chaos reigned ashore. The men had no food, clothing, utensils, arms, or vehicles. We temporarily borrowed some supplies from a Seebee group. I didn't get to Guadalcanal till March 1943.' [N2]

Second Lieutenant Charles Schubert praised those on shore. 'At first everyone had thought that the ship was beached, and that we would be back the next day and start unloading her. Therefore, we got off with only the clothes we were wearing. What a logistical problem for the shore-based personnel. They were marvellous and shared any and everything they had with us. We acted as service troops until late February 1943. We unloaded ships and refuelled aircraft which flew to and from Guadalcanal daily. When we were finally re-equipped with weapons, we did go to Guadalcanal; by that time fortunately for my outfit, the Japs had evacuated Guadalcanal.'

Water was a problem. Although plentiful on the island, it was necessary to transport additional fresh water to the now inflated units. Gasolene tankers were cleaned out and converted to waster carriers, but it was impossible to completely eliminate the taint of petrol. 'We could tell whether the tank carried regular gas or 100 octane,' one soldier quipped.

Elmer Nisley, who was on board the *President Coolidge* with 'E' Company, 172nd Infantry Battalion, writes, 'Every man had nothing but the oil soaked clothes on their backs on landing. They had to cut holes in their clothes to remove the oil stains because the sun would have burnt blisters on their skins through the oil. They made shoes out of the cork life rings and the Seebees gave them as much as they could in the way of replacement clothing from their own kit bags. It must be remembered that they had all been fully equipped to land on Guadalcanal. Once they sank they were out of the War. No one paid any attention to them for months. There was little or no food left over in the mess. They were given what could be spared and supplemented with coconuts. There were very few natives around, so they had no other help with food - we were poor for a long time. At night we slept under the platforms built two feet above the ground as a base for the tents of the 7th CB Battalion.'

The landing of 5,000 or so troops in a remote base which at times itself had difficulty in subsisting in the manner that the US soldier believed he should have been accustomed to did nothing to boost morale, of neither the stranded troops nor the settled residents. But the troops did have their war hero, and Elwood Euart, the 'capable young Captain of Pawtucket, Rhode Island' had died a war hero, 'saving the lives of many men by quick thinking and self sacrifice beyond the call of duty.' It was something the Army men could justifiably be proud.

Within a few weeks the 'lost battalion' was busy performing a multiple of duties, such as manning anti-aircraft positions, defending a strategic outlying island, aiding in servicing an air base, furnishing details to serve with the base quartermaster or bakers to assist in all the important task of providing bread for the island, divided as they were and all working closely with a number of diverse units. They were employed as a work units to unload ships on their way to Guadalcanal, and to assist in the construction of air strips and roads.

Stephen Parisi recalls, 'When brought to shore we were assigned areas along the coast. My unit, the Third Battalion 172nd Infantry, was assigned to an area next to a US naval construction battalion, and they fed and clothed us until our supplies arrived from the USA. The supplies came by liberty ships, and when they arrived they were unloaded by men of the 172nd working around the clock. When our rifles arrived and were distributed, Sgt. Ed Ponder, and I, plus our twelve-man squads were sent on outpost duty in a high area overlooking the harbor. The outpost was on land belonging to a plantation owner named Mr. Morris. He befriended us, and kept us supplied with fresh meat and eggs. He also invited Sgt. Ponder and myself to his home for dinner on two occasions after our tour of duty on outpost was over.'

'Thanksgiving, Christmas and New Years Day, were celebrated as festively as conditions permitted. Mosquito bars had become the most revered item of equipment and as the weeks passed, slumber was possible despite the noisiest efforts on the part of the rats, bats and the myriad of other jungle creatures which come to life each night. Cattle and horses roamed the length of the island grazing on the abandoned coconut plantations. Shortly after the first of the year, we were re-equipped with the arms of the field artillery. Trucks, howitzers and small arms were hastily assembled and training programs, tactical missions and firing problems schedule. There were numerous handicaps, not the least of which was the mire of mud in all areas, due to the continuous rains. During the tropics worst months of January, February, and March, fevers raged through out the islands, Dengue fever was responsible for quartering and weakening large percentage. Atabrine had proven its effectiveness in combatting malaria, otherwise white men could not have survived in the numbers they did. Only one man in the battalion had contracted malaria fatally and it was pretty throughly proven that he had scorned the little 'yellow pill'.

Henry Schumacher makes further comment. 'It was to Espiritu that the battle casualties from Guadalcanal were evacuated. During the height of that fierce battle the air force and the Navy operated largely from this advance base. Many a battle scarred vessel and machine gunned riddled bomber was hastily repaired and returned to flight. Submarines, transports, freighter, aircraft carriers were constantly arriving and departing. Espiritu Santo played a necessary and integral part in the battle of Guadalcanal. Saw the *San Francisco* limp into port. In the four months the battalion lived and worked on the Island, it had been under only a few scattered air-raids. These were the nuisance type, being only small scale and causing little damage. Mammoth air bases, recently constructed operated unhampered by the enemy.'

Stephen Parisi again, 'We continued our jungle training during our stay on Espiritu Santo. Four months later we left Santo for Guadalcanal, February 1943, where we had our baptism of fire, then further we fought through the Solomon Islands, New Guinea, and finally the Philippine invasion in the Lingayan Gulf on 9 January,1945.' The men of the 172nd Regimental Combat team paid their dues.

Warrant Officer R. Moshimer and Captain W. Covill, who were involved in the attempted rescue of Captain Elwood Euart, were taken by boat up the channel to a Navy advance hospital, 'hardly more than a few tents', and were given a can of mineral oil and a package of cotton. 'It was suggested that we should take off all our oil soaked clothing right down to our birthday suits, and proceed to remove as much oil as we could. Captain Covill and I were driven to a navy bivouac area in the back of a dump truck, and what a sight we must have been! Both naked except for oil soaked shoes. What a way to spend your first few hours on dry land!'

He was extremely disappointed at the turn of events, and no doubt expressed his feelings accordingly. 'Having been trained as a lean, mean, fighting machine we now were mere pussy cats. We didn't even have marsh-mallows to throw at an enemy. So, we had to wait about and attempt to look busy. Supplies were scarce and slow in coming. It seemed to be common knowledge that the United States entire war production was being sent to Europe with a bare minimum for the Pacific campaign.'He was, however, extremely appreciative of the Navy for taking care of his men after the loss of the ship.

THE CONSEQUENCES

The assistance provided by the U.S. Navy and Army units on Espiritu Santo to the 'shipwrecked' troops begs a very interesting question. What had the Army planned to do with their 5,000 troops when they arrived at Espiritu Santo by the customary method of landing by boat and not swimming ashore? If there was any intention to keep the troops on Espiritu Santo, and then dissipate them as required to the battle-front in the Solomons, surely prior arrangements would have been made to suitably quarter them. It appears however that no quarters were available, which gives rise to the conclusion that the Army intended to take them on to the Solomons as soon as possible, perhaps even without the opportunity to disembark. If this was so, the troops would have been send directly into the fray on Guadalcanal. Whereas the US First Marine Division took Guadalcanal relatively easily on 7 August 1942, the Japanese had retaliated in a number of severe attacks, most of which were not in their favour, but kept the Americans on their guard as they defended the major air-strip near the present town of Honiara. Bloody Ridge was not given that name for nothing. The 'Coolidge troops', members of the 172nd Infantry Regimental Combat Team, would have made a significant contribution to American land strength, and no doubt would have assisted to repel Japanese attacks.

We will never know of course, but perhaps the sinking of the *President Coolidge* claimed more than the lives of fireman Reid and officer Euart, for how many young marines died on Guadalcanal whilst waiting for troop support? The marines were equipped with light arms and equipment necessary to establish a beachhead, but not with the proper equipment to occupy and hold a large section of the island. No doubt this was the task of the 172nd Infantry.

They would not have arrived in time for the Battle of Bloody Ridge over September 12-14, 1942 when forty US troops were killed (and hundreds of Japanese infantry), but they may have made a contribution in the determined Japanese advance across the Matanikau River over 20-23 November, 1942, when 117 men of the US 164th Infantry were killed. The loss of the *President Coolidge* explains why the marines were not relieved until 21 January 1943 at the earliest. Indeed, some of the men destined for Guadalcanal in October 1942 did not arrive till March 1943. By then, the intensive land battles on Guadalcanal were over, with the US forces in complete control.

The other interesting matter to ponder is - how were the troops going to get to Guadalcanal? Were there other troop ships waiting at Espiritu Santo to whisk them up north to the Solomon Islands, under suitable protective convoy one could assume, or was it the Army's intention to direct the *President Coolidge* north with all 5,000 troops on board. This would have been a most dangerous practice - placing all of ones eggs in the same basket so to speak, particularly if the ship was to travel unescorted as it had done from San Francisco. Japanese naval presence was well known in Solomon waters and in several naval battles had the better of the Americans. A single torpedo could have put the troopship on the seabed and taken most of the men with it.

These are purely matters of speculation, but there is no doubt that the loss of the *President Coolidge*, and the military equipment and ammunition on board, and the guns and fighting equipment of the troops, would have been a major blow to US military strategic planning, and put the allied war effort back several months. The sinking came at a critical time in America's initial military deployment in the South-West Pacific and sent reverberations of anxiety throughout the theatre. The race was on to establish forward fighting bases backed by reliable logistical support networks before the Japanese, seemingly catching their breath following their spectacular invasion of the Philippines, main-land South-East Asia, and the islands north of Australia, continued their drive south. The loss of equipment and huge consignments of ammunition that had all been crammed into the *President Coolidge*'s cargo holds was a devastating blow to the establishment of allied defences on Espiritu Santo, to say nothing of having five thousand weaponless men stranded on the island. [N3]

CHAPTER NINE

NELSON'S BLOOD

I t was inevitable that an Inquiry be held in the loss of the *President Coolidge*, and rightly so considering the magnitude of the disaster. But rather than keep an open mind as to the cause, it was apparent that the Navy wanted to protect its own integrity and competence, and thus a suitable scapegoat was required. Who better than the skipper of the ship, Captain Henry Nelson. Remember that Nelson was not Navy - he was a civilian employed by American President Lines, so if he could wear the blame, the Navy would be off the hook.

Nelson of course didn't see matters the same as the Navy. In a letter to Captain Walter H. Roberts, Commanding Officer, Naval Forces Base Button, dated 28 October 1942, just two days after the loss of his ship, Captain Nelson defended his actions, as he should, and as would be expected. He writes:

Dear Sir.

Sailing from White Poppy [Noumea] for Button [Espiritu Santo] on October 24th, we arrived at a point called Hypo off the island outside of the port of Espiritu Santos [*sic*] and not having had any instructions as to any other dangers to this port, proceeded on a course as I thought to the harbor of Button. We contacted two destroyers prior to the entry where the ship struck the two mines. No information was given to us and no challenge was made by either of the two ships, and the first intimation was from a signal station further in the harbor telling me to stop, that we were approaching danger. I in turn stopped the engines and backed the engines, but with the speed that we were carrying, we still went too far and we struck two mines. I immediately, with the speed we had left, headed the ship for the beach, and ordered 'Abandon Ship', which was done and completed in forty-five minutes of 5000 personnel for which there is only a loss of one crew member.

Sailing from White Poppy, no one mentioned to me, no one informed me, that there was a mine field at Espiritu Santos. Had there been some knowledge of mines, I never would have approached anywhere within miles of the port. There was no guard boat anywhere visible.

(Signed) Henry Nelson, Master, S.S. President Coolidge. [N1]

This document was later admitted to the Military Commission, as an exhibit.

A preliminary Court of Inquiry was held on 12 November 1942, on board *USS Whitney* in Noumea, convened by order of the Admiral William F. Halsey, Commander, South Pacific Area and South Pacific Force. The court sat for five days and sought to establish the cause of the sinking of President Coolidge. [N2]

(See Appendix 3, page 243 - Inquiry papers, for 'Record of Procedure of a Court of Inquiry Convened on Board USS Whitney, 12 November 1942.)

The Navy Port Director, Lt. Commander John D. Andrews, U.S.N., stated that the sailing orders for Mr. Nelson, the Master, had been prepared the day before, lacking only the exact time of departure. He did not explain the 24-hour delay in transmitting the orders to the ship nor his failure to warn the master of the ship that there were mines in the harbor at Buttons. He implied that the matter (of the mines) was 'too secret to be passed on to civilians'. Expecting his sailing orders to be scrupulously carried out, he relied entirely on the 'Special Information' sheet to be appended to the general Routing Instructions, as adequate. This document is the vital element in the loss of *President Coolidge*. The first dispute of significance is whether Captain Nelson ever received the 'Special. Information'. Even though he signed for the whole packet which supposedly contained them, the question remains as to whether he knew or should have been told of the mines at Espiritu Santo, and whether his instructions were sufficiently unambiguous.

Colonel Arthur G. King, Chief of the Medical Unit and Surgeon of the Espiritu Santo Service Command, comments, 'In the transcript of the Court of Inquiry two important facts stand out. When questioned, as they all were, every officer, both military and civilian, testified that he had no criticism whatever of the conduct of the Master, Henry Nelson, or any other Army, Navy or civilian personnel in charge of any operation. A few officers volunteered that they would be glad to serve under Captain Nelson again on another voyage. Secondly, not a single witness who had been aboard the ship stated when questioned under oath that he had ever seen the crucial and mysterious "Exhibit B, Special Information" which was supposed to direct the S.S. President Coolidge safely through the mine-field.'

No charges were officially laid prior or during the Court of Inquiry, although it could be argued that the underlying intent of the Court, or at least of Admiral Halsey, was to find a scapegoat, preferably a civilian, who would could divert the blame away from the Navy. Halsey of course would only have been in a position to make judgement based on reports he had himself received from his officers. It would appear reasonable to think that the findings of the Court of Inquiry would establish that the sinking was the end result of a sequence of incidents for which different individuals and the U.S. Navy itself were responsible.

However, despite the excellent performance of the ship's master in beaching the ship close to shore, despite the evidence which cast grave doubts if the proper instructions were ever given to him, and despite the Defence Counsel's affirmation that the loss of the vessel was caused 'by the system which sent the *SS President Coolidge* into the area without notifying the Master that there were mines there,' the official finding of the Navy Court of Inquiry was that the loss of the ship was caused 'by the gross negligence and culpable inefficiency' of Captain Nelson, and that 'he and he alone was responsible for the loss'. Their recommendation was for further proceedings and prosecution.

This suited Admiral Halsey who, it could be assumed, wished to keep the high reputation of the U.S. Navy intact, particularly during this first year of the Pacific War. Halsey formally charged Captain Henry Nelson, and directed Rear Admiral Calvin H. Cobb, U.S. Navy, to convene, and preside over, a Military Commission be held in Noumea on or after 2 December 1942. The formal charge against Captain Nelson was laid in a memo directed to the proposed judge advocate, Captain Richard Fagan, US Marine Corps, Retd. on 29 November 1942.

It stated: 'Through Negligence Suffering a Vessel of the United States to be Lost. In that Henry Nelson, master of the S.S. President Coolidge, a merchant ship of the United States owned by the American President Lines and chartered by the War Department, while so serving as master of the S.S. President Coolidge, under orders and control of the United States navy in the zone of military operation and an actual theatre of war in the South Pacific Area, making passage from Noumea, New Caledonia to Segond Channel, Espiritu Santo, New Hebrides, with United States Army and Navy personnel, combat equipment, and supplies aboard, on or about October 26, 1942, having previously received a complete set of routing instructions, including special information for safely entering Segond Channel, from the duly constituted port authority at Noumea, New Caledonia, did, while conning said ship, nevertheless, neglect and fail to follow, or cause to be followed, the aforementioned instructions in approaching Segond Channel, and did negligently, carelessly, wantonly, and recklessly cause said ship to make a wrong approach to Segond Channel at an excessive rate of speed which precluded him from receiving a pilot aboard and acting upon timely warnings that his ship was standing into danger; and he, the said Henry Nelson, through said negligence, did suffer the said *SS President Coolidge* to strike two mines in a wrong approach to Segond Channel, Espiritu Santo, New Hebrides, at or about 9:35 a.m., on the day aforesaid, in consequence of which the said *SS President Coolidge*, two lives, and a vast cargo of combat equipment and supplies were lost to the detriment of the success of United States military operations, the United States then being in a state of war.'

And so, Captain Henry Nelson, a civilian, at the age of sixty-three and with nearly half a century of impeccable service in the merchant marine, appeared in a U.S. Navy-convened court in Noumea.

It is reasonable to question what right the U.S. Navy had to convene a military Commission, and to charge Captain Henry Nelson, a civilian, with negligence. The Seventh Paragraph, section 333, Naval Courts and Boards, states, 'The officers, members of crews and passengers on board merchant ships of the United States, although not in the Naval service of the United States, are, under the laws of the United States, the decisions of the courts, and, by the very necessities of the case, subject to military control while in the actual theater of war.' Rest assured that the 'Military Commission' was a full court, not a commission in the layman's general understanding of the term, and was in a position to impose penalties if the charges were sustained.

It is obvious from Halsey's charge that negligence was the key word, although Halsey does not hesitate to add emotive language like 'carelessly, wantonly and recklessly' to the charge, just in case the message wasn't clear. The US Navy wanted Nelson's blood and they were determined to get it, through a court preceding convened by themselves.

132

Captain Henry Nelson, master of the *President Coolidge*, and Commodore of the American President Line on his retirement.

At the risk of being facetious, Halsey could hardly have charged himself with 'having negligently failed to ensure that those under my command and responsible for the laying of mines at least tell someone about it when the mines are laid'. Surely the U.S. Navy would have learnt something from the loss of their destroyer *USS Tucker* just twelve weeks prior to the loss of the *President Coolidge*. But then, the point being made by the Navy was that Captain Nelson was indeed informed of what procedures to take in approaching Espiritu Santo, and that he simply failed to follow instructions.

It may have appeared expedient to suggest that Captain Nelson, with all his years of maritime experience, would not have disobeyed any instruction, particularly as he was entering the waters of Espiritu Santo for the first time and would have welcomed any instruction to assist his docking. So, the case before the prosecution was to ensure that the Commission panel appreciated that entry documents were indeed handed to Captain Nelson and that he had acted *negligently* in not carrying out these instructions. Other factors also arose during the Commission which the prosecution would use against Captain Nelson, but several of these in effect 'backfired' and were shown to be detrimental to US Navy procedures.

An 'Objection to the Specifications' of the charge laid by Admiral Halsey was immediately presented by the Council for the accused, Captain Gordon B. Parks, US Navy, and Chester C. Hosmer, US Naval Reserve, the indication being that, 'In this specification no facts are properly alleged which supports the charge therefore the specification does not state a triable offense. It is fatally defective in at least four particulars.' This was a legal defence which debunked the actual charge worded against Captain Nelson, on the grounds that, in laymen terms, the charge could not be proven one way or the other because of the vagueness of the charge. (See Appendix 3, page 246- Inquiry Papers, for a summary of the Objections.). The Objection was not successful although Hosmer raised the 'Objections to the Specifications' once again during his Written Argument (a summation at the conclusion of the trial).

Rear Admiral Cobb convened the Military Commission as directed, and conducted the trial. Captain Richard Fagan was appointed Judge Advocate. The Military Commission was held at College La Perouse, Noumea, New Caledonia over six days from 8 December to 14 December 1942.

Needless to say, Captain Nelson continued to deny the charge, and in the formal 'Statement of the Accessed' states, *inter alia*, 'I did not cause the loss of the *SS President Coolidge*. I received no special instructions for entrance to Segond Channel. I directed my ship to that channel in the safest manner possible with due consideration for the information that I had regarding it. With the information I had, it would have been poor seamanship to have directed my ship through the narrow Bocacyo [sic] passage when a wider and less navigationally hazardous entrance was available. For then, it would have been folly on my part under these circumstances to have delayed my arrival at Buttons by taking the longer Bocacyo [sic] passage route and thus longer expose my ship to open water and submarine attacks.' (See Appendix 3, page 247 - Inquiry Papers, for the full Statement of the Accessed, and a summary of the daily Testimony).

Over four full days of witness testimonies, and two subsequent days of summary, the prosecutions main direction was to convince the Commission Members (the jury, so to speak), that certain documents were delivered to Captain Nelson, and that Captain Nelson took no notice of the documents. The direction of questioning continued on the line of that taken at the previous Court of Inquiry.

In essence, two vital documents should have been delivered to Captain Nelson from the Port Director's office in Noumea. One was what may be called 'General Routing Instructions', the other 'Special Instructions', the latter giving specific details as to how to approach Segond Channel. Ensign John DeNovo, assistant at the Port Director's office in Noumea, testified that he delivered both documents to Captain Henry Nelson aboard *President Coolidge* on 24 October 1942. Captain Nelson and his officers denied the existence of the 'Special Instructions'.

To emphasise again - the 'Special Instructions' was the crucial document that gave Captain Nelson specific directives as to how to safely approach and enter Espiritu Santo through the minefield, although, and it is important to note, that no mention of the presence of a minefield is made in the document.

The relevant section of Special Instructions, Exhibit 3, is as follows: 'Ships approaching Segond Channel, Espiritu Santo, are to use EAST Entrance only. White Rock has been located on South shore Espiritu Santo Island in Long. 167° 13' 27" East. Approach Eastern entrance from Bogacyo Island passages to point with White Rock bearing 345 degrees distance two miles. Steam toward White Rock until North tangent Ayre Island bears West which is danger bearing, then head into channel.'

Bogacyo Island should read Bogacio Island, and Ayre Island should read Aore Island. Whether these were typo errors in the official copied document presented to the Military Commission, or whether an actual error of geographic identification is not know. Either way, they are errors by the Port Director's Office in Noumea.

The Military Commission took considerable time to establish how the documents were delivered, how they were packaged and held together, and how Captain Nelson received and receipted the documents - as did the Court of Inquiry the previous month. It appeared important to the prosecution and to the defence as to how the documents were held together - by staple, or paper clip, thus determining some measure of 'permanency' of the attachment. Thus the Special Instructions (marked Exhibit # 3) is the vital element in the first part of the tragedy.

The first dispute of significance is whether Captain Nelson ever received the 'Special Information'. Even though he signed for the whole packet, which allegedly contained this document, it is important to determine whether he knew of, or should have been told of, the mines at the entrance to Buttons, and whether his instructions were sufficiently unambiguous. The vital document was seen only by the Navy messenger, Ensign DeNovo, who was confused about his own check-marks on the check-off list. Could he have accidentally picked up the 'Special Instructions' when he gathered together the duplicates of some documents in Captain Nelson's office?

The ultimate key to the *President Coolidge* disaster lies with the mystery of the missing 'Special Instructions'. According to the US naval authorities in Noumea at the time, the orders handed to Captain Nelson, and for which he duly signed, consisted of a set of general routing instructions to get the vessel safely to point Hypo, plus five separate enclosures, one of which supposedly gave precise directions for entering the harbour at Button. It was this particular enclosure listed as 'Special Information' that all senior officers aboard the *President Coolidge* would later adamantly testify they had never seen.

Perhaps the Port Director's office in Noumea, the responsible authority for issuing sailing orders to the master of the *President Coolidge* simply omitted the 'Special Information' document from the package carried aboard by Ensign DeNovo. This possibility was not queried in any depth.

The prosecution took pains to convince the Commission Members that even in the absence of the 'Special Instructions', Captain Nelson acted negligently by not questioning the whereabouts of the 'Special Instructions'. The prosecution argues that because of the statement in the General Instructions,

'*Thence to Button noting attached instructions for entering Segond Channel, Espiritu Santo,*' Captain Nelson should have questioned the whereabouts of these 'special instructions'. It is apparent however that other documents delivered to Captain Nelson could reasonably have been regarded as being the 'special instructions' so referred, and Captain Nelson would have thus been satisfied that he had all the required documents.

It is relevant to note that the Noumea Port Director, Lt. Commander Andrews, immediately he received a report of the sinking of the *SS President Coolidge*, modified the sailing instructions for other ships about to leave Noumea to make them less ambiguous, to announce the presence of mines at Buttons, and to change the wording to make the information more mandatory. He changed 'noting', which means merely to see or observe, to 'following' (orders) which means to obey. He agreed also that sailing orders should have included the mention that in approaching Buttons ships would use 'only' the southeast passage between Bogacio and Tutuba Islands. These matters however were not brought out during the Military Commission.

The sighting of destroyer *USS Sterett* (DD407) at 0730 hours when *President Coolidge* was about 6-8 miles southeast of Tutuba Island solicited the communication from *President Coolidge* 'Have you anything for us?' to which the destroyer replied 'Negative.' (The Navy Port Commander at Buttons, Captain Walter H. Roberts, USN, testified at the Court of Inquiry the previous month that the destroyer *DD407* was on anti-submarine duty and had nothing to do with the arrival of the *President Coolidge*.)

The other major direction of questioning was in regard to the actions of patrol craft *PC479* under the command of Lieutenant John Davis. *PC479* was patrolling south of Bogacio Island and saw the *President Coolidge* heading toward Espiritu Santo when ten miles distant. The prosecution attempted to prove that *PC479* made every effort to prevent *President Coolidge* from entering into dangerous waters, and had signalled *President Coolidge* that she was entering the 'wrong entrance'. The defence argued that Davis did not make every effort from preventing *President Coolidge* from entering the 'wrong' entrance to Segond Channel, and the appropriate signals, if indeed sent, were sent too late and were not in any case received by *President Coolidge*. The evidence given did not sit well for Davis even though the prosecution indicated that *PC479* had acted appropriately. The prosecution attempted to convince the Members that the *President Coolidge* was travelling too fast for *PC479* to provide a pilot however it is apparent in evidence that *PC479* could have intercepted the *President Coolidge* prior to entering the channel.

Appendix3, page 248 provides a summary of testimony taken from witnesses over the six days of the Military Commission, giving a more detailed insight into the directions being taken by the prosecution and the defence. Together with the 'Written Opening Argument of the Judge Advocate', and the 'Written Argument of the Accessed', the reader may like to draw a conclusion.

FINDINGS

The Military Commission acquitted Captain Nelson of all charges. The personal damage however had been done. Although Henry Nelson was acquitted of negligence and culpability, the Opinion of the Navy-controlled Court of Inquiry held on board *USS Whitney* in November 1942, which completely exonerated the Navy system and Navy performance, had been

TIMING

From the testimony at the two inquiries, and other accounts, it is possible to compile a schedule of events within an error of plus or minus a minute. It is appreciated that this, however, may be only of academic interest, as it has little bearing on the allegations against Captain Nelson and his officers.

0730   Destroyer *Sterett* sighted by *President Coolidge*, and signalled with question, 'do you have anything for us; destroyer replies negative.

0845   *PC479* sights *President Coolidge* at distance estimated of ten miles bearing 092°.

0900   *PC479* challenges then unidentified ship with IBUB. No reply received. IBUB was spelt out - Interrogatory, Baker, Unit, Baker.

0910   *PC479* signals IBUB again. (IBUB is the man-of-war challenge to an unidentified ship).

0912   *PC479* receives message 'what does IBUB mean'.

0913   *PC479* signals again using challenge code for unescorted merchant vessels, OE. (Option Easy). *President Coolidge* replies within 35 seconds with KDMX. PC479 replies 'roger'.

0914   *PC479* sees *President Coolidge* make turn 'to the left', ie due west.

0915   *PC479* signals *President Coolidge* 'what is your destination'. No answer received. Distance between *PC479* and *President Coolidge* is estimated at 4 miles.

0917   *President Coolidge* signals letter K, hoists two identification flags.

0918   *PC479* signals *President Coolidge* 'wrong entrance' once again.

0919   *PC479* looses sight of *President Coolidge* behind Tutuba Island.

0935   *President Coolidge* hits first mine, and within thirty seconds, a second mine.(There is some dispute as to whether the *President Coolidge* hit the first mine at 0930 or 0935. Even the Military Commission does not establish exactly what time it was. Judging by other events, it seems that 0935 is the more likely.)

0938   *President Coolidge* is aground on edge of reef.

0940   *PC479* sights *President Coolidge* again and notes her still in water and down at stern (This was recorded in the initial log as at 0933 but it is later noted that there is a clock error of seven minutes).

0947   *PC479* arrives at *President Coolidge*. Departs soon after.

1038   US Coast Guard official time of sinking.

1052   *President Coolidge* sinks - disappears underwater.

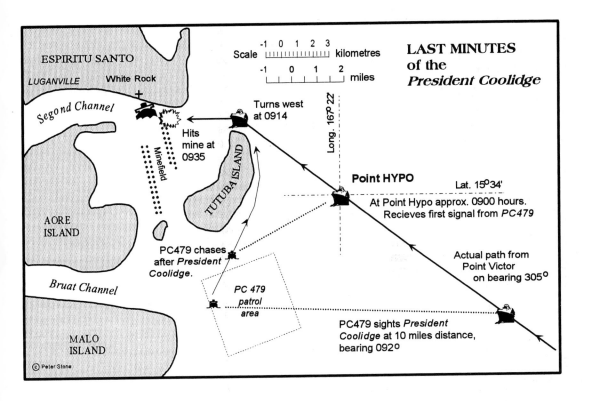

LAST MINUTES
of the
President Coolidge

Scale -1 0 1 2 3 kilometres
-1 0 1 2 miles

ESPIRITU SANTO

LUGANVILLE   White Rock

Segond Channel

Turns west
at 0914

Hits
mine at
0935

Minefield

TUTUBA ISLAND

Long. 167° 22'

Point HYPO   Lat. 15°34'

At Point Hypo approx. 0900 hours.
Recieves first signal from *PC479*

AORE
ISLAND

PC479 chases
after *President
Coolidge.*

Actual path from
Point Victor
on bearing 305°

Bruat Channel

PC 479
patrol
area

PC479 sights *President
Coolidge* at 10 miles distance,
bearing 092°

MALO
ISLAND

© Peter Stone

widely publicised. Colonel Arthur King writes, 'It was war-time and the good name and reputation of a distinguished mariner was considered just another sacrifice on behalf of maintaining the U.S. Navy morale.'

Admiral Halsey had no option but to accept the Military Commission's decision in the trial against Captain Nelson. Although the captain was acquitted and an open finding was found, Halsey was clearly ready to defend any possibility that the Navy could have been in any way responsible. After the Inquiry, Halsey made available his own document, titled 'Finding of Facts', listing thirty-four points that he believed relevant. Some of these were clearly incorrect considering the evidence given at the Court of Inquiry and the Military Commission. Other points he raised indicated some possible lack of responsibility on the part of the Captain, carefully avoiding any further accusations against Captain Nelson, and the possibility that the Navy could have been in any way responsible. (See Appendix 3, page 244 - Inquiry Papers, for a full record of Halsey's 'Finding of Facts'.)

The US Navy was in no rush to publicise the acquittal of Captain Nelson, which of course implied probable negligence on the part of the US Navy for the loss of President Coolidge. Records of the Military Commission were finally sent through channels to the U.S. Secretary of the Navy who approved them on 26 April 1943, a full four months after the hearings.

It could also be suggested that the US Navy preferred to publicise the findings of the Court of Inquiry held in November on board *USS Whitney*, which were favourable to the Navy, rather than the Military Commission findings at which Captain Nelson was acquitted. For example, the Navy Department, Office of the Chief of Naval Operations, Washington issued a 'Memorandum For File' on 19 January 1943, with reference to the loss of the *President Coolidge*, which was an exact duplicate of the 'Record of Procedure of a Court of Inquiry Convened on Board *USS Whitney*, 12 November 1942'. No mention is made of the findings of the Military Commission held in December. One could be forgiven for thinking that the Navy was prepared to completely disregard the Military Commission, and simply disseminate information on the loss of the *President Coolidge* as determined by the earlier Court of Inquiry. The Navy's Memorandum is a most mischievous document, and, if purporting to be an up-to-date record of facts as of the release date of 19 January 1943, is incorrect in several aspects and likely to mislead the reader into thinking that the US Navy was not, in total or in any proportional way, responsible for the loss of the *President Coolidge*. The Navy Department was still trying to protect its hide despite two formal hearings, the last of which completely exonerated Captain Nelson. [N3]

CONCLUSIONS

To summarise the facts as indicated in the two official hearings:

(a) It was never proven, beyond a reasonable doubt, that Captain Henry Nelson did in fact receive all of the pertinent enclosures contained in his routing instructions, particularly the 'Special Instructions' for entering Segond Channel.

(b) Even if the 'Special Instructions' for entering Segond Channel had been sighted by Captain Nelson, there was no indication that a minefield had been laid, nor that the *President Coolidge* should await instructions at point Hypo, or seek a pilot to enter the channel.

(c) A Navy patrol vessel, off the entrance to Espiritu Santo, contacted the *President Coolidge* but did not warn her of danger until two minutes before the *President Coolidge* was out of sight, this in spite of the fact that the *President Coolidge* had been in sight for some 35 minutes.

(d) The Navy shore signal station on Espiritu Santo attempted to warn the *President Coolidge*, 'Stop you are standing into mines', but before the complete message was received, *President Coolidge* struck mines. Here again, the action taken came too late.

(e) That destroyer *USS Sterett* had communicated with the *President Coolidge* but did not indicate any warning, nor should it have been required to do so, according to the Port Director. It may be reasonably assumed that the destroyer was aware of the minefield.

(f) That no Naval vessel was patrolling near the eastern end of Segond Channel in order to prevent the very disaster that did occur, particularly in consideration that Base Buttons knew of the impending arrival of the *President Coolidge*.

(g) That Point Hypo was north of the safe entrance between Bogacio and Tutuba Islands, and it would have been illogical for the *President Coolidge*, travelling in a northerly direction, to have to turn back south. As enemy submarines had been known in the vicinity, the objective should be to get the ship in safe waters as soon as possible. If there was the intention that the *President Coolidge* enter the safe passage between Bogacio and Tutuba Islands, then Point Hypo should have been designated at least ten miles south of where it was.

The loss of the *President Coolidge* threw light on the pressures faced by merchant navy officers as they struggled to adapt their normal seagoing lifestyles to the new demands of war. The intervening decades have done little to settle the issues and there remains a strong argument supporting the theory that Captain Nelson, held solely responsible for the disaster in the eyes of the US Navy, was in fact the merchant navy scapegoat demanded by the US Navy command who had no intention of letting the *President Coolidge* incident tarnish their performance.

If a fair judgement is to be made on the decisions taken by Captain Nelson, one important psychological factor must be appreciated. Throughout the long days and nights of circuitous steaming from the time the *President Coolidge* left San Francisco outward bound, the over-riding fear in the minds of the merchant marine officers aboard had always been the possibility of an enemy submarine attack. The thought of running into a 'friendly' minefield was given little or no consideration if only for the fact it was naturally assumed that any such dangers would be made abundantly clear in the official routing instructions handed down by the US naval authorities.

Reality, however, was a very different story. Extraordinary though it now seems, US naval logic at this comparatively early stage of the Pacific War reasoned that as the locations of 'friendly' minefields constituted such sensitive information, merchant navy officers operating US military transport vessels should be denied access to it. And so it was that the secret sailing orders for the *President Coolidge* made no mention whatever of the danger from mines, even though two separate patterns of the weapons had been laid in the immediate vicinity of the eastern entrance to the Segond Channel. There is also the question of why Point Hypo was designated at such an inappropriate position?

Back in San Francisco, Captain Nelson had to face further enquiry from the United States Coast Guard, attending an 'A' Marine Investigation Board on 6 February 1943 before Coast Guard Marine Inspection Officer Lt. Cmdr. Henry V. Barbieri. This was merely a formality. The US Coast Guard was satisfied with the details of the inquiry held in Noumea, and took no further action, as the U.S. Coastguard was then part of the U.S.Navy. It confirmed formally that the *President Coolidge* was lost and that the insurance coverage was $7,500,000. All but for the want of a staple. See also Appendix 3, page 262 - Inquiry Papers, Coast Guard Findings.

The U.S. Coast Guard, in a report on the incident issued in 1963, commented: 'From the paucity of information available, we can only assume that the *SS President Coolidge* was instructed to proceed to Espiritu Santo from Noumea, and, when arriving at point Hypo or other designated point off Espiritu Santo, await pilot or instructions how and when to enter port. Apparently, no pilot or instructions were immediately available, or seen, when the *SS President Coolidge* arrived near vicinity of harbor entrance at about 0900 or 0930 October 26. There is almost no information available concerning what specific action was taken by the Master in attempting to obtain instructions prior entering port or what specific warnings or instructions were attempted by about 0900-0930, October 26, 1942, to time vessel struck mines, at or about 0935, October 26. The Master claims he did not see or hear any warnings until too late to stop vessel from passing over mine field.

'The specific location of our own mine fields were highly classified and never positively identified to individual commanding officers. This lack of information was never any serious handicap to vessel skippers, so long as they knew the danger areas existed beyond specific coordinates described in routing instructions. The specific routing instructions provided to Captain Nelson at Noumea were never made public. Captain Nelson claims and implies, in effect, that his routing instructions failed to warn him of mine fields or other dangers at or near the entrance of Espiritu Santo. It was also not clearly described as to which entrance to be used. Although we may never know all the true facts contributing to the loss of the President Coolidge, it is clearly established and documented, over Admiral Halsey's signature, that Captain Nelson was acquitted of all blame for the sinking of the *SS President Coolidge*.'

The war effort was impeded and the monetary loss was in the millions but the most poignant tragedy was the career of the ship's master. Captain Henry Nelson was tried by the Military Commission which returned a finding of 'Not Guilty' on 14 December 1942. Understandably, Captain Nelson, and other senior officers of his ship were very bitter about the treatment they and all the Merchant Marine people had received from the U.S.Navy.

On the stand, Captain Henry Nelson quoted his age as 'past 63', and had been at sea since he was a boy 'in the neighbourhood of forty-seven or forty-eight years'. He had been a seafaring man since he joined the Coast Guard as a youth and had first served with the Pacific Mail. He received his masters license in 1905, and since 1921 had been master of *President Wilson, President Pierce, President Cleveland*, and *President Coolidge*, the latter for two and half years.

He was given another command by the American President Lines and later made Commodore of the American President Line. He soon reached retirement age, and in 1948, after fifty-three years at sea, retired to live the rest of days peacefully in San Francisco. He had only recently married one of the stewardesses with the line, and they lived a quiet life until he died in July, 1952.

CHAPTER TEN

MONUMENT TO THE FUTILITY OF WAR

As the Americans gained the upper hold in the Solomon Islands and bombed Rabaul into isolation, forward bases such as those in the New Hebrides and New Caledonia were gradually downgraded. Bomber and fighter airfields ceased their constant activity and gradually fell silent. Only transport and supply aircraft used the strips on Espiritu Santo as the war came to a close. Out of the seven major airfields in the New Hebrides only two remained fully operational at the end of the war in August 1945, while two others were reserved as alternate airfields. Three fields, Fighter One, Bomber One and Havannah (on Efate), were allowed to return to nature, the jungle quickly and quietly devouring all but a narrow strip. The only evidence now remaining of the once flourishing seaplane bases are cement slabs.

Soon after the end of the war, Bomber One (Palekulo) was used by a now defunct airline named TRAPAS, flying between Noumea, Vila, Santo and return. Eventually however the jungle won the battle, and Bomber Three was used until the 1970s for commercial flights. But as Bomber Three was on higher ground, it was often clouded in when it rained, and delays were frequent. This resulted in the resurrection of Bomber Two which had been allowed to return to its 'native' state. The strip was cleared and Pekoa became the commercial airport, as it remains today.

QANTAS soon arrived, using Catalinas and afterwards Sunderland flying boats, as did TOA (Trans Ocean Airlines). Both companies flew from Sydney, Noumea, Vila, Santo, returning to Sydney the next day. They used some of the war-time moorings opposite the old Burns Philp store site at Luganville, which is close to where British Petroleum now have their tanks. It is interesting to note that the watering system located at Bomber One, used by the Americans, is now being used by the Japanese fishery at Palekulo. The main war-time watering system for the township and the wharves has become the present Santo town water supply.

Hundreds of Quonset huts remained on Espiritu Island when the U.S. Army and Navy departed in 1945 - many were full of equipment. With initial caution, lest the Americans return, the equipment was eventually command-eered by local expat-riates. The photo shows the Navy's main dock area, Pier 3, with ships at anchor in Segond Channel.

Before the former PT base at Luganville had been cleared of all equipment, it was the site of the first Santo Club, set up in one of the war-time Quonset huts. New Zealander Reece Discombe who made his home in Port Vila two years after the end of the war, recalls, 'A very nice meal was to be had at the restaurant. Further up the road, where New Hebrides Motors now stands, the late Tom Harris had a cinema. This was set up in the old huts at the torpedo repair base which later became the home for Asco Motors, and he used and American projection equipment. Base CB101 was above the main wharf on Andre Naturel's property - most of the huts are still in their original position. The church was first used as a cinema prior to Tom Harris opening his theatre. I later converted this building into a house in which I lived with my wife.'

Most American serviceman had probably seen enough of Espiritu Santo to last a lifetime and were glad to get out of the heat, humidity and mosquitos,. But not Ray Jenkins. As soon as he was demobilised, Jenkins returned to Espiritu Santo and set up a business repairing radios and electrical equipment. Reece Discombe comments, 'Ray couldn't believe it was the same place because when he was stationed at Espiritu Santo there were fifty thousand bods tearing up and down and now there was nobody. Ray told me he was there when the Coolidge went down and he said when you have 4,000 or 5,000 guys suddenly arriving there wasn't much in the way of stores. They had to clothe and feed these fellows. They drained the stores and the guys had to wait for more ships to come in to take them on to Guadalcanal.' [N1]

During World War II, James A Michener, then a lieutenant in the American Army, was stationed in Santo. Michener, in his excellent *Return to Paradise*, mentions that life in Santo after the war was 'delightful, free, riotous, happy'. He notes that 'the black men' have changed considerably, and now wear tailor-made shorts and T-shirts. 'They work a few days and then knock off for a good time.' He mentions the Club Civile, once the officer's mess at the American base, now refurnished and enlarged. 'The food is terrific!', and it is a place where 'people of all colours belong'.

Michener mentions both Tom Harris and Ray Jenkins. Harris is described as having 'a face like Punch, and a belly laugh like Falstaff'. Despite being raided many times for selling grog to enlisted men, he was, apparently, applauded many times for his assistance to the Americans. Ray Jenkins is mentioned as being a thirty-year old from Hollywood, a quiet and balding fellow. Michener suggests that Luganville was at its boisterous best when the movies were on, held in a '... huge Quonset by the sea. On Saturday nights after the movies the seats are pushed back, jazz records are played, and everyone has a whale of a dance till three or four in the morning.'

Michener writes that of all the islands in the Pacific, Espiritu Santo made the most impression on him. It is here that he observed island life and was inspired to write *Tales of the South Pacific*, from which the musical South Pacific was derived. It is said that Michener would gaze across the sea to the volcanic island of Ambae far on the horizon, often with its summit shrouded in cloud, and dream of his famous and fabled Bali Hai. And, his famous character Bloody Mary was not totally a character of fiction. [N2]

On the present town side east of the Sarakata River, no houses nor shops existed before nor after the war; the only buildings in this area were hundreds of Quonset huts, most still containing wartime equipment. Squatters later moved in and it was not until the 1950s that the present town of Luganville was established. The social centre of 'Santo' was the Corsica Hotel, run by the Rossi family. This hotel consisted of Quonset huts left behind by the Americans, and was later destroyed by fire. A modern hotel, the Hotel Santo, now stands on this site. [N3]

The last of the US troops left Santo in August 1945, but various transport units remained, shipping out their material to northern bases at Guam and Leyte. After 12 June 1946 there were only two Americans left behind to sell what they could: They remained till the following year.

Reece Discombe, resident at Port Vila, was one of the earliest post-war salvors who came to Espiritu Santo in 1947. He remembers, 'Soon after the war an American "major" arrived at Santo saying that he was employed by a large American construction firm. His role was to collect all the old aeroplanes, which he did with the help of many of the local people. A furnace was set up at Bomber One to melt down the metal, which was reduced to ingots. After the export of hundreds of tons of ingots the Condominium Government discovered that no export duties had been paid. In spite of exhaustive enquiries, the '"major's" whereabouts have never been discovered!'

Buyers arrived from Noumea, Tahiti, New Zealand and Australia to purchase war equipment such as jeeps, trucks, lighting plants, bulldozers, Quonset huts and anything else useful and available. A lot of the material was bought locally and shipped throughout the New Hebrides. Some of the small Piper aircraft-were sold to the Noumea Aero Club, with large amounts of spares.

Reece continues, 'When I came in 1947 there were a couple of Yanks cleaning up, and a few auctions sales. They soon left but we were too scared to do anything about what was left as we thought the Americans would be coming back. But they didn't, so finally buildings and equipment started to disappear. The local planters would come in. Some took the frames, but mainly they went for the galvanised iron and took them back to their island plantations. Iron was at a premium.'

Million Dollar Point lies in a direct line from the extension of the Pekoa airstrip runway, seen in the photograph. This photograph was taken prior to the equipment being dumped into the sea. The wreck site of the *President Coolidge* lies some 400 metres to the west (left) of Million Dollar point. The base at Luganville is to the far left of the photograph, with ships anchored in the Segond Channel.

'One of my first tasks when I arrived in the New Hebrides was to purchase war materials from the land owners, drag it out of the jungle and have it shipped to Sydney, usually aboard the BP ship *Marinda*, for restoration to working order. When most of the material had been shipped from the land, we took it out from the sea at Million Dollar Point.'

Frenchman Andre Naturel bought a complete army base just above the wharf, # 1007, complete with vehicles, fire engines, generating plants, huge amounts of general equipment, machinery and spares - and 'enough flour to make bread for two years'. As he had gained experienced in hard hat and aqualung diving in New Caledonia, Reece Discombe was initially employed by Naturel to oversee a number of land and sea salvage projects. [N4]

In 1948 Reece Discombe shipped out over 500 tons of steel plate and fittings from Aesi Island This was the remains of one of the largest naval repair bases in the Pacific during the war. A huge floating dock was anchored adjacent to the remains of the existing wharf. Marston matting removed from Pekoa airfield (Bomber Two) by Reece was shipped to Sydney on the ship *El Retiro* in the late 1940s.

MILLION DOLLAR POINT

Santo was the largest U.S.base outside of Honolulu in the Pacific during World War II. As the war was nearing a victory for the Allied troops, the US forces based in Santo had no need for the tremendous amount of equipment used over the preceding three years to build five airstrips, miles of roads, and a small township. As soon as the surrender was declared, army and navy moved to rid themselves of the burden of equipment so that they could all go home. The easiest solution was to simply dump it all in the sea. And so, Million Dollar Point was created, a landmark of waste and a monument to the futility of war.

Million Dollar Point juts into the Segond Channel and marks the northern entrance to the channel from Scorff Passage. When Espiritu Santo was under

Rusted equipment is spread along the coast for a hundred yards, and into the sea down to 140 ft. The scene is looking west along the Segond Channel, toward the wreck site of the *President Coolidge.* *(Photo taken 1988)*

U.S. Army occupation, the land here was scared with huge pits where coral had been removed by the army to surface new roads. There were no trees lining the shore, so this was a logical place to simply dump anything and everything that was no longer required by the army. [N5]

As the bulldozers, cranes, large trucks, forklifts, engines, bucket dredges, tyres, and all kinds of auxiliary earth-moving equipment was dumped into the sea, thousands of tons of coral fill was pushed in on top of the sub-merged equipment, thus forming a ramp from which further equipment could be dumped. Almost every conceivable object was dumped at the point. Material that was not dumped was buried in trenches or burnt. Installations and material left behind eventually became the property of the owners of the land, but that was not known at the time the U.S. forces moved out. As Reece has mentioned, the locals thought the Americans would return, even though they could have surmised the attitude of the Americans from the destruction of equipment at Million Dollar Point. Tons of equipment still remained in the jungle, which slowly smothered the rusting remains of trucks and bulldozers.

It took four months, till the end of 1945, to rid Espiritu Santo of most, but not all, of its valuable military equipment and spares. The sooner the job was done, the sooner the men returned to their homes. On shore, thousand of tyres, small aircraft and all manner of disposable equipment were burnt. Crockery, glassware and the ubiquitous green Coke bottle littered the foreshore and covered the rejected equipment.

Dumping of valuable equipment, spares and ordnance was a common occurrence throughout the Pacific at the end of the war. It is only reasonable that local New Hebridean natives would ask the question - why? Was this another one of the idiotic white-man's ways, a measure of his wealth, an expression of his inconsideration to those natives, and British and French expatriates who could make good use of the equipment to develop their post-war land? Perhaps it was.

REECE DISCOMBE, OBE.

Reece was one of the first divers to dive the *President Coolidge* after the war. His reward was the foremast bell off the ship which was found on an early dive.

Reece Discombe did his stint in the New Zealand Army and after the war, started his own marine engineering business in Auckland, repairing war damaged ships sufficiently to allow them to get to the major repair docks in Singapore and Hawaii. 'After the war, war surplus was the order of the day. By that I mean there were lots of bargins to be bought cheaply. A bunch of blokes who were up here during the war reckoned if they only had a ship to come to the islands to collect all the equipment that was left on the beaches etc, they would make a fortune. So they bought a ship at disposals, and then asked my firm to make it sea worthy to get sea going certificates. This we did. As the group never had an engineer, I decided that I would go with them. So off we went. First stop Norfolk Island, then New Caledonia, Loyalty Islands, Warpole Island, Vila, Santo etc, picking up cargoes all along the way. In Santo a Frenchman named Andre Naturel wanted to buy the ship on the condition that the engineer stayed behind and changed the engines, so I did. After I had changed the motors, Andre Naturel offered me a job at £100 a month and keep. The basic wage in New Zealand after the war was £20 a month and taxed. What could I do? I went back to New Zealand, sold the business and have been here ever since.'

Reece astutely realized that the world ran on wheels and rubber; that the marketplace had been rationed and starved for six years, and that no new manufacturers could find their way into New Zealand or Australia for quite some time.

Reece and wife Jean came to the New Hebrides in 1947. Because of his engineering and maritime background, Reece was soon appointed a Lloyds Surveyor by Burns Philp and did most of the surveys and salvage for Lloyds and Queensland Insurance.

Underwater salvage at the time was achieved with the use of standard dress, ie hard-hat diving, with which Reece was familiar. In 1947 however he was one of the first persons outside Europe to use the recently developed demand regulator developed by Gagnan and Couseau, which we now know as SCUBA, and used it at Million Dollar Point to recover bulldozers and other war surplus equipment.

He befriended the French Resident Commissioner Pierre Anthonioz and suggested that an expedition be mounted to 'have a go at finding the wreck sites of your comrade in Vanikoro'. Reece was of course referring to La Perouse and the loss of his two ships *Astrolabe* and *La Bouselle*.

A 'skilled and utterly fearless' diver with a penchant for adventure, Reece re-discovered the ships of the missing French explorer. He found the *Astrolabe* off the island of Vanikoro in the Solomon Island's Santa Cruz group in 1958. The wreck had not been pinpionted since the Irish sea captain Peter Dillon located it in the mid-1820s. In 1962 Reece discovered La Perouse's second vessel *La Bouselle*, which had never been sighted since it went down in 1788. *La Bouselle* had come to grief in a deep, wedge-shaped chasm, about one kilometre from where the *Astorolabe* was wrecked.

For these achievements he was made an Officer of France's National Order of Merit, the civilian equivalent of that country's Legion Of Honour. The honour was personally conferred on Reece Discombe by President Charles de Gaulle during a visit he made to the New Hebrides in 1967.

Reece recalls that as the great man hung the order round his neck he said, 'What a pity you are not a Frenchman...'

In 1972 he was awarded the British Red Cross Silver Medal for his services to the Red Cross. In 1978 he was 'gonged' once again, this time with the Queen's Jubilee Medal, marking the 25th year of her reign. On the eve of Independence he received the Resident Commissioner's medal for services to the country, and an OBE was confered in the 1980 Queens Birthday Honours.

Reece is a remarkable man with many honourable achievements to his name. He continues to live in Port Vila and has a remarkable knowledge of the history of the New Hebrides. Jean sadly passed away in 1998.

But like most actions, there is a reason, even if an unacceptable one. Indeed, two reasons. First, the equipment had been used and paid for and was no longer required for military purposes. It would have cost more money in fuel and manpower to ship the equipment back to the United States, an exercise that nobody would have volunteered for as all were anxious to return home, including the commanders. Second, had the equipment returned to the United States, and sold on the open market, it would have created a glut that would have set back many of the manufacturing companies for years, some possibly not being able to overcome the immediate post-war period. It was important for Caterpillar, Westinghouse, General Motors, Hyster and all the other manufacturers to get back on their feet and establish new markets. Indeed, many military contracts stipulated that the equipment would not be sold on the open market at the end of the war, for the very reason mentioned. This of course begs the question: why wasn't the equipment donated or even sold to countries like New Hebrides, Solomons and New Guinea where the people suffered death and destruction in a war that was not of their concern? [N6]

Why didn't the US Forces simply leave the equipment for the people of New Hebrides? After all, America had brought the war to the islands, and used native land. This is a reasonable enough question and is often asked. There is no official statement providing an answer. As mentioned, the equipment could not be returned to the U.S.A. and sold. Most likely the manufacturer had also stipulated that the equipment must not be donated or sold to a third party, as such sensible generosity would have also delimited potential commercial markets for this same equipment in the Pacific.

A bulldozer lies upside down amongst other equipment rubble about 30 ft down in the entrance to Segond Channel, at Million Dollar Point.

Perhaps the U.S. forces thought that if they simply left the material, the local inhabitants would help themselves. This eventually occurred but only after it was quite apparent that the Americans would not return. Native people are honest and the concept of theft is new to them and brought about only recently as the war introduced them to material possessions. Sharing an item is common, but the New Hebrideans would not have contemplated simply taking what was not their own. Certainly, there was no formal offer to the Condominium government to assume possession of the material until many years after the end of the war. The only reasonable explanation is that dumping the equipment was the most expedient solution, and allowed the homesick troops to head home as soon as possible. This was confirmed by a soldier who returned to Espiritu Santo many years after the war. Asked the same question, he laughed and said that it was common practice because if there was no equipment to account for the officer in charge would be able to get home quicker. If he had to itemise it all he could have been there for ever. This would account for why some of the equipment that was clearly useful, such as the crates of aircraft engines and spares, was unceremoniously dumped.

Some equipment was indeed salvaged in good condition as not all was consigned to a watery grave. And even then, a few feet of seawater was not going to stop the determined entrepreneur. Once the Americans moved on from Espiritu Santo, Million Dollar Point became a favourite fishing spot, and it wasn't mackerel they were after. Reece Discombe recalls, 'Some of the people who were fortunate enough to own the then new fangled apparatus called 'aqualungs' used them to full advantage for salvaging non-ferrous metals and any other useful objects. Several tons of items such as brass propellers and copper pipe and wire were removed from Million Dollar Point. Hundreds of tyres still attached to submerged vehicles were removed and sold for five pounds each.'

The bow of the *El Retiro* looms out of the gloom at Million Dollar Point. She ended up on the bottom whilst trying to salvage war surplus material dumped in the Segond Channel.

Reece raised some two hundred tyres from trucks, and no less than fourteen bulldozers. Seawater won't stop a Caterpillar, and Reece got them all working and shipped them off to Australia. Many others also removed equipment from Million Dollar Point, some with more imagination than good sense. The truck tyres were in good condition, as would be expected of submersed rubber, but why not take the whole axle? Some did. And within a few kilometres of fitting the equipment to their trucks, they were walking again.

Reece Discombe recalls, 'The only thing that was there when I arrived was all the junk sticking out of the water. Thats how it was when the Yanks left it. They burnt tyres for a week and you could see black smoke for miles around - they left miles and miles of wire beading off the tyres where they had burnt them.'

James Michener, in *Return to Paradise*, mentions the waste at Million Dollar Point. 'The engines coughed, and the giant procession crawled along the ramp' and the 'lumbering dinosaurs of modern industry plunged into the sea.' Michener suggests that the French were made offers to purchase the equipment at ridiculously low prices, by they kept stalling final negotiations in the belief that the Americans would simply give up and move on, leaving all the equipment up for grabs. If this is so, the frustration of the Americans is not recorded, but their patience finally ran out, and the equipment was dumped.

Reece again: 'The Yanks would fill trucks with all sorts of material and drive them into the sea. As they descended into the water the driver would jump out and let 'em go. Bulldozers were the same. You name it, its down there. In 1948/49 I took out the bulldozers. They were about the last to go in. We used one to drag out the others. All I had to do was wash them in fresh water and change the oil, batteries and electrical gear. Some never had starters in those days - they had a small engine on the size of the Caterpillars - and they used to crank that up. I changed the magnetometers and got the things going. They were all shipped down to Australia to the Joint Coal Board. In those days all the coal was dug with tunnels underground but in the age of the bulldozer they changed to open cast mining, which was easier. So that is why they wanted the bulldozers. In Santo I got all the lighting plants and shipped them out. Trucks and cranes - shipped them out. You name it. I used to get equipment out of the jungle. Unfortunately I was wet behind the ears and I was doing it for somebody else - some of these war fellows that knew their way around. I was employed at one time by an Australian syndicate, headed by the local manager, Alex Jamieson. My job was to get it out of the jungle and put it alongside ship's slings. As soon as the material was alongside the slings you could get a Bill of Lading for it - and once you have the bill you can get insurance. With the Bill of Lading, Jamieson used to fly down to Sydney and present the bill. Everything was sold and the money was in his pocket before the ship arrived. That is how the war asset guys made their money.'

As mentioned, there was always the fear that the Americans would return and recover what was rightfully theirs, even though it was quite obvious that the equipment had been dumped, particularly that at Million Dollar Point. Reece Discombe comments, 'There were huge reels of copper electrical cable, one inch and two inch thick, some reels six feet in diameter, but everyone was too scared to touch it. After a year or so a fellow by the name of Pascal Michel came along and one day rolled all the wire onto his trucks. He was game enough to do it but it all belonged to the US Government. But he shipped it out. He later told me he got ten thousand pounds for all that copper wire in those days. Then a fellow by the name of Donald Gubbay came along with a ship called the *El Retiro* - about 600 tons. I used to run that ship to Sydney with all the (Marston) matting taken off Pekoa airfield - that's the airfield used now. I was paid a thousand pounds to take all that matting off and stack it for the land owner, Leon Wright.

'Gubbay used his boat to work over the wreckage at Million Dollar Point, but the silly bugger didn't put moorings out to hold the boat off shore. Of course, when a decent south-easterly got up it blew his ship up closer to shore and when the tide went out all this material went through the bottom of his boat. Somebody said it was a bulldozer blade but I never saw a bulldozer in there at that time. But there was certainly enough material there to punch a hole in the bottom. Gubbay took out a lot of scrap metal and sent it off to Japan after the war and he worked Million Dollar Point quite a bit.

'For myself, I took dozen of tyres off vehicles - a lot of the tyres off the trucks were spare wheels and had never been on. I think I took about two hundred tyres out of that lot - and I was getting five pounds a pop. There were two ways of working this - if you took the wheels off and filled them up with air they were all okay and a fellow could get his five pounds worth - but it wouldn't last - once you got a flat tyre that was it because the rim had already rusted up. Or the other way, you could take them out, completely strip the tyre off the rim, clean all the rim off and get rid of all the salt water, paint it, put the tyre back on then you have got a reasonable wheel. I was very much involved in that.'

'Over the edge it is about 140 ft deep and if you take the amount of vehicles piled on top of one another until they stick out the water plus the distance of fifty-sixty metres on a point - thats a hell of a lot of vehicles. And then we took out a lot of propellers, tobin-bronze, propeller shafts, copper, copper wire, and anything else of use.' [N7]

Melbourne diver Phil
Cherici takes the wheel
of a vehicle 40 ft down
on Million Dollar point.
Marine growth covers
war detritus in a
colourful coating, adding
to the interest in diving
the site.

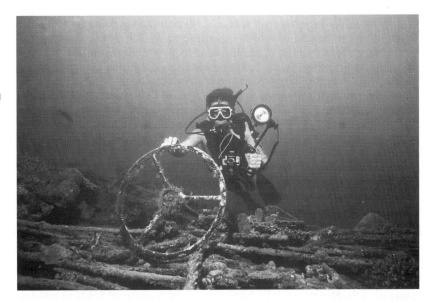

DIVING MILLION DOLLAR POINT

Million Dollar Point lies six kilometres east of town, a few hundred metres
past the coral path leading to the President Coolidge. The beach is strewn with
rusted machinery, spare parts, vehicle axles and tyres, broken crockery, glass
and old green Coca-Cola bottles. But it is beneath the surface that the sheer
waste of war material can be appreciated. The seabed drops down to 140ft in
a gradual slope. The amount of machinery is difficult to visualise, even when
diving on the site. There are bulldozers, cranes, large trucks, forklifts, engines,
bucket dredges, tyres, iron girders, and all kinds of auxiliary earth-moving
equipment on the site making it a truly unique dive. A huge gun barrel with an
internal diameter of some six inches can be seen pointing to the surface from
the rubble. The photographic capabilities are enormous although there is only
limited growth on the wreckage and the visibility is usually from 10 to 25
metres.

Scattered amongst the larger items are thousands of cases of equipment and
spares, their wooden crates now deteriorated and their contents concreted into
a hard rusted conglomerate, aided by tons of cement that was also dumped over
the site. The tons of crockery and coke bottles dumped on the site slipped
slowly through the mass of equipment to the bottom.

A walk along the foreshore will provide shards of crockery and the
occasional intact Coca-Cola bottle with the base stamped Oakland or San
Francisco. Oakland seemed to be the most popular Coca-Cola bottle found near
the surface at Million Dollar point. A date can be seen on most bottles, about
mid-way up the bottom curve of the bottle. All the bottles I have observed
show the date 1943, but there would have been earlier and later bottles no
doubt. It must be realised that Million Dollar Point is now a National Park, and
nothing must be removed from the site.

Adding to the excitement of a dive at Million Dollar Point are two small ships lying on the pile of rubble - the ill-fated *El Retiro*, and the scrapped island trader *Dedelle*. It is perhaps amusing to dive on the *El Retiro* and think of the frustration of the owner poaching materials at Million Dollar Point and then to find his boat on the seabed keeping company with the very equipment he was attempting to steal - sorry, salvage. One of the attractions of the 160-ft *El Retiro,* and *Dedelle*, is that they are so shallow, and virtually upright, that a snorkeller can have the pleasure of seeing a real-live-genuine shipwreck *in situ*. To a non (scuba) diver, this can be a real thrill, and adds to the attraction of Espiritu Santo as a general tourist destination. [N8]

To snorkel or dive Million Dollar Point, first determine the tide flow and enter up-tide so that you can drift back to the point, particularly if snorkelling. A full tank is not required, and many divers visit the site in between diving the *President Coolidge*, ensuring that they keep within only a few metres of the surface. There is always the temptation to go deeper, to the seabed beyong a hundred feet. Needless to say, any dive beyond thirty feet will affect the acceptable bottom time for a subsequent dive. My enthusiasm is such that I would sacrifice a dive on the *President Coolidge* each trip to Luganville, just to have a good long exploration at Million Dollar Point. Indeed, it would be a good first dive for anyone who has not dived for a while, or needs to build up some confidence at depth - but this is rarely done as the attraction is always the magnificent *President Coolidge*.

Even a snorkel at Million Dollar Point between dives on the *President Coolidge* is better than nothing. There is always something interesting to see, the challenge to identify the type of equipment and the manufacturer. Although the mass of machinery is conglomerated into one massive structure and appears immanently stable, it would be wise not to penetrate into or underneath any structure just in case corrosion has taken its toll. [N9]

"No Magic Carpet Ever Moved So Swiftly and So Easily". *S.S. President Coolidge* soon after launching. From the Dollar Steamship Lines' promotional brochure *Anchors Aweight*.

Deck sports and relaxation on the Sun Deck of the *President Coolidge* - restricted to First Class passengers of course.

"Thus More Than One Has Swum Across the Long Pacific". The First Class swimming pool on the *S.S. President Coolidge* is now at 190 ft under the surface and is visted by experienced divers. The caption is from the Dollar Steamship Lines' promotional brochure *Anchors Aweight*.

"Captain's Dinner", in the First Class Dining Room of the *S.S. President Coolidge*.
From the Dollar Steamship Lines' *Anchor's Aweigh* brochure.

"Club Without Dues - Smoking and Games Room", on the S.S. President Coolidge.
Note 'The Lady' in the background.

"Corner of a Roving Continental Lounge", on the S.S. President Coolidge.
The caption is from the Dollar Steamship Lines' promotional brochure Anchors Aweigh.

Although badly damaged, the destroyer *USS Tucker* is an excellent dive with a few sections that may be penetrated safely.

Melbourne diver Phil Cherici examines Coco-Cola bottles stamped 'San Francisco' and 'Oakland', and dated 1942, at Million Dollar Point, Espiritu Santo, at the eastern entrance to the Segond Channel.

"A Monument to the Futility of War". A forklift truck lies on top of the rubble at Million Dollar Point. In the vicinity lie trucks, cranes, bulldozers and a mass of other disgarded war material.

Allan Power enters a doorway from the Promenade Deck of the *President Coolidge*. The deck, actually the wall of the Continental Lounge and Smoking Room, is litered with rifles, bayonets and helmets abandoned by the troops as they left the sinking ship.

The barber's chair hangs precariously from the 'wall' of the crew's barber shop on B Deck. It was noticed several years ago when section of the metal panelling corroded.

The forward locker right in the bow of the *President Coolidge* contains paint, portholes, chain, rope and wire.

The 3-inch gun on the bow of the *President Coolidge* is covered in colourful marine growth. Cantilevered from the 'side' of the ship, it has remained in position for over fifty years, a testimony to the strength of its mountings..

'The Lady' is the most photographed item on the *President Coolidge*. Located in the First Class Smoking Room of the President Coolidge, the wall relief of a unicorn and a lady with Elizabethan collar still retains its colour. The diver is Selena Layden.

These beautiful ceilings lights are in the First Class Smoking Room of the *President Coolidge*.
The diver is Allan Power.

Crockery litters several dining areas within the ship. Allan Power shows these items in an area in front of the First Class Dining Saloon on C-deck.

CHAPTER ELEVEN

BLASTING
FOR BRASS

During 1943, as the fighting moved further north to the island of Bougainville, salvage operations on the *President Coolidge* commenced, to raise vehicles and weapons that had been carried on the deck, as well as cargo in the holds, by cutting through the starboard plates. An attempt to salvage the howitzers down in a hold of the ship had since been abandoned although some guns were recovered. Special efforts were made to recover huge amounts of currency known to have been put aboard, and also there is record of the mail being recovered, and dried in the sun over acres of land.

Chief of the Medical Unit and Surgeon of the Espiritu Santo Service Command, Colonel Arthur G. King, MD was concerned at the loss of medical supplies. Colonel King recalls: 'On October 23,1942 an urgent telephone call from Major James R. Lowell, our medical Supply Officer [in Noumea], begged me to do something administratively to modify an order he had just received. It was to place all his available quinine sulfate, amounting to 519 lbs., some 250,000 doses, aboard the *President Coolidge* which was to sail from Noumea the next day. As far as he knew it was all the quinine left in the depot for the Army troops in the South Pacific Area. He felt that putting it all on one ship going north was risky, and recommended that only half the quinine be sent on the Coolidge and the rest on a later ship. At that time quinine was the only medication which could cure malaria. Atabrine, a synthetic drug was readily available in huge quantities but it was useful only as a prophylactic for the disease. There was no malaria on New Caledonia and we had enough quinine in the individual hospitals to treat the malaria cases being sent to us. On the other hand the yearly incidence of malaria was 400/1000 on Vanuatu, and an official report stated that on Guadalcanal there were eight cases of malaria for every gunshot casualty. My appeal to the G-4, Colonel John W. Homewood, was turned down with the assurance that nothing could happen in the short run to our advance depot, code-named 'Buttons' at Luganville on Espiritu Santo in Vanuatu.'

All available quinine was placed aboard the *President Coolidge* in Noumea, and all went to the bottom of the Segond Channel. On 14 January 1943, Colonel King received orders to proceed the next day to the wreck site of the *President Coolidge* and to make a dive with the Navy professionals to identify and if possible to rescue the large amount of quinine.

'I spent the morning on the diving barge being trained to use the diving gear, including the huge bolted-on helmet now considered very old-fashioned but then strange and fearsome to me. About noon it was discovered that at least one of the old mines had broken loose from its rusted chain and the salvage operation was postponed as well as my part in it.' King never got to make the dive; there is no record that the quinine was ever recovered.

Although millions of dollars worth of important equipment went down with the *President Coolidge*, very little was recovered. U.S. Navy divers raised some of the more accessible equipment and munitions from the forward holds during the American occupation of Espiritu Santo, but no immediate post-war salvage operation resulted, and the once proud passenger liner was left to the next generation of salvage entrepreneurs to desecrate her grave.

The wreck site of the *President Coolidge* was initially marked with four large buoys. Reece Discombe recalls that the planters would come down and use the buoys as a target for their makeshift firing range. 'They would blaze away and see who could sink the first buoy - so there were a lot of bullet holes in them. Not much later, the buoys disappeared - they are still down on the bottom with all the chain on them. After that we had no idea where the Coolidge was and the only way we could pick it up was to go back and forth on a boat with a grapple.'

Reece continues, 'My impressions of the Coolidge? Remember that after the war no one had seen the ship. We had no idea of it's size and knew nothing about it, so we did not know what to expect. We were so scared by the size of the damn thing. Nobody had been on it since the Yanks dived on Number Two hold and took out three long range guns to send to the Solomons. There is still one left in the hold. We dived from our boat. Before the growth built up on it, you could see the wreck from the surface - you could see the port holes. When we hit the water you let yourself slowly sink getting used to the situation, can't see much, then you sink slowly. All of a sudden this huge object comes at you like the Great Wall of China. It was so huge we did not know as to which way to turn. We just hovered over it in amazement. We had no idea as to how it was laying so we gradually started to explore. The whole dive was mind boggling.'

'We had always wanted to have a look at it. I was in association with a couple of French guys who had done a bit of diving, and I had plenty of experience around New Caledonia on wrecks and what have you. Robert Charles had set up the baker shop in Santo and was also the first man to start the electricity in the town. The other chap was John Desplat, an engineer living in a Quonset hut where the PT base was. We used to do a hell of a lot of diving, plenty of spearfishing, going after big grouper. We would dive off the oregon wharves, and pick up [military] shells - and found a couple of wooden boats on the bottom.'

Reece Discombe recovered the 'prize' of all ship's - the bell, located at the base of the forward mast. The 20-inch high brass bell has the markings 'Pacific Brass Oundry of San Francisco 1940'. Repeat - the word is 'Oundry', not 'Foundry'. [N1]

The location of the *President Coolidge* however was never forgotten, and her nearness to the shore in depths accessible to hard-hat and later, scuba and hookah divers, encouraged ambitious thoughts of raising the ship, or at least to recover some off her cargo, and non-ferrous metals. Always on the look-out for badly needed metal of all kinds, the resolute Japanese made approaches to work on the ship, just as they did in Rabaul during the 1950s.

The main bell from the *President Coolidge*, located near the fore mast by Reece Discombe. It is still in perfect condition.

After salvaging material from Million Dollar Point and within the jungles of Espiritu Santo, Reece Discombe had gained a reputation for achievement which apparently reached Japanese awareness. In 1947 the Japanese Government expressed an interest in refloating the *President Coolidge* by blocking off all openings, and floating it down the Segond Channel where they could beach it at the flying boat base near the Renee River. Reece was contacted by a Japanese syndicate to do an underwater survey of the vessel to determine whether it would be feasible. Reece recalls, 'Their idea was to plug up everything and put some air in it and refloat it and as the tide was drifting through the canal - it ran at about 5 knots - beach it well down near the far end of the channel. It might sound stupid to a lot of people when you look at the feasibility of it. The idea was to get the boat into shallower water so you could cut out your decompression time when working on it. That was the whole bugbear with the Coolidge. Even if you had got the stern up another sixty feet or something, look at the decompression times it would have saved.' The conclusion was that whereas it could be done technically, it was doubtful whether the proposition would be economical. Of course it begs the question as to whether the condominium government would have permitted the Japanese to salvage the ship. [N2]

As mentioned, the United States government took no action to salvage the ship after the war and showed no further interest in the ship nor her cargo. Remember that the *President Coolidge* was a government ship when she was sunk, not by virtue that she was an Army troop transport, but because the American President Line was a government-appointed company under the control of the US Maritime Commission, formed after the demise of the Dollar Line. The USA Certificate of Registry, Official Number 231219, shows that the ownership of the *President Coolidge* was surrendered by the owners, Dollar Steamship Lines, Inc., in favour of the United States Department of Commerce on 20 July 1938.

On 8 May 1953, and ex-employee of the Dollar Line, Mr. Burton Kent Jaquith, who had been a steward on the *President Cleveland* in 1935, purchased the *President Coolidge* from the US Department of Commerce for the consideration of $10.00, on an 'as is, where is' basis, '*together with all her engines, boilers, machinery, the masts, sails, boats, anchors, cables, tackle, furniture, and all other necessaries thereunto appertaining and belonging, except lead and other metallic ballast covered by Section IX (G) of the sales agreement more fully described on page 2 hereof, and leased or licensed equipment, if any, on board.*'

It was also mentioned in the sales agreement that Mr. Jaquith '*shall not at any time operate nor cause nor permit the vessel or any part thereto to be operated*'. This was not likely. But the clause of some concern and confusion is that '*the Buyer shall completely scrap, dismember, dismantle or destroy the hull of the vessel within two years of the date of delivery thereof, so as to prevent further use of it in any manner whatsoever*'. It could be argued that the vessel was in such a condition that it could not be 'operated' in any case.

In accord with the requirement of the sales agreement, Jaquith contracted with Miyachi Salvage Co. of Kobe, Japan, in 1957, to salvage the *President Coolidge* for the purpose of breaking her up. The British-French condominium government denied the request for permits to allow Miyachi to undertake salvage, and 'after much correspondence and litigation', the project was abandoned. Why the Condominium refused permission is not documented, but it is highly unlikely that the government would have recognised, at the time, the enormous tourist potential of the ship. It is probable that strong anti-Japanese feeling still remained (as it did in New Guinea and Australia when the Japanese attempted to salvage vessels during the 1950s). Had Jaquith approached a non-Japanese salvage company, the ship may not have been as intact and as attractive as she is now. It was a fortuitous decision by the New Hebridean government.

THE PROP JOB

For the next sixteen years, the *President Coolidge* lay at rest, with schools of barracuda as company, and the occasional French resident diver, before coming to the notice of an adventurous Australian. Barry May had been an active wreck diver and salvor prior to establishing a commercial diving business in 1958. Coastal Diving and Engineering in Sydney continued until 1967 but by then Barry became restless and with scrap metal prices rising he yearned for the opportunity to seek and dive on remote wrecks. May had heard of opportunities in New Caledonia, and with new partner Des Woodley, 'had a practice run on a few South Australian wrecks to sharpen up old but not forgotten skills', prior to taking a ship to Noumea where they set up base camp for eighteen months.

Barry May recalls, 'I first found out about the *President Coolidge*, and the *Tucker*, from an article in a diving magazine, perhaps a New Zealand magazine. I made some enquiries through friends and contacted Captain Emile Savoire who ran the ship *Jacques del Mar* from Sydney to Noumea via Lord Howe Island and Norfolk Island. Savoire knew a little about the Coolidge and also told us about wrecks in New Caledonia. He took Des Woodley and myself to Noumea on his ship and we worked there for about two years until we were told to leave.'

New Caledonia proved profitable, but what was good for the Aussies was also good for the French, so Barry May left Noumea after a rival French company arrived on the scene. At the end of 1968, May and Woodley arrived in the New Hebrides with the 45 ft. workboat *Danielle,* bought in Noumea. Later they bought an ex Australian Navy dive support boat, the 66 ft. *Seal,* and renamed her *Pacific Seal*. 'Des and I bought the *Seal* in Sydney. It was very run down and we partly fixed it up and went to Middleton Reef and got the propellers off the *Runic*, returned to Sydney, finished off repairing the renamed *Pacific Seal* and took it to Santo. She became the workboat for the extensive salvage on the *SS President Coolidge* and other wrecks in the area.'

The *Pacific Seal* left Sydney in November 1969 with Sydney diver and photographer Allan Power on board, arriving in Luganville the following month. Power recalls, 'I had known Barry for many years - spearfishing with him - and joined the *Pacific Seal* predominantly to take photographs, not to work on salvage - but inevitably I had to do some salvage work. The main task was to raise the two huge bronze props off the wreck of the *President Coolidge* which until that time had seen very few divers.' [N3]

Barry May.

The *President Coolidge* offered great rewards, and an enormous challenge. Apart from her massive bulk, her stern lay in deep water, 240 ft, and it was the stern that May was interested in for she had two huge brass propellers each weighing over fourteen tons each, and 20-ft in diameter.

Appropriate protocol had to be observed in order to salvage the wreck. Barry May contacted the US War Shipping Administration who provided the name of the owner, Burton Jaquith in Florida, but May advised that he received no reply to his correspondence. He then contacted the New Hebrides condominium government who advised that they had no interest in the wreck as their jurisdiction ended at low water mark. However, after May had successfully removed the props, the government decided they did indeed have jurisdiction and let tenders for salvage of the wreck. This was merely a technicality, as Barry May was awarded the contract, and an 'export duty' was paid to the condominium thus contributing to the country's economy. Barry May suggests that 'the oil that floated into Santo harbor after we blew the props probably triggered their interest'.

Barry May and Des Woodley recruited an excellent team of Australian divers to assist in this very difficult operation, including Allan Power who remained in Luganville. [N4]

With information from Port Vila engineer, diver and salvage expert Reece Discombe, it was not too difficult to locate the huge ex-luxury liner. The greatest difficulty faced by Barry May and his team was of course the depth. Standard equipment was twin 72 cubic ft. bottles which allowed twelve minutes bottom time plus decompression time using Australian Navy tables. This severely limited the work time required to remove the huge propellers and raise them to the surface. The starboard prop was at about 180 ft (55 m), the port prop at 220 ft (67 m).

Barry May was presented with a formidable task, requiring unique procedures to be adopted. Added to their difficulties was the fact that accurate (air tank) contents gauges were not known at the time; the diver had to work out his air consumption as best as possible, and rely on a 'reserve' lever which gave just a few minutes more of air, the useful amount depending on the depth of the diver. As the prop job was at such a deep level, the 'reserve' was virtually useless. As one diver said, 'At that depth, it just gave you an indication that the next breath would be your last - enjoy.' [N5]

May recalls, 'They were three-blade 20 ft diameter 14 ton single piece propellers on their shafts. Number three hatch contained bolt-together four-blade spare props, iron bosses and bronze blades. The blades weighed four and a half tons each. A couple of blades were not recovered, assumed buried under other cargo. To deal with the props on the shafts we started on the shallower prop and attached slings from the prop to the lifting lugs on the hull and loosened the nut holding it onto the shaft with a small explosive charge. The idea was to avoid dropping it into 240 ft of water on the sand and to acquire some expertise at extended deep water work.'

The propellers on the shafts had three blades and were fully cast, not bolted on. A small explosive charge placed on one side of the propeller nut loosened it on the thread in the same manner as one would hit a tight nut on one or more sides with a hammer. The propeller had a taper fit on the keyed shaft. Thesmall charge also loosened the prop on the shaft, and as the ship lies on a significant angle, gravity allowed it to slip off easily once the nut was removed from the end of the shaft. The charges, using Hydrogel, were electrically detonated from the surface.

Allan Power recalls, 'To remove the phosphor bronze props - each blade was about nine feet long - we worked in teams of two divers down at a time. Each diver had a twelve minute bottom time for 185-200 ft (56 - 61m). One dive per person per day only. We used mainly 72-cf twin and single sets, with various regulators of dubious reliability - and no contents gauges. The tanks had a 'five minutes reserve' - when it worked. [Actually a 300psi reserve 'J' valve, operated by a lever on the first stage of the air supply]. Surprisingly there were no bends cases. The group used US Navy tables. There were no repetitive dives. Before taking the nuts off, the cone-nut had to be removed with dynamite. These were made of gunmetal, and were full of grease. There was no corrosion on the steel nuts holding the props on - big steel nuts shining like they were chrome. The nut - about eighteen inches - was keyed in. We had to remove the key - hammered it out.'

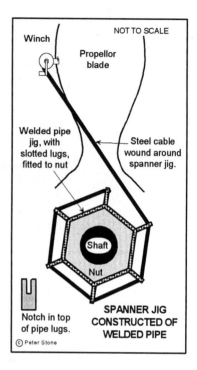

SPANNER JIG CONSTRUCTED OF WELDED PIPE

© Peter Stone

Initially a very large chain wrench with an extended chain and a pipe extension to the handle was used in an attempt to remove the huge nut on the starboard shaft. This proved very difficult to use and a special spanner was made. 'Barry May constructed a special purpose spanner made of steel pipe. A steel cable was wound from the spanner on the nut and then the cable was attached to a boat-winch which in turn was secured to the nearest prop blade. A few turns on the wrench handle gradually unwound the nut. It was a slow and labourious - and dangerous - procedure and it took a week to get one nut off - several months to do the whole job. The starboard nut was first to be unwound. The huge propeller shaft nut was unscrewed till it was nearly off the shaft, then bumped off with a light explosive charge. The [starboard] prop was then pushed off the shaft with dynamite, and fell to the bottom intact in 240 feet.' Barry May recalls that the prop was on a tapered shaft and the weight of the propeller pushing down on the nut made it very difficult to unwind. 'It jammed part way off and a small "push" with explosives was necessary to allow it to come of the shaft. The propeller was attached to the ship with wire slings onto the propeller lifting lugs. As I recall, these slings broke when the prop came off and it fell, intact, to the bottom in 240 ft. From there it was lifted under the *Pacific Seal* into shallower water where it was broken up.' [N6]

Barry May continues the saga, 'About this time - after the starboard prop came off - I had to go to Sydney to sell a load of scrap metal. While I was away the rest of the crew decided to get the deeper prop off quickly and they put a fairly large explosive charge behind it to blow it off nut and all. When I got back I found one prop in two pieces on the sand in 240ft, a hole leaking oil in the stern of the Coolidge, a fair amount of oil in Santo Harbour, and a rather unpopular salvage crew.'

The port propeller was concealed under the stern and some twenty feet deeper than the upper starboard prop - remember the ship is lying on her port side. Attempts to use the spanner were labourious and slow, so in Barry May's absence, a 'quicker' method was devised by his enthusiastic team. A case of dynamite was strung around the back of the prop and the whole lot was blown off the shaft. The explosion loosened a few hull plates and fuel oil escaped. Explosives were not used on the *President Coolidge* after this.

Allan Power remembers the port prop being blown off , '... too much dynamite was used - lazy- put a dent in the arse of the ship. The prop blew to pieces and went to the bottom. One blade speared into the seabed some 30 ft away. Two blades remained on the hub, now on the bottom also. The excessive dynamiting of the port prop started some of the oil leaks.'

Barry May again: 'We got the props okay, but digging in the sand at 240 ft is not easy. All the diving on the props was done on tanks, mostly twin 72s, working up to 30 minutes decompression times, which as I recall is about 12 minutes bottom time. We experienced some problems with narcosis but no bends problems at that time.'

It took four months to remove both propellers. Although nobody experienced any serious problems relating to decompression, the team had its anxious moments. The greatest diving safety problem was that of experiencing tunnel-vision, apparently caused by a CO_2 build-up coupled with fast descent and exertion. The team was well prepared, but luck was certainly on their side.

New Zealander Peter Spurdle returned from a voyage to Japan on board the *Whai*, and called in to Espiritu Santo just one week after Barry May and his team had removed the props. 'We hunted and hunted, the echo sounder rolling out miles of squiggly lines but no sign of a wreck. I was sure that the Aussie in Luganville was wrong in his directions but then a launch came up and guided us further down the channel to point out the buoys marking the liner's grave. An oil slick stained the greenish sea and escaping fuel stank in the still air. We dragged the grapnel over to catch on the wreck's hull and climbed down the ladders over the stern and slipped into the sea, ducking under the oil film. At about 30 feet we passed through the thermocline and into the cooler waters of the deep. There it was! Huge beyond belief!

'She lay on her side. We could see about a hundred feet along its deck with the bulk of the big ship vanishing into the misty distance. Small mortar bombs and 50-calibre ammunition lay scattered across the coral-encrusted plates and sand. Big salmon and groper lazed past stanchions and beams and huge silver and green trevally circled the flak nests with their rusty guns pointing at crazy angles. A long ragged gash split the starboard side near the bow.

'Black oil seeped from cracks and floated away up to the surface in slowly twisting goblets to spread and spread in an iridescent film. Even after twenty-seven years she bled, with hundreds of tons of fuel yet to escape. On down past the bridge, with its gaping ports, past the empty davits and wreckage of ventilators and yet more gun mountings. At over 200 feet the huge stern lay exposed , the shattered propeller hubs shorn bare by explosives removing the massive bronze blades.

'We were awed by the huge shafts, the black mass of the stern rearing overhead like a cliff. Air running short we swam regretfully back to the surface taking care to avoid the spiralling fuel bubbles. Back on board it was a long time before we calmed down after this fantastic dive.'

Englishman Peter Cole was one of the team on the *President Coolidge* project. Cole was employed by a metal merchant in Sydney and came to work for May to supervise packing and shipment of the recovered metal. Cole recalls, 'I first landed on Santo in June 1970, ferried from Noumea aboard a shaky old DC3. The airstrip was an old US bomber field, and at a casual glance looked very much in original condition. The terminal, for want of a better word, was a two-sided tin shack containing two school desks. Behind one sat a French gendarme, and behind the other an English policeman. Behind each inspector was a local 'police boy' in French and English uniforms respectively.' By the time Cole had arrived, the two props had been removed and the *Pacific Seal* was on its way to New Guinea on another salvage project. This left the 22-metre *Onewa*, a former New Zealand coaster, to continue the work on the *President Coolidge* and the *Tucker.*

Cole recalls, 'Our first job after setting up a scrapyard and sorting and packing the tonnes of scrap metal was to pull out four 4.25-tonne propeller blades from the Coolidge's hold. These were spares and were bolted to the bulkhead of the vessel. The hold was at a depth of 43 to 50 m.' Six blades were recovered from No. 3 hold.

Peter Cole's work on the *President Coolidge* is all the more remarkable as he was a complete novice diver. 'My previous diving experience had been an hour or two spent about a week before swimming around the small ships wharf on Santo. I had never used an aqualung in my life, and had learned to swim in a small pool at school in England. Fortunately, I took to diving instantly, and loved every minute of it. This was just as well, because my first dive was down 138 ft (42 m) to sling up the first prop [which had been brought up to shallower water], and then I stayed at about 80 ft (25 m) relaying winching signals from the diver in the hold to the winch driver at the surface. The whole job was a tricky one, and took several days. But we eventually got them out and dumped them just off the small ships wharf in town.'

Most of the material recovered by Barry May and his team was sold to Australian metal merchants and refineries. The props were take to Simonsons, the main wharf at Luganville, and prepared for direct shipment to Japan as they were too big for Australian smelters.

Life in Luganville during the 1970s appears to have been a bit more lively than the later years after the Coconut Revolution of 1980. Peter Cole recalls, 'The highlight of Santo's social life in those days was the monthly dance at Maos bar on the arrival of the *Polynesie,* a small, neat freighter that plied the Australia-New Caledonia-New Hebrides run. A noisy rock group belted out the latest songs, the French girls danced (with each other), and the men drank. Drinking was the major activity on Santo, and it didn't take long to become an active member of this informal club. There were two hotels on the main road - Maos run by a Tahitian, and The Corsican, run by an expatriate Australian. A third bar, Goodyns Bar, off the main road, was run by a Belgian Gaullist who preferred to swear in English because it had more swearwords than French. The town was full of "characters", mostly English, French and Australian expatriates who had lived and worked on the island for most of their lives, some for more than 30 years.' [N7]

After the spare blades were retrieved from the hold of the *President Coolidge*, Barry May extended his operations to the Solomons and New Guinea (Bougainville) and worked his way back again to Espiritu Santo in

Propeller blades
recovered from the
President Coolidge by
Barry May and his team,
lie on a wharf at
Luganville ready for
despatch oversea.

1971, where he resumed another assault on the *President Coolidge,* this time raising over fifty tons of field gun shells and rifle cases. The world metal prices had hit a peak but soon dropped.

Peter Cole arrived back in Santo in 1972 to asist with the salvage and recalls, 'Life on the island was unchanged. A nightclub had been added to the local attractions in Luganville, the Hog Harbour Hotel had a bit of weekend life, and the French and English were still bickering. An earthquake had dropped the small ships wharf below low water mark and demolished the building of CFNH, the French trading company (it was only two US Quonset huts side by side). Back on the Coolidge we opened up No 1 hold and pulled out thousands of live 105 mm shells which had to be defused aboard the workboat. Other cargo in the hold consisted of dozens of spare wheels and tyres. We sold the tyres locally as there were still quite a few trucks around which the 'as new', water-preserved tyres fitted. One ambitious driver bolted a complete 30-year-old steel wheel and tyre on his truck. The wheel collapsed with the first load he carried, although the tyre was OK. Cases and cases of Springfield bolt-action rifles came to light. We winched a case on board and examined the contents. Every single one had suffered corrosion, although some looked all right. Numbers 2 and 3 holds had already been opened by the Americans: they had removed two complete plates from the hull. In No 2 hold there were dozens of trucks, jeeps, halftrack vehicles, boxes of spares, kitchen equipment, enormous aluminium pressure cookers, and all sorts of general ,campaign equipment. No 3 hold contained thousands of cases of small arms ammunition and hundreds of 105 mm and 75 mm shells. We salvaged as many of these as we could and then rigged up an air lift dredge to suck up the small shells. These were 'deloused' ashore in a home-made furnace of 44-gallon drums and sheet metal. We fed compressed air and diesel fuel into the furnace and burned great piles of shells at a time. The brass cases were separated from the projectiles and packed into 44-gallon drums for shipment to Australia.' [N8]

Allan Power adds to the description, 'Shells on the Coolidge were packed in cardboard tubes - in the forward holds. Some are still there. No cutting was done by Barry [May] on the Coolidge. We raised 105 mm cartridge cases. We would fill a basket with full rounds and haul them to the surface, knock out the heads, screw out the heavy brass fuse from the front, and then throw the valueless steel projectile overboard - you can see them scattered on the bottom. Some shells leaked - water and cordite formed a gas on the surface - the gas expanded and blew the lighter cartridge cases off. At times it was quite dangerous to raise the shells.'

'We never opened the engine room,' Barry May recalls. 'I did an inspection inside it - via the ventilator shafts - and found about twelve feet (3.6 m) depth of free oil in the top of the engine room which had leaked out of the bunkers. About this time scrap prices fell dramatically and oil prices had not started to escalate. We therefore suspended our operations after we had recovered viable scrap from the holds and external pipework.' [N9]

THE OIL JOB

By 1974 it became apparent that the bunker oil seeping from the wreck of the *President Coolidge* was increasing, and thus threatened the ecology of the Segond Channel. There is little doubt that the removal of the port propeller by dynamite hastened the problem of oil escaping from the great liner. An article in the local publication *Nabanga* stated that Santo and the whole archipelago was at the mercy of the breaking-up of the wreck of the *President Coolidge*, 'an occurrence which would release 800 tons of oil, killing coral, plankton and fish, and polluting the beach'.

Reece Discombe comments: 'Now, with all that blowing and dynamiting on the Coolidge, that naturally loosened up the rivets and plates and then the oil really started to pour out of it. On a calm day you could see the wreck quite clearly on the bottom - the bow section at least - and you could smell the oil. It got worse and worse after Barry May had had a go at it with all that dynamiting. It had to loosen up something. All the planters - especially around Aore and Malo [islands] - and around town - when the tide went out it would take a slick of oil with it and everybody could smell it and they started to complain to the government. But the Condominium didn't do anything about it and finally they got hold of Ian Lockley and Ian Perrott [at Salvage Pacific in Fiji]."

Whilst doing the 'prop job' in 1969, Barry May did a comprehensive survey of the ship and as mentioned, found bunker oil floating free in the engine room and boiler room. This prevented any thought of further salvage within these areas until the oil was removed. His research had shown that the ship could have been carrying upwards of 6,000 tons of fuel oil, so he was understandably concerned about the pollution potential with the ship gradually deteriorating.

About a year after Barry May left Espiritu Santo in 1972, he was approached by the Fiji-based marine salvage contractor Ian Lockley to take over the salvage rights of the *President Coolidge* as assigned by the Condominium to May. Lockley had heard of the complaints from the locals in Luganville, and came to Espiritu Santo to do a survey, at his own expense. Lockley's company, Salvage Pacific Ltd., was strategically placed for South Pacific salvage, and did well from recovering oriental fishing boats that managed to plaster themselves on the Fijian reefs. May agreed to the transfer of salvage rights. He had previously approached the condominium government for a subsidy to remove the oil - it was not viable to do the job for the value of the oil alone. Bureaucracy dogged the application with the government and by the time the required permits came through oil prices had started to rise and recovery of the oil became viable in its own right. But no subsidy was forthcoming and May assigned his salvage rights to Lockley.

By now oil started appearing in the Segond Channel. It was obviously heavy bunker oil and the sizeable volume spurred the New Hebrides condominium government to take action - well, to at least listen to complaints from the residents. Not only was the seepage polluting the waters, but there was the even greater threat that an earthquake could break up the wreck and create a major oil spill. Following complaints from local residents, the Condominium government decided to take the initiative and called in Lockely's Salvage Pacific (Fiji) to make a thorough survey of the wreck with a view to determining the quantity of oil that remained and the possibility of its salvage.

The concept of recovering oil from a once proud liner fired Lockley's imagination, for no other reason that a salvage operation of this type was unique and presented a new challenge. The task was formidable. The bottom sloped from the bow at 100 ft (30 m) to the stern at over 240 ft (73 m). She was 654 ft (199.5 m) long with an 81 ft (24.7 m) beam and seven decks. Amongst this once floating skyscraper were secreted thirty-four oil tanks, some with double bottom plates, some deep within the ship, some in the bow and some in the stern. All could contain oil.

In February 1974, Salvage Pacific quoted the Condominium government a price to do a formal survey on the *President Coolidge*, and received a down payment to do the job - otherwise they would not have commenced the survey. Lockley and Perrott were required to determine how much oil was left on the ship - but not to remove it as this was not part of the contract. As engineering plans were available, they knew exactly where the tanks were within the double-hulled ship, and could mark them out on the bottom and starboard side of the ship As oil floats on water, the survey team need only commence drilling from the lowest level of each tank. As soon as oil seeped out, they knew where the oil level was. The top surface of the oil could be determined by the shape of the tank and how the tank lay - remember that the ship is lying on her port side. By knowing the cubic capacity of the tank, the quantity of remaining oil could then be determined. [N10]

Ian Lockley made several inspection dives on the wreck, then initiated survey operations to determine the amount of oil remaining in the vessel and the best way to remove it. Lockley, an Australian who had learnt the salvage business on the Australian coast, rightly figured the job impossible by conventional means, and some ingenuity and intelligence was required. Lockley lacked neither. With the permission and no doubt encouragement of wife Betty, he designed a four man submersible decompression chamber on his lounge floor in Fiji, using kitchen chairs and anything else appropriate from the home. The chamber was rolled and completed in Suva. Designed for use as a submersible decompression chamber it was intended to anchor it to the bilge keel of the *President Coolidge* and with a system of pulleys and counter weights raise and lower it by means of a turfor block operated by one diver inside. The chamber was supplied with 10 cubic feet of flushing air per minute from the 45 ft salvage boat *Salmar*, piped music, telephone, banks of air and oxygen bottles for emergencies (independent of the support ship), and a set of plans of the *President Coolidge* - and more important, a handful of *Playboys*.

Allan Power exits the four-man submersible decompression chamber built by Ian Lockley for use during the oil survey. Allan has just completed his decompression time and is free ascending to the surface. The chamber is tethered to the hull of the *President Coolidge*, and may be raised or lowered as required from within the chamber.

Thirty-foot hookah lines and regulators for emergency use hung below the chamber and a shark cage with independent air supply was also built. The shark cage was never used. Allan Power comments, 'A bit of an overkill really. We didn't see any sharks whilst we were working on the job.' [N11]

The survey got underway in earnest in October 1974 when the company's salvage vessel *Salmar* arrived at the wreck site with six divers. The submersible decompression chamber was attached to the bilge keel of the wreck by a counterweighted chain and block system enabling the divers to regulate chamber depth from 40 to 10 ft according to their decompression requirements.

After placement of the submersible decompression chamber and a protective shark cage, dives were made to locate and drill into the double bottom oil tanks extending from the bow to slightly aft of midships. This phase proceeded smoothly since the ship is lying on its port side and the entire bottom of the hull is exposed. The only difficulties encountered were in controlling diver buoyancy as the drilling was conducted in open water on the vertical 'wall' of the ship bottom. Next the margins of the starboard deep tanks were outlined on the starboard hull and holes, were drilled through the forward high corner of each tank.

Allan Power recalls the arrival of Salvage Pacific. 'Ian Lockley came to Santo in 1974 to salvage the oil from the *President Coolidge* which was now seeping out at an alarming rate and threatening to damage the ecology and the channel. The condominium government of the then New Hebrides asked Lockley to remove the oil as by now there was a huge slick covering the foreshore. With a south-easterly blowing you could smell the oil in Santo. The foreshore was getting slabs of oil residue, and you could see a big oil slick from the air. I worked with Lockley for six months on that task, and learnt how to use repetitive tables, doing three dives a day. Lockley had a diving chamber. During this time I didn't take many photos - too busy.

'We would find out where the tanks were by counting lines of rivets, and try to work out the highest point of a tank and drill a quarter inch hole through one-inch thick steel with an air drill and see if oil came out. If no oil, the air (under pressure) would roar out and the deck would vibrate for twenty minutes. If oil came out we would immediately plug it.' If air, then the tank was empty - assuming that they had drilled at the highest point of the tank. If oil seeped out, the hole was plugged and successive holes were drilled lower in the tank to determine the depth of the oil.

With exterior drilling concluded, the team commenced the more difficult task of the internal ship survey, to assess the condition of structural members, locate oil pockets, and check the port-side tanks. As would be expected, many of the bulkheads were in an advanced state of deterioration and in several places oil was observed seeping through the bulkheads. Leaking oil, trapped by the starboard inner plating, formed pockets in the boiler room and No. 2 cargo hold. The boiler room pocket was 14 ft thick. The internal survey was the longest phase of the survey operations because the working depth was increased to between 140 and 180 ft (42 - 55 m) necessitating shorter working dives and longer decompression periods.

A series of drill holes were required in one of the aft tanks, going higher each time until it struck oil and then measurements were taken. Access to many of the port deep tanks was obstructed by 10 to 30 ft of debris. This required that access be gained by other routes and so a series of dives was made through one of the mine holes at 180 ft (55 m) to drill into two port deep tanks. Access to this tank could only be made through the jagged mine hole in the ship, but it was too small to get through with tanks. Three of Lockley's divers, John Whitman, John Hickman and Jim Prescott had the job. They set off with over 300 ft. of air hose for the drill, twin 70s on their backs, plus torches and two spare 70s each with a 100 ft. hookah line and regulator tucked under an arm. Down to 180 ft. - Whitman took off his tanks, switched to the bottle-supplied hookah and with drill and torch in hand eased through the narrow opening and threaded his way through the ship to the tank. Jim stayed outside paying out the hookah line from the entrance. He succeeded in drilling the necessary holes till

The old New Zealand tug *Tui Tawate* is loaded with 250 tons of bunker oil from the *President Coolidge*, and awaits the arrival of the P.&O. liner *Arcadia*. Salvage Pacific's salvage boat *Salmar* lies at anchor behind *Tui Tawate*.

he struck oil, took measurements then worked his way back, coiling the air line as he went. Bottom time, 70 minutes at 180-ft. A three hour session in the chamber was required, with five stages commencing at 50-ft, to 10 ft. [N12]

Toward the same end, a hole was cut with oxy-arc through the starboard plating into a cofferdam above No. 7 deep tank, which if clear, would have provided transverse access to several port deep tanks. The cofferdam was obstructed 15 feet in. It was hoped that working in the boiler room could have been avoided because of the tangled maze of piping and general deterioration, but all other routes were blocked so divers entered the port boiler room and engine room to determine the amount of oil in the last of the ships' tanks.

Allan Power: 'We had to get to the bottom double holds with an oxy-carbon arc - had to cut through the outer hull enough for one to get in - and had to do the same cutting on a vertical level. I worked between the hull and the tank wall on the double bottom. Dive profile - working for thirty or forty minutes at 160 ft (49 m) deepest. Did up to three dives a day - using the chamber to recompress - two dives per day was quite common. US Navy tables were used - 30 ft then 20 ft then 10 ft. The longest time that Ian Perrott and I did was on a survey of the back hold - twin tanks - 190-ft one hour - 183 minutes decompression.'

Long dives were one thing, but nature also added to the hazards. Three divers were in the submersible decompression chamber when and earthquake hit. The chamber bucked and danced and water poured in through a hatch. The noise added to the divers discomfort and they considered baling out with decompression time to go. What a choice - stay there and drown or escape and get bent. Not sure of exactly what was happening, they elected, wisely, to stay and ride it out. When they finally surfaced Ian Lockley described the heaving shoreline and swaying trees while they all agreed that it was lucky no one was actually inside the *President Coolidge* at the time. The ship had been 'shaken like foxy with a rat', the visibility reduced to zero inside, a large section of

The *Tui Tawate* is anchored over the wreck site of the *President Coolidge*, awaiting another load of oil to transfer to the *Arcadia*. Note how close she is to the reef edge which drops off steeply.

ornate tiled fountain had torn from its place against a wall in the main lobby and crashed 60 ft to the other side of the ship. And a seven ton anchor plummeted over the bow to the sand below.

It was the presence of Lockley's submersible decompression chamber that made the oil survey and recovery task possible. Three dives a day to over 150 ft (46 m) for nearly an hour at a time would have been impossible without the chamber. After several weeks investigation it was determined that 600-800 tons of oil still remained in the tanks. Samples of oil were also taken and proved still to be in excellent condition after more than thirty years under water.

Some six weeks of decompression diving had taken place during the survey, with over 1,500 hours underwater. Divers were down three dives a day with torches and equipment into the innermost recesses of the ship, yet not one bend or debilitating accident occurred. Lucky? Lynton Diggle doesn't think so. 'The attention to detail and safety that Ian Lockley displayed was infectious and the faultless working of the chamber was testimony alone to Ian's ability as an engineer/diver/salvor.' In the event of an accident a one-man chamber was always at the ready on board *Salmar*.

Despite these assurances, there were several close calls. Salvage Pacific partner Ian Perrott had an equipment problem that was very close to being tragic, and he landed in hospital. Allan Power recalls, 'Ian was pushing the time while working in the engine room, cutting. Just that little bit more. He became entangled in the umbilicals for (cutting) oxygen and electricity for lighting. Allan Cain, a Fijian mixed-race diver got him to the chamber. I was on board *Salmar* when Allan rang from the chamber to say that Mr. Perrott had run out of air. I had visions of Perrott trapped in the wreck. When I dropped off the duckboard of *Salmar* with a tank tucked under my arm, I could see Ian's long legs hanging below the chamber. I squeezed past his legs and got the upper part of my body into the chamber. Allan Cain had managed to get Perrott halfway into the chamber but Ian was over six foot tall and he could not lift him right in. I told Allan that I would brace myself under Ian and push upwards while he pulled him up under the arms. This got him into the chamber, up over Allan's knees. Perrott promptly vomited all over me. I thought, the lousy buggar, how come he had fruit salad for lunch - I didn't get any. Ian came round after he had pumped large quantities of water out of him. We had to complete his decompression of course and then get him off to hospital.'

British District Agent Dick Baker recalls, 'I vividly recall being called to the hospital one Saturday evening to find Ian very ill as a result of a diving mishap. The French doctors did not know how to treat him as although they had all the necessary drugs they

A diver exits a small hole in the hull of the *President Coolidge* that allowed access to the boiler room during the removal of the oil.

had no specialised knowledge of these problems and had no idea of what dosage to administer. Being Saturday evening in those days the entire communications system had come to halt and the only way we could establish any contact with the rest of the world was via the ham-radio network. With the help of this we managed to get hold of a ham in Sydney who lived not far from the hospital where Ian Lockley's medical adviser was based. Luckily he was on duty that night and the Sydney ham managed to get him on the telephone and relayed advice to us with which our doctors were able to resuscitate young Ian by the following morning.'

Allan Cain, also had a close call. Diving in the engine room for the first time, he was left alone by his buddy for some reason. Entry to the engine room at the time was through the rear funnel vent, and in complete darkness. Ross Jenkins, in the chamber, could hear Allan's low-air sonic alarm going off way below, somewhere within the ship. There was little that could be done from the chamber nor the surface. It was touch and go. But Allan found his way out, much to the relief of the rest of the divers.

In total, thirty-four oil tanks were tapped; Lockley worked out that there was some 650 tons of oil to be recovered. He wasn't too far off, and some six hundred tons of bunker C-grade oil was later recovered.

Reece Discombe comments, 'That was a great effort. They made their report back to the Condominium but of course the government did nothing immediately about it. Lockley was keen - all set to go to take the oil out - and had given the Condominium a price to do that.'

Lockley was in the box seat to be awarded the contact having completed the survey successfully. He advised the government that they had better make up their minds soon as the plugs inserted during his survey would eventually deteriorate through electrolysis and the oil would leak out. The story goes, and nobody seems to deny it, that the imaginative Lockley decided to give the Condominium government some incentive to overcome their procrastination

A suction hose has been connected to a flange and valve to withdraw bunker oil from the *President Coolidge*.

and make up their mind to award the contract. As the survey holes in the hull were stopped with wooden plugs, he sent down a diver to remove a few of these.

Reece Discombe comments, 'I don't know for how long - maybe overnight or so - but that swamped the canal with oil and everyone jumped up and down and then the government made their mind up and said go ahead.'

The official story, and probably the true account although the mischievous events as indicated above are far more interesting, is that the plugs had deteriorated. It would appear that some plugs were wooden, and other of steel. The *New Hebrides News,* 29 March 1976, reported that 'Santo beaches have been polluted recently by the oil leaks from the wreck. As a result, the Condominium Public Works employed a diver recently to block some of the holes in the oil tank.'

In May 1976, the respected *Pacific Island Monthly* reported that 'The oil leaks from the sunken former US navy vessel *President Coolidge* have been plugged by marine divers working on the wreck off Santo, in the New Hebrides. The oil, which was causing a serious problem of pollution, was found to be seeping from deteriorating plugs inserted in the vessel's hold after a survey had been made of its fuel reserves. This study was made over fifteen months ago by a Fiji company Pacific Salvage, investigating the possibilities of salvaging 800 tonnes of oil trapped in the ship. After the salvage investigations, holes made in the ship's hold were plugged again, awaiting the expected pumping operations. However, as time passed the stoppers have corroded, provoking the oil leaks. The authorities engaged a diving specialist, [a] Mr Martin, to study the situation which revealed an estimated 1,200 litres of oil escaping each day. New bronze stoppers were set in place to replace the iron ones, with a sealing of concrete added for good measure.'

In March 1976, the *New Hebrides News* announced that work was due to start soon on pumping out the 850 tons [*sic*] of fuel oil in the Coolidge, by Salvage Pacific Limited based in Suva, Fiji. The joint project was to be financed by a British Government grant of $60,000, and carried out by Savage Pacific Limited, which had made the full survey of the wreck in late 1974.

With the contract firmly in his grasp, Lockley prepared for the removal of the oil. It was necessary to locate the highest point in each tank, already done by the survey drilling, and position a valve so that a hose could be connected and the oil pumped out. A 4-hole pipe flange with a threaded core was taped and bolted to the hull at the appropriate high point of the tank. The hull was then cut through within the flange core with a special cutter of some three inches diameter. As soon as the cut broke through, a 3-inch nipple gatevalve was screwed onto the flange as quickly as possible to limit escaping treacle-like oil. Once the valve was in place it was only a matter of attaching the pumping hose and opening the valve.

Allan Power recalls, 'We needed to use a jig to apply pressure - the flange was used to hold the cutter. There were only two cutters on board and it was instant death if we lost one. Once cut through we would ease off, leave the drill cutter in place, take away the jig, and fit the gatevalve.'

Of course the problem then arose as to what to do with the oil. Fortunately, tests indicated that it was excellent C-grade bunker oil and had not 'deteriorated' in any way over the years. British District Agent Baker at Luganville recalls, 'As you know, our main concern was to get rid of the oil before the leakages became even worse and gave rise to major pollution. Even in those days this was a very sensitive subject and I remember being very worried about the problem of actually disposing of the oil assuming we could get it out without precipitating some disaster. Burning was the original intention until we considered the quantities involved and the likely ecological results of this. Then someone suggested that we pump it into some of those underground tanks and caves that the Americans had used around the Palikulo area. This was kyboshed because the experts considered that due to the porosity of the local rock and the possibility of cracks in the concrete tanks the oil would seep into all sorts of areas, possibly large quantities of it eventually back into the sea - not at all the sort of outcome we were hoping for. I don't know who suggested sending a sample to Shell in Sydney or whoever it was (although of course I could claim credit for it myself) but it was an excellent long shot and we were all amazed to learn that they considered the stuff still to be of commercially useable quality. Even luckier, given the rather primitive nature of the fuel, was the fact that one of the few remaining large vessels which could still burn it called at Santo every few months, namely the old *Arcadia* - and that we were able to sell it to her. So not only did we get rid of the stuff but were even able to get at least a little money back from it to help defray the costs of the project.'

Reece Discombe reflects, 'Now the problem arose - what are they going to do once they got the oil out. There were no containers around - no barges to put the oil in. So they bought an old triple expansion steam engine tug that was made in Scotland in 1942 for the Ministry of Defence and was called the *Empire Shirley* - Empire was the class of tug, and they had a big gun up at the bow. So after the war all this stuff was sold and this particular boat was bought by B.P. Petroleum and came down to New Zealand where it was used in Wellington Harbour for towing the oil barges around to all of the ships. It was later sold to an Indian syndicate in Fiji to be used for salvage work. Lockley was just starting to get going [on his salvage business] - he had done a few small jobs - but the Indian didn't have half the nous that Lockley had and so the tug just lay there. Lockley managed to get some money from the Condominium to buy the tug and use it to store the bunker oil. Okay - so the Condominium government bought the tug and Lockley got it going again. By now the name had changed to *Tui Tawate*. The tug towed Lockley's other boat, the *Salmar* to New Hebrides. On the way, the *Tui Tawate* ran out of boiler water so they started filling it up with salt water. I don't know how much further they would have got with the salt water because you can imagine what the salt build-up would have been but they made it over here.' [N13]

Needless to say, the *Tui Tawate* was in a sad state when it arrived at Espiritu Santo. Now powerless, the tug was prepared for accepting the oil. She was completely gutted, and every available space below decks made sound to accept the oil. Crews quarters up front were cleaned out and storage lockers and hatches sealed. The only place not to be filled were the engine room and the boiler room.

Lockley's responsibility was to recover the oil, which he could do so by using the *Tui Tuwate*. But one could hardly take the lot out to sea and dump it; a safe ecological method was required.

The salvage vessel *Salmar* is dwarfed by the tug *Tui Tawate*, in turn dwarfed by the P. & O. Liner *Arcadia*, waiting to transfer the bunker oil recovered from the *President Coolidge*.

The initial idea was to use the oil fired burners in the *Tui Tawate* and simply burn the oil. Lockley had to put a reasonable proposal to the Condominium before he was awarded the contract. It appeared however to be waste to dispose of the oil, which tests proved could be used as C-grade bunker oil. In 1977 the government, presumably the British component, quite wisely negotiated with P. & O. Lines, the owners of the passenger cruise liner *Arcadia*. The oil could be used directly by the *Arcadia* thus providing a satisfactory ecological and economic solution. Powerful hydraulic pumps transferred the oil first to the *Tui Tawate*, to await the arrival of the *Arcadia*. Timing was important, for the cruise liner did not care for any delay longer than necessary. The *Arcadia* was loaded with approximately 200 tons of oil at the rate of 30 tons an hour on each of three trips. The P. & O. Line paid the Condominium for the oil. Some 600 tons of oil was removed from the *President Coolidge* in 1977 completing what ranks as one of the world's most unique salvage jobs.

With the *President Coolidge* now 'environmentally safe', and the oil being used effectively on the *Arcadia*, questions were asked Luganville as to what happened to all the money that was to be made from the deal. Leaders of two Espiritu Santo political parties questioned the Resident Commissioner, asking who made the profit from the sale of the fuel oil, and why had it not gone to the Condominium treasury or to a Santo organisation.

In the *Hebrides News* it was clearly stated that '*Far from there being a profit from the sale of the oil, it had cost a great deal to extract the oil, and [also] recalled that there had been demands from the Santo population for a long time to remove the oil to prevent pollution.*'

The *New Hebrides News* reported that the operation cost some $92,000, whilst the sale of the oil to P. & O. amounted to only $17,000, so the removal of the oil cost $75,000. '*The revenue helped to pay for the cost of getting the oil out but there was a loss on that aspect, not a profit. Finally, the Condominium will benefit by duties payable it any of the scrap metal, such as copper alloys from the condensers and feed pipes is exported.*'

The $60,000 grant from the British Government reduced the out-of-pocket cost to the Condominium to $15,000, a very fair price considering the pollution disaster that was averted. [N14]

Lockley's contract only allowed for the actual removal of the oil, but he also had a permit to work the *President Coolidge* for scrap up until 1981. Once the oil removal was completed, he recovered non-ferrous metals. 'The windings on the motors are as thick as your finger', Lockley is reported to have said, his eyes sparkling at the prospect of recovering tons of copper and brass from the ship. The crew cut out the side of the engine room to remove the condensers and the electric drive propulsion motors that drove the screws.

There was also a report of a 'mystery cargo' aboard the *President Coolidge* that was listed simply as - ballast. This was later defined as being pure nickel ingots. Ian Lockley believes there were three on the ship, 'two of which were "stolen" and the third salvaged'.

Allan Power recalls, 'The *Salmar* [Salvage Pacific's salvage tug], kept leaving to tow boats of reefs. Lockley's five year option ran out. He was ready to renew but by then tourism had started. He had cleared the side of the engine room - lifted sections to one side, took out catwalks, junction boxes, copper tubing, electric motors - dynamiting and lifting. Non-ferrous metal was dumped on the side - and is still there. We worked on the engine room for several months, but nothing was raised to the surface. The engine room had huge lathes - still there. We cleaned out the engine room - perfect for tourist divers now as there is easy access and no obstacles.' Two lathes were actually raised from the engine room in 1977 and lie on the starboard hull of the ship next to the holes made by Lockley's team to gain entry to the engine room.

The attempt to salvage the engine room was not profitable and Lockley stopped operations after he received a bend in the shoulder whilst working at 120 ft removing nuts on a piece of equipment. He recovered as the chamber was still on site. He offered to take a 3-inch gun off the bow and mount it in the park opposite the Santo Hotel (next to Allan Power's home). The local Minister thought it was a good idea, but Allan recognised the potential of dive tourism to Espiritu Santo and had the idea quashed when New Hebrides gained independence and became the Republic of Vanuatu in 1980.

On 18 November 1983, the Vanuatu government declared the wreck of the *President Coolidge* a protected National Park site and no salvage or recovery of any artifact is permitted.

CHAPTER TWELVE

A LADY
IN WAITING

Allan Power turned off the gravel road onto a narrow track through the bush and pulled up in a clearing next to the beach.

'This is it', he said.

I jumped out of the Toyota cab with unashamed enthusiasm and looked across Segond Channel.

'Where is it ?' I asked.

'See that pole out there?', Allan said pointing to a spot some sixty metres offshore. 'It's about another 200 feet beyond that. She's lying on her port side, her bow is at seventy feet and her stern below two hundred. C'mon, let's go'.

Allan doesn't like to waste words. His enthusiasm is infectious. I didn't need much encouragement. Within minutes we had kitted up and were standing in a metre of water at the iron rod Allan had embedded in the reef.

'Hang your camera on one of the hooks, and put your mask and fins on here. Then follow me. It drops off to about twenty feet - we'll pick up a rope that leads us to the bow of the ship. Stick with me. If I hold up my [contents] gauge you do the same. We'll swim along the top of the ship to the bridge, then down along the promenade deck. Keep an eye out for the three-inch gun on the bow. The bridge is at a hundred feet. Just to be on the safe side we'll only do the top of the bridge for the first dive and do a twenty minute deco at ten feet. Okay ?'

With my camera in hand I dropped below the surface, commencing one of the most incredible dives one could experience.

That was sixteen years ago and I have been back many times since. Each time a feeling of excitement, of anticipation, grips you as Vanair's Twin Otter from Port Vila flies over the wreck site just before touching down on the old Bomber Two strip at Pekoa. It is not usual to see a line of divers making their way to the beach after the first dive of the morning. You can actually see a path worn through the coral reef made by thousands of divers over the years. [N1]

There is little that Allan Power does not know about the ship. He has explored well into the interior and is as familiar with the saloons, passageways, berths and engineroom, moreso perhaps than would have been Captain Henry Nelson. He has logged thousands of dives on the *President Coolidge* and has prepared dive plans for all the major points of interest. Remember that the ship lies on her port side and on an incline so to penetrate to the lower decks does not mean a deeper dive, unless the diver swims further toward the stern

Access to the wreck of the *President Coolidge* could not be easier. At low tide, coral heads are exposed, allowing an easy walk to the edge of the reef. From there it is a simple descent down to a rock which has a rope attached to the bow of the ship. Alternatively, a boat may moor to one of the buoys - note how close it is to shore, and how calm are the waters.

of the ship. Timber pannelling and partitions have long deteriorated and the wide staircase amidships has collapsed and deteriorated, leaving an easy access 'tunnel' into the lower decks.

As I first entered these calm waters of the channel I had no idea what to expect. Just what does a huge liner look like underwater? It stretches the imagination to think of a six hundred foot ship ship lying on her side on the seabed. You approach cautiously as if the ship itself posed a danger. With reasonable underwater visibility of 80 feet (at the time) it is of course impossible to appreciate the full 654 feet of the vessel. Like the consumption of a good meal, each morsel must be taken in turn. But I was diving in February, not the best time as rainwater washing down the nearby rivers emptying into the Segond Channel can reduce visibility down to 40 ft. I was lucky. But from June through to mid-November, 150 ft is not unusual. [N2]

At twenty feet down we followed a rope tied to a coral head which led down at a forty degree angle off the reef edge. As we descended the visibility cleared slightly and at forty feet the extremity of the bow loomed into sight. I followed Allan along the starboard bow and slipped down away from the ship to admire the magnificent sight. I immediately spotted the 3-inch starboard gun, its barrel pointed forward, covered in delicate corals. As the wreck is lying on an angle, the hull near the bow is fairly horizontal. Over the curve of the bow, the hull decends at a fourteen degree angle toward the stern. A huge lathe, and a second smaller one, lie on their side on the hull, the result of an aborted attempt at salvage. The shark cage, another reminder of earlier salvage attempts, still lies on the hull, surrounded by hundreds of military shells and smaller cartidges.

Two angelfish followed us as we dropped over the edge of the hull and down the 'side' of the ship and entered number one hold with its cargo of Army jeeps and trucks, their distinctive grills still clearly identifiable. The ship had over 10,000 tons of equipment and supplies on board, including trucks, jeeps, field guns, artillery guns, ammunition and long-range fuel tanks for planes.

First sight - the bow of the *President Coolidge* looms out of the underwater gloom. Note the rope attached to the bow.

Moving on to the second hold, Allan pointed toward a bulkhead and motioned that I should look inside. I could see nothing of interest until I shone my torch between two beams, and saw the crew's barber's chair, on its side still bolted to the decking. The *President Coolidge* has seven holds (see plans); four of these had large central hatches, two each on the bow and stern of A-Deck, and can be entered without difficulty. Holds 3 and 4 were loaded from side cargo doors, whilst hold 5, the refrigeration hold, was loaded via two smaller port and starboard hatches on A-Deck. Hold No. 7, rarely visited because of its depth, contains spare bolt-on propeller blades, a 105mm Howitzer, 37mm anti-tank guns, .50 cal bullets, 30.06 bullets (not .303 as often thought) and a few trucks.

Allan was not rushing but he wanted me to see as much as possible on this first dive. As we swam aft the bridge gradually emerged like an image in a fog. We ascended to level off at one hundred feet and followed the line of the enclosed promenade deck until we reached the first of the lifeboat davits. Allan dropped down into the promenade deck and turning around, pointed a 45-Colt pistol in my direction. It had been carefully secreted amongst the rubble and as I swam off, was discretely returned to its secret place. I found out later that Allan moves the gun from place to place so that divers wont be tempted to give it a new home - in their vest. Some are. None succeed. [N3]

By now our twenty minutes was nearly up and Allan was preparing to return - over the starboard hull. Ladders used by the troops to leave the ship when she was sinking still lay on the hull as they had fifty years ago. The ladders are made of aluminium rungs, and steel links. A school of barracuda and a lone shark circled overhead whilst a rather friendly and inquisitive turtle follows us for a few minutes along the starboard hull.

It seemed like just minutes before we were at the bow again, and heading up the rope to the deco stop. It had been a short dive, shorter than most, but I had

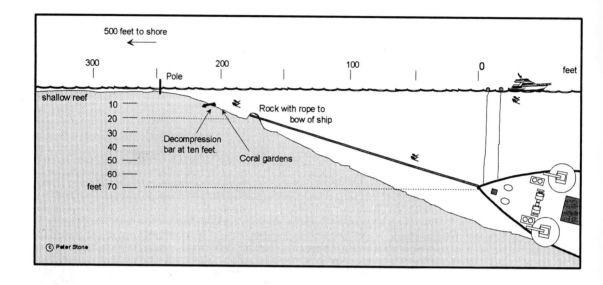

a few days in Santo and I expected to dive every day. Of course I realised that Allan was checking me out. As I returned with plenty of air left in my tank and hadn't demonstrated a total lack of diving ability, I presumed I passed the test. Allan said later that the main problem that visiting divers have is air consumption. He watches them like a hawk, and has a completely independent 'pony bottle' system on his main tank. He has never had to use the 15 cf (cubic ft of air) system himself but visiting divers have had to on the odd occassion. There is also a backup/deco tank at 20ft. Regulator failure has been a problem on a few occassions. Allan commented that he has had problems with some instructors and experienced divers who have run out of air but feel too proud to use his system, or the backup tank on the deco stop, and several have actually come to the surface prematurely.

Allow me to describe the 10 ft 'deco stage'. In Allan's inimitable fashion he has actually created a coral garden so divers would not get bored doing their deco. He has collected coral and even an anemone with its associated clownfish and placed them around another coral bombie. The area is a kaleidescope of colour. Fortunately I was prepared for this and switched over to another camera and another tank for an hour of macro photography. Every few years Allan's 'garden' is destroyed by heavy seas but he keeps coming back and rebuilding it. Thousands of fish await his arrival at the ledge. They know it is time for a feed. Allan has taken down a plastic bag of bread scraps. He is joined by Boris, a huge grouper, named by Allan Power after the horror movie actor Boris Karloff. Allan first saw Boris when he came to Vanuatu in 1969. During these years he grew slightly fatter and looks in better condition, due, no doubt, to the marvellous company he keeps.

For the first dive you tend to be oblivious to the marine life and a shark may pass by as totally unconcerned of you as you are of it. The total mass of the ship is stunning, and an euphoria not unlike narcosis can set in as you swim along its length. The first dive is always the most memorable, particularly if it

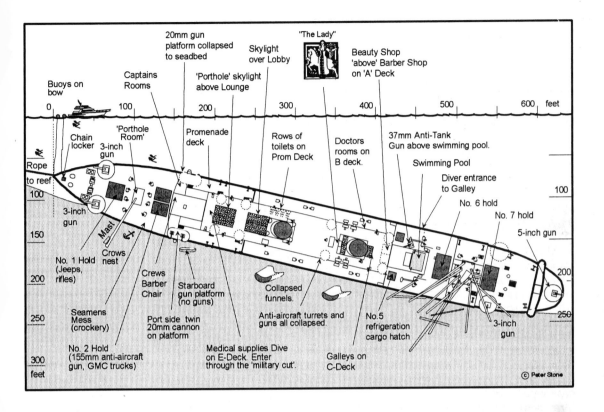

20mm gun platform collapsed to seadbed

Skylight over Lobby

"The Lady"

Beauty Shop 'above' Barber Shop on 'A' Deck

'Porthole' skylight above Lounge

Captains Rooms

Buoys on bow

0   100   200   300   400   500   600 feet

Chain locker

'Porthole Room'

3-inch gun

Promenade deck

Rows of toilets on Prom Deck

Doctors rooms on B deck.

37mm Anti-Tank Gun above swimming pool.

Rope to reef

100

3-inch gun

Swimming Pool

Diver entrance to Galley

No. 6 hold

100

Mast

No. 7 hold

150

Crows nest

5-inch gun

No. 1 Hold (Jeeps, rifles)

200

Crews Barber Chair

Starboard gun platform (no guns)

Collapsed funnels.

No.5 refrigeration cargo hatch

200

250

Seamens Mess (crockery)

Port side twin 20mm cannon on platform

Anti-aircraft turrets and guns all collapsed.

3-inch gun

250

No. 2 Hold (155mm anti-aircraft gun, GMC trucks)

300

feet

Medical supplies Dive on E-Deck. Enter through the 'military cut'.

Galleys on C-Deck

© Peter Stone

includes an introduction to the Lady. Usually however, The Lady has to wait, as the first dive tends not to include a penetration of the interior of the ship. The dive operator will plan a series of dives, and as most divers visit the *President Coolidge* for a dive session over several days, there is no need to be impatient. The Lady will still be waiting, and her company will be all the more enjoyable if the diver is relaxed and confident having had a few dives on the exterior of the wreck.

It is easy to manage two dives per day on the *President Coolidge* even if each dive is to below one hundred feet. Great care must be taken not to induce an attack of the bends which is derived from a combination of time and depth. A second, or 'repetitive' dive must take into account the 'surface interval' between the two dives . By diving at, say, around 9.00 am, a second dive is possible later in the afternoon, at around 3.00 pm, giving sufficent surface interval (of about five hours) to allow a reasonable second dive without the need for excessive decompression time - that is, the time spent at various depths from 20ft to the surface at the end of a dive to allow the nitrogen 'bubbles' to gradually dissipate into the body. For the dives planned by Allan, it is not always necessary, according to the dive tables, to 'do deco' but just on the safe side Allan spends at least twenty minutes at ten feet below the surface. Alan is concervative with his dive plan. And so he, and now other dive masters, should be. His meticulous attention to safety is such that in nearly thirty years of taking thousands of divers through the wreck, he has never had a mishap nor has any one of his diver guests.

That is not however to suggest a perfect record for the *President Coolidge*, for the ship has claimed three lives. A visiting Dutch yachtsman on a world trip with his wife and seven-year-old son anchored over the ship on 5 November 1980 on their way to settling in New Zealand. With no guidance, Oskar Schwitter dived the wreck, taking his young son down to the top of the bridge at about 100 ft. His first dive was trouble-free but curiosity got the better of him. He returned to the wreck after only a few minutes surface interval with the aim of raising an artifact that he had spotted. Fortunately the son stayed on board the yacht. Within minutes of returning from this second dive, the yachtsman collapsed on the deck in agony, writhing and foaming at the mouth. His wife, thinking her husband had had a heart attack, sailed the yacht back to Simonsend's wharf at Luganville where locals put him in the back of a ute to be taken to hospital. He was alive but only just - as the locals put it, he 'had small wind left'. He died on the back of the ute, the result of a massive cerebral bend, ie a bubble in the brain. He was burried next day in the pitiful Luganville cemetery.

Allan had no idea that someone was on 'his' wreck and was called by the harbour-master and police to assist with identifying the cause of death. Allan's knowledge of the wreck was such that he could positively state the depth that the unfortunate diver had descended by identifying the particular artifact raised. Allan recognised a brass cap on board the yacht that had been on the promenade deck at 160ft. Oskar Schwitter had dived back to this depth for the second time within minutes of the first dive. This terrible tragedy, so unnecessary as the *President Coolidge* is such an an 'easy' dive, left Mrs. Schwitter and her son in a terrible dilema. The yacht was sold in Vila and mother and son returned to her homeland, abandoning what was to be a new life for the family. [N4]

Although this was a most unfortunate accident, it does serve to tragically illustrate the need to dive with an experienced guide if you yourself are not fully familiar with the wreck. This was born out in another tragic incident over sixteen years later.

The *Vanuatu Trading Post* reported the incident as follows: 'Two experienced divers visiting Vanuatu on holiday died in an accident on *President Coolidge* in Santo on Friday [8 November 1996]. Australian Andrew Gunst from Cairns, and Stephen Rayner from Wales, United Kingdom were in their early 30s and both experienced divers. Gunst was certified a Master Instructor, had done saturation diving which involves spending long periods of time under water and was also a Commercial Diver. Rayner was an experienced diver qualified in Dive Rescue.' [N5]

An alert went out when they failed to appear at the end of the dive time period. The divers had said they were interested in exploring the engineroom of the ship, so the search commenced there. Santo Dive Tours divemaster David Tischenko, and visiting divemaster Rodney Sales from Dive 2000 in Sydney had the harrowing task of searching the engineroom for the two lost men. Gunst and Rayner had been in the engineroom on previous dives, but always with a guide. This time however they had gone deeper into an even more restricted section of the engineroom, more toward the stern at a depth of 180 ft (55 m), where they were found by Tischenko and Sales. Allan Power was later reported in the *Vanuatu Trading Post* as having said, 'In all my 27 years of diving the Coolidge, I would never go in where they went as it is too dangerous because of the silt.'

Allan Power retrieves a heavily encrusted Colt 45 pistol from the silt. Any movement within the confines of the ship disturbs a fine siltation which can quickly obscure all vision. This is the gun that a diver tried to steal. "You must think I am a f.... idiot", Allan said when he appre-hended the culprit.

'The normal route in the engine room is through a shaft 60 ft. high and 30 ft. wide and down a safe passage but they had gone around tight corners and narrow passageways. They had just got silted out. If you disturb silt in a wreck like that, no matter how powerful your torch is you cannot see a thing and totally lose visibilty.' They had simply ran out of air trying to find a way out.

It was late in the day when Tischenko and Sales found the two bodies, and with insufficient air left in their tanks, a recovery was not possible; another dive immediately would have added to the personal danger of the rescuers. A night dive to the area would have been too dangerous, hence Tischenko and Sales, together with local experienced diver Phil Smith from ER Engineering in Santo and one other diver, Ken Braithwaite, recovered the bodies the following Saturday morning. [N6]

A novice diver/journalist reporting in an Australian newspaper travel supplement wrote, 'It appears that one of the pair has panicked, stiring up a blinding cloud of silt from the floor of the wreck that prevented them from finding their way out. The rescue team found scratch marks on the metal roof where one of the men had tried to claw his way out. His body was found nearby, his fingers bloodied from the struggle. The other was found some distance away, just a few metres from an exit that would have led him to safety.' [N7]

The possibility of accidents such as these were far from my mind when Allan and I returned for our second dive that afternoon. I knew I was in safe hands and all I needed to demonstrate was commonsense, utmost obedience to Allan's directions, and safety was assured. We swam immediately to the bridge, and entered a large window area at the forward section of the once glass-enclosed promenade deck. The feeling was eerie to say the least. On the 'floor' of the deck, which in fact is the wall of the passageway (as the wreck lies on its side), hundreds of steel helmets, rifles and bayonets lay in the soft silt. Allan raised a gas-mask from the silt, and with the sleight-of-hand of a magician, produced a beautiful gold crucifix. Possibly one of the troops had clasped the necklace with silent fear as the ship rocked with the mine explosions. Allan replaced the crucifix where it shall remain for many more divers to see.

In fact it is now illegal to raise any artifact from the wreck. The government of the Republic of Vanuatu have wisely protected the wreck from what is commonly known as the 'wreck basher'. Allan can tell many a humourous story about divers attempting to return with a souvenir. But they rarely succeed as he knows every inch of the wreck and where all the artifacts lie. Allan relates the tale of one diver who tried to outwit him. 'They must think I am wet behind the ears. I knew this guy had taken something by the way he was acting. At the deco stop he went behind a rock. I followed him and he moved on to another rock, so I backed off. On shore he went straight to his dive bag. The others were in on it and all had smug looks on their faces. I waited till everyone had changed and then went up to his bag and pulled out a pistol.'

Allan was fuming, and said to the diver, 'You must think I am a f.... idiot'. He got the point. As I said, Allan does not waste words.

Until the late eighties, Allan Power was the only dive operator taking divers on the wreck, and hence Allan could control pilferage. Now that there are several dive operators visiting the *President Coolidge*, there is a less control. But no dive operator tolerates pilferage and anyone caught could end up in the local prison for more than a few days. [N8]

Divers swim over the starboard hull above the Promenade Deck. Note the rope ladder that would have been used by some of the troops to disembark.

I had no intention of slipping a pistol into my pocket, although I must admit to an inherent desire to take home a souvenir. After swimming for about seventy metres along the promenade deck, Allan dropped down through a doorway and into the interior of the ship. The diver will note no glass now encloses the promenade on the Premenade Deck. All glass was removed when the ship was converted to military use in 1942, and replaced with panels of timber for quite obvious reasons. Glass would have caused untold personal damage if the ship had come under attack. The wood has now rotted, hence allowing easy access to the promenade.

To the inexperienced diver it is here that claustrophobia can take a grip although there is always an exit to be seen in the gloom. But with Allan leading I was not concerned. Within moments we had stopped at a bulkhead, and turning back on ourselves, went through another opening and dropped down into the gloom of another abyss.Allan swung his torch around. As though some invisible hand had switched on a projector lamp, The Lady came to light. What a magnificent sight. Here in the depths of this once luxury liner, here in the First Class Smoking Room where silk jacketed First-Class passengers lounged, talked and read, The Lady stood watching every movement.

Melbourne diver Selena Layden admires *The Lady* in 1992. Note that *The Lady* is actually lying on her side; Selena is posing in a horizontal manner above *The Lady.* For a true orientation of the photo, turn the book sideways. Refer also to the colour section.

Note:
The Lady took a tumble in the early hours of 26 January 2000 after a slight earth tremor.'She' was found that same afternoon, in 60 m. It appears that instead of falling straight down onto a mass of steel at the 'bottom' of the Smoking Room, she glided head first toward the stern, missing all obstructions, and fell through an open door onto fine silt. Aside from a piece of corner frame that remained in the original position there was absolutely no damage. In a joint effort by all dive operators she was raised and taken to a shed behind Hotel Santo, cleaned, and the broken piece replaced. Again, in a joint effort, *The Lady* was returned to the ship within a few days, but not to her original position; she was placed in a more accessible location, above the door to the galley in the first class dining room.

Allan found The Lady in July 1981. Quite surprising actually considering the number of times he had penetrated into the interior of the ship since first diving on the ship in 1969. 'I had been down to the stern through the Smoking Room and suddenly saw this white horse. I had never seen it before. I never saw the Lady - just the horse - probably a bit narced. It took me a couple of dives to find it again'. She is something very special to him, a true love that will never fail. Most visiting divers get to meet 'his' Lady providing they are sufficiently competent and comfortable to dive inside the ship.

The 'Lady on Horseback' is a decorative ceramic three-dimensional wall fresco just inder three feet square. The 'horse' is in actual fact a unicorn (the tusk has broken off), and the Lady is standing not sitting. Despite her submersed state for over fifty years, the baked-on colouring is still vibrant. She really does look magnificent - and so large, or is it the narcosis having some effect?

It is most likely that The Lady and her friend, the Unicorn, were covered by a timber hording to protect them when the ship was converted for military use. All decorative features of the ship were removed where possible, but The Lady was built into the bulkhead of the Smoking Room and could not be easily removed. It would have been simpler to protect her with a timber covering. Over the years, this would have rotted and finally collapsed leaving The Lady exposed. This explains why Allan Power, an extremely observant diver, would have not seen her for twelve years. When found, The Lady had a metal frame but this was puled off 'by bloody stupid divers' who had hung on to the frame.

Indeed narcosis can and does have an affect on many divers meeting The Lady for the first time, particularly prior to the mid-eighties. For those not familiar with the term, *nitrogen narcosis* is caused by the partial pressure of nitrogen gas (the major element in normal air), which, under increasingly greater pressures as would be the case as a diver decends, causes an euphoric state not unlike being intoxicated by alcohol. In this state, the diver can act irrationally and the imagination and memory tend to be affected. The symptoms are 'caused' by depth, but vary from diver to diver, and the diver 'environ-ment', and are relieved immediately by returning to a shallower depth. Be that as it may, many divers became 'narced' when visiting The Lady because of the simple fact that they would need to enter a dark space through a narrow opening and then twist and drop down a further twenty feet. This twisting and turning encouraged narcosis in the less experienced diver, the disorientation adding to the narcotic effect.

Since the mid-eighties however, a much lesser number of divers become even mildly 'narced'. This is simply because a section of the ship had corroded, thus allowing easier access into the interior Smoking Room. The procedure now is simply to swim down the Promenade Deck and enter the First Class Smoking Room on the Premenade Deck level from the forward bulkhead (which has completely corroded), and dropping down to the 150ft (45m) level of The Lady. The diver is always swimming forward and down, and with the divemaster in the lead, a light is shone directly on The Lady, so the diver has a focus and is not dissoriented. 'They home in like moths to a flame,' Allan comments. 'The approach used now lets the divers see The Lady in the distance, gradually approaching while increasing depth. Once they see The Lady they forget their apprehensions.' By having something to concentrate on, this has virtually eliminated narcosis, and although 150ft is ample to bring on the effect, the sense of being narced is often confused with the euphoria of seen The Lady. Thus, a visit to the Lady is not a particularly hazardous dive, and there is always penetrating light and thus an easy exist.

The Lady gazes down at First Class passengers relaxing in the Smoking Room. (See also colour section).

Narcosis has resulted in the estimates of the height of The Lady to be from 2 ft to 10 ft. Sydney diver and photographer Mike Scotland reports that in order to clarify the situation and eliminate further arguments at the bar of the Hotel Santo, one of his group had the foresight to take a measuring tape down in order to check out The Lady's vital statistics. The wall figure is exactly 800 mm by 730 mm (31 1/2 x 28 1/2 inches). [N9]

I don't know if I was narced or not this first time I was introduced to The Lady, but I certainly was experiencing a wave of euphoria. I thought The Lady was about a yard square, so I wasn't too far off the mark. She was, and still is, remarkably beautiful. She stands solemly next to the unicorn with a somewhat glazed look in her eyes. Her full breasts appear to burst from the ruff on her bodice, but contrary to the observation of my Canadian friend Stan Combs, her nipples are not showing. 'I confirmed down there by grope that her nipples are exposed. Sick, I know, but I just had to do it. Blame the nitrogen.' It *was* the nitrogen Stan, but I am sure it was good for her too. I think more than a few divers have touched The Lady for luck, but the dive operators frown in it. At the end of the last dive for the day, a dive operator may lighly brush off any silt on The Lady by simply waving the hand in front of her, but not touching any part of the wall ornament. The silt will settle by the first dive the following day and leave The Lady bright and clean for the photographers.

The Lady as she is now. Note that her hand, and the tusk of the Unicorn, have broken off, and the ornamental frame has perished. (See also colour section). Below is the artificial fireplace, lit with red bulbs to simulate the warmth of the flame.

Just what is the significance of the Lady and the Unicorn? Why would an American shipping line feature something so apparently British? Bill and Bettina Douglas of Brisbane have proposed the theory that the female figure represents Queen Elizabeth 1. This would explain her Elizabethan gown with ruff and also the reddish hair, albeit slightly faded. The presence of two Tudor roses, one above The Lady's left arm and another below the unicorn's left hoof strongly supports the argument; the Tudor rose was adopted by Elizabeth's grandfather Henry VII and appears frequently in portraits of Elizabeth 1. Also - in mythology, only virgins can see unicorns. The *President Coolidge* was built and launched in Virginia, named by Sir Francis Drake in honour of his "Virgin Queen", Elizabeth 1. In view of the fact that no other explanation is available, the Douglas Theory seems most plausible.

Allan Power admires
one of the brass
'mushroom' lamps in the
Continental Lounge.
(See also colour
section).

A powerful torch is necessary to see The Lady in all her glory. She was placed above an artificial fireplace which may be clearly seen by moving horizontally (ie it is at the same depth). In the days when 'first-class' gentleman smoked their pipes and read their newspapers, a warm artificial glow eminated from the fake fire, the illusion of flame coming from red bulbs in the fireplace.

A greater perspective of The Lady can be appreciated by seeing her in juxtaposition with the fireplace, and with some effort, you can imagine the Smoking Room for what it was, even though it is necessary to adjust your vertical perception. I was enthralled by The Lady and can understand why she has become an icon of the wreck of the *President Coolidge*. But like all encounters with beautiful women, time passed far too quickly.

Peering down into the gloom I could see strange lines on the 'bottom' of the Smoking Room at a depth of about 175 ft (53 m) I made the traditional hand signals to Allan as if to say 'what's that'. Allan wrote on his slate - 'bunks'. Of course ! With 5000 troops on board they had to sleep somewhere and even the Smoking Room was not imune to be turned into a dormitory. Down below lay hundreds of triple-decker steel bunks, crumpled together like a pack of fiddlesticks. And below the mass of steel tubing would lie the personal belongings of the hundreds of troops who once called this ship their home for twenty days.

Before exiting the interior of the ship, Allan pointed out the huge seven-ft long by eighteen-inch electric lights in the Smoking Room. Exiting the Smoking Room, we passed by 'The Dunnies', three long rows of toilet bowls, (one row of thirteen, and two rows of fifteen bowls), installed on the starboard side of the ship to satisfy the needs of the troops on board. (There are no equivalent rows on the port side). These were constructed in the passageway from the Smoking Room to the lobby just before the Continental Lounge when the *President Coolidge* was converted to a troopship, and replaced a womens toilet, cabin and passageway. The toilets seem so close to each other that

The Dunnies - three rows of toilets installed in the *President Coolidge* on the Promenade Deck level when the ship was converted to military use.

privacy was virtually non-existent. The four feet high wooden partitions between them have long deteriorated.

We now passed into a huge open area where Allan pointed out the porthole skylights - hundreds of small portholes set in the roof of what was the First-Class Lobby and the Continental Lounge. At least some light can penetrate the darkness at this point. A sign in the lobby provides direction to the 'Promenade Deck'. A mosaic fountain in the lobby is a favourite stop for a photograph. Allan also pointed out the Chinese-style brass 'mushroom' lanterns on the ceiling of the Continental Lounge, and several huge portholes - they are nineteen inches across the glass.

We exited the Continental Lounge through the front windows of the bridge face, and dropping down, swam above the sand bottom next to the port side decking, passing machinery, lamps and deck fittings strewn on the seabed. The masts spear into the seabed at a forty-five degree angle, the crows nests a platform for corals and a habitat for tiny fish.

Allan pointed to a seven ton anchor. It had been strapped to the bow but came crashing down after an earthquake a few years previous. The 3-inch gun on the port side seemed to be resting on the sand, whilst its starboard counterpart hovered high above us. We ascended to the starboard gun precariously canterlivered over the deck. How on earth can this be ? The mountings must be enormous. Allan stoped above the gun (never under it for obvious reasons), and taped on the hull. Within moments two yellow and black pennant fish appeared from nowhere and greeted Allan like some long lost friend. Puzzled, I soon find out why. Allan has picked up some shellfish on the way and proceeds to feed his finned friends. We then dropped down under the bow to see the huge gorgonia and dendrophyllia, then up along the bow rope to a deco stop at ten feet on the edge of the coral ledge. [N10]

When the visibility is good, above the 100 ft mark or so, which it can be at times, a most enjoyable dive may be had by swmming down along the starboard side of the ship, over the promenade deck and then down past the broken-off funnels and on to the seabed. Then look back and see the huge ship spread before you. Two smaller anti-aircraft guns lie on the sand seabed after breaking from their mountings on either side of the bridge. Domestic type fans, fire extinguishers and thousand of other items litter the seabed. Occassionally a large turtle will swim overhead and smaller reef sharks are common. And if The Lady has brough her luck, a dugong may glide over the reef edge.

In subsequent dives over many years I have had the unique pleasure of venturing further and deeper into the ship. When there is only Allan and I, he tends to wander off into some deep nook and cranny. Occassionally we would turn our torches off and in the pitch darkness see a faint stream of light in the distance through a porthole or hatchway. We penetrated deep into the galley of the ship, and explored the engineroom, the bridge and swimming pool. But it is not necessary to penetrate deep in order to enjoy the immensity of the ship. The Continetal Lounge on the Promenade Deck level, with its huge skylights consisting of hundreds of portholes, is an excellent dive and doesn't involve excessive depth.

In recent years, experienced divers have ventured further toward the stern, visiting the first-class swimming pool at a depth of 160ft. Note also that the plans of the ship show a second swimming pool, on B deck. This is Tourist Class swimming pool, and was located above No. 6 hatch. It was probably a canvas pool that could be easily removed to allow access to the hold below.

To dive these deeper stern sections of the ship from shore requires a long swim of over 200 metres each way, which expends energy and uses up valuable air. This is not a dive for the casual visitor. Highly qualified and experienced divers have used battery-powered scooters to reach the stern and the bare prop shafts. The scooters allow a greater distance to be travelled with minimum exertion, but the depth still has to be considered, and a dive to 240 ft is not for the sport diver. [N11]

My first dives of the *President Coolidge* were in 1982. By then, Allan Power's Santo Dive Tours had been established, and diving the wreck was simply a matter of following Allan's directives. This of course has added to the safety aspect of diving the ship. New Zealander Lynton Diggle was engaged to do an underwater film for Ian Lockley's Salvage Pacific in 1974. His recollect-ions give a diferent aspect of diving the *President Coolidge*. Indeed, even getting to Espiritu Santo was an adventure. 'After a two night stopover in New Caledonia at the Chateau Royal, I arrived at Vila in the New Hebrides, the world's only condominium government, run jointly by England and France. There was a choice of customs - Poms to the left, Frogs to the right. There are the two flags of each nation - neither an inch higher than the other - set with a theodolite they say. I took the short flight north, past the Island of Pentecost where the locals leap head first from a 60-odd ft tower with only vines tied to their ankles to break their sickening fall. Past the island of Aoba with smoking volcano, right over the *Salmar* already anchored over the Coolidge site, and landed at Santo. It was a bit chaotic in Luganville, the 'capital', as the previous day they had a larger than usual earthquake, breaking shop windows and throwing stock to the floors.' [N12]

'My first dive with Ian Lockley was to be a sort of Cook's tour of the ship and introduction to the chamber. As we suited up and donned twin 70s Ian explained that if you're inside the ship and you get separated and your torch goes out there's only one thing to do - panic! "Great", I thought, "Bloody

Allan Power swims past the crows nest on the forward mast, which has collapsed to the seabed.

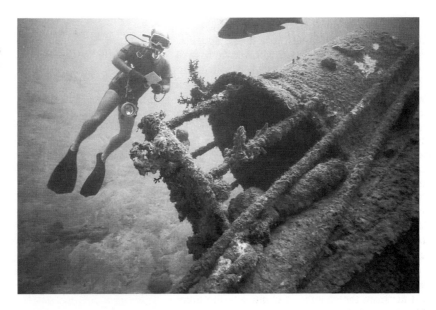

great". As we swam down the 70-odd feet to the starboard side of the Coolidge I just felt plain scared. It wasn't until we reached the enormous expanse of flat steel that was the ship's side that I started to relax. It was vast, a couple of football fields would fit on its side comfortably. I love portholes and here were rows upon rows of them, solid bronze and all intact, measuring 19-inches across the glass. On over the side and my neck was getting a permanent lean trying to bring the ship on an even keel. Down past the bridge at about the 120-ft. mark - there was the maker's plate - along to the foredeck where a massive 3-inch gun stuck out like a great phallic symbol. Back up on the side again Ian pointed out the ship's name, foot-high brass letters stretching some 20-ft towards the bow. I was beginning to grasp the enormity of the ship. We swam over a massive gash in the side where the U.S. Navy salvaged some important equipment and I peered into the black void below.'

Diggle continues: 'There was the shark cage ahead, appearing to sway as it floated anchored to the bilge keel. We went in and Ian demonstrated the hooka air supply inside. We had been down over an hour below the 100 ft mark and I guessed Ian's air was getting low. I followed Ian like a leach up the anchor chain of the submersible decompression chamber. We stopped at the 30 ft. mark and consulted the U.S. Navy tables on a plastic card. Ian went on up past a school of large tropical barracuda to the chamber entrance, casually hung his bottles on a snap hook and free ascended up into the chamber. Thank God he couldn't see me floundering with two buoyant 70s which immediately flew above my head when I undid the strap, nor able to watch me try to go up the ladder with my regulator neck strap still on. I finally emerged into the eerie light of the chamber and tried to look cool and nonchalant. In 20 years of diving I'd never had a dive like this one and the adrenalin had been working overtime. I was pleased to learn that none of the divers regarded their first dive there a breeze. Once inside we took off our suits and made ourselves comfortable in the humid atmosphere.'

'Ian phoned up for some music and Burt Bacharat came thumping through the speaker. Bole, one of the Fijian boys, came down to take our bottles back for refilling and to collect our suits for drying. We poured a drink and stretched out plans of the Coolidge to trace our dive. Time went amazingly quickly and Ian was soon cranking the turfor to raise the chamber to the 10 ft. level. We had something over half an hour here then with only mask and fins swam out and up to the *Salmar* above. A hot shower, a coffee and a couple of hours later we were ready again for our second dive.' [N13]

Lynton Diggle again: 'Ross Jenkins, a fellow New Zealander, [an ex-wrestler and 'an excellent companion both above and below the water'] joined Ian and I for my second dive, this time to be inside the ship. My initial heebies had faded and I set off confidently to the ship's side. Here, not far from the chamber's chain was the main gangway entrance - a sort of 7 x 5 ft hole that dropped straight down to nearly 200 ft. on the other side of the ship. It was like going down a lift well head first. The visibility had returned almost to normal and our torches pierced the crystal water. This was a storybook wreck - not the heaps of twisted junk on storm-tossed coasts that I was accustomed to. The *President Coolidge* is virtually intact, each deck level clearly definable. We peered into corridors and passenger accommodation and down to the crockery department. Plates, cups and glasses were heaped up in stacks enough to stock a hotel.'

The shark cage was positioned on the hull of the *President Coolidge* by Ian Lockley in preparation for the oil recovery project, but was never used. It is now a haven for fish, and the curious diver.

'Here in the vestibule, where once the purser would have directed first class passengers, and wealthy Americans would have sat and gazed at the huge ornate fountain, the expensive brass lamps and fittings were still hanging free on their wiring. A chandelier was lying at a crazy angle, it's patterned glass still visible beneath a layer of crud and coral. I sat on a beam, torch in hand, and just surveyed the scene. Ross, a perpetual comic, was trying on a gas mask for size and talking away through his mouthpiece. Ian was cleaning the fountain base with his gloves - its mosaic tiles glistened gold in our torch light. I was busy planning angles and shots when I heard Ross's sonic reserve going off. I glanced at my depth gauge - 120 ft. We quietly drifted to the shaft entrance, up and out to the bright light and up to the 30-ft. mark to study the tables. Decompression time seemed halved in the chamber whenever Ross was with us, his endless mirth, good humour and fund of dirties had us at times almost rolling out the hatch with laughter. I've watched him almost drown trying to laugh with a regulator in his mouth.'

'One memorable dive took Ian, Ross and myself into the aft vestibule at the 150 ft. level. Another black shaft, this time past the Post Office with its empty pigeon holes. Letters, picked up for Santo from wives and girlfriends, long since disintegrated in the silt. Down we dropped to 180 ft. Here was the first class dining room, table bases sticking out from the floor which formed the right hand wall. An electric fan lay in the corner and Ian picked up some heavy serving dishes covered in black silver sulphide from the plating. Yet further down the shaft we dropped past corridors and cabins. Beautiful ship's fittings were caught in the torch beams. Daylight was long gone. I looked at my gauge - 210 ft. My decompression meter registering a 40 ft. stop! I had never dived below 150 ft. before, yet here I was at two-ten by torchlight inside an enormous ship - I felt tremendous yet very aware that I couldn't possibly be operating on all six at this depth. Further through the ship we went. Suddenly an enormous hole opened up and we could see daylight. We were swimming out the aft hold to the deck. Aircraft wing tanks - tyres, cases, all the impedimenta of war were strewn out the hold. On to the deck and the stubby remains of the aft wheel and binnacle. The visibility was about 80-ft. As I stood behind the wheel and looked along the deck. I could make out both sides of her 81-ft. beam. The *President Coolidge* is one hell of a shipwreck.' [N14]

Yes, I must agree. The *President Coolidge* is indeed one incredible shipwreck. And all but for the want of a staple. [N15]

DIVING THE *PRESIDENT COOLIDGE* - IS IT SAFE?

Although the deaths of the three divers should not be dismissed lightly, the wreck of the *President Coolidge* is a safe dive. This can be confirmed by the thousands of dive hours spent on the wreck by thousands of divers. This is not to suggest that a measure of complaceny could be adopted, for the safety record has only been maintained by the dilligence of all the dive operators who now visit the wreck, and the ability of their clients..

If I am prepared to judge the ship as a safe dive, I should perhaps elaborate on my assessment. By safe I mean that under accepted sport diving standards of skill, the wreck *per se* does not significantly add to the danger of the dive. If a diver is fully trained to at least Open Water standard of a recognised school standard, (but preferably a higher standard), and has had sufficient dives to make him or her confident and aware of their own limitations; if a diver is properly equipped with diving gear of a high quality and air of an acceptable standard; and if the diver feels comfortable in the water and demonstrates a level of common sence, the ability to dive with a group and a negligible measure of bravado, then the *President Coolidge* is indeed a safe dive. In fact, I would rate it as one of the easiest (and of courst most enjoyable) dive sites in my twenty years of diving.

It goes without saying that the dive operator, and in particular the divemaster leading the dive, must demonstrate an unconscionable desire for quality leadership and possess an extremely high level of ability. As important perhaps is the ability of the divemaster to sense impending problems and to prevent a disaster from happening rather than resolve the problem when it does. The ease of entry from shore, the positive orientation and sence of direction at all times, the generally excellent visibility, the lack of significant current when on the wreck, and the back-up systems for air, all add to the enjoyment and safety of the dive. Most dives on the wreck will be beyond 100 ft (30 m) so should be treated with the respect that a deep dive demands. This means precise attention to dive planning with appropriate decompression stops.

Having said this, I don't believe it is appropriate for a novice, who has just qualified, to dive the *President Coolidge* unless additional attention to safety is considered. It would be inadviseable to quantify the number of previous

MR. PRESIDENT - ALLAN POWER

If ever a man should be called Mr President it is Allan Power. Since arriving in Luganville in 1969 to assist with the removal of the propellers from the *President Coolidge*, Allan has logged over 15,000 dives on the ship, for a bottom time of over one and a half *years*. He knows every inch of the ship, and has taken over 20,000 divers from all over the world to visit The Lady.

Allan Power was born in 1933 in Sydney. In 1949 he was at Balmoral when he spied a man spearfishing and immediately placed a Sheen speargun on lay-buy for £3-10. In 1953 Allan finished his apprenticeship as a pastry-cook, but leaving what he called 'a crazy business', got himself a job in a foam rubber factory. Allan worked there for no less than fifteen years, from 1953 to 1968. He recalls, 'I soon realised in these very early days of Australian diving that indescriminate spearfishing was a waste. I saw many big grouper shot off Heron Island - and all wasted. I became sick and tired of the killing of big fish, so I concentrated on natural history, reading the masters - Dakin, Grant, Whitley, Roughley.'

In 1954 he went on holidays for four weeks, travelling to Lord Howe Island by flying boat, and was one of the first to dive this magnificent island.

In 1956, Allan bought his first underwater camera for £300 - a Rolleimarin, and went to Heron Island on the Great Barrier Reef every year during the early sixties. In those days spearfishing competitions were held on Heron Island during the 'off' season to encourage divers to visit the tourist resort. On one occassion a 450 lb grouper was taken off Wistari. 'A total waste', Allan recalls, who was by now well into underwater photography, so much so that in the mid-1960s, he won the coveted Levanto prize for underwater photography in Italy. [N19]

By 1967 Allan's expertise as an underwater photographer had developed to the point where book publishers were asking for photographs, and he spent five months on Nor'west Island in the Capricorn Group, Great Barrier Reef. He left the rubber factory in 1968 to concentrate full-time on underwater photography, stationed on Tryon island for five months. This resulted in the best selling publication *The Great Barrier Reef*, published by the Hamlyn Group.

Back in Australia in 1969, an opportunity arose for Allan to visit Vanuatu with old spearfishing friend Barry May on his recently acquired *Pacific Seal*. In November 1969, Allan left Sydney on what was to be a trip setting his destiny. Arriving in December, Allan worked with Barry May's salvage team on the *President Coolidge* for a year or so, successfully raising both propellers from the wreck. When the *Pacific Seal* went off to the Solomon Islands for further salvage, Allan stayed on in Santo mainly for the photography. He observed that were many different species of corals and fishes to that which he had seen on the Great Barrier Reef. Allan was now selling his photographs to private authors, publishers and libraries, and lived off his photography using two Rolleimarines and bulb flash units. During these early days on Espiritu Santo he dived with a hookah unit from a 14-ft Quintrex aluminium boat powered by a 33 hp motor.

In 1978 Allan was offered the position of Diving Director at the new resort on Bokissa Island. A few divers were starting to come up to Espiritu Santo to dive the *President Coolidge* but the resort was not doing too well and in 1979, Allan returned to Luganville as the tourist trade was virtually non-existant. He had however the foresight to remain in Santo, and established his own dive operation. But trouble was brewing on Espiritu Santo, and in 1980 the Coconut War erupted, a revolution stage-managed by Jimmy Stevens. Needless to say it was rather quiet on the *President Coolidge* for a few years but Allan stuck it out until the tourist divers started coming back a few years after independance. Allan went back as a caretaker of Bokissa in July 1980, remaining till early 1981. By this time New Zealand divers had 'discovered' the *President Coolidge* and diver numbers were increasing.

Australian divers soon became aware of the *President Coolidge* through a number of articles in skindiving magazines. With the development of organised dive travel, established in Australia by the late Anthony Newley of Always Travel in Melbourne, and promoted extensively by Janis Stone at Aquarius/Dive Travel Australia, diving 'the world's largest accessible shipwreck' became just a matter of a phone call. The *President Coolidge* had been 'rediscovered'.

Allan recalls, 'I wasn't initially interested in taking people on dives - more interested in photos. Then more and more divers came. I (initially) didn't have a compressor. A Frenchman here, Martine, had a compressor and

tanks. New Zealanders started overseas dive travel - organised groups - long before the Australians. Sometimes twenty-five or thirty at a time. 1982 to 1985 were the boom years - 45 groups booked one year, many from Aquarius. It made the Hotel Santo financially viable - everyone gained - bus drivers, taxi, restaurants - they all rely on the Coolidge. It brought in millions of dollars into the economy.'

Since Allan Power established Santo Dive Tours in Luganville, thousands of divers from throughout the world have been through the *President Coolidge* under his guidance without a single accident. Allan lives opposite the Hotel Santo in a comfortable and tastefully decorated home overlooking Segond Channel. There are no photographs of his on the walls, and the visitor is generally unaware of Allan Power's achievements in underwater photography. Over a coffee and a bun at his home after a dive, The Lady and the President dominate the conversation. Allan will wax lyrical about his beloved ship, but there is no mention of the past, and little offered on his personal life.

It is difficult to estimate just how long Allan has spent in the *President Coolidge* over the past twenty-eight years. He spent 12 minutes a day bottom time, plus decompression time of some thirty minutes, for two months raising the props, and 660 hours on the Lockley oil job alone. Also, it has been estimated that Allan has done over 15,000 dives on the *President Collidge* for a total dive time of about year and a half. Little wonder he is affectionately called 'Mr. President'. Asked in 1982 what he saw as his future, he laconically replied, 'to last out as long as I can.'

And this he has done remarkably well. After a five-way heart bypass, Allan still dives his beloved ship, but not as frequently as before. Dive guides take over his reponsibilities at Santo Dive Tours, and there are other dive operators in town who lessen the load.

The author first met Allan Power back in 1982. He hasn't changed much over the years. Indeed, Allan is one of those mercurial souls who will never age. At the expense of uttering a cliche, it could be said that Allan Power is now a legend in his own lifetime. Considering the number of total dive-hours on the wreck that he has been directly responsible for, all without any incident, Allan's achievements are unique and should there ever be a diver's Hall of Fame (God forbid!) Allan's balding pate and cheeky grin would have to greet the visitors at the door.

dives that raises a novice to an 'experienced' diver, but the concept of attending a dive training course and immediately diving the wreck is fraut with danger. If circumstances are such that this is inevitable, then the novice should be 'hand-held' by a divemaster on a one-to-one basis, particularly on the first dive. The novice and the dive operators owe that much to themselves and other divers and dive operators.

My comments have been based on access to the *President Coolidge* from shore. Vertical diving from a dive boat anchored above the wreck is another matter. As any good divemaster is aware, the anxiety factor increases significantly in open water, and added precautions need to be made. There is also the possibility of a surface current in Segond Channel which needs to be considered. Open water decompression is no major problem provided the diver has something to grasp and to maintain constant depth, but it is certainly not as much fun as pottering around on a coral garden. And because of this there may be a tendency to limit the decompression time. An extra ten minutes at ten feet on a reef is much more pleasant than hanging from a line. For the experienced diver however, vertical diving does have the advantage of a quicker accent to a deeper part of the wreck, with maximum true bottom time.

Springfield rifles litter the wreck of the *President Coolidge*. Note the extensive crustation of calcium-base products that engulf metal objects after immersion in seawater.

The wrecksite of the *President Coolidge* is very easy to find, from shore and sea, and it is a simple matter to moor right over the wreck (anchoring is not permitted), or drive to the shore clearing. But if you do decide to go visit The Lady take with you the gifts of common sence and skill. Don't dive unless you see one of the dive operators in Luganville first. Experience in diving is no substitute for local knowledge of the ship. It is strongly recommended that you always dive with a divemaster/guide, but if circumstance and opportunity are such that you choose not to, do not penetrate the ship other than through and along the promenade deck, and exercise every caution and consideration for a deep wreck dive. Although it is not necessary to 'book' with a dive operator prior to arrival, it is nevertheless recommended as you may find that that the dive operator has his or her hand's full with a large group, and a slight change in the schedule by a day or so may be beneficial. As the site is a designated National Park, there are strict laws that prevent anchoring over the wreck. Mooring buoys have been placed on the wreck for use by the registered dive operators. These are not for public use.

As previously mentioned, an acceptable plan is to have a dive in the morning around 9.00am and a second dive at about 3.00pm. This gives a reasonable surface interval between dives allowing for a bit of local sightseeing, or relaxing at the hotel or resort. A general shore dive profile consists of about twenty minutes bottom time on the wreck, generally defined as being from the time of descend down the rope to the bow and back to the

This spare anchor was strapped to the deck near the bow but became dislodged during an earthquake and crashed to the seabed.

bow, and up to thirty minutes decompression time at various depths at the reef edge. Boat dives may have a number of dive profiles depending on the depth. Many divers use dive computers which are particularly useful in determining a dive plan for repetitive dives. But at all times, follow the plan and instructions of the divemaster.

The size of the ship is awesome, and it would take many dives to thoroughly explore the wreck. Most divers visiting Luganville have pre-paid for a set number of dives, or have a limited time period over which to do their diving. A ten-dive package gives some opportunity to see most of the main sections of the ship, and because of the limited time and hence number of dives possible, dive operators have selected specific dive plans to ensure that the best areas arevisited within the constraints of what is acceptable for normal sport diving. Visibility can range from 15 to 35 metres. The sea is always warm and usually flat calm. A light 3mm wet-suit or a lycra suit is suitable for diving. Shorts and a T-shirt are possible but discouraged as there are a few stinging hydroids on the ship, and even a slight scratch on a sharp piece of rusty metal can end the dive trip if not treated immediately for infection. I have always used an anti-biotic ointment (and powder) called Neosporen, which is readily available. Most experienced divers bring their full kit except weights and tanks of course. Dive computers are not mandatory but are extremely useful. Octopus rigs (twin regulators) are sometimes required by individual dive operators, and are now common equipment in any case. All dive operators have equipment to hire, so don't be put off from diving the *President Coolidge* because you do not want to lug a dive bag of gear half way around the world. Dive operators will require proof of qualifications and experience, hence at least an Open Water dive card is mandatory, and a logbook is always accepted as proof of experience.

A final word of caution concerns the use of scooters. In the hands of an experinced diver, they can be loads of fun and increase the safety of the dive through limited exersion. But in the wrong hands they can encourage bravado and could lead to tragedy. Scooters are not a panacea for deep diving.

CUT-AWAY THROUGH CENTRE LINE OF SHIP

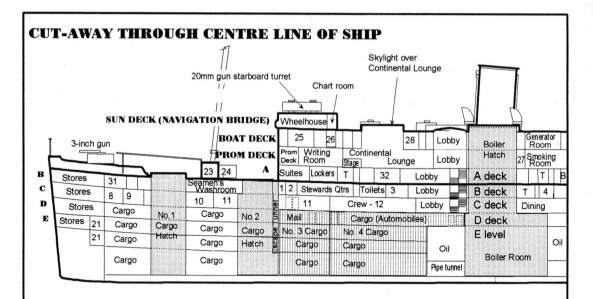

20mm gun starboard turret

Chart room

Skylight over
Continental Lounge

SUN DECK (NAVIGATION BRIDGE) Wheelhouse

3-inch gun

BOAT DECK

PROM DECK

KEY

1. Doctor's Office (offset behind crew's barber shop).
2. Crew's barber.
3. Purser's Office.
4. Musician's Balcony overlooking First Class Dining Rm.
5. Tourist Class Barber Shop.
6. Tourist canteen.
7. Steerage Social Hall (surrounds Light Vent. Shaft).
8. Brig (on port side).
9. Steward's washroom.
10. Steward's Messroom.
11. Automobile space (surrounding No. 2 Cargo Hatch).
    Entry via side doors.
12. Crew and Musician's Quarters, Barber, Toilets, Linen.
13. Tourist Galley and Main Galley.
14. Steerage (Third Class) accommodation.
15. Third Class Dining Saloon.
16. Chinese Storerom.
17. Refrigerated Cargo.
18. Tourist Baggage.
19. Steerage toilets.
20. Cargo area or Steerage Passenger accommodation.
21. Refrigerated Cargo.
22. Chain Locker.
23. Power Station 4.
24. 3-inch gun (on starboard side).
25. Senior Officer's quarters. (Captain's Office and Room
    on starboard side; Chief Officer on port side).
26. Gyro Compass Room in Officer's Lobby.
27. Beverage Room.
28. Clerk's Office.
29. Deck pantry.
30. Power Sub-Station 3.
31. White Boys (thats what it says on the plans!)
32. Novelty Shop.
33. Captain's Office.
34. Captain's Cabin
35. First Officer's Cabin.
36. Chief Officer's Cabin.
37. Third Officer's Cabin.
38. Radio Operators.
39. Cadets.
40. Spare Room.
41. Clerks.
42. Sub-Staion No. 1
43. Engineer's Room.
44. Engineer's Room.
45. Engineer's Log Room.
46. First Assistant Engineer's Room
47. Chief Engineer's Room.
48. Second Assistant Engineer.
49. Electrician.
50. Third Assistant Engineer.
51. Second and Third Assistant Electrician.
52. Junior Engineer.
53. Deck pantry
54. Battery Room (Emergency Generator Room).
55. Clerks' Rooms.
56. Second Officer..
57. Junior Officers.
58. Tourist Purser.
59. First Class Purser.
60. Theraputic Room.

© Peter Stone

Note new location of *The Lady* - see page 181.

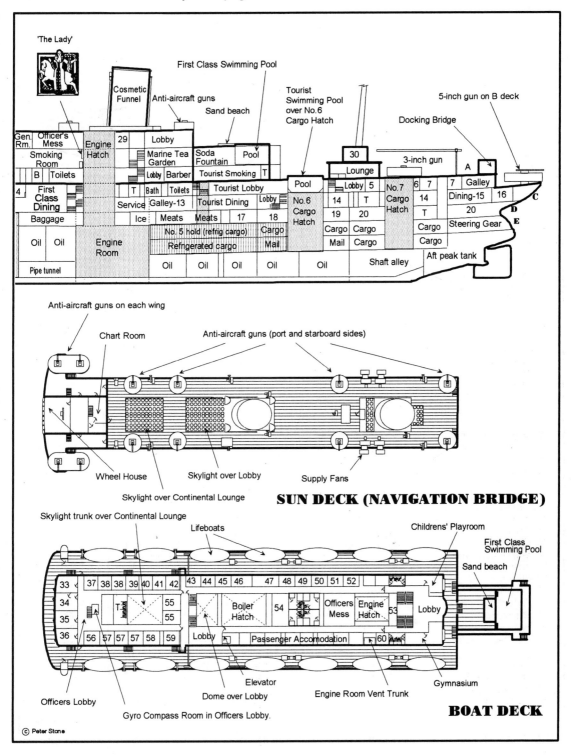

SUN DECK (NAVIGATION BRIDGE)

BOAT DECK

© Peter Stone

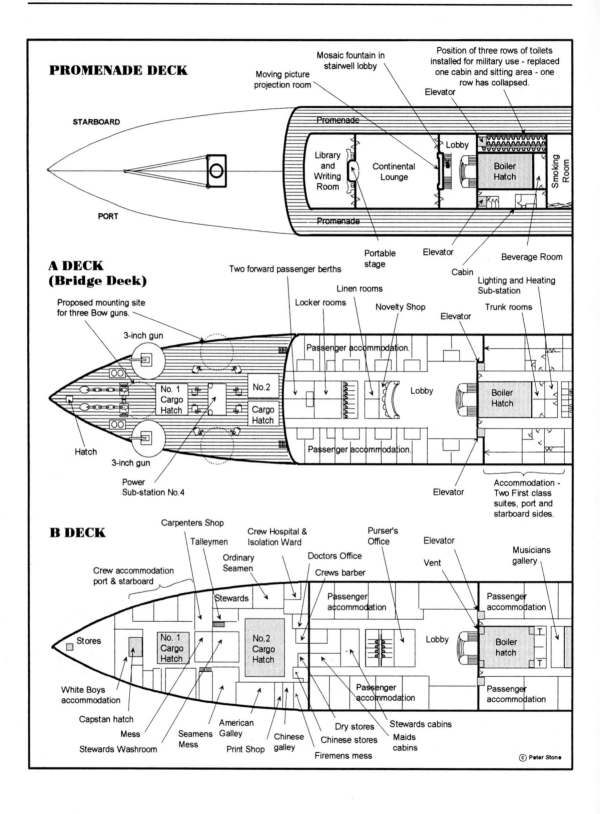

PROMENADE DECK

STARBOARD

PORT

Mosaic fountain in stairwell lobby

Moving picture projection room

Position of three rows of toilets installed for military use - replaced one cabin and sitting area - one row has collapsed.

Elevator

Promenade

Lobby

Library and Writing Room

Continental Lounge

Boiler Hatch

Smoking Room

Promenade

Portable stage

Elevator

Cabin

Beverage Room

A DECK (Bridge Deck)

Two forward passenger berths

Locker rooms

Linen rooms

Novelty Shop

Elevator

Lighting and Heating Sub-station

Trunk rooms

Proposed mounting site for three Bow guns.

3-inch gun

Passenger accommodation.

No. 1 Cargo Hatch

No.2 Cargo Hatch

Lobby

Boiler Hatch

Hatch

Passenger accommodation.

3-inch gun

Power Sub-station No.4

Elevator

Accommodation - Two First class suites, port and starboard sides.

B DECK

Carpenters Shop

Talleymen

Crew Hospital & Isolation Ward

Purser's Office

Elevator

Musicians gallery

Ordinary Seamen

Doctors Office

Vent

Crew accommodation port & starboard

Crews barber

Stewards

Passenger accommodation

Passenger accommodation

Stores

No. 1 Cargo Hatch

No.2 Cargo Hatch

Lobby

Boiler hatch

White Boys accommodation

Passenger accommodation

Passenger accommodation

Capstan hatch

Mess

American Galley

Dry stores

Stewards cabins

Seamens Mess

Chinese galley

Chinese stores

Maids cabins

Stewards Washroom

Print Shop

Firemens mess

© Peter Stone

Note new location of *The Lady* - see page 181.

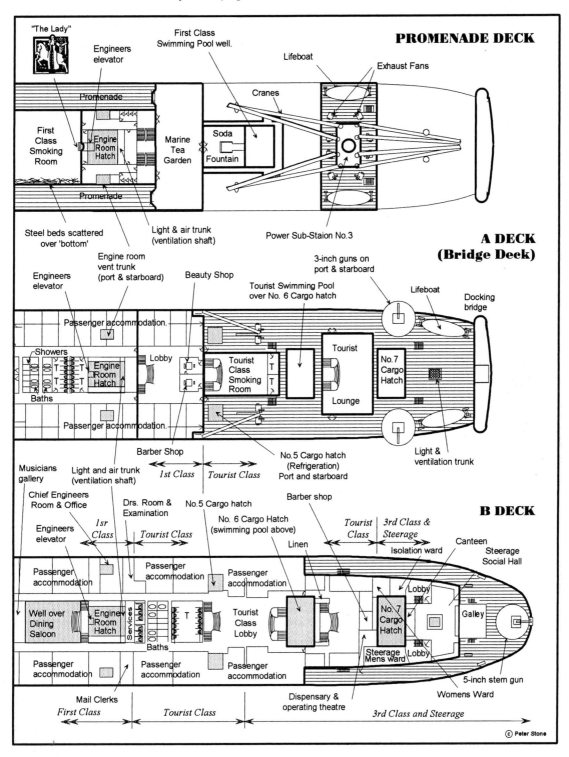

PROMENADE DECK

"The Lady"
Engineers elevator
First Class Swimming Pool well.
Lifeboat
Exhaust Fans
Cranes
Promenade
First Class Smoking Room
Engine Room Hatch
Marine Tea Garden
Soda Fountain
Promenade

A DECK (Bridge Deck)

Steel beds scattered over 'bottom'
Light & air trunk (ventilation shaft)
Power Sub-Staion No.3
Engine room vent trunk (port & starboard)
Engineers elevator
Beauty Shop
3-inch guns on port & starboard
Tourist Swimming Pool over No. 6 Cargo hatch
Lifeboat
Docking bridge
Passenger accommodation.
Showers
Lobby
Engine Room Hatch
Tourist Class Smoking Room
Tourist
No.7 Cargo Hatch
Baths
Lounge
Passenger accommodation.
Light & ventilation trunk
Barber Shop
No.5 Cargo hatch (Refrigeration) Port and starboard
1st Class | Tourist Class

B DECK

Musicians gallery
Light and air trunk (ventilation shaft)
Chief Engineers Room & Office
Drs. Room & Examination
No.5 Cargo hatch
Barber shop
No. 6 Cargo Hatch (swimming pool above)
Tourist Class | 3rd Class & Steerage
Canteen
Steerage Social Hall
Engineers elevator
1sr Class
Tourist Class
Linen
Isolation ward
Passenger accommodation
Passenger accommodation
Passenger accommodation
Lobby
Well over Dining Saloon
Engine Room Hatch
Services
Tourist Class Lobby
No.7 Cargo Hatch
Galley
Baths
Steerage Mens ward
Lobby
Passenger accommodation
Passenger accommodation
Passenger accommodation
5-inch stern gun
Womens Ward
Mail Clerks
Dispensary & operating theatre
First Class | Tourist Class | 3rd Class and Steerage

© Peter Stone

198

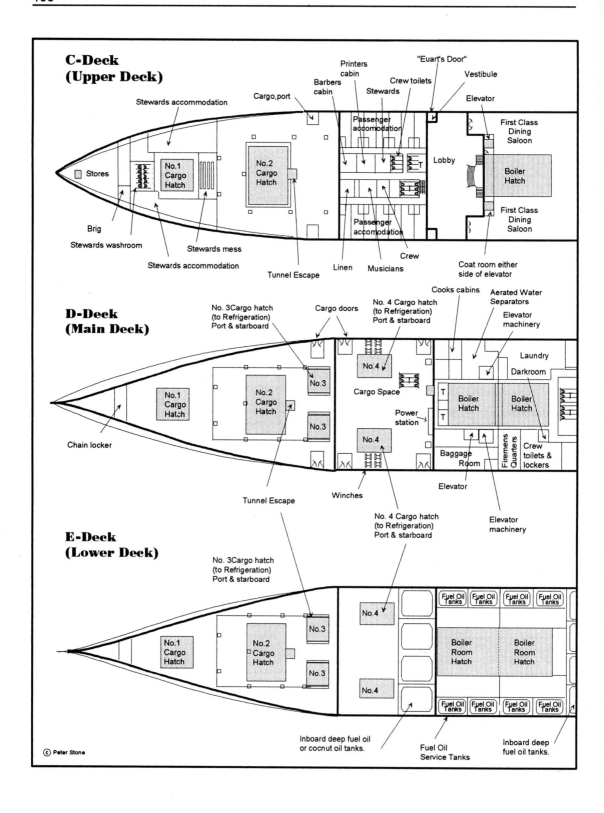

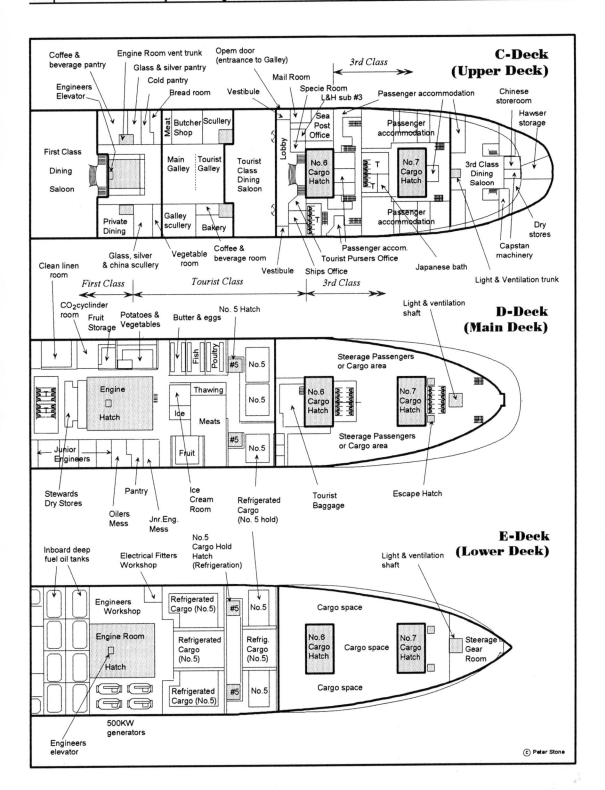

C-Deck (Upper Deck)

Coffee & beverage pantry
Engine Room vent trunk
Opem door (entraance to Galley)
3rd Class
Glass & silver pantry
Mail Room
Engineers Elevator
Cold pantry
Specie Room L&H sub #3
Passenger accommodation
Chinese storeroom
Bread room
Vestibule
Hawser storage

First Class Dining Saloon
Meat
Butcher Shop
Scullery
Main Galley
Tourist Galley
Tourist Class Dining Saloon
Lobby
Sea Post Office
No.6 Cargo Hatch
T
T
T
Passenger accommodation
No.7 Cargo Hatch
3rd Class Dining Saloon

Private Dining
Galley scullery
Bakery
Passenger accommodation
Dry stores
Capstan machinery

Clean linen room
Glass, silver & china scullery
Vegetable room
Coffee & beverage room
Vestibule
Ships Office
Passenger accom.
Tourist Pursers Office
Japanese bath
Light & Ventilation trunk

D-Deck (Main Deck)

First Class
Tourist Class
3rd Class

CO_2 cyclinder room
Fruit Storage
Potatoes & Vegetables
Butter & eggs
No. 5 Hatch
Light & ventilation shaft

Fish
Poultry
#5
No.5
Steerage Passengers or Cargo area

Engine Hatch
Thawing
No.5
No.6 Cargo Hatch
No.7 Cargo Hatch

Ice
Meats
Junior Engineers
#5
Fruit
No.5
Steerage Passengers or Cargo area

Stewards Dry Stores
Pantry
Ice Cream Room
Refrigerated Cargo (No. 5 hold)
Tourist Baggage
Escape Hatch
Oilers Mess
Jnr.Eng. Mess

E-Deck (Lower Deck)

No.5 Cargo Hold Hatch (Refrigeration)
Light & ventilation shaft

Inboard deep fuel oil tanks
Electrical Fitters Workshop

Engineers Workshop
Refrigerated Cargo (No.5)
#5
No.5
Cargo space

Engine Room Hatch
Refrigerated Cargo (No.5)
Refrig. Cargo (No.5)
No.6 Cargo Hatch
Cargo space
No.7 Cargo Hatch
Steerage Gear Room

Refrigerated Cargo (No.5)
#5
No.5
Cargo space

500KW generators
Engineers elevator

© Peter Stone

Note new location of *The Lady* - see page 181.

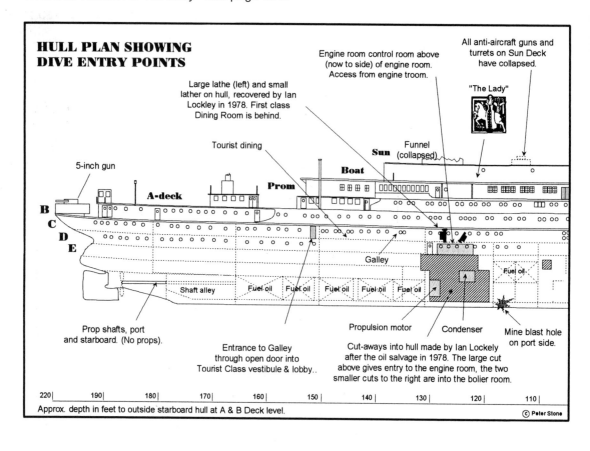

HULL PLAN SHOWING DIVE ENTRY POINTS

Engine room control room above (now to side) of engine room. Access from engine troom.

All anti-aircraft guns and turrets on Sun Deck have collapsed.

Large lathe (left) and small lather on hull, recovered by Ian Lockley in 1978. First class Dining Room is behind.

"The Lady"

Tourist dining

Funnel (collapsed)

Sun

Boat

Prom

5-inch gun

A-deck

B
C
D
E

Galley

Fuel oil

Shaft alley

Fuel oil · Fuel oil · Fuel oil · Fuel oil · Fuel oil

Prop shafts, port and starboard. (No props).

Propulsion motor

Condenser

Mine blast hole on port side.

Entrance to Galley through open door into Tourist Class vestibule & lobby..

Cut-aways into hull made by Ian Lockely after the oil salvage in 1978. The large cut above gives entry to the engine room, the two smaller cuts to the right are into the bolier room.

220| 190| 180| 170| 160| 150 | 140 | 130 | 120 | 110 |

Approx. depth in feet to outside starboard hull at A & B Deck level.

Ⓒ Peter Stone

The hull of the *President Coolige,* clearly showing the enclosed Promenade Deck. Note also the two open doors, both on C deck. The stern door provides entry to the Tourist Class lobby, whilst the forward door is for First Class passengers. This became known as Euart's Door.

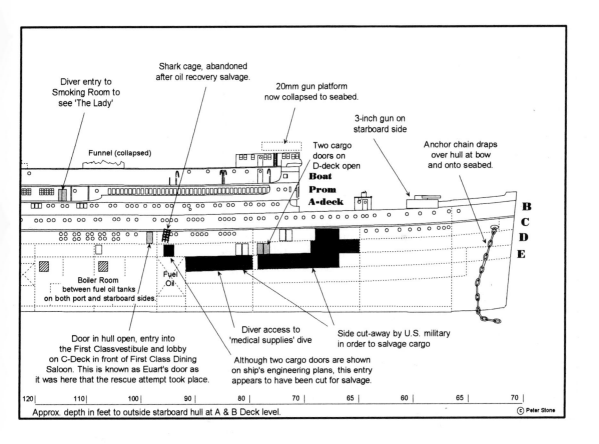

Diver entry to
Smoking Room to
see 'The Lady'

Shark cage, abandoned
after oil recovery salvage.

20mm gun platform
now collapsed to seabed.

3-inch gun on
starboard side

Anchor chain draps
over hull at bow
and onto seabed.

Funnel (collapsed)

Two cargo
doors on
D-deck open

Boat
Prom
A-deck

B
C
D
E

Boiler Room
between fuel oil tanks
on both port and starboard sides.

Fuel
Oil

Door in hull open, entry into
the First Classvestibule and lobby
on C-Deck in front of First Class Dining
Saloon. This is known as Euart's door as
it was here that the rescue attempt took place.

Diver access to
'medical supplies' dive

Side cut-away by U.S. military
in order to salvage cargo

Although two cargo doors are shown
on ship's engineering plans, this entry
appears to have been cut for salvage.

| 120| | 110| | 100 | | 90 | | 80 | | 70 | | 65 | | 60 | | 65 | | 70 | |

Approx. depth in feet to outside starboard hull at A & B Deck level.

© Peter Stone

The *President Coolidge*
exposes her lower hull
as she lies on a forty-five
degree angle. Most of
the crew have escaped
by now. Note the anchor
chain, and the rope
ladders. The gun turret
above the bridge is also
clearly seen. It is in the
area shown that the
U.S. Navy cut into the
ship in order to salvage
cargo from Holds 2, 3
and 4.

DIVE SITES

Important Note: Dive profiles indicated here are shown as an example only and should not be used for actual dive planning. Visiting divers must follow the dive plan outlined by the divemaster. When using the words 'top' and 'bottom' the author means in a vertical sense as the ship is now lying. Hence, the top of the bridge would actually be the starboard wing. Within the ship, the 'top' and 'bottom' will be walls and bulkheads, whilst the 'sides' will be ceilings and floors. If only the ship had slipped off the reef upright we wouldn't have this problem! The use of 'he' and 'himself' is meant to include both sexes. The mention of US Navy Dive Tables does imply a recommendation, and indeed, more conservative tables should be used by sport scuba divers. The decompression times mentioned are as an indication only, to give further description and meaning to the text and must never be used as a basis for a dive plan. Likewise the depths indicated are for illustration only, and should not be used for dive planning - refer to the divemaster for details. There is a 3 ft (1m) rise and fall of the tide, so reported depths can vary slightly. Descriptions given are predominantly shore dives, which vary from boat dives only in their access to the dive site mentioned.

THE PROMENADE DECK

This tends to be one of the first dives for a visiting diver as it does not involve penetration of the body of the ship, and yet gives an awesome appreciation of the size of the ship and what she has to offer. Slip down the rope to the bow, saying hello to Boris and the angel fish on the way, and along the side of the ship past the 3-inch gun to the front of the bridge. Enter through one of the windows into the Promenade Deck. The Promenade Deck was restricted to first class passengers in the days when the *President Coolidge* sailed the northern Pacific, but as a troopship, it was lined with bunks. The promenade deck was enclosed with glass, but the panels have all gone so entry to the deck is no problem. Avoid the hydroids growing on the structure as they can cause an annoying sting.

When the troops abandoned ship many tried to take rifles, helmets and person effects with them, but were ordered to abandon anything and everything for good reason. Apart from the possibility of drowning the possessor of such items, there was also the opportunity of dropping something on some poor unsuspecting soldier clinging desperately to a cargo net. As a result, the decks were littered with all manner of personal and military gear. Most of the material is still there to this day. Rifles, bayonets, helmets, boots, rounds of ammunition, gas masks, plates, cups, cooking utensils, medicine phials and phials of cat-gut for sutures, and 30-06 rifle rounds (not .303 which are rimmed). A pistol is often presented to the diver by the divemaster, securely hidden afterwards. A Thompson sub-machine gun, previously located on the Promenade Deck, is now left on the hull for easier access. Even a set of false teeth and a crucifix may be found on the Prom-Deck. It is important not to touch any of the artifacts and to keep well off the bottom to avoid silting. The divemaster usually has a few items that are retrieved and passed around for inspection.

The rifles are U.S. Springfield .30-06 rifles, model M1903, a rather ancient weapon built first in 1903, and now resurrected for World War 2 use as

Helmets, rifles, bayonets and other war material lie on the 'floor' of the Promenade.

demand for the newer M1 rifle was too great. The new production of the Springfield was designated Model M1903A1, with the M1903A2 being a slightly modified weapon altered to suit modern production techniques. It had a five-round box magazine, and a calibre of 7.62mm (.30 inch).

At 105 ft (32m) depth, about 100 ft (30m) along the promenade deck, look down to the rows of toilets without going down to them, and then exit the Promenade Deck and swim over the hull. The shark cage used during the oil removal is still there, now a cleaner station for fish. Allan Power has observed grey whaler sharks being cleaned here. A large coral trout is often seen observing the surroundings from inside the cage, whilst a school of barracuda hovers above.

From the shark cage at about 80 feet (25m), inspect the nearby holes in the side of the hull where the U.S. military had pulled out equipment from the front hold soon after the ship went down. Then swim back to the bow within twenty minutes, and up to the deco stops, taking five minutes at 20 ft and 10 minutes at 10 ft.

PORT BRIDGE WING

This dive is often used by divemasters to check out a new group of divers and see how they handle depth without the added anxiety of penetration. It is an interesting dive, with a maximum depth of 150 ft (46m), and gives an opportunity to check out one of the two 20mm Oerlikon guns on the port bridge wing near the seabed. Even after more than fifty years, they can be swivelled slightly. These had a crew of three plus two loaders and could blast out 650 rounds a minute, using a sixty-round drum magazines, several of which can be found scattered about. It had an effective range of 1000 yards (900 m), and a maximum range of 4000 yards (3.6 km).

A swim over to the crows nest on the main mast is interesting and provides an opportunity for natural light photography. A large hatch cover lies on the seabed, and another leans up against the bridge. A large anchor, once strapped to the forward deck, fell to the seabed in 1991 after an earthquake. Perhaps the greatest danger to the *President Coolidge* is the possibility of an earthquake, which could dislodge bulkheads. Fortunately however there is no chance that the ship would slip further into deeper water, as the stern is on the flat bottom of the channel. Scattered around on the seabed are numerous objects that cascaded out of the holds when the ship turned turtle - typewriters, fire extinguishers, fans, 37mm and 105mm ammunition.

THE LADY

The Lady is at 150 ft, (45m) well inside the ship, so this must be regarded as a deep penetration dive, and is not for an inexperienced diver. A typical dive profile allows for only twenty minutes from the commencement of decent to the bow and back to the bow at 70 ft, then up the rope to the decompression stop at twenty feet for five minutes and ten feet for fifteen minutes.

From the bow, the diver follows the side of the ship past the 3-inch gun to the top of the bridge, over the top of the Promenade Deck to a point above the doorway that enters into the Smoking Room. It is best not to enter the Promenade Deck at the Bridge as there is the temptation to dawdle and look at artifacts on the bottom of the promenade deck which is not part of the objective of the dive. From above the First Class Smoking Room doorway, the diver drops down into the Promenade Deck and straight through the doorway into the Smoking Room. The diver is now in a large room with the bottom 48 ft below. Although some light penetrates the room, it is necessary to become accustomed to the gloominess. The divemaster should be ahead and by now has shined a torch directly onto The Lady, 25 ft (8 m) below and in front of the diver. This will allow the diver to become orientated again and to focus on the object, thus lessening the possible effect of narcosis. Then, as Allan Power puts it, the punch-ups start. Everyone wants to get there first, particularly the underwater photographers. And God help anyone who touches or fins too near to The Lady and disturbs any silt.

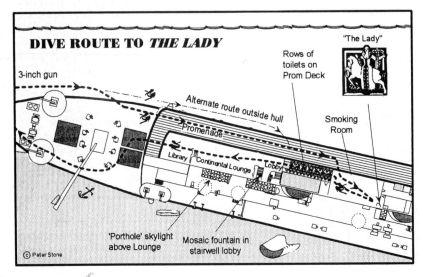

The Lady has been relocated.
See page 181.

The small mosaic
fountain in small tiles of
green, white and
orange, is in the Lobby
on the Promenade Deck
in the stairwell that leads
up to the Boat Deck.
In the lower photograph,
the fountain may be
seen just above the
chair in the lower centre
of the photograph
below.

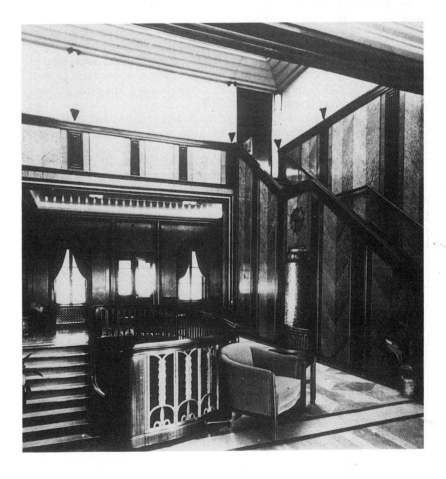

It is particularly important that divers above The Lady do not get too near the bulkhead wall, otherwise silt will rain down on the divers and photographers below. Such an act is punishable by severe ostracisation back at the hotel. Note the fireplace that was once beneath The Lady. This once glowed in imitation of a cozy fire with red bulbs to give the impression of a flame.

The introduction to The Lady is polite and swift. There is no time to explore the bottom of the Smoking Room, littered with the metal frames of 'bunks troops for the use of', and besides, the depth of 175 ft (53 m) is way out of the dive plan. It is time to return to 120 ft (36 m) and admire the 18 inch by 6 ft (450 x 1830 mm) ceiling lights that are of course on their side, and to pass by the rows of toilets before entering the Vestibule outside the Continental Lounge. The upper set of toilets turned through 90 degrees as a result of an earthquake in mid-1991 and have now fallen to the floor (wall) below. The wooden stairways have long deteriorated, but a delightful mosaic fountain may be seen in what used to be the Lobby before the Continental Lounge.

It is time to exit the interior of the ship, from the fountain in the Lobby, through the Continental lounge and out through the windows at the front of the Library and Writing Room. A good divemaster would be waiting as the diver exits the ship into open water, checking each diver's air content; a good diver will assist by holding up his contents gauge. The diver then proceeds directly to the bow, and the ascent begins. There is no time to inspect the gun or the forward holds - the objective now is to return to the deco stops as quickly as possible. The bottom time back to the bow should be 20 minutes, but you are still 70 ft (22m) down, and need to ascent up the rope at an acceptable ascent rate of no more than 30 ft/min. At the 30 ft (9 m) mark a short safety stop of five minutes is appropriate, and with a bit of luck, Boris will be there to meet you. Boris, a huge grouper indeterminable weight and age, has greeted divers at the site since Allan first saw him in 1969.

The final decompression is at 20 ft (6 m) for five minutes, and 10 ft (3 m) for fifteen minutes. The decompression time may seem ultraconservative, but it is always best to err on the side of safety. U.S. Navy Tables show that a bottom time of 20 minutes at 150 feet is two minutes at 20 ft and seven minutes at 10 ft, but these are designed for fit, navy divers (with a military acceptable redundancy factor) so a safety factor is mandatory for sport diving. Besides, there is always the possibility of a diver dropping down below the dive plan level, or being a bit tardy in returning to the decompression level in time. One of the roles of the divemaster is to ensure that each diver performs adequate decompression stages.

THE JEEP HOLD

This is the shallowest dive of interest on the wreck, with a maximum depth of 100 ft (30m). The Jeep Hold is the first hold (from the bow), and contains several Willys jeeps (truck utility, 4x4 quarter ton), originally packed in wooden crates which have since rotted, and packed in such a way that all the wheels were removed and placed on the back seat. The windscreen was on top of the wheels, and the steering wheel packed in one of the rims of the wheels. They were stacked on top of each other, but as the ship lies on her side, they are now on their rear ends. A book of instructions showed how each one was to be unpacked, with specific procedures as to opening the crate and assembling the vehicle. A much photographed jeep lies on its side at the entrance to the hold.

Number One hold contains a number of Willeys Jeeps. This much photographed vehicle is at the entrance to the hold.

On the edge of the hold there is a crate of Springfield rifles, a typewriter, and at one time a lot of office equipment like rubber stamps and various items but these seem to have mysteriously vanished over the years. No filing cabinets have been found.

THE GUN HOLD

This is the number two hold, the biggest of all the holds. With a maximum depth of 115 ft (35m), it generally allows a longer time to explore, but the usual conservative dive plan of twenty minutes bottom time and fifteen minutes decompression is still observed. Penetration into the hold is unrestricted and there is no need to delve into every nook and cranny to see something of interest. The hold contains a 'Long Tom', a large 155mm anti-aircraft gun, and a number of ten-wheel General Motors Corporation trucks (two wheels up front, eight in tandem pairs on the back). This is an excellent dive as there is very little travelling required, and the equipment offers an excellent opportunity for interesting underwater photography. [N16]

About ten years ago, Allan Power removed a rusted panel at the stern of the hold and found a barber's chair, adding further interest to the dive. The white chair is canterlevered from its base and makes for a good photo. It is not possible to get right inside the barber's shop, but by squeezing between two steel structures, it is possible for one person at a time to see and photograph the chair. This was the crew's barber shop, on B-deck. Next door to the barber's shop (now above) was the crew's doctor's office and hospital where ampules of medicine, instruments, and various bottles may be found.

On the same deck, on the port side of the cargo hatch (now below) is the seamen's mess and galley, where cups, saucers, plates, jugs, and a stainless steel urn can be seen.

If time is available and it has been scheduled on the dive plan, a visit to the chain locker on return to the bow is interesting. This rather confined area is full of tins of paint, spare oars (for lifeboats), spare portholes, coils of red and black steam hose, wooden pulley blocks, ladders, a large coil of manila rope, heavy chain, shovels - and at the bottom locker, which means a deeper penetration (but even depth), a marvellous collection of beautiful old bulbous lamps, made of glass and brass, just like those seen on old sailing ships.

Because of the restricted space, the Locker is not a dive for a large group, or for anyone with even a twinge of claustrophobia.

MEDICAL SUPPLIES DIVE

This is another 120 ft (36m) dive with twenty minutes bottom time, requiring direct penetration of the ship through the hull. The dive commences from the bow once again and proceeds past the shark cage and to a large rectangular cut in the hull made by the Americans into what used to be the automobile cargo section. This is in fact cargo hold No. 4 which, unlike the front two holds, has no vertical cargo hatch to load materials. Access to the hold from the outside was through a pair of large twin doors in the hull. Now however access is through a large long hole cut in the hull of the Lower Deck for salvage purposes.

It was here that all the medical supplies for the troops on Guadalcanal were stored. US Navy divers recovered what they could of the medical supplies - ampoules of morphine, sulpha drugs, vitamin K, bottles of plasma, sutures in small glass phials, and various ointments, bottles and jars, and a few instruments. At 110 ft (34 m) drop into the hole and enter a large section of the ship which has ample penetrating light. The Navy divers didn't recover all the medical supplies, so there is still plenty to see, including plates, cups, cooking utensils, phones and other items on the floor between decks while dozens of aircraft drop tanks and more ammunition can be seen in the cargo area. Australian diver Mike Scotland reports seeing, '... two large ampules containing powder. The yellow one was sulphur used as an anti-bacterial agent. The white powder was penicillin, the freshly discovered wonder antibiotic that was responsible for saving so many lives during the war. Both drugs are vital in the treatment of the wounded. More interesting still was a smaller ampule containing a yellowish liquid. This was morphine, an essential painkiller for the treatment of the wounded.'

The diver will also see a large number of small field cookers, various types of ammunition, and field telephones scattered about. The dive leader will guide you through a doorway into the large cargo hold, leading toward the bow. There is a temptation to dally and explore the contents of the hold, but this should be left for another dive as time is critical. Leave the forward hold by exiting above the main forward mast, and head back to the bow in open water.

ENGINE ROOM DIVE

Although the engine room has claimed the lives of two divers, it is nevertheless a dive that can be made by the experienced diver who follows the basic rules of deep penetration diving. And with a competent divemaster to lead the dive, the safety aspect is further increased. There is no need to explore every nook and cranny in the engine room and by staying in an open area, the incidence of disorientation and claustrophobia, and silting is reduced.

From the bow, cut down diagonally across the starboard side of the ship toward the bottom of the ship and follow the bilge keel down past a large heap

The Control Room on the
President Coolidge is a
tight squeeze for divers,
but easily accessible from
the Engine Room. The
top photograph shows
just a few of the control
dials that were positioned
in the control panel
(below).

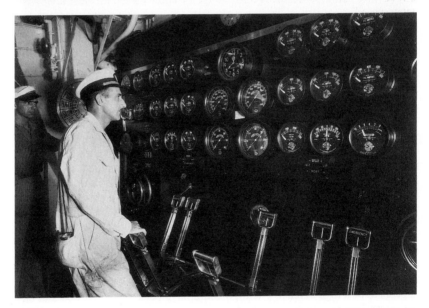

off rubble pulled out of the engine room in 1976 by Ian Lockley and his team.
The whole side of the engine room has been cut away for salvage and a large
amount of ducting, cables, and catwalks have been cleared. This allows for
easy penetration. The diver can peer down and see one of the huge propulsion
motors and large condenser at about 130 ft (40 m). Drop down to the condenser and then twenty feet further down to a small entrance hatch to the control
room which was actually above the engine room. This is a confined space and
at 150 ft (46 m), narcosis will have an affect.

An electrical panel inside the engine room on the *President Coolidge.*

The divemaster will place himself at the narrow doorway entrance to the control room, and illuminate the whole panel. Divers can enter and examine the control panel closely, and see the three engine telegraphs. Exit the engine room through the engine room hatch that leads up to the rear funnel. This was a false (cosmetic) funnel, used as an air-vent. There is an engineers elevator from the engine room up nine levels to the funnel on the sun deck, but divers generally go up the huge airshaft and come out at the top (Sun) deck - depth at this stage is still 150 ft.

There are other exits from the false funnel shaft into the ship, however alternative routes through the interior are strongly discouraged as it means further penetrating the ship when it would be wise to exit the ship as soon as possible after having been within the Engine Room. As a general rule, any penetration of the ship should be at the commencement of the dive, so that should a problem occur later, the diver may be at least in open water.

Both funnels have collapsed on the seabed, a flat heap of rusted metal, and are hardly recognisable as such. The only identifying feature is the top ring of the funnel. The American President Lines eagle logo on the funnels cannot be determined. They may have been painted on, but photographs show what appears to be a logo in relief. The logo could have been made of wood and has since rotted away. It is best not to drop down and inspect the funnels in detail as the depth would be beyond the dive plan depth of 150 ft. Better to rise and make your way back to the bow.

THE GALLEY

A dive to the galley requires a deep penetration, and is at 170 ft (52m). From the bow, the diver goes straight down the starboard side of the ship to the loading door at the end of the passenger and Mail section on C or Upper Deck, and drops down to 160 ft (49m) until a doorway is reached. This provides entry into the tourist class dining saloon. A galley off the dining room has electric cookers and a large bakers-dough mixing machine. Another section has heaps of green crockery, plates, cups, and mugs. Drop down to 170 ft and pass by the china scullery, and you will see three large stainless steel steam cookers, and a potato peeling machine, then break out into the huge first class dining saloon with its brass ceiling lamps. To exit the interior, swim through the dining salon into the front lobby and emerge out of what is now called Captain Euarts doorway. The diver will now be right next to the shark cage. It is an easy swim back over the hull to the bow.

SWIMMING POOL

There were two swimming pools on the *President Coolidge* - after all, we couldn't have the riff-raff from tourist class messing up the pool with the first class passengers, so each had their own space. In fact the first class pool on the boat deck even had a small sandy 'beach'. It is this swimming pool that is visited, as the tourist class pool was over the No. 6 hatch and was probably made of canvas for easy removal for access to the hold below.

The maximum depth of the dive is 196 ft (60m), and does not require any penetration, except for along the promenade deck if you so wish. After swimming alongside the top (Sun) deck of the ship you pass by the funnel openings and anti-aircraft emplacements before dropping down to the pool. Amazingly, the pool still holds water, and it is a strange feeling to swim a lap of a vertical pool. Above the pool is the soda fountain which has old Coca-Cola scattered about. From here you can enter the beauty shop and the barber's shop, with its chair still bolted to the floor and thus now cantilevered.

Above the pool is a 37mm anti-tank gun. These single axle two wheel guns were used on Guadalcanal, firing anti-personnel canister shot. They had a range of 12,850 yards (12 kilometres), with a rate of fire of four rounds per minute.

DOCTOR'S OFFICE

This is another interesting dive but certainly not for the inexperienced diver as it involves depth, penetration and confined quarters.

This Doctor's Office and Examination Room, one of several on the ship, is on the starboard side of B-Deck, and is at 150 ft (45 m). Entry is made through 'Euart's Door' in the hull on C-Deck then through the Dining Rooms and up again to the Doctors Office. The room lies in almost total darkness, but with the aid of a torch, such curiosities as an old-fashioned telephone and tiny glass ampoules containing white powder can be found. As the dive requires a rather long penetration of the ship into an enclosed, darkened space, it is not a dive for a novice, or anyone with a problem with claustrophobia. An Australian newspaper journalist, who had just learnt to dive in Port Vila, taken here on only her third dive, reported, 'There in the blackness I began to feel slightly claustrophobic, sensing a terrifying flash of what it would be like to be trapped there. I couldn't wait to get back outside to where at least a chink of sunlight could filter through the gloom.'

Once again, is important to stress that divers must feel comfortable and competent to dive deep, and penetrate into enclosed, darkened areas. It is the divemasters responsibility to ensure that the diver is well briefed before the dive, and to be given every opportunity, without any indication of intimidation, to pull out of the dive if it is beyond the experience and desire of the diver.

VOYAGE TO THE BOTTOM OF THE SEA

Two prop shafts on the *President Coolidge* lie at depths of 210 ft (64m) and 240 ft (73 m) - at the tips where the props were. This is way beyond the limit of the casual sport diver and is thus not a dive planned by the local dive operators. Very experienced divers have swum from shore to the bow and down to the prop shafts, but they do so with strict dive planning and additional equipment. Twin tanks of air are used, and additional tanks are 'staged' along the way for safety reasons. The consumption of air is critical, and a gulp of air at 240ft is the equivalent, in terms of surface cubic capacity air used, of about eight gulps on the surface, so a tank of air will diminish very quickly at depth. Twin tanks provide twice the normal capacity of air, of course.

The introduction of 'mixed gas' diving using Nitrox for example may open the way for the experienced, specially trained sport diver to descend to these depths with relative ease, but at the moment, plain ordinary air is all that is available in Luganville. That means that special precautions need to be addressed in addition to the mere depth of the dive. The onset of narcosis can hit anywhere from around 100 ft (30 m) down, and at 200 ft (61 m) everyone on air is affected to some extent. [N17]

The combination of depth and time require the dive plan to include adequate decompression 'staging' to eliminate the potential of the dreaded 'bends'. A dive to 240 ft (73 m) for fifteen minutes bottom time would require, according to US Navy tables, decompression stages of four minutes at 30 ft, six minutes at 20 ft, and twenty-one minutes at 10 ft.

Considering that true bottom time is taken from the moment of decent from the surface, to the beginning of ascent, it is important, if diving the props for example, to reach the stern of the *President Coolidge* as quickly as possible. In this instance, the experienced diver could descend, preferably down a shot line, from a dive boat right over the stern of the wreck, and would reach the bottom in a matter of minutes. To swim from shore to the stern of the ship is a long and strenuous task, eating up bottom time that would be preferred to be spent exploring on the stern, and consuming air. The addition of the need for exertion adds to the air consumption problem. To overcome this, divers are using underwater scooters to reach their destination with the minimum of exertion. Air consumption is dramatically reduced, and the scooter-diver can reach the stern in five minutes from the bow, a quarter of the time it would take for a rapid swim, and with the greater majority of tank air still available. But it must be emphasised that any deep diving, even with the use of a scooter, must be undertaken by only a skilled, experienced diver, and is not an option generally offered by dive operators in Luganville. [N18]

The stern of the *President Coolidge* is indeed a fascinating dive. It gives the diver the opportunity to once again appreciate the enormity of the ship. Past the bridge, the diver will note the first class swimming pool and the lifeboat davits, then the stern gun and the enormous rudder. Schools of barracuda and golden trevally pass by but these are not noticed in the concentration to reach the tip of the stern in as quick a time as possible. The higher end of the starboard shaft is at 185 ft (56m). The diver may decide, wisely, not to proceed lower than this depth. By moving away from the stern, an opportunity is given to see the stern in all its glory, complete with the two bare prop shafts. It may be at this point of time that you curse Barry May and his successful salvage of the props, as they would have looked magnificent *in situ*.

The stern of the *President Coolidge* now lies on the seabed at 240 ft. This is an extremely deep dive, and is not encouraged. Note the two 3-inch guns, on A-Deck, and the 5-inch gun on the stern, on B-Deck.

The more adventurous diver may decide to drop down further beyond the 200 ft level, below the rudder to the second prop shaft, and note the remains of a lifeboat on the sand bottom at 230 ft (70 m). From the seabed, the stern is an awesome sight.

The dive has taken twenty minutes from ascent to a return to the bow. Bottom time is roughly divided into five minutes ascent, seven minutes on the stern, and eight minutes to return to the bow. Acceptable decompression adds another forty minutes - five minutes at 40 ft (12 m), five minutes at 30 ft (9 m), ten minutes at 20 ft (6 m), and twenty minutes at 10 ft (3 m).

Rodney Sales, Manager of Dive 2000 in Sydney recalls several memorable dives to the stern of the ship using an Apollo scooter. 'Once past the engine room cut we start to head over toward the keel. We see the starboard prop shaft appear in the distance at 57 metres and drop down for a close up look. It is a foot in diameter. Looking down we can see the huge rudder blade. It is tempting to continue to drop but the planned depth is 60 metres. Now is an important time for us to watch our depth and check air and time. Heading around stern to the deck we find the huge 5-inch gun. The controls are still intact and below we can see the 3-inch guns, the starboard side (top one) having fallen onto the sand. Being careful not to exceed 60 metres and with a planned return to the bow in 20 minutes we need to be very careful. Heading up the deck we pass the rear hold and arrive at the swimming pool. The tiles are still there and you can still find the ladders. A quick swim and we head up while being careful not to exceed our computer ascent warning, We find the anti-tank gun above the pool. We make our stops along the way short as we only have 20 minutes and it is easy to over stay our planned time, but if ahead of time we continue from the pool up the centre of the deck, past the funnels and front bow. This gives a great perspective of the whole wreck and its size and deck layout.'

'For those with the appropriate experience and equipment, an extension with a planned depth of 70 metres allows you to see the keel of a lifeboat ten metres off the stern of the ship. You will also be able to took up at the stern. It is an awesome sight, huge, and you can see the whole shape and layout of the prop shafts, rudder and rear 5-inch gun. There is also an unusual black coral tree on the sand. We are very careful not to lose sight of the wreck at any time.'

Twin tanks are used for a dive to the stern. It is to be emphasised that this is an extremely deep dive, beyond the boundary of acceptable sport diving, and on the boundary of standard air diving. Rodney comments, 'For many people this is the deepest they have been before. The reason to go to the stern should not be because you want to go deeper. With this attitude divers do silly things once they hit the planned depth. Plan your dive and dive your plan - don't exceed your planned depth. If you don't understand this you should not be doing this dive.'

There are specialist courses that train the sport diver in the requirements for deep diving, and modern diving equipment is capable of performing to a high standard at the depths required. As mixed-gas diving becomes more popular and accessible, a dive to the stern of the *President Coolidge* will present only the normal challenges of a deep, well-planned dive. There is great training and equipment available to dive to this depth safely. 'If you don't know how to plan this dive yourself you should not do it. Obtaining the appropriate training is the answer. You can always return and do this dive once you are prepared,' Rodney comments.

As somewhat of a Stop Press, Reece Discombe contributed the following comments on being inside the Number One (Jeep) hold, when an earthquake hit. 'I was checking out the huge gun in the hold when all of a sudden the fish started swimming like bats out of hell, and I thought that shark or large fish may have been chasing them. Then I heard a low rumbling sound, then a rubbing noise like squeaking or two pieces of metal being rubbed together. I turned around when I heard one of the GMC trucks in the hold crash down and from then on I could not see a thing as the silt engulfed me. I knew I was not trapped but could not see a thing, but I looked up and could see a hole that had been made by the in the side of the ship to take the guns out. I managed to get out through the hole, and when I looked back into the hold I could not see a thing; it was like a fog. Just as well the truck hadn't crashed down on top of me.'

CHAPTER THIRTEEN

A
CHAMPAGNE
AFFAIR

Espiritu Santo is one of my favourite Pacific destinations and with the wreck of the *President Coolidge*, and its war history, there is a special attraction. But there is more to the island than just diving. Its history, culture, casual 'tropical Pacific' attitude and natural beauty is something to admire and appreciate.

It has a fascinating history. Archaeological evidence has shown that human habitation of Vanuatu began several thousand years ago. For many centuries the people lived a subsistence existence in small tribal groups, with many different languages and cultural practices. The first European to 'discover' the New Hebrides was the Portuguese explorer Pedro Fernandez de Quiros, who arrived in the northern islands on 3 May 1606, in the service of the King of Spain. Thinking he had found the great southern continent which geographers had surmised must exist to balance the globe, he called it *Austrialia del Espiritu Santo*. Quiros attempted to establish a model Christian settlement in the northern part of the island which has retained part of the name. However he did not stay long, his visit marred by the massacre of local people and the abduction of some of their children so as to demand food by ransom. The French navigator, Louis Antoine de Bougainville, and the British explorer, James Cook, were the next Europeans to pass by in the last half of the 18th Century; Bougainville in 1768, and Cook in 1774.

Throughout the 19th Century, Espiritu Santo was visited by a succession of European traders and Christian missionaries. French and British citizens also arrived to set up cotton, coffee and coconut plantations. Espiritu Santo and many other parts of New Hebrides suffered at the hands of the notorious 'blackbirders', who took away thousands of people to work as virtual slave labour on sugar plantations in north-eastern Australia and Fiji. In 1887, France and Britain set up a Joint Naval Commission to protect their interests in the islands. This led to the establishment in 1906 of an Anglo-French Condominium to jointly administer the New Hebrides, a cumbersome and expensive arrangement which, with some modifications, was to persist for seventy-four years.

After the war most of Santo's plantations remained French-owned and many more Vietnamese labourers were brought in to work them; the first had arrived in 1923. Later, as the struggle for independence grew, the New Hebrides Cultural Association was formed on Espiritu Santo which would eventually be renamed the New Hebrides National Party and then the Vanuaaka Pati. In elections in November 1979, the Vanuaaka Pati had an overwhelming victory, and the New Hebrides was renamed Vanuatu on July 30, 1980. Santo was the scene of a short-lived secessionist rebellion led by Jimmy Stevens soon after the declaration of independence.

Santo's hinterland remains largely unexploited and the whole island retains a unique natural splendour. The population is predominantly ni-Vanuatu with less than 2% being made up from Chinese, Vietnamese and Europeans of various nationalities. Some ni-Vanuatu still live according to the customs of centuries past, refusing tinned food, rice and bread, and preferring the custom ways, hunting with bow and arrow and growing their own vegetables.

European involvement in the history of Santo has been colourful, to say the least, but nothing can surpass the natural environmental beauty of the island. The east coast where most of the island's agricultural and commercial developments are located has a tropical climate. The interior has large areas of tropical bush and extremely rugged terrain while the West coast is drier with sheer high mountains and narrow plains. Some of these areas, such as the village of Wousi, famous for its traditional pottery, are accessible only by boat. People living on the west coast are relatively isolated and agricultural land being limited means that vegetable gardens are often established on the steep, bamboo covered hillsides facing the sea. Santo's main industries remain agricultural, notably copra, coffee, cocoa, fish and beef.

An hour flight north of Port Vila by Vanair brings you to Pekoa airport on Espiritu Santo. Your hotel or resort will probably have transport waiting, but there are plenty of taxis. Five minutes from Pekoa airport and you are in the main street of Luganville, a once prosperous commercial town, now a shadow of its former glory but gradually showing signs of prosperity as new buildings are constructed. The old Chinese stores are still there and well worth a browse. The restaurants come and they go, and unlike those in Port Vila, are not known for their cuisine, but there is a measure of variety, and you can get a fine cappuccino in the main street.

Luganville is the second largest town in Vanuatu (after Port Vila). During the French-English condominium government, the French plantation owners ensured that Luganville had a number of restaurants and cafes but those times have long past. Nothing is permanent any more. There are a few cafes, over thirty interesting Chinese shops which have resolutely remained in business, and a number of Ni-Vanuatu shops. It is worth an afternoon to potter around town, dropping in to some of the Chinese stores and seeing their wares. Duty free shopping is also available in Luganville, and there are also a few places that sell excellent artifacts and gifts. A visit to the morning market is also very interesting, with the opportunity to buy fresh exotic fruits.

Luganville has taken more than a decade to recovered from the Santo Rebellion in 1980. Most shops and cafes closed down, never to re-open. It may not be correct to blame solely the rebellion. With the proclamation of independence, reluctantly granted by the French but supported by the British, the French plantation owners moved out, many abandoning their properties. Commerce deteriorated, and Luganville reverted to a somnolent village. In the

There may be no such thing as a 'typical' south Pacific town, but if you have read James Michener or Somerset Maugham, you could easily imagine Luganville as fitting the cliche. In recent years however the somnolent town has shown signs of life, with new buildings being erected, and an air of optimism. The 'Three Bears' has defied demolishers however. Some say that during the war years it was a nightclub and later a brothel. Note the Quonset hut on the left.

past few years however, modern new buildings have been constructed in the main street and the town has an air of prosperity about it.

The visitor to Espiritu Santo has a choice of accommodation. The Hotel Santo is popular with divers as it is right in town. A few kilometres out if town along the road that skirts the channel is the Bougainville Resort, a delightfully tranquil resort of comfortable fares (bungalows) in landscaped gardens of wild orchids, frangipani and bougainvillea. If you refer an island resort, then Bokissa Island is only half an hour by boat from Luganville, and the new resort on Aore Island is only across the channel directly opposite Luganville. Divers may be picked up from all the resorts.

There is also primitive but comfortable accommodation at Lonnoc Beach Resort near Champagne Beach, but this is to relax after a few days of diving as it is too far to commute to Luganville on a daily basis. [N1]

The majority of tourists to 'Santo', as the island and town of Luganville are casually called, are scuba divers, but those who do not dive will still be able to experience the beauty of the island and appreciate its rich early and military history. Port Ory and Hog Harbour to the north of the island have some of the most beautiful beaches in the world. And as previously described, Champagne Beach is most appropriately named. Simply magnificent and tranquil - if you are the only one there and not amongst the hundreds on a Pacific cruise.

Although it has been over fifty years since the American military presence in Luganville, there is still evidence of their three-year stay. A huge Coca-cola dump just outside town containing millions of bottles is a significant reminder of their stay. The familiar domes of Quonset huts have survived nearly half a century, now used as workshops or warehouses, and one of the airstrips is the main airport. But their greatest legacy was of course the wreck of the *President Coolidge* which has brought thousands of divers to Vanuatu and has significantly contributed to the economy of the republic, and in particular to Espiritu Santo.

Jimmy Stevens and his family greeted us warmly on a visit to his compound near Vanafo village. The charismatic leader of the 'Coconut Rebellion' or the 'Santo War' as the news-papers have called it, died at his village in 1994.

Million Dollar Point is an interesting visit even for the non-diver. There is a particular fascination in snorkelling over this dump of military equipment, and the two small wrecks in shallow water add to the interest.

It was inevitable that independence be granted at some stage to the New Hebrides but it was not given with good grace by the French who had most of the plantation land and outnumbered the British three to one. Independence came in 1980. Then came the revolution headed by the charismatic Jimmy Stevens, part Scottish, part Samoan, on Espiritu Santo in what was called the Coconut War. Stevens was supposedly supported by the French who did not want independence - certainly they did nothing to put the revolution down. In August 1980 Papua New Guinea troops were called in to quell the unrest; Stevens' son Eddie was killed in a brief skirmish, Jimmy was arrested, and the revolution ended.

Many years ago on my first visit to Espiritu Santo I was taken to Vanafo village, just north of Luganville. This was Jimmy Stevens' village, and it was under the huge banyan tree that he arosed his people. Jimmy was then serving a sixteen year sentence for being a puppet to the French landowners and was only let out in November 1991 when all prisoners , political or otherwise, were released from jail when a new government came to power. I wonder what happened to the petty crime rate after such a magnanimous gesture?

Jimmy Stevens returned to his beloved village, his family, and his loyal 'army' of followers, and vowed to give up politics. He probably had little choice. On a recent visit to Santo I asked if it were possible to visit the village once more as I remember it as being somewhat primitive. I was told rather firmly that Mr Stevens did not like tourists gawking at his people. I could appreciate this. I had no wish to intrude on their privacy but it was suggested that if I ask at his compound, he may provide permission for a few photographs.

Although Jimmy Stevens and his family wear western dress, his 'soldiers' and the people of is compound dress traditionally. Note the arm bands indicating membership of the Nagriamel movement.

On our way up to magnificent Champagne Beach I stopped at the village with three friends and our taxi driver, Timmy Rovu. At Jimmy Stevens' compound gate I left a message with one of his uniformed guards, asking permission to take a few photographs in the nearby village, not wishing to disturb Mr. Stevens nor intrude in his private compound. I realised that permission may be refused, but I was not prepared for what was in store.

The guard, in minimalist dress suited to the climate, wearing a bark mal-mal down from the waist, trotted off, returning five minutes later. He beckoned for us to come inside. A gate mysteriously opened. Surely not automatic, I thought, until I noticed another guard discretely hidden in the bushes pulling a rope attached to the gate. Somewhat hesitatingly we entered a long grassy clearing.

Jimmy Stevens came out of a communal building followed by a large gathering of family and followers, hand outstretched with a broad smile. He introduced himself. I did likewise, and introduced my friends. 'We would like to welcome you with a song,' Mr Stevens said. They sang beautifully in their native language. We were overwhelmed. Some sixty or so men, women and children, lined up to be individually greeted. We shook each hand. Only Jimmy, his son and daughter with babe in arms wore western dress. The men wore a tight loincloth covered with a coconut-weave mal-mal (lap-lap). Women, old and young, wore nothing but a leaf skirt.

'Come inside', the ex-revolutionary beckoned . We chatted for a while - life, in and out of prison, of family and the future. 'You must look around the village,' Jimmy offered. We were on first name terms by then. His son, Frank, dressed conspicuously in western clothes, escorted us around the village, introduced us to all and sundry, and explained village life. They were all about to leave the compound to attend to their fields when we arrived.

Village lifestyle is extremely primitive by our standards. They tend their garden plots during the day and live a very secluded life without even the basic utensils. What makes this all the more remarkable is that the village is only ten minutes by vehicle from Luganville where jeans and T-shirts are standard attire. As we parted I was presented with a mal-mal, which I treasure to this day, and invited back any time. 'We would like to sing you a farewell song,' Jimmy said. Only a small group remained. In English, and with perfect diction and harmony, they sang, 'Now Is The Hour'. It was beautiful, and there was not a dry eye amongst our group. This was the last time I saw Jimmy Stevens. He died in 1994.

There are a number of excellent tourist guides on Vanuatu, so there is little need to repeat a detailed description of local tours and places of interest. I would probably be doing a disservice if I did not mention the Lonely Planet Publications book on Vanuatu which is excellent and available worldwide.

It is always a pleasure to take a day off from diving the *President Coolidge* and head up along the east coast toward Champagne Beach. The following is a short account of an actual itinerary that could be enjoyed by any visitor. There are a number of ways of travelling north. You could hire a car and do it yourself, or join a regular tour group. As there was only my wife, brother-in-law Greg and wife Nita, we decided to make private arrangements with one of the local taxi drivers. I had met Kenneth at the airport on our arrival a few days earlier and arranged for him to meet us where I was staying in Luganville. My old friend and taxi driver from 1992, Timmy Rovu, has apparently gone up in the world and has his own bus and taxi, but I couldn't find him.

We commenced the day with breakfast at Leslie Conklin's Natangora Cafe on the main street, about a hundred yards down from the Hotel Santo, enjoying eggs and toast, muffins, toasted sandwiches, and the only cappuccino available in town. At one of the supermarkets, we bought fresh bread and cheese, ham, salami and tomatoes - our picnic lunch was assured. Kenneth was waiting for us at 9.00 am as planned and we headed of for the north-east coast.

My aim was to stop first at the Blue Holes near the Matevulu College, but for some strange reason the pond had turned grey due to something to do with cows polluting the water, or so we were told, the excessive catching of the eels which had kept the pond clear. In actual fact, it was due to recent land clearing. Another fable associated with the pool is that Dorothy Lamour spent many hours swimming in the pool during the famous Hollywood actresses visit during World War Two to entertain American troops. In actual fact, she was never on Espiritu Santo. (The Blue Holes have now returned to their crystal clear condition.)

To reach the Blue Holes it is necessary to travel along the runway of Fighter Strip One, which has not been overgrown and with relatively little effort, could be serviceable. Aircraft parts lie in the long grass off the runway.

As the Blue Holes no longer lived up to its name on this occasion, we went on to another 'Blue Lagoon', this one near the Coconut Research Station on the east coast road. The delightful grounds around the pool were well maintained and we had no hesitation in having a swim in the cool, crystal clear pond. I had the others put on a mask and they gasped with delight at being able to see so far in the clear water, following small fish, and noticing the algae strings on the overhanging branches. It was an excellent refreshing start to the day. Divers tend to not to visit this pool as it is shallower than the sixty feet that may be reached in the main pond of the Blue Holes.

On the way, Kenneth gave an excellent commentary as he drove us through a research coconut-palm nursery, and stopped at a copra kiln. He pointed out several rivers, ponds and villages on the way, stopped occasionally so that we

The Blue Holes are crystal clear and one pond reaches to a depth of some sixty feet. As it is located next to Fighter One airstrip, it was a popular place for a cool swim to allay the effects of the tropical heat.

may take photographs. He was the perfect driver/guide. The drive in to Port Ory was superb. This is the end of the road along the east cost of Espiritu Santo. The village lies on the shore of a beautiful beach, with several offshore reefs and islands. (I believe this is also called Sunset Beach, probably for tourism reasons). Men were fishing from out-rigger canoes, and children crept cautiously toward us. Kenneth showed us the remains of a US bomber aircraft completely buried in the sand - only a small part of the engine was visible. It was difficult to image that a complete bomber, a US war relic, lay beneath us.

As I was taking a few photographs I saw a gentleman stomping up the beach and waving excitedly. 'I think we have problems,' said Kenneth with a bit of a grin. The man approached us and spoke angrily to Kenneth who replied calmly but this did nothing to alleviate the agitation of the fellow. He was not the chief of the village but a politician of some local party. I thought perhaps that I should have asked permission to take photographs. I said 'sori tu mas'. He gestured that he had no quarrel with me, but Kenneth should get the Hell out of here - and, I presume, take us with him. Kenneth was from a neighbouring village who supported an opposing political party - so Kenneth wasn't welcome at Port Ory. We were being evicted from paradise. It was not a major problem as the other beaches we were to visit could offer fine swimming, but I would have liked to have stayed and made friends with the kids, and even had a walk through the village. But we were unwelcome guests. Wendy's reaction was sensible. 'Good on him,' she said, recognising that tourists are not always the best type of visitors to such a pristine village. And I tend to agree. But the quarrel was not with the tourists, although I later heard that Port Ory was not the most welcoming place. Pity it was like that. I also heard that the Port Ory village is Catholic; some of the young folk would come into Luganville and harass the Protestants. Now where have I heard that before? I wasn't impressed by being evicted for political reasons, and would have liked to hear what the

Fighter One airstrip near Turtle Bay provides access to the nearby Blue Holes.

chief would have said. But we must always remember we are guests on private property, and I did not seek permission from the chief in the first place.

It was only a short drive back down the coast to Golden Beach. Some prefer it to the more popular Champagne Beach, and I wasn't going to argue the point. Huge trees splayed their branches over the golden sand. The water was crystal clear with slight wave movement. The local land owners had built a few comfortable benches, and an enclosed fale. We had no hesitation paying the requested 100 vatu (200 vatu for the group) into the honesty box, and we had the beach to ourselves. But it wasn't quite the same without the kids and the village ambience.

We had our picnic lunch at Golden Beach and moved on to Champagne Beach. As always, the beach looked magnificent, and I still rate it as my favourite, the finest beach I have seen. I think it is the coconut palms that give it the edge on Golden Beach and others, although the palm huts built to house the artefact sellers and drink vendors when the cruise ships come in detract from the beauty of the scene. These are a recent addition as Champagne Beach is often the 'mystery island' that is offered on some Pacific cruises. Another small group of tourists were leaving as we arrived, and a European couple in a canoe were also preparing to leave after sunbaking on the beach. It was now our own. A trimaran lay at anchor in the bay. It was a beautiful setting. Kenneth went off to visit his father in a nearby village. We opened a bottle of champagne to drink on Champagne Beach. I cannot imagine what this place must be like when a thousand or so cruise-ship tourists disgorge themselves onto a beach less than a kilometre long. Kenneth said that it is not a pleasant sight as many get drunk and carry on loudly. But at least all the rubbish is removed by the ship's crew and the beach was absolutely spotless.

Champagne Beach was once owned by the Grazziani family, the son of whom, Yves, now runs the Bougainville Resort. There is now the proverbial land dispute now, and two entry fees are required. One of the 'disputes' was,

There is, surely, no finer beach in the whole Pacific Ocean than palm-fringed, crystal clear, golden sand, Champagne Beach. Of course, such accolades predisposes that there is no one else on the beach but you, your partner and friends.

however, Kenneth's uncle so we had only to pay one fee - I think it was 100 vatu each. When Kenneth returned, we drove the short distance to the neighbouring beach and had a drink at Lonnoc Beach Resort. There is no power, evening lighting being by candle and kerosene lamp. The rooms have coral rubble floors and the beds looks rather spartan, but what does one need in paradise? It would be a wonderful place to just unwind for a few days.

We were back in Luganville by 4.45pm having had a full and memorable day. After drinks at the Hotel Santo we adjourned to the Formosa Restaurant over the road, serving some of the finest Vietnamese food you could imagine. Their deep friend prawns are out of this world. They also serve, dare I say, a magnificent Coconut Crab, but I refuse to have this as the animal is becoming rarer each day and could be wiped out if its consumption continues at the present rate.

This gives you some indication of what could be regarded as a 'typical' day trip to Champagne Beach. It is possible to travel across to Big Bay and return via an inland road, but I have not done this.

Shorter trips around the south-east corner of Espiritu Santo can comfortably be made in a morning or afternoon. The coast road takes you eastwards, past the main wharf and copra docks on the right, and then Simonsen's wharf, where smaller inter-island vessels are moored. Keep travelling east and you will come to a bend heading north to the airport. Continue straight on however, on an un-made road, and you will reach Million Dollar point. On the way you will pass an obscure track to the wreck of the *President Coolidge*, and some fifty metres past, on the left, you will see a memorial. Steps lead up to a simple, white-painted concrete structure which reads, *In Memory of Capt. Elwood J. Euart, 103 Field Artillery Battalion, U.S.A., October 26th 1942.*

About 400 metres beyond the memorial, a narrow coral track on the right leads to Million Dollar Point, opposite the island of Tutuba. The ramp, built out into the water by the American forces as they dumped their equipment, is

The memorial to Captain Elwood Euart lies just off the road passing the site of the President Coolidge, near Luganville. The inscription states: *In Memory of Capt. Elwood J. Euart, 103 Field Artillery Battalion, U.S.A., October 26th 1942.*

deteriorating badly - take care when walking near the edges as rusted metal protrudes in places and can cause a nasty cut. Entry for divers and snorkellers is best made from the beach just to the left (east) of the jetty. The two wrecks will be found right in front of the beach and the jetty.

The coast road continues around the south-east point of the island and heads north, winding through bush invaded by American liana vine which forms a thick green canopy over the trees and shrubs lining the road. These vines grow all over the south and east of the island, smothering other foliage. They were introduced by the Americans during the war for camouflaging installations, a role that they achieved competently. But they have taken over the island.

A road to the right takes you along a narrow peninsula to Palikulo Point, with Palikulo Bay on the left. As you drive along the narrow peninsula, you can see the open sea breaking on the exposed shore to your right, while on the left, the water in the sheltered bay is calm, and safe for swimming. The Club Nautique, on the left, is an ideal picnic spot, with a sandy beach. Although it is, strictly speaking, a private club, casual visitors are made welcome. It is undoubtedly the best beach for swimming, especially for young children, within easy reach of Santo town. The road, such as it is, hugs the shore and in clear weather you should be able to see the island of Aoba on the horizon. This volcanic island was, it is said, the inspiration for Bali Hai, in Michener's *Tales of the South Pacific*.

Beyond the Club Nautique is the Palikulo Fishery. Permission to visit may be obtained at the office near the entrance. The fishery is run by the South Pacific Fishing Company (SPFC), and was established in 1957. Although the company is Japanese, the fishing boats are mainly Taiwanese. The track down to the quay takes you past the refrigerated warehouse where hundreds of tons of fish of the tuna family are stored at minus 30°C. Larger vessels transport the fish to Japan and elsewhere in the Pacific. This is well worth a visit. The Taiwanese fishing craft provide an unusual spectacle in the waters of Vanuatu.

If you return to the main road, and then turn right, ie north, you can head back to town at a junction at Surunda. The coast road to Surunda crosses the golf course, with the club house and beach on the right. A sign gives some indication as to how hazardous the rough can be - 'Watch for Crocodiles near the 7th Tee'.

If you were to continue north, you would pass by IRHO, the Coconut Research Station, where different types of coconut from all over the world have been introduced. Hybrids have been produced, in an effort to find insect and disease resistant species. The nearby Blue Pool, previously mentioned, provides an opportunity for a cool swim in crystal clear water.

The airstrips are spread over the southern part of the island and all can be visited quite easily. On arrival, you will land at the old Bomber Two, now Pekoa airport. Further north near the Matevulu Blue Holes is the old Fighter One strip previously described. Bomber Three to the north-west of Luganville is also worth a visit and is still in excellent condition.

A visit to the traditional village of Vanafo can be arranged. This was Jimmy Stevens' village, and the flag of his Nagriamel Movement stands on the spot where his son Eddie was shot while trying to outrun a roadblock in 1980. The Steven's compound is further on from the village and as indicated, is not generally visited. But arrangements can be made to meet the people of Vanafo and have a look around the village. Best to make enquiries in Luganville first as to the appropriate protocol. I am always concerned that western visitors to native villages that follow a traditional, or 'kastom' way of life, should not be overly influenced by western traditions. Native villages are not zoos. Visitors must at all times respect the people and their customs, and the only objective in visiting should be to learn and appreciate the way of life of another culture.

In expressing such concerns, I have been impressed with the observations and opinions of those who have worked closely with the Ni-Vanuatu. One such person is Canadian Stan Combs who worked closely with the Ni-Vanuatu on Malekula and other islands. Stan comments, 'I wouldn't worry too much about

Bomber Three airstrip has defied an attemp by nature to smother the airstrip. This was used as the main commercial airstrip immediately after the war, but due to its elevation, it was abaandoned in favour of Bomber Two, Pekoa.

American built Quonset huts of iron and corrugated sheet metal were put to good use after the departure of the US forces, and have withstood the test of time.

having spoilt many ni-Vanuatu by sending divers to Vanuatu. Actually, the only parts of Vanuatu that I discourage people from visiting is custom areas such as the interior of South Malekula, where a hundred or two Small Nambas were living the kastom life. There may also be some areas of Santo and Tanna where people have chosen to keep their distance from the West, and I think their wishes should be respected. The rest of Vanuatu has pretty well been exposed to us, and I actually favour the kind of people who are self-sufficient and culturally sensitive seeing the "real Vanuatu" and spending some money there, rather than in Vila.' [N2]

Whatever the reason for visiting Espiritu Santo, do take the time to learn something of the island's history and culture. You will not be disappointed.

CHAPTER FOURTEEN

IN
MEMORIAM

O n 26 October 1992, fifty years after the loss of the President Coolidge, a church service was held at the Euart Memorial near the site of the wreck of the *President Coolidge*. A Melanesian pastor said a prayer, after which a delightful choir sang several hymns. The gathering of a few US servicemen, and visiting scuba divers adjourned later to the Hotel Santo where Allan Power said a few words about Captain Elwood Euart.

In 1993 Col. (Retd) Stephen Parisi, was invited to lay a wreath on the memorial commemorating the 50th anniversary of the tragedy. As mentioned in Chapter Six, Parisi was a Sergeant with 172nd Infantry on board the *President Coolidge* when she hit the mines. He was representing all the servicemen who fought in the South Pacific area during World War 2, and was accompanied by the U.S. Ambassador to New Guinea, Robert Farrand, and Brigadier General Eugene Imai, Commanding General of the 25th National Guard Division in Hawaii.

Parisi reports, 'I was selected to represent all army units that served in the South Pacific during WWll, for a wreath laying ceremony at the memorial that had been erected for Captain Elwood Euart on Espiritu Santo. The ceremony didn't take place until May 1993, because Ambassador Farrand would not have been available earlier. The trip and the ceremony were organized by Major Schowalter and Captain Cox based in Hawaii. The participants were the 25th Division Color Guard, Brigadier General Eugene Imai commander of the 25th Division, Major Schowalter, Captain Cox, U.S. Ambasssador to New Guinea, and myself. I left Saturday May 22, 1993, with stops in Washington, DC, Los Angeles, and Honolulu. I was met in Honolulu by Major Schowalter. I had a six hour lay-over, so I spent some time with the Major, and his family, and we all left for Sydney at 12:05 Sunday morning. We had a six hour layover in Sydney also, before leaving for Noumea, New Caledonia. We changed planes there and left for Port Vila, Vanuatu. The following day we met with President Timakata, the Deputy Prime Minister, the Police Commissioner, and the Commander of the Military Forces. The next morning we left for Espiritu Santo a little more than one hour flight, by a twin engine commuter plane. We were met at the airport by the mayor and his staff, and we went to his office for a short meeting. We then left for the ceremony.'

Colonel (Retd) Stephen Parisi is flanked by U.S. Ambassador to New Guinea, Robert Farrand, and Brigadier General Eugene Imai, Commanding General of the 25th National Guard Division in Hawaii., at Million Dollar point in 1993.

'The Euart memorial was erected after the war and situated off the road, overlooking the area where the Coolidge lies. The mayor and dignitaries, plus approximately ninety natives were in attendance. The island bishop and his choir were present and sang during the ceremony. The mayor, the Ambassador, the General and myself all spoke. I spoke of the Coolidge, the people of Santo, and my stay there after the Coolidge sank. It was a very nice ceremony lasting about an hour. We then went on a tour along the coast to Million Dollar Point, a former Japanese fishing village, and the bomber runway built in 1942 by U.S. engineers for use by our B-17 Bombers, and still in fairly good condition. We went to the Bougainville resort where we were staying and had lunch with the mayor and officials of the island. After lunch we participated in the dedication of a medical building built by U.S. engineers for the people of Espiritu Santo for the friendship shown our service men and women.'

'We went into town afterwards to the market area, and I was introduced to Jimmy Stevens. After dinner that evening at the Bougainville Resort I gave a talk on what I remembered of the Coolidge. I met Franki Stevens that evening, the son of Jimmy Stevens. We had one full day on Santo with a full schedule. I was disappointed in that I didn't have the time to talk to some of the people on Santo that may have observed the tragedy, nor to travel the island to visit some of the places of interest where I was stationed in 1942. Of course some of the areas may not be recognizable after fifty years. At any rate I decided as I left Santo that morning that I would return and spend more time there, which I did in 1994.' [N1]

Reminders of the American military presence on Espiritu Santo during the Pacific War are gradually disappearing as old Quonset huts collapse, and new buildings are erected in a rejuvenated Luganville. Indeed it is remarkable that even after fifty years in a climate not conducive to longevity of unprotected steel and iron buildings that so many have survived for so long.

Wayland Bennett's Corsair was badly damaged when it crashed into the jungles of Espiritu Santo. The US emblem is clearly seen.

In recent years, Espiritu Santo has been the centre of several investigations as the jungle has given up its secrets. It is known that some forty or fifty planes 'rammed into the island's tangled heart'. Not all were located, and many airmen were simply posted missing, their bodies left to rot quickly in the tropical humidity. The posting of a 'Missing in Action' is particularly hard for relatives, and as time progresses, the uncertainty is harder to bear than a confirmed loss. For this reason, there is no statute of limitations enacted to cease recovery of a serviceman even after half a century. In respect of operations in the Pacific, the United States unit responsible for recovery and recording of their military personnel is the Central Identification Laboratory team based in Hawaii - CILHI.

Wrecked aircraft are still being found in the dense jungles north of Luganville, some by chance, others as a result of a determined search - and then with a considerable amount of good luck. Considering the terrain, it is a wonder that any have been found at all. As Vanuatu competes in the realm of world trade, it can offer timber as a prime export, and there is no finer timber than in the northern sector of Espiritu Santo. The area north and north-west of Luganville is sparsely populated, even along the coastal fringes, due to the dense jungle. Occasionally, a native party will wander into these remote areas in search of wild boar, and it was as a result of such a hunting party that a ten year search ended.

On 22 October 1943, 2nd Lt. Wayland E. Bennett took off on a training flight from Fighter One airfield to do dive bombing practice on a hill in the remote central jungles of Espiritu Santo. According to a report of an accompanying aircraft, Bennett's F4U-1 Corsair spun into the jungle after his right wing buckled, and he slammed into the ground at 400 knots. This partially buried the engine in the ground and set off ammunition which penetrated a wing. (When the aircraft was located, they found more than 2,000 rounds of live ammunition at the site). A search was conducted but as there were no landmarks in the flat green terrain, and the aircraft did not explode and burn on impact, all searches were unsuccessful, and Wayland Bennett was officially listed as Missing in Action.

On 28 June 1948, a Missing in Action (MIA) team located what was believed to be Bennett's aircraft which 'yielded human remains and artifacts', and were thought initially to be those of Bennett. But there was insufficient evidence to be conclusive, so Bennett remained, if not officially, missing in action. Certainly his family and friends were not convinced, and yet little could be done. As far as the U.S. Army was concerned, the matter was closed and no further searches were taken.

Police and Vanuatu Military Force men search the site of the wrecked Catalina, but very little was recovered apart from what the village people had already taken and returned.

In 1988, a chance meeting between an old schooldays friend of Bennett, and an amateur aircraft enthusiast, Dr. Dan Bookout, resulted in a determined effort to locate the remains of Wayland Bennett. Bookout solicited local Port Vila rancher Ken MacGowan to assist and although Bennett's aircraft was not found, MacGowan located a further six aircraft. Bookout lay claim to finding eight aircraft.

In the meantime, Port Vila resident Reece Discombe was aware of the loss of the F4U and had conducted several searches of his own. Several aircraft had been located, but none that could be identified as that of Bennett. Reece co-operated later with Bookout in the search and organised regular forays into the jungle following up native finds. In June 1993, after yet another rumour, Reece flew to Espiritu Santo and recovered the ID plate off an aircraft, #02608. It was Bennett's. The aircraft was relatively intact, considering its reported impact, with the tail section and one wing separated from the fuselage. A skeleton lay partially out of the cockpit.

From 2 to 5 April 1994, a U.S. Army search and recovery team from the Central Identification Laboratory in Hawaii, conducted an excavation on the site. Human skeletal and dental remains were recovered, along with personal items and equipment, and taken to Hawaii for further inspection and identification. Although human remains were fragmented and weathered, there were sufficient for further identification.

Bennett's remains were returned to his home town of Texarkana, where he was interred after a memorial service on 16 September 1994. Reece Discombe and wife Jean were invited, and attended the ceremony. Judging by newspaper reports in the Texarkana Gazette, it was Bookout who received the accolades.

The year 1994 saw another amazing find in the jungles of Espiritu Santo. On 14 January, timber cutters working on the eastern slope of Tarok mountain near Matantas village discovered the remains of a United States Catalina flying

The two wing emblems show the peacetime and wartime markings on the Catalina, one painted over the other but time has faded them into one.

boat and crew. The aircraft was completely burnt out, having hit the top of the mountain only ten feet below the tree line

The aircraft, serial number 2389, with eight crew on board, was lost on 6 August 1942, a day before the US assault on Guadalcanal. The Catalina was returning from a regular patrol when it hit the mountain during a rain storm. It was later positively identified by a vendors data plate recovered from site:
BREWSTER AERONAUTICAL CORP, LONG IS, CITY NY
PBY-5 8775LBS CONT. 70496C.

It turned out to be a PBY-5 Catalina, built 21 April 1941, operating as one of the Black Cat Squadron, VP-23, so-named because their tails were painted black.

After having been located by a logging company bulldozer driver, the authorities were notified. Ken MacGowan was asked to conduct an investigation with the approval and support of the Vanuatu police and military. 'When I got there all the bones and firearms had been removed by the natives. The police and myself went down to the village and recovered them and they were taken to the police station'.

Little remained of the wrecked aircraft. The port and starboard engine assemblies and a section of the starboard wing were identifiable. Two insignia could be clearly seen on the wing - a neutrality red disc within a white star on a surrounding circular blue field, and a war time insignia of a white star within a blue field. The later could have been painted over the peacetime insignia, with weathering allowing the two to be seen after fifty years.

A 500 lb live bomb was located some twenty metres forward of the starboard engine, causing some concern to later investigators. A Colt 45 revolver, two ,30 calibre machine guns, and an assortment of personal and navigational items were recovered from the site and from the village, including portion of a gold watch band, flight goggles, pocket knives, and a navigational watch. The recovered human remains appeared to make up five bodies. No dog tags were recovered.

If controversy dogged the recovery of Wayland Bennett, the finding of the Catalina brought it all to a head. Because the CILHI team had removed the skeletal remains from Vanuatu without proper authority, a second team from the Central Identification Laboratory in Hawaii was denied entry visas, causing some concern between the two Governments. It was noted that the first CILHI team had 'breached agreement by not submitting a report, and removed articles from Vanuatu.'

Custom land owners came in to the act, and after seeking court action, an order was granted forbidding foreigners from collecting bones and remains from their custom land. The remains of the victims of the crash were all later returned to the USA for burial, and identified.

Espiritu Santo has not attracted many of the half million or so American servicemen who passed through Luganville during the Pacific war to return to the island for a nostalgic visit. It was not a war theatre, and no men were lost due to enemy action. There are no pilgrimages by members of the various unit associations to relive old times, nor any need to pay respects to old comrades. Perhaps the men do not have special memories for the island, despite its beauty. Perhaps they had little time to enjoy its charms. Whatever the reason, very few American ex-servicemen return through curiosity.

It is left to the scuba divers to show their appreciation, for if a ship is to be lost, let it be close to shore, in shallow water, and with no loss of life. The *President Coolidge* meets two of these demands.

STOP PRESS

In June 1998, Colonel (Retd) Stephen Parisi of Massachusetts, USA, fulfilled a half-century ambition by returning to Espiritu Santo and diving on the *President Coolidge*. After successfully completing a dive course in his home town, he was taken down to the ship by Allan Power. Such was Allan's confidence in Colonel Parisi's new-found skills, and his enthusiasm for seeing the ship once again, that Allan's divemaster took the Colonel on further dives, as far down as the bridge area, and a penetration into No.2 hold. Colonel Parisi, at 82 years of age, is the oldest person to have dived the *President Coolidge*. What a wonderful, rewarding achievement this must have been, for both Colonel Parisi and Allan Power.

S.S. PRESIDENT COOLIDGE
Statistics & Departures

DIMENSIONS & STATISTICS

Length Overall	654 ft 3 in.
Length on 32-foot water line	630 ft.
Beam, moulded	81 ft.
Length between perpendiculars	61 ft 5 in.
Depth, moulded, to Boat Deck, at side	79 ft 6 in.
Depth, moulded to Promenade Deck, at side	70 ft.
Depth, moulded to Bridge Deck, at side	61 ft.
Maximum draft, to bottom of bar keel	34 ft.
Displacement at Maximum draft,	33,350 tons.
Tons per inch at maximum draft	94.9
Midship Section coefficient	.979
Black Coefficient (on water line length)	.675
Gross Tonnage	21,936
Net Tonnage	12,986

Capacity:

Fuel oil (all available tanks), tons	6240
Water ballast (all available tanks), tons	5670
Coconut oil (tanks available for fuel or coconut oil), tons	1181
Fresh water, tons	2320
General cargo - bales, cu. ft.	556,000
Refrigerated cargo, cu ft.	59,500

Power Plant:

Propellers	2
Shaft horsepower	26,500
Speed at rated power, knots	20.83
Cruising radius (full speed), nautical miles	14,500
Cruising radius (cruising speed) naut.miles	19,500

Passengers:	First class	307
	Special class	133
	Third class	170
	Steerage	378
Crew		324

DETAILS

Ordered in 1929.
Keel laid in April 1930.
Built in 1931 by Newport News Shipbuilding & Dry Dock Co., Newport News, Virginia.
Customer: Dollar Line for the trans-Pacific passenger service.
At the time of her building she was rated as a 21-knot vessel and was the largest liner ever constructed in an American yard.
Built to compete with Japanese lines in the Pacific
Cost US $7,050,000
President Hoover and *President Coolidge* were the only two vessels designed and built from the keel up for the Dollar.
Launched 21 February 1931.
Completed 10 September 1931. First sea trials.
Delivered: 1 October 1931.
Maiden voyage: 15 October 1931. New-York-San Francisco-Far East.
Inaugural commander: Captain K. A. Ahlin
Home port San Francisco.
First commercial Far East voyage, from San Francisco: 6 November 1931
The Dollar Line was taken over by the US Government and continued as the American President Line in 1938.
Taken over by Maritime Commission: 2 June 1941.
First voyage under U.S. Army control: 15 July 1941.
War Shipping Administration takes over from Maritime Comm.: 21 Feb 1942.
Sunk by striking a mine at entrance to harbor, Espiritu Santo: 26 October 1942.

DESCRIPTION

There were nine decks in all, containing the sun deck, three of them being for the full length. The forecastle deck was known as the bridge deck, with promenade and boat decks above. Twelve watertight bulkheads divided the ship. The after funnel was a dummy over the engine room. No. 4 hold and between decks were insulated and served by side hatches. There were side doors on the main deck into Nos. 2, and 4 cargo spaces. Provision was made for three guns forward and two aft, and four A.A. guns between the funnels. Two masts and two stacks. Complete superstructure combined forecastle and bridge deck.

The ship had twin screws and a turbo-electric drive, the turbines driving two huge generators which supplied current to the two main motors coupled directly to the shafts, all built by the Westinghouse Company. Each motor was capable of producing 13,250 hp but the normal s.h.p. was 24, 250.

Design speed was 20 knots in service, with 21 as a maximum (but the *President Hoover* reached 22 knots in her trials). Steam for the turbines was provided by twelve Babcock and Wilcox watertube boilers, at 300 psi, burning oil fuel from the 6,250 ton bunkers.

In 1938 the '$' insignia was removed from the smokestacks of the fleet, replaced by the proud eagle of the newly-born American President Lines. The new funnel colours were blue with a broad red band on it, a white American eagle and four white stars, while the hulls were changed to grey.

VOYAGES

The following sailing list has been compiled from a number of sources, including Sailing Cards, and the Ship's Log held by the San Francisco Museum. These however are incomplete. The list has been supplemented from other sources, some of which may lack credibility. The gaps are intentional - where no data is available.

DEPARTURES		ARRIVALS	
1940			
12 Sept	Shanghai	Honolulu	
22 Sept	Honolulu	San Francisco	27 Sept.
29 Sept	San Francisco	San Pedro	30 Sept.
1 Oct	San Pedro		
5 Oct		Honolulu	10 Oct.
10 Oct	Honolulu	Manila	28 Oct.
30 Oct	Manila	Hong Kong	1 Nov.
3 Nov	Hong Kong	Shanghai	
6 Nov	Shanghai	Kobe	8 Nov.
	Kobe	Yokohama	10 Nov.
10 Nov	Yokohama	Honolulu	17 Nov.
17 Nov	Honolulu	San Francisco	22 Nov.
24 Nov	San Francisco	San Pedro	25 Nov.
26 Nov	San Pedro	San Francisco	27 Nov
4 Dec	San Francisco	Honolulu	9 Dec.
9 Dec	Honolulu	Manila	
24 Dec	Manila		
	Shanghai	Kobe	3 Jan 1941
1941			
18 Jan	San Francisco	San Pedro	19 Jan.
20 Jan	San Pedro	San Francisco	21 Jan.
24 Jan	San Francisco	Honolulu	29 Jan.
29 Jan	Honolulu	Hong Kong	
23 Feb	Hong Kong		
26 Feb	Shanghai	Kobe	
28 Feb	Kobe	Honolulu	8 Mar.
8 Mar	Honolulu	San Francisco	13 Mar.
15 Mar	San Francisco	San Pedro	16 Mar.
17 Mar	San Pedro	San Francisco	18 Mar.
21 Mar		Honolulu	26 Mar.
26 Mar	Honolulu	Kobe	
5 April	Kobe	Manila	14 April
	Manila	Hong Kong	
22 April	Hong Kong	Kobe	
27 April	Kobe	Honolulu	6 May
6 May	Honolulu	San Francisco	11 May
14 May	San Francisco	San Pedro	14 May
16 May	San Pedro	San Francisco	17 May
20 May	San Francisco	Honolulu	25 May
25 May	Honolulu	Orient	
	Orient	Honolulu	28 June

2 June 1941 - taken over by Maritime Commission.

28 June	Honolulu	San Francisco	3 July
7 July	San Francisco	San Pedro	10 July
	San Pedro	San Francisco	

VOYAGES (continued)

DEPARTURES		ARRIVALS	
15 July 1941 - first voyage under contract to the Army.			
15 July	San Francisco	Honolulu	20 July
20 July	Honolulu	Manila	
	Manila	Shanghai	12 Aug.
	Shanghai	Honolulu	23 Aug.
23 Aug.	Honolulu	San Francisco	28 Aug.
8 Sept.	San Francisco	Honolulu	13 Sept.
	(Orient)	Honolulu	18 Oct.
18 Oct.	Honolulu	San Francisco	23 Oct.
1 Nov	San Francisco	Honolulu	6 Nov.
6 Nov	Honolulu	Manila	
3 Dec	Port Moresby	Honolulu	5 Dec.
20 Dec	Honolulu	San Francisco	25 Dec.
1942			
1 Jan	San Francisco		
12 Jan	San Francisco	Melbourne	
	Melbourne	Wellington	
	Wellington	San Francisco	7 March
	San Francisco		
15 Feb	Melbourne	Wellington	18 Feb
	Wellington	San Francisco	6 March
19 March	San Francisco	Melbourne	
	Melbourne	San Francisco	8 May
	San Francisco	Melbourne	17 April
21 April	Melbourne	Bora Bora	
	Bora Bora	San Francisco	5/8 May
26 May	San Francisco	Suva, Fiji	9 June
16 June	Suva, Fiji	Auckland	19 June
24 June	Auckland	Suva	27 June
(30 June discharging in Suva).			
2 July	Suva	Auckland	6 July
11 July	Auckland	Suva	14 July
20 July	Suva	Auckland	23 July
	Auckland	Suva	
10 Aug.	Suva	Auckland	12 August
	Auckland	San Francisco	29 August
6 Oct.	San Francisco	Noumea	20 October
24 Oct.	Noumea	Espiritu Santo	26 October

The *President Coolidge* sank off Espiritu Santo Monday, 26 October, 1942

AMERICAN PRESIDENT LINES'
Role In World War 2.

By Eugene F. Hoffman
Vice President-Public Relations
American President Lines
15 June 1957.

In the late Fall of 1940 - more than a year prior to Pearl Harbor - almost the entire facilities of the globe-girdling American President Lines were made available to the United States Government by request of the State Department. It was then that the thunder clouds of the Sino-Japanese War threatened to extend to the Western World. France had fallen, and with Hitler seemingly assured of victory, there was gathering evidence that Tojo might lead Japan into active military alliance with Germany and Italy, against Britain and America.

There were thousands of United States citizens scattered throughout the Orient, and the State Department felt that they should be brought home at the earliest possible date. Thus it was that during the first week in October, 1940-exactly 14 months before Pearl Harbor-the SS *President Pierce* sailed from San Francisco on regular schedule to the Orient with instructions to bring home the first evacuees-the wives and children of Americans stationed in the Far East.

The *President Pierce* arrived in San Francisco in late November with the first trickle of what later was to become a heavy stream of evacuees from the Orient, the great mass of whom were brought home in vessels of the American President Lines. This stream reached tidal proportions and was climaxed on January 16, 1941, when the liner *President Coolidge* arrived in San Francisco with a total of 832 passengers aboard to set an all-time record for number of passengers carried by a merchant vessel in regular trans-Pacific service.

Thus for many months before the United States entered the war as a belligerent, the entire merchant fleet of the American President Lines was already engaged in war work, or more appropriately at that time, 'defence work'. Not only were her big trans-Pacific carriers bringing home American repatriates and evacuees of other nationalities, but these same vessels and others in the Company's Round-World service were coming home with their holds laden with essential and strategic raw materials needed for national defence and the war which was soon to be upon us.

Even as far back as the Fall of 1937, two years before Hitler invaded Poland, the American President Lines felt the sting of war and sensed the 'shape of things to come.' The Sino-Japanese war was new then, but its pace was furious and awful. After the bombing of Shanghai many Americans besieged the office of the Company for passage home. One of the Company's two capital ships, the big luxury liner *President Hoover*, was dispatched on an errand of mercy to pick up these passengers when, off Woosung, she was mysteriously bombed and severely damaged. It was a daylight attack, and the Hoover was not armed; but her gallant commander, Captain George Yardley, and other deck officers, seized the ship's side arms and stood upon the bridge and fired away at the dive-bombing planes. One bomb struck the sun deck on the port side of the after funnel and penetrated to the A-deck staterooms. Fortunately the staterooms were unoccupied at the time and no passengers were killed.

I

But several of the ship's crewmen were injured, one fatally, and the vessel was damaged to the extent of a half-million dollars.

A few months later, the *President Cleveland*, on a similar errand of mercy, was fired upon from shore and strafed from the air while in the Yangtze River, but no casualties resulted.

Following the *President Hoover's* return to San Francisco where the bombing damage was repaired, the Company, on advice of the State Department, charted a new course for her which would bypass the turbulent China Sea. Hereafter, she would take the 'outside' passage, sailing South to Manila in the open sea east of Formosa. On her first voyage over this new course, the 22,000-ton *President Hoover* ran aground on a tiny rocky island off Formosa and became a total loss. It was said that the Japanese had always maintained a light on this rocky island, but on the night the Hoover went aground the light was out. After her abandonment, the Hoover hull was reported salvaged by the Japanese for its scrap value.

The *President Hoover* went aground with 1000 souls aboard, approximately 600 of them passengers. The seamanship of the officers and crew was so expert that not a life was lost, and many not even had wet feet. This happened on December II, 1937. The following day the United States gunboat *Panay* was bombed and sunk near Nanking by Japanese planes. This was almost exactly 4 years before the attack on Pearl Harbor.

Prior to America's entry into the war, and after the *President Hoover* was lost, the American President Lines operated the following ships and services:

TRANS-PACIFIC. San Francisco-Honolulu-Yokohama-Kobe-Shanghai-Hong Kong - Manila - Hong Kong - Shanghai - Kobe - Yokohama - Honolulu - San Francisco - Los Angeles.
Steamers: *President Coolidge, President Pierce, President Cleveland, President Taft.*

'ROUND-WORLD. New York - Havana - Los Angeles - San Francisco - Honolulu - Kobe - Shanghai - Hong Kong - Manila - Singapore - Penang - Colombo - Bombay - Suez - Port Said - Alexandria - Naples - Genoa - Marseille - Boston - New York
Steamers: *President Harrison, President Garfield* later renamed *Madison, President Polk* later renamed *Taylor, President Adams* later renamed *Grant, President Van Buren* later renamed *Fillmore, President Monroe* later renamed *Buchanan, President Hayes* later renamed *Tyler.*

In 1938, the Company ordered seven new combination passenger and freight vessels of a special

type known as C3P, to be built under provisions of the Maritime Commission construction program, at Newport News, Va., to replace the seven older vessels in the Round-World trade.

During the last half of 1940 and the first half of 1941, American President Lines took delivery of the following new vessels: *SS President Jackson, SS President Monroe, SS President Hayes, SS President Polk, SS President Van Buren, SS President Garfield.*

The Navy took delivery of the seventh vessel, the *SS President Adams*, directly from the yards at Newport News, and subsequently the Government requisitioned for purchase the *Jackson, Hayes, Van Buren* and *Garfield*. At the same time the Navy took over on a bareboat charter basis the *Monroe* and *Polk*.

Also owned and operated by the American President Lines were the: *SS Ruth Alexander, SS President Johnson* (ex-*Manchuria*).

Several of the Company's larger combination passenger and freight vessels taken over by the government performed distinguished service in the various invasions in the European theatre of war. American President Lines' vessels in the trans-Pacific and Round-World service were particularly well suited for quick conversion into troop transports. The *President Coolidge* and the 535-type liners were outfitted and on berth to load troops within a few days after being requisitioned.

As a result of the war in Europe in September 1939, regular trades and services of many Allied Nations in competition with American President Lines were either disrupted or completely suspended. In order to offset this serious loss of ship tonnage and at the same time cope with the abnormally heavy movement of critical strategic materials and the general cargo movement, American President Lines, through various charter and agency agreements, supplemented its own ship tonnage with vessels of other American flag owners. This supplemental tonnage was placed on the American President Lines' vital routes between this country and China, Philippines, Netherlands Indies, Malaya, Burma, India and Ceylon. Thus prior to Pearl Harbor, American President Lines, in addition to the above named vessels, were operating agents for ships owned or controlled by: American Pioneer Line, Coastwise-Far East Line, Baltimore Mail Line, Lykes Brothers Steamship Company, Luckenbach Steamship Company, U.S. Army Transport Service, U.S. Maritime Commission (Danish Ships).

While the majority of these ships were freighters, which during 1940 and eleven months of 1941 were pouring essential raw materials into the United States, the big passenger carriers, such as the *Presidents Coolidge, Pierce, Cleveland* and *Taft* were shuttling back and forth across the Pacific, bringing home capacity loads of evacuees and refugees. On. their outward voyages these same vessels were carrying Army and Navy personnel and needed supplies to bases overseas. General Macarthur and his staff originally sailed to Manila on the *President Coolidge*.

Meanwhile, American President Lines' Round--World vessels were bringing into Atlantic Coast U.S. ports similar capacity loads of evacuees from Mediterranean ports and war-torn Europe.

Chronological stepping stones that marked the path to Pearl Harbor and the American President Lines operations in the Pacific increasingly difficult and restricted were the following:

July 26 1939 -The United States notified the Japanese Government of the former's decision to abrogate the American Treaty of- Commerce and Navigation.

March 30, 1940 -Wang Ching Wei's Puppet Government was established in Nanking.

October 16, 1940-The United States placed an embargo on scrap iron and steel exports to Japan. (It was in this month, October, 1940, that the U.S. State Department urged all non-essential men and all women and children to leave the Far Eastern danger zones. Immediately following this order, American President Lines undertook the enormous task of citizen evacuation. A few ships of other Companies, notably the *SS Monterey* and *SS Mariposa* of the Matson Line, and the *SS Washington* of the United States Lines, cooperated in this undertaking, for which American President Lines acted as -Far Eastern Agents.)

July 29, 1941-Japan officially occupied all of Indo-China.

November 14, 1941 - President Roosevelt ordered the evacuation of American Marines from China.

November 27, 28, 1941 - *SS President Harrison* and the *SS President Madison*, respectively, sailed from Shanghai to Manila with contingents of United States Marines aboard.

When on December 8, 1941, Japan formally declared war on the United States and Great Britain, the steamer *President Harrison* which had previously delivered a complement of United States Marines at Manila, was on her way back to Chinwangtao, North China to evacuate additional Marines from Peking. The *President Harrison* was overhauled by Japanese naval units off Woosung and seized as a prize of war. When the Captain and crew

saw that capture was inevitable, they risked their lives by running the ship hard aground on a rocky island in the East China Sea, deliberately wrecking the vessel in order to render her useless to the Japanese. Her crew was interned and all officers and passengers aboard with naval or military ratings were transferred to prison camps. Thus, the *President Harrison* became the first gold star in American President Lines Service Flag for floating equipment lost.

As evidence of the measure in which the American President Lines used its facilities to aid the Government in going to the rescue of distressed citizens, we quote the following letter dated September 2, 1941, from Secretary of State Cordell Hull to Henry F. Grady, who was then President of the American President Lines:

'My dear Mr. Grady:

I have learned that recently when the Department's officers were in consultation with you regarding the possibility of diverting the SS President Coolidge on her homeward voyage from Shanghai to a Japanese port to embark Americans desiring to return to the United States, your company, in addition to offering the services of the ship for that purpose, voluntarily, on its own initiative and at its own expense, ordered the necessary material placed aboard the ship at Shanghai to provide additional accommodations for the Americans in Japan in the event that arrangements could be made to embark them. As you know, it was not possible, to make these arrangements, but I wish to thank you and your Company for the fine spirit of patriotic cooperation with the Department which you have shown.

Sincerely yours, (Signed) Cordell Hull'

After the die was cast at Pearl Harbor, the entire physical resources and facilities of the American President Lines, plus the experience and energy of the management and personnel, were placed at the disposal of the United States Government and consecrated to the task of winning the war at the earliest possible moment.

Upon creation of the War Shipping Administration, all Company-owned vessels were bareboat chartered thereto, and key members of American President Lines' staff with special training in the shipping business were made available to the War Shipping Administration for important overseas assignment. Some APL staff members were already on loan to the Government in such positions as administrator for China Defence Supplies Corporation and Lend-Lease in India and Burma.

Three American President Lines' vessels were in or near Manila when the bombs fell on December 8. These were the: *SS Ruth Alexander, SS President Grant, SS President Madison.* The *Ruth Alexander* and the *Grant* were in port in Manila when the shooting started. There they became the principal target for aerial bombardment.

The Navy notified Company officials that they would not be able to give protection to ships in Manila Harbor and suggested that it would be safer for the vessels to 'make a run for it'. After consultation with the Masters it was decided to sail. Consequently, under cover of darkness, both ships departed. The President Grant, under Command of Captain W. S. Tyrrell, made good her escape and after an exciting and eventful voyage made safe port in Australia. The *Ruth Alexander*, under Command of Captain F. P. Willarts, was not so fortunate. She escaped at night some time after the *President Grant* departed but was caught by Japanese bombers in the Celebes Sea off Balikpapan. Defenceless against the merciless bombing, the gallant little steamer was blasted to the bottom of the sea, and so became gold star No. 2 in the Company service flag. One member of her crew was killed and a half dozen others were wounded. After tossing about in open boats for many hours, survivors were sighted and picked up by a Dutch Dornier flying boat and taken to Balikpapan.

The rescue was heroic. The Dutch pilot of the Dornier ordered all his bombs and supplies jettisoned to make room for the 46-man crew of the an sunken vessel. At that, the only way this number could be accommodated was to have them stand close together, like sticks of cordwood. Even the wounded had to stand straight up. The plane's load was so heavy the pilot had to taxi five miles before he could get his ship into the air.

The *SS President Madison*, commanded by Captain Vaidemar Nielsen, was south of the Philippines when the war broke out. This vessel played hide and seek, through the Dutch East Indies, sailing mostly at night, and eventually made home port safety.

When the *SS President Taylor* sailed from San Francisco January 5, 1941, it marked the 17th anniversary of the inauguration of the Company's famous 'Round-World' service. In 17 years 'President' liners, sailing every two weeks westward from San Francisco, had completed more than 350 circumnavigations totalling 10,000,000 miles. This record had been achieved without loss of a single passenger's life as a result of accident.

But even before the 17th anniversary was celebrated, events were happening that were to jeop-ardize that famous route of the 'round-world ships. The great Mediterranean Sea, an important segment of the circuit, was being claimed by Italy's Il Duce as *mare nostrum*. The hazards of the war were increasing constantly and although American President Lines used the Mediterranean route as long as possible, it finally became necessary for it to abandon the regular course and route its vessels from the Far East around the Cape of Good Hope, a deviation of more than 3,000 miles which lengthened the voyage by some 10 days additional steaming, a serious matter when speed was vital in building up the nation's stock pile of strategic material.

An example of how American imports of these materials jumped during 1941 is offered in the statistics of crude rubber. Prior to 1940, America imported an average of 400,000 tons of rubber per annum. In 1941, rubber imports exceeded one million tons, a substantial portion of which was carried in ships owned or operated by American President Lines. Comparable increases reflected in the figures for tin and other war-making commodities.

After the Neutrality Act was repealed, American President Lines, along with many other American steamship companies, diverted much of its tonnage to carrying Lend-Lease cargoes to the Red Sea, and to Murmansk and Archangel.

With America's formal entry into the war, this famous 'Round-World' service, like the Company's trans-Pacific service, was completely disrupted, and all APL tonnage then became consolidated in the newly formed War Shipping Admin-istration pool.

In the Summer of 1941, due to mounting tension and repeated hostile actions of Japanese toward American and British nationals in China, American President Lines moved its Far Eastern headquarters from Shanghai to Manila. Already the Company had discontinued steamer calls at Japanese ports, first curtailing them and finally bypassing Japan entirely.

The headquarters staff, then under the direction of Vice President Oscar G. Steen, arrived in Manila in late August, 1941, and in January, 1942, all staff members, except four who had previously joined the U.S. Armed Forces, were interned at Santo Tomas prison, Manila. Of the four APL employees who 'joined up', one was reported killed in action, a second drowned when a Japanese prison ship went down, and the other two were interned by the Japanese. The Company's Singapore staff escaped by plane to Java, and eventually made their way to Australia. The Hong Kong staff was interned in Stanley Prison for a period of six months and then re-patriated on the first Gripsholm to America.

Although the headquarters office had been re-moved from Shanghai, a skeleton crew had been retained there to look after the Company's interest. This staff was not immediately imprisoned, but was confined to a restricted area in the International Settlement. However, in February, 1943, the Shanghai staff members were placed in various prison camps. In September, 1943, three of them were repatriated to the U.S. Three others remained in internment. In September, 1943, three of the staff at Manila were also repatriated, leaving fourteen still interned there.

Creation of the War Shipping Administration brought a demand for experienced shipping exec-utives to serve the Administration at various world ports. No less than ten American President Lines officials were loaned to the Government for this purpose. They served at Allied control ports in India, South America, Europe, Australia, Hawaii and various ports in the continental United States.

In addition to these men with the War Shipping Administration, American President Lines had 131 of its regular shoreside staff serving with the Armed Forces-Army, Navy and Marine Corps.

In the meantime, American President Lines, in common with other U.S. merchant ship operators, was receiving its full share of Liberty ships and others that began sliding down the ways in ever increasing numbers in our nation's shipyards.

At the time over eighty vessels had been assigned to American President Lines as agents for the War Shipping Administration. However, from December 7, 1941, cargo operations on various other vessels assigned to Army, Navy and Lend Lease, for which American President Lines also acted as agent, ran well into the hundreds of ships. Contrast this picture with American President Lines' normal peacetime operation of less than 20 vessels, and one begins to appreciate the enormity of the wartime operation. And like any other phase of modern warfare, the operation of so many units of equipment implies a certain ratio of casualty. American President Lines had its share, and its log books and other Company records are replete with accounts of marine disaster and glowing tributes to the heroism and expert seamanship of officers and men.

There was the brave young purser whose sense of duty was so acute that he went down with his torpe-doed ship - the *MS Chant* in the Mediterranean in a vain attempt to save important documents of military value.

There was the young assistant purser of the bombed *Ruth Alexander*, who, although injured and badly shaken, went back to sea as soon as he had

recovered, only to have another ship shot out from under him, following which he tossed in an open lifeboat for 16 agonizing days before being rescued. This same lad went back to sea for a third and a fourth time, before finally being 'grounded' for the duration. He is Robert Feder, later the Company's Claims Agent at Manila.

There was the glorious episode at Dutch Harbor, where the officers and gun crew of the *SS President Filmore* were cited for Inconspicuous gallantry and intrepidity" after they had shot down three Japanese bombers and damaged a fourth during a bombing and strafing attack on the ship. Merchant Marine crewmen aboard ship were also cited for their part in fighting off the attack. The ship's officers and crew members "passed the ammunition" to the hard-pressed gunnery crew.

The gallant *SS President Filmore*, incidentally, along with the *President Madison,* was taken over by the Navy and converted into a hospital ship. As such she was re-christened the *SS Marigold* and the *Madison* was re-christened the SS *Refuge*. In addition to eleven Liberty ships and other agency-operated vessels, American President Lines lost as casualties of war a total of five of its own former peacetime fleet of vessels.

The loss of the SS *President Harrison*, captured in the China Sea, and the *Ruth Alexander*, bombed off Borneo, we have already described. In addition to these two, the Company also lost the big trans-Pacific liner, *President Coolidge*; the *SS President Taylor* and the *SS President Grant*.

The *President Coolidge*, commanded by Captain Henry Nelson, with 4,000 U.S. Army troops aboard became a war casualty off Espiritu Santo, New Hebrides, in the South Pacific. Due to the expert seamanship and the high morale of the troops, all hands were saved except one crew member and one soldier, who were reported missing. The tragic loss of this big troop carrier was a severe blow to the Army transport service.

The *President Taylor*, with 1334 souls aboard, became the Company's fourth vessel casualty on 'Friday, the 13th' of February, 1942, off Canton Island in the South Pacific. No lives were lost. The *President Grant*, mentioned earlier as having escaped from Manila after the Japanese attacked the Philippines, became the Company's fifth war casualty, also in the South Pacific. It was loaded with troops and a full crew, but all hands were saved.

Several other distinguished 'President' liners, which had been taken over on requisition by the Armed Forces early in the war, also became casualties of battle. These included the *SS President Cleveland* and the SS *President Pierce*, troop carriers, which were lost in the North African invasion; and one of the C3P combination 'Presidents' taken over by the Navy and used as a supply ship. This latter vessel was grounded in the Eastern Mediterranean and became a total loss.

Thus there are eight known gold stars in American President Lines' service flag of ships; and several thousand stars - a revered number of them gold - in the Company's service flag of personnel.

In summary, prior to Pearl Harbor American President Lines had twenty (20) owned vessels. All twenty 'went to war' ... and only three came back. The Company's pre-war fleet consisted of these vessels: seven Old 'Round-the-World '502s'; seven New 'Round-the-World 'C3Ps'; one Luxury passenger liner - *President Coolidge*; three Trans-Pacific '535s' - *Cleveland, Pierce, Taft*; one SS

President Johnson (then 37 years old), and one SS *Ruth Alexander* (former Pacific Coast Passenger Carrier).

Of these 20 vessels, only the old *President Johnson* (which had advanced in age to 42 years), and two C3Ps, the *SS President Polk* and the *SS President Monroe,* were returned to the Company.

It is a stirring testimonial to the American Way that within a period of little more than a decade this humble fleet of three war-weary ships could evolve into the mighty merchant armada that now fans out over four major world trade routes under the American President Lines' flag.

Like the winning of the war itself, this notable achievement of building a peace-time merchant fleet would not be possible without the three-way partnership of Government, Private Industry and Labor - all working together for the common good.

RECORD OF PROCEDURES
and other papers.

HEARINGS

1. A preliminary Court of Inquiry was held on 12 November 1942, on board *U.S.S. Whitney*, convened by order of the Admiral W.F. Halsey, Commander, South Pacific Area and South Pacific Force. The court sat for five days and sought to establish the cause of the sinking of *President Coolidge*. The Inquiry lays the blame on Captain Nelson and recommended further proceedings and prosecution.

2. A Military Commission was held at College La Perouse, Noumea, New Caledonia over six days from 8 December to 14 December 1942, to hear a chargee laid by Admiral W. Halsey against Captain Henry Nelson. Captain Nelson was acquitted.

3. A U.S. Coastguard 'A' Marine Investigation Board sat in San Francisco on 6 February 1943 to consider details on the loss of the *SS President Coolidge*. The Board accepted the findings of the Military Commission and no further action is taken.

RECORD OF PROCEDURE OF A COURT OF INQUIRY CONVENED ON BOARD THE *U.S.S. WHITNEY*. 12 November 1942.

1. The *President Coolidge* was sunk by mines in a mine field, at 0935 ship's time, on October 26, 1942, while the vessel was proceeding from Noumea to the harbor at Luganville Bay, Santos Island, with 5050 U.S. troops aboard. The vessel was beached upon a ledge, several hundred yards from the beach, by the Master, listed over on her port side, gradually filled, slipped entirely off the reef and sank, at 10.45 ship's time. It is stated her bow was down in 70 ft of water and her stern in 270 ft.

2. The vessel, employed in transporting troops, was reported under orders to proceed to the Buttons, as the waters of Luganville Bay are known, where she was to meet a small boat with a pilot out side the mine field. The location of the mine field was refused the Master. The vessel was reported by the 2nd. Officer, who was on the deck, to be making 15 knots but others believe that speed excessive. Weather fair and clear: sea smooth: wind not stated: visibility good: daylight. Ships in vicinity of the harbor.

3. The vessel approached Santos Island at about 0850, ship's time, stopped one half hour to talk to a destroyer, anchored at the spot marked x on Charter No. 2833. The destroyer instructed the Master to proceed into Luganville Bay to the east and around Tutuba Island. The vessel then proceeded, evidently following the destroyer's instructions, without waiting for a pilot and had reached the position marked No. 1 on the when the first explosion occurred. The 2nd. Officer stated the vessel did not wait for a pilot as it was not healthy outside. The first explosion, at 0930 ship's time, was amidships port side at the after fireroom as the water rushed into that compartment first according to the men on watch. One half minute after the first explosion, there was a second explosion on the starboard side of the engine room. These explosions were not on the sides of the vessel but on her double bottoms. Engines were at standby at the first explosion, but it is uncertain how long they had been at that point. The vessel had

enough headway to permit the Master to turn her to the beach 300 - 400 yards away. In three minutes the water had entered the fireroom and had reached the operating controls. Watertight bulkheads had already been closed. The Master immediately ordered right rudder and headed for shore. The vessel ran the distance to shallow water, pushed herself upon a ledge, several hundred yards from the beach and sank in one hour. As vessel now lies, she is completely out of sight upon coral reefs that drop off very fast.

4. Almost immediately, the Master gave orders to abandon ship. Life rafts and lifeboats were used; Navy vessels, of which there were a number in the harbor, gave assistance. Some of the men swam the short distance to shore. It is reported one in the crew and four among the troops were lost. The crew of vessel was ashore for 6 or 7 days, and then taken aboard the *SS Island Mail* and *SS Cape Fairweather*. Twenty-six of the crew 'hitch hiked' on Army planes from Santos Island to Noumea, where they boarded the *SS Lurline*, sailed November 6, 1942, and later arrived in San Francisco. Most of the cargo was aboard when the vessel and a small amount of the cargo only having been discharged at Noumea.

5. The Master, Third Mate, who was on watch; and the members of the Purser's Department, went to Noumea, where a hearing was held. The Master of

the *SS Joseph Stanton* (U.S.) in Espiritu Santo, on October 25, 1942, reports that at about midnight all hands were called to battle stations and firing was heard in the distance. It was later ascertained this firing came from a Japanese submarine shelling the airport. When the *President Coolidge* entered Espiritu Santo the next day the Master of the *Joseph Stanton* stated the *President Coolidge* was ordered to stop by the patrol vessel outside in order to pick up a pilot, but did not do so and steamed toward the wrong channel entrance at about 15 knots in a northerly direction, instead of a westerly direction which she should have followed. The signal tower operator at the Port Director's Office, is reported to have ordered the vessel to stop and go full speed astern in order to avoid the mines. But this order was likewise ignored. It is also stated that while the Navy tried its best to avert the accident, the command was heeded too late. Because the cargo and side ports were open, a breach of regulations, the ship sank much faster than had they been closed.

Authors comment: Several details presented as facts above were later disproved or disputed at the Military Commission convened a month later in Noumea on 8 December 1942. For example, the destroyer (*USS Sterett*) did not instruct the *President Coolidge* to enter the channel; nor did *President Coolidge* 'ignore' any warning signals.

FINDING OF FACTS - ADMIRAL W.F. HALSEY

Document prepared by Admiral W. F. Halsey, US Navy, Commander South Pacific Area and South Pacific forces, 'based on his understanding of testimony given at the Court of Inquiry on board *U.S.S. Whitney*, on 12 November 1942, the Court of Inquiry having been convened by order of the Commander, South Pacific Area and South Pacific Force'.

Author's comment: In the absence of a date appended to the document, it could be assumed that Halsey's Finding of Facts were compiled after the Court of Inquiry, but before the Military Commission. The timing however is irrelevant as there is no record that these 'facts' were presented as evidence during the Military Commission in Noumea on 8 December 1942. They do however show the misunderstanding, or perhaps prejudice, of Admiral Halsey.

1. That the S.S. *President Coolidge* was lost as the direct result of having struck two mines in the

approaches to Segond Channel, Espiritu Santo, New Hebrides, at about 0935, October 26, 1942.
2. That after striking the mines the ship was intentionally beached on a reef near shore.
3. That at 1053, October 26, 1942, the ship slid from reef and sank in the approximate position, latitude 15°31'20" south, longitude 167°13'00" east. where she now lays.
4. That the *S.S. President Coolidge* was a seaworthy passenger steamship of the following characteristics: Length 654 feet. Beam 81 feet. Displacement 33,035 tons. Screws 2 (electric drive). Full load draft 34 feet. Normal cruising speed 26 knots. Builders cost approximately $9,000,000 when completed in 1931.
5. That the ship was owned by the American President Lines and chartered by the War Department.
6. That the officers and crew of the ship were civilians in the employ of and paid by the owners.
7. That the master of the *President Coolidge* was

Henry Nelson, the defendant before this court.

8. That at about 1330, October 24, 1942, prior to sailing from Noumea, New Caledonia, to Segond Channel, Espiritu Santo, New Hebrides, the defendant received and receipted for a complete set of routing instructions issued by the duly constituted authority Noumea, New Caledonia.

9. That the aforesaid routing instructions were complete when delivered and therefore included the "Special Information", a copy of which is appended marked "Exhibit 3"

10. That about 1520, October 24, 1942, the ship sailed from Noumea, New Caledonia for Segond Channel, Espiritu Santo.

11. That the original of the routing instructions (Exhibit 2) delivered to the judge advocate by the defendant, contains the last sentence of paragraph one, page one, the follow 'Thence to Button. noting attached instructions for entering Segond Channel, Espiritu Santo'.

12. That at about 0800, October 26, 1942, the ship passed through a point of 'Espiritu Santo, designated as Point Hypo in the routing instructions.

13. That from 0800, October 26, 1942, until the ship sank the defendant had the conn of the ship.

14. That the detailed routing instructions furnished the defendant required him to enter Segond Channel by courses leading through Bogacio Island passages, south and west of Tutuba Island.

15. That at about 0730, October 26, 1942, when he ship was in a position about ten miles south of Point Hypo, she was challenged by a destroyer, DD407, then on offshore patrol duty. [The destroyer is identified as *Sterett*. The *President Coolidge* would not have been south of point Hypo, but south-east.]

16. That after passing through Point Hypo the ship was challenged by a patrol craft cruising in the waters between Tutuba and Malo Islands.

17. That after completion of the challenge by the patrol craft further communication was prevented by the *President.Coolidge* having attained such a position that Tutuba Island intervened between the two vessels.

18. That the patrol craft had on board a pilot for transfer to the *President Coolidge*.

19. That after passing through Point Hypo the defendant set course approximately 305° true heading to the east and north of Tutuba Island, preparatory to entering the Segond Channel.

20. That this course was altered to the left to, approximately 275° true and the ship rounded the northern end of Tutuba Island with the north end of said island abeam to port, distance about 1500 yards.

21. That the decision to enter Segond Channel on this score and through this entrance, without a guide vessel or pilot and in disregard of the 'Special Instructions' requiring entry through Bogacio Island passages, was made by the defendant, after doubt as to the proper approach to Segond Channel had been brought to his attention by the first officer K.I. Davis.

22. That the ship at this time was making 122 r.p.m.. or a speed of about 17 to 19 knots.

23. That the ship's position as she approached the entrance to Segond Channel was not plotted continuously.

24. That services and facilities were available to the defendant whist his ship was off port, by use of which he could have obtained entry instructions in addition to those contained in his written 'Special Instructions'.

25. That the defendant made no effort to obtain specific entrance instructions after his ship arrived off port.

26. That the first mate, Mr. Kilton I. Davis, of the S.S. *President Coolidge*, the navigating mate of the S.S. *President Coolidge*, did have knowledge of the presence of mines in the western entrance of Segond Channel as evidenced by his knowledge of the loss of the U.S.S. Tucker caused by these mines.

27. That sufficient time during the voyage was available to the defendant to thoroughly study his instructions.

28. That approximately 10 other vessels following exactly the same instructions as given to the defendant made safe entrance into Segond Channel, Espiritu Santo, and one of these vessels sailed from Noumea the same day as the *President Coolidge*.

29. That after having been informed that his ship was standing into danger, the defendant took prompt measures to kill the ships headway by first stopping the engines and then attempting to book.

30. That despite the defendant's efforts to kill the ship's headway, she struck a mine which caused loss of excitation of the ship's main generators and precluded engine room response to the booking bell.

31. That immediately upon hitting the first mine the defendant ordered right hard rudder, close all-watertight door's, and ordered the announcement over the public address system 'Abandon Ship'.

32. That the aforesaid action caused the ship, with her remaining headway, to take the ground in the approximate position, latitude 15°31'20" south, longitude 167°13'00" east.

33. That upon beaching one anchor was dropped with approximately 15 fathoms of chain.

34. That disembarkation of all passengers and crew was accomplished in about one hour, in a seamanlike manner.

MILITARY COMMISSION MEMBERS AND WITNESSES
8-14 December 1942, College La Perouse, Noumea, New Caledonia.

Accused: Henry Nelson.

Council for the accused: Captain Gordon B. Parks, US Navy; Chester C. Hosmer, US Naval Reserve.

Judge Advocate: Captain Richard Fagan, US Marine Corps, Retd. (First Marine Amphibious Force, Noumea, New Caledonia).

Commission Members: Rear Admiral Calvin H. Cobb, USN (President); Captain Schuyler Mills, US Navy; Captain George H. Bahm, US Navy; Commander Alexander F. Junker US Navy; Commander; Louis T. Young, US Navy.

Witnesses for the Prosecution:

John A. DeNovo, Ensign, USNR. (Assistant in the Port Director's office, Noumea, New Caledonia); Stanley H. Dunn, Yeoman 2c, USNR (Port Directors Office, Noumea); George E. Doyle, Cqm, USN (Chief quartermaster attached to naval Advance base, Noumea); Robert Lyons, civilian (Third Officer, *President Coolidge*); Doran S. Weinstein, Ensign, USNR (Communications officer, on board *President Coolidge*); Kilton I. Davis, civilian (First Officer, Navigating Mate on board *President Coolidge*); Milton McManus, civilian (Chief Officer on board *President Coolidge*); Dinsmore Alter, Colonel, USA (Coast Artillery Corps, United States Army. Commanding officer of troops aboard *President Coolidge*).

Witnesses for the Defence:

Doran S. Weinstein, Ensign, USNR (Communications officer, on board *President Coolidge*); John K. Davis, Lt, USNR (Commanding officer of PC479); Alexander J. Gray, Jr. Cdr, USN Retd. (U.S. Naval Advanced base, Noumea, New Caledonia); George E. Doyle, Cqm, USN (Chief quartermaster attached to naval Advance base, Noumea); William A. Benton III, Lt (jg), USNR (was stationed aboard *USS Whitney* (in Noumea) and had acted as pilot on occasions).

OBJECTION TO THE SPECIFICATION
Of the charge against Captain Henry Nelson, to be heard at the Military Commission, 8 December 1942.

1. The specification is objectionable in that it attempts to allege three distinct offenses in a single specification: First, did neglect and fail to follow instructions; second, did cause said ship to make a wrong approach to Segond Channel; third, did proceed at an excessive rate of speed which precluded him from receiving a pilot aboard or to act on timely warning.

2. The specification is objectionable in that it contains the following conclusions of fact:

(a) The allegation that: he did proceed at an excessive rate of speed which precluded him from receiving a pilot aboard or to act on timely warning; is a conclusion of fact. There are no facts set out to support such allegation. It would be impossible for the accused to prepare a defence against this allegation unless it is shown at what point the vessel should have slowed down and what speed would have been a safe speed.

(b) The allegation that: (he) "did negligently...... cause said ship to make a wrong *approach*" contains no information upon which the defendant could prepare a defence since no facts are alleged wherein the approach was "wrong".

(c) The conclusion of the pleader regarding a "vast" amount of cargo is so obviously conclusion that no argument is necessary.

3. The recital that: "having received a complete set of routing instructions including special information for safely entering Segond Channel, from the duly constituted port authority at Noumea, New Caledonia, did, while conning said ship, nevertheless, neglect and fail to follow or cause to be followed, the aforementioned instructions in approaching Segond Channel", does not identify in what particulars the accused is alleged to have neglected to follow the instructions. It does not state that the accused had been directed to, or that it was his duty to, follow any instructions hence no offense is alleged.

4. In this specification no facts are properly alleged which support the charge therefore the specification does not state a triable offense. It is fatally defective in at least four particulars.

STATEMENT OF THE ACCUSED

The sea has been my life for over 44 years. I received my unlimited master's license in 1905. Since that time I have been master of many vessels sailing in all parts of the world - since 1920 the President Wilson for 3 years, the President Pierce for 13 years, the President Cleveland for 1 year, and the *President Coolidge* for 3 years. I have sailed under various instructions from both private and governmental agencies. In all that time I have neither disregarded nor violated any instructions received unless they would have imperiled the safety of my vessel. I am at present the senior master and Commodore of the APL. I have been master of the S.S. *President Coolidge* since early 1940, a period of over 2 1/2 years. My affection for that vessel was as great as that a man may have for an inanimate object. My patriotism and love of country has never been questioned. I am not a young man, having reached the age of retirement even for Naval Officers. It was because of my feeling that my country needed me in its time of crises that I continued at sea rather than to seek retirement to enjoy with my family the few remaining years of my life.

I did not cause the loss of the S.S. *President Coolidge*. I received no special instructions for entrance to Segond Channel. I directed my ship to that channel in the safest manner possible with due consideration for the information that I had regarding it. With the information I had, it would have been poor seamanship to have directed my ship through the narrow Bocacyo (sic) passage when a wider and less navigationally hazardous entrance was available. For then, it would have been folly on my part under these circumstances to have delayed my arrival at Buttons by taking the longer Bocayco passage route and thus longer expose my ship to open water and submarine attacks.

I have been subjected to this trial by Military Commission at a foreign place and have been without the advice and comfort of my friends and family during this period. I have not been allowed to communicate with my company in order to receive advice, instruction, or aid. It has been necessary for me to entrust my defence of the charge before the Military Commission to those who were not previously well known to me either personally or by reputation.

I re-affirm my innocence of the charge and specifications. My whole life, career, and activities have been foreign to such.

Henry Nelson, Master.

EXHIBIT - SPECIAL INFORMATION

Author's comment: This is the contents of the document referred to as Special Instructions in the proceedings, as is the document at the centre of the Inquiries. It is this document that Captain Nelson was supposed to have received in order to safely enter Segond Channel, but which he maintains he never received.

Ships approaching Segond Channel, Espiritu Santo, are to use EAST Entrance only. White Rock has been located on South shore Espiritu Santo Island in Long. 167° 131' 27" East. Approach Eastern entrance from Bogacyo Island passages to point with White Rock bearing 345 degrees distance two miles. Steam toward White Rock until North tangent Ayre Island bears West which is danger bearing, then head into channel.

Entry into SEGOND CHANNEL is to be made only during daylight hours, from 0600 to 1800.

When clear of the port all lights are to be extinguished and dimmed Navigation lights only are to be exhibited to avoid collision. Paravanes, if fitted, are to be streamed in mineable waters. Zig-Zag during daylight and moonlight.

Note: When within 500 miles of an Allied Nation's base or territory, vessels are cautioned not to open fire on single aircraft unless actually attacked, as these patrol planes are most apt to be Allied patrols seeking to establish the ship's identity.

RECORD OF PROCEEDINGS OF A MILITARY COMMISSION CONVENED AT COLLEGE LA PEROUSE, NOUMEA, NEW CALEDONIA.
By order of Commander, South Pacific Area and South Pacific Force.
Case of Henry Nelson, Civilian, December 8, 1942.

Author's comment: This is a summary of evidence given at the Military Commission, extracted from the full text of the proceedings. As with most inquiries, there is a great deal of swearing in, administrative text and duplication of evidence which has not been included. Where similar evidence is given by more than one witness, only one extract is documented, unless there is conflicting evidence.

DAY ONE - Tuesday, 8 December 1942.

Ensign John DeNovo, assistant at the Port Director's office in Noumea, took the stand, and testified that he had delivered routing instructions to Captain Henry Nelson aboard *President Coolidge* on 24 October 1942. Of particular importance was a sheet of 'Special Information', (Exhibit 3), which DeNovo advises the commission was given to Captain Nelson along with general routing instructions (Exhibit 2). This is the crucial document that gave Captain Nelson specific instructions as to how to approach Espiritu Santo. Yeoman 2c Dunn testified that Exhibit 3 (Special Instructions) was attached to Exhibit 2 (General routing instructions). Considering the crucial aspect of this document, the prosecution established that the Special Instructions were joined to the General Instructions by a paper clip. The evidence that the Special Instructions were attached to the General Instructions is given by Ensign Dunn, who attached the documents, and Chief quartermaster Doyle, who received the documents from Dunn. It is also significant that the Special Instructions sheet is not the last sheet in the batch documents under question, ie those to be ultimately handed to Captain Nelson. The batch of documents were placed in a brown manila envelope, and then in an unlocked safe in the Port Director's office. Doyle testified that seven ships prior to the *President Coolidge* had received the Special Instruction providing them with information to make safe entry into Segond Channel. The question was asked of Doyle as to where point Hypo is in relation to the eastern entrance to the Segond Channel and the southern end of Tubata Island. (Point Hypo is on an apex of a triangle between the three points (see map) and is north-east of the southern point of Tubata, and hence the 'safe' entrance into Segond Channel. This is significant to some extent, as it indicates that the *President Coolidge* would have had to turn south-west from Hypo to enter the channel west of Tubata. he point was not however taken up by the defence.) DeNovo as recalled to the stand to testify on the matter of whether the papers were stapled together or held with a paper clip. DeNovo confirmed that they were held with a paper clip. DeNovo also testified as to his delivery of the papers to Captain Nelson on board *President Coolidge*. DeNovo states that he pointed out each of the six documents handed to Captain Nelson, and on specific questioning, recalls that 'Item 6', (Exhibit 3 - Special Instructions), was delivered to Captain Nelson. DeNovo testified that he left Captain Nelson's office with carbon copies of some of the documents.

The relevant section of Special Instructions, Exhibit 3: 'Ships approaching Segond Channel, Espiritu Santo, are to use EAST Entrance only. White Rock has been located on South shore Espiritu Santo Island in Long. 1670 131 27" East. Approach Eastern entrance from Bogacyo Island passages to point with White Rock bearing 345 degrees distance two miles. Steam toward White Rock until North tangent Ayre (sic) Island bears West which is danger bearing, then head into channel.'
[Author's note: Ayre Island should read Aore Island. Whether this was a typo error in the official copied document presented to the Military Commission, or whether an actual error of geographic identification is not know.]

DAY TWO - Wednesday, 9 December 1942

DeNovo was again called to the stand and repeated that the documents handed to captain nelson were clipped together. He removed the clip in the Captain's presence but could not recall if he clip was re-affixed when the captain took possession of the documents. Under cross examination, DeNovo was asked could the special instructions be stapled to the regular instruction, to which he replied that they could be as there was a stapling machine in the (Port Director's) office. The defence is not specific however and there is ambiguity in the reply from DeNovo. The fact that the two documents could have been stapled together implies that it was possible that an act could take place but does not indicate that it actually did take place. The defence (nor the prosecution) followed up on this to determine if the two documents were actually stapled together. DeNovo does not offer the advice that they were. DeNovo is questioned on the relevance between the number of documents delivered to Captain Nelson and the checklist required to ensure receipt of documents by the recipient, in this case Captain Nelson. it is noted that the checklist does not allow for all documents to be checked, although Exhibit 3, Special Instructions, is listed. DeNovo is adamant that Captain Nelson received the Special Instructions along with the other documents.

Third Officer Robert Lyons is called to the stand. Lyons was on the bridge when the *President Coolidge* approached Espiritu Santo, and testifies that Captain Nelson had the conn. Lyons testifies that *President Coolidge* passes a destroyer coming out of Segond Channel, and sights 'another vessel' toward Tutuba Island (later identified as *PC479*). Lyons testified that he was given the General Instructions to read soon after leaving New Caledonia, and denies, on questioning, that Exhibit 3 - Special Instructions was attached to the General Instruction. (Mr Lyons is then asked if he is related to the accused!)

Third officer Lyons confirms that the *President Coolidge* exchanged signals with 'the vessel near Tutuba Island', but does not know what the signals were. Speed of the ship when entering the channel was 17 1/2 knots. Lyons suggests that the ship 'went down' at 10.55 am. Lyons is questioned on his recollection of the statement 'Thence to Button noting attached instructions for entering Segond Channel, Espiritu Santo'. Lyons states that "As I see it, any part of paper attached to or on file with sheet 1 of Exhibit 2 (General Instructions) is attached instructions to that file. The suggestion here is that Lyons didn't seek or question the absence of the specific attachment that referred to safe entry into Segond Channel. Lt. John K. Davis, commanding officer of *USS PC479* was called to the stand. Davis testifies that *PC479* was patrolling 4 miles off Bogacio Island, bearing 160°. Testimony is given that PC479 sees *President Coolidge* at ten miles distant travelling approximately due north, and challenges the *PC* at 0900 hrs, and receives no reply, and challenges again at 0910 hrs and received a reply at 0912 hrs from *President Coolidge* asking PC479 what the original message meant. After some confusion, call signs were established, and the *President Coolidge* was recognised. At 0914 hrs, PC479 requests information as to *President Coolidge*'s destination. No reply is received but it is soon apparent that the *President Coolidge* is heading for the eastern entrance to Segond Channel. *PC479*

signalled 'wrong entrance' three times before loosing sight of *President Coolidge* behind Tutuba Island at 0919 hrs. *PC479* chased after *President Coolidge* and by the time *PC479* rounded the northern tip of Tutuba and sighted *President Coolidge* again, *President Coolidge* was still in the water and down at the stern. Davis testifies, "By this time (0947 hrs) numerous picket boats, motor launches, motor boats etc had stood out from the main anchorage and were also standing by the *President Coolidge* to assist survivors. I saw that our services were not needed at that task so we turned around and again assumed our position as patrol."

[Author's note: Third Mate Lyons testifies that the (PC479) boat was in view for some 45 minutes; Lt. Davis on board PC479 testifies that PC479 signalled *President Coolidge* 'wrong entrance' just two minutes before losing sight of *President Coolidge* behind Tutuba Island.]

Davis testifies that he was not advised prior to the arrival of the *President Coolidge*. Duties of PC479 were to conduct sound searching for submarines, and 'also acting as a vessel, as a matter of convenience to incoming ships, something like a pilot vessel'. *PC479* was not instructed to place a pilot on board all ships approaching Espiritu Santo, however Davis 'had orders to make available pilots to all ships desiring them coming into the channel'. (However), 'I made it my practice to offer one (a pilot) to each vessel I saw approaching the harbour'. *PC479* was aware of the minefield and had two pilots aboard. Davis testifies that he did not send a signal to *President Coolidge* advising *President Coolidge* that *PC479* wished to place a pilot on board, and did not do so because of lack of time. It is determined that although *PC479* first sighted *President Coolidge* at 0845 hrs, *President Coolidge* did not answer a signal until 0910 and hence the *President Coolidge* was definitely in sight of signals from 0910 to 0919, a time period of nine minutes. (In actual fact, Davis contradicts his previous testimony - *President Coolidge* replies at 0912 and hence is only, definitely, within signalling for seven minutes. Davis testifies that *President Coolidge* 'may have been within signalling distance before 0910 but she did not answer my signals'. Davis agrees that the duty of PC479 was to warn *President Coolidge* that she was entering a wrong entrance. Davis is questioned on why a radio signal was not sent to *President Coolidge*, and states that "I did not know what frequency she was guarding". Davis testifies that he was aware that 'all large ships guard 500 kc', and that he could have sent a message on that frequency.

On being questioned that the *President Coolidge* might have been headed for the eastern entrance to Segond Channel, Davis replies that he thought *President Coolidge* was heading further north toward Palikulo Bay. Davis is questioned as to when he instructed *PC479* to increase speed to intercept *President Coolidge*, and notes a change of speed at 0914 hrs (9 knots), and 0915 hrs (12 knots). (Maximum sustained speed of *PC479* is 17.3 knots). Questioned as to why *PC479* did not seek to place a pilot aboard *President Coolidge*, Davis testifies that 'mainly because the Coolidge did not approach close enough. She was considered to be eastward of the track of vessels of approach to the harbour, and until she made her turn at 0914...' Davis testifies that PC479 was not flying a pilot flag, and *President Coolidge* could have no way of knowing that a pilot was on board. Davis is questioned intensively by the Prosecution and the Board as to why he was not alarmed (my words) that the *President Coolidge* could have been heading for dangerous waters until such time as she turned due west. Davis said that he believed the *President Coolidge* (read, all vessels) approaching Espiritu Santo would have been instructed as to how to approach the safe entrance. The Judge Advocate, 'Well, Mr. Davis, if there was no possibility of anything going wrong, how and why were you on patrol as well as submarine duty?'. Davis replies, 'I have no answer to that one.'

[Author's note: Davis' testimony does not ride well for him. It appears that as commander of PC479, Davis does not exercise the utmost responsibility in preventing *President Coolidge* from entering dangerous waters.]

Ensign Doran S. Weinstein, communications officer on board *President Coolidge* is brought to the stand. Weinstein testifies that a destroyer is seen and signalled at 0730 hours, and an hour later another vessel (PC479) is sighted, and no signals seen until IBUB received (at 0900). Weinstein testifies that after sending KDMX (at 0913), '3 or 4 minutes, 5 at most' passes before PC479 is out of sign (behind Tutuba Island). Weinstein testified that a signal from a shore station was received stating 'stop, you are standing into mines'. As soon as the word 'stop' was signalled, the word was yelled down to Captain Nelson on the wing bridge. As soon as the rest of the signal was completed, *President Coolidge* hit the first mine. Weinstein testifies that *President Coolidge* identification was flown by signal flags KDMX, Jig pennant 3 Jig, hoisted the previous night and were still flying when *President Coolidge* approached Espiritu Santo and when she hit the mines.

Author's note: Such pennants would have identified the *President Coolidge* from a distance of several miles, through binoculars. Davis makes no mention of identifying the ship through flag signals.

DAY THREE - Thursday, 10 December 1942

First Officer Kilton I. Davis takes the stand. Kilton (first name used to distinguish from John Davis) testifies that he had plotted the chart of *President Coolidge* to point Hypo, but not beyond this point toward the Segond Channel. The speed of *President Coolidge* as she turned west toward Segond Channel was 'between 18 and 19 knots'. Davis recalls reading the words 'Thence to Button, etc' on the general Instructions, but did not raise the question of special instructions with Captain Nelson. Kilton testifies that Captain Nelson indicated his intention to enter the Segond Channel by the eastern entrance 'unless he was stopped or given an escort to go in another channel'. Kilton suggests that the eastern channel, for a ship (the size of the *President Coolidge*), 'that would be the only logical channel for him to take'. Kilton recalls testimony at the previous Court of Inquiry that he asked Captain Nelson, 'Are you going to lay off and wait for a pilot or guide?', to which Captain Nelson is alleged to have replied that ';it was too dangerous to be playing around outside with probable submarines in the area'. Kilton testifies that he saw the papers given to Captain Nelson in Noumea but that he did not see Exhibit 3 - Special Instructions, nor did he question the statement 'Thence to Button, noting attached instructions etc', nor seek the 'special instructions' that were indicated. Kilton was questioned as to whether he had heard what had happened to USS Tucker, to which he replied he had heard a rumour to that effect. The defence asked, 'Did it not ever occur to you that if the western approach was mined that it was quite possible that another approach was mined?' to which Kilton replied 'No, it did not enter my mind, but on thinking it over if one channel is mined it leads me to greatly believe that another would not be in order to make a safe entrance to the harbor'.

Chief Officer Milton McManus took the stand. McManus was questioned on the cargo and personnel aboard *President Coolidge*, including the loss of fireman Robert Red.

The Judge Advocate, U.S. Marine Corps Captain Richard Fagan took the stand as a witness for the prosecution, and introduces Exhibit 9 - a written report by Captain Nelson on the loss of *President Coolidge*.

Colonel Dinsmore Alter, commanding officer of troops aboard *President Coolidge*, took the stand, and testified to the loss of Captain Euart.

DAY FOUR - Friday, 11 December 1942

Doran Weinstein was called as a witness for the defence. He denies receiving a message 'wrong entrance' (from PC479). John Davis is called as a witness for the defence. Under questioning, Davis indicates that *President Coolidge* was first sighted at distance ten miles, bearing 092, travelling 330°, and asked 'If you had kept the *President Coolidge* bearing 090o would you have intercepted her before she reached the channel...' to which he replies 'Yes sir. I would have been between her and either side of Segond Channel'. David makes a statement, in which *inter alia* he states, 'I submit that before the time that the *President Coolidge* committed herself to definitely enter the passage between Espiritu Santo and Tutuba Islands, no conversation between that ship and ours was warranted beyond establishing identification. I further submit that from the time she made her turn until the time she passed from our sight there was ample time for us to send and her to receipt for a warning that she was approaching the wrong entrance to Segond Channel. It is not usual to send any warnings to a ship before she is observed to be doing something wrong. Furthermore I believe that we would have been exceeding our authority and duty , not to mention creating a breach of etiquette and custom to warn the Coolidge of the presence of this mine field before she made her turn at 0914, and that such warnings before she made her turn at 0914, would hardly have been expected by the Coolidge.' Davis again testifies that *President Coolidge* made no response to the 'wrong entrance' message from PC479.

Commander Alexander Gray was called to the stand. He testifies that the port authorities (at Espiritu Santo) were advised by radio of the arrival of *President Coolidge* 'between 1100 on the 25th, and 1100 on the 26th, local time'.

Chief quartermaster George Doyle was recalled to the stand, as a witness for the defence, and testifies that ships departing Noumea for Espiritu Santo are no advised that the water (of Espiritu Santo) are mined.

Lieutenant William Benton, stationed on board USS Whitney, was called to the stand and questioned on matters of piloting (which appeared to be quite irrelevant).

The accused, Captain Henry Nelson takes the stand at his own request, and testifies of the circumstances of his receipt of the papers from Ensign DeNovo. Captain Nelson testifies that he did not witness DeNovo making 'any red check marks' on the check-off list. Asked specifically if he received Exhibit 3 - Special Instructions, Captain Nelson indicates negative. Asked 'Were you informed prior to the time the Coolidge was mined, that there were mines in the area of Espiritu Santo?', Captain nelson replies, 'Not even a whisper.' Asked, 'If you were informed that there were mines there, even a possibility of mines, what effect would it have had upon your actions on the morning of October 26th?', to which Nelson replies, 'I would not have gone near any entrance until I was informed of the safe way to go. By that I mean I would have turned the ship, kept up sufficient speed and contacted the destroyer for information'. Nelson testifies that the PC boat had time to advise *President Coolidge* that a pilot was available but did not do so. In the fact that no pilot was offered (by PC479), Nelson testifies that this 'indicated that there was no necessity for a pilot'. Nelson is questioned by the prosecution about his recollection of the papers delivered to his office by DeNovo, and gives unconvincing replies to his ability to remember exactly what documents were present, and what was checked for. 'Can you explain to the court how it happens that you are extremely vague as t the presence of one document and at the same time so positive of the absence of another document?', to which Nelson replies after further questioning, 'Well, I don't quite understand it myself. It is not vague in my answer to the other papers which should have been there and the Coolidge would have been afloat today.' Nelson testifies that the entrance he chose was 'the logical way', and although he had not been to the area previously, the charts showed no danger to the approach made. Nelson is further questioned on his choice of approach, and it is well to reproduce the details here.

Q. 'Captain Nelson, what did you consider the significance of these words, page 1 of Exhibit 2 (General Instructions), "Thence to Button noting attached instructions for entering Segond Channel, Espiritu Santo?'

A. 'I have been puzzled ever since the ship went down.'

Q. 'Were you puzzled before the ship went down, Captain?'

A. 'No'.

Q. 'From point Hypo as you proceeded 'Thence to Button', did you note or attempt to note any attached instructions?'

A. Yes, I looked all over for it and there were none.

Q. And after finding none, you preceded without them, is that correct?

A. 'There was none there and I preceded.' Captain Nelson later testifies that because there were no specific instructions he presumed there were no dangers.

Asked why he chose the particular route from point Hypo to the Segond Channel, Captain Nelson replies, 'In the first place it is the logical passage for any ship to come in. This shows clear entrance into the harbour. Why should I proceed from Hypo a longer distance down to Bogacio when there was no necessity for it?'

The prosecution asks, 'Did it not occur to you Captain Nelson that it was quite likely that the logical, as you call it, approach to Espiritu Santo would also appear logical to the enemy and that for that reason it might quite understandably be mined?', to which Captain Nelson simply relied, 'No'.

Comment: With this question, the prosecution, ie the US Navy, shoots itself in the foot. If the US Navy mined the eastern entrance to Segond Channel because it was indeed the most logical entrance to the channel, then all the more reason to ensure that friendly boats would not enter through this channel by providing adequate warnings by way of patrol craft appropriately positioned, and by a fail-safe procedure of documented warnings, and by an appropriately positioned warning post with adequate signal possibilities.

Asked why he did not ask for a pilot before entering unfamiliar waters, Captain Nelson replies 'No reason I should ask for one. As I said before, the approach appeared clear and no information to the contrary.'

DAY FIVE - Saturday, 12 December 1942

The Judge Advocate requested an adjournment until 14 December.

DAY SIX - Monday, 14 December 1942

The record of proceedings of the forth and fifth day are read to the commission. The Judge Advocate desired to make no closing argument. The trail was finished.

WRITTEN OPENING ARGUMENT OF THE JUDGE ADVOCATE MILITARY COMMISSION, 8-14 DECEMBER 1942.

May it please the court:

It is my intention in the early stages of the summary of this case to break down and completely analyse the specification, allegation by allegation, in order to prove conclusively to the commission that no point has been overlooked, that every point has been proved and to cite the testimony or evidence supporting each point.

In connection with this procedure, I respectfully invite the members to follow the points through from the copies of the specification which they have in front of them.

1. That the Coolidge was a merchant ship of the United States, owned by the American President Lines. Here we have the test of the third officer and navigating mate, Mr. Kilton I. Davis, and also the covers of the log book and the bell book.

2. That it was chartered by the War Department. Colonel Alter satisfied this allegation completely.

3. That Henry Nelson was the master of the Coolidge on October 26, 1942. Lyons, Kilton Davis and Ensign Weinstein testified to this.

4. That he was under orders and control of the Navy in a zone of military operation. Ensign DeNovo's testimony supports this point, and, even more strongly, Captain Nelson's own signature on his orders and routing instructions prove that he acknowledged that he was under the orders and control of the Navy, and the nature of his passengers and cargo proved that it was a military operation.

5. That the Coolidge was in an actual theatre of war in the South Pacific Area. This is clearly established by the very nature of Exhibit 2 and the enclosures thereto, and by the statement of the accused to Lyons that he suspected submarines in the vicinity. The geography is a matter of judicial notice.

6. That the Coolidge was making passage from Noumea to Segond Channel. Lyons, K.I.Davis and Weinstein all covered this.

7. That she had aboard Army and Navy personnel, combat equipment and supplies. Mr. Manus Colonel Alter and Ensign Weinstein all supported this.

8. That Captain Nelson, on or before, October 26, 1942, received a complete set of routing instructions. In addition to Captain Nelson's signature on Exhibit 2, Ensign DeNovo, of course, unshakably proved

this allegation, supported in the preliminary stages by Dunn and Doyle. For the court will recall that Mr. DeNovo, in answer to the question, "Then you are sure that you delivered Item 6 of the check off list to Captain Nelson?" replied, "I am positive". That Mr. DeNovo reaffirmed this statement on various occasions despite innumerable abstract questions dealing with addition and subtraction, and finally that he positively identified Item 6 as being represented by Exhibit 3, and that said routing instructions contained special information for entering Segond Channel.

9. That Captain Nelson was personally conning the ship at the time of the explosions. Both Lyons and K.I. Davis testified to this.

10. That Captain Nelson was personally conning the ship for at least one hour before it struck the mines. Lyons, the watch officer who was relieved by Nelson is enough here.

11. That Nelson made a wrong approach to Segond Channel in that he did not follow the directions contained in Special information. Here we have but to read "Special Information" to discover that Bogacio passages are the directed and hence the only right approaches. Then consider the testimony of Lyons, J.K. Davis, K.I. Davis and the accused himself that he passed north of Tutuba Island to find, Q.E.D., that this latter approach was a wrong approach.

12. That he was careless and reckless in making the approach at an excessive rate of speed. In connection with this allegation we have the Bell Book, K.I. Davis, the Cahill stipulation and the accused himself, to support that part that the ship was making something around 19 knots. We also have Lieutenant Benton's testimony as an expert, that the greatest speed he undertook through a channel which he had navigated twenty times before was 15 knots. From here it is only for the court in its wisdom and long experience to decide whether it was careless and reckless to make a completely strange approach at nearly 20 knots, and I ask the court to bear this word "careless" in mind for future consideration.

13. That his speed precluded him from receiving aboard a pilot who was at that time aboard the PC 479. Lieutenant Davis has established that there were, in fact, two pilots aboard the PC 479 available for the Coolidge. It surely has been more than clear that the speed of the ship was the primary factor which precluded receiving the pilot aboard, coupled with the other factor that Captain Nelson did not ask for a pilot although he himself testified, at long last, that he wanted a pilot.

14. That his speed and wrong approach precluded

his acting upon timely warnings from a shore signal station and the PC 479 that his ship was standing into danger. In the first place, had the approach not been wrong, no warnings, timely or otherwise would have been necessary. We have ample testimony that both PC 479 and the shore station did warn the Coolidge and it is simple arithmetic that, had the speed of the ship been halved, the time to act on the warnings would have been doubled.

15. That the Coolidge, with Captain Nelson conning, struck two mines in the wrong approach to Segond Channel. Here we merely cite Lyons, K.I. Davis, the Bell Book and the testimony of the accused.

16. That the mines were struck at about 9.30 a.m. on October 26, 1942. Again we have Lyons, K.I. Davis and the Bell Book.

17. That the Coolidge was lost. Lyons, Davis and Weinstein actually saw it disappear.

18. That two lives were lost. Under this point we have the testimony of McManus, the Cahill stipulation and Colonel Alter's testimony. In connection with this point, however, it may be said that, considering sections 311 and 429, Naval Courts and Boards, a substitution of words might be in order.

19. That a vast cargo of combat equipment and supplies was lost. Here we need only recall Mr. McManus' recitation of the cargo aboard to realize that it consisted of combat equipment and supplies and that it was, in very fact, vast. Then it will be recalled that McManus and at least two others testified that it went down with the ship.

20. That the losses were to the detriment of the U.S. Military operations. The judge advocate feels that it is clearly inferable from the very nature of the losses that they were to the detriment of U.S. Military Operations.

21. And finally that the United States was in a state of war, which is an allegation of which the court may take judicial notice.

Now gentlemen, those are all the points of the specifications. They are covered thoroughly without any omission and without evading any issues. In short they prove the specification completely and far beyond any reasonable doubt.

We may now consider some of the circumstances, some of the testimony, some of the aspects of the case in greater detail.

From a standpoint of proof, no possible doubt may be entertained as to whether the accused received "Exhibit 3".

However, from a standpoint of argument, and solely from this standpoint, we may consider two possibilities regardless of how remote one of the possibilities may be.

They are of course that the accused did receive "Exhibit 3" and that the accused did not receive "Exhibit 3".

If he did receive it, he ignored it, he lost it, or he threw it away. In any case he neglected to carry out the provisions of the document and through this negligence the Coolidge, her cargo and two human lives went to the bottom of the ocean.

If he did not receive it, the purely argumentative possibility, it immediately becomes apparent that the offense of negligence has been committed with equal degree of carelessness, recklessness and wantonness in that (a) he neglected completely to make any effort to obtain the vitally necessary information as to approaching Segond Channel although he testified that something seemed to be missing, (b) he neglected completely to seek the council of his officers, (c) he neglected completely to ask for assistance from either of the vessels he contacted near the approach despite the fact that he testified that he did want a pilot (d) he neglected completely to take the precautions on approaching the harbor which any reasonable man under the circumstances (the circumstances of war) might be expected to take and (e) he neglected completely to accept and be guided by the precautionary words, "Thence to Button, noting attached instructions for entering Segond Channel, Espiritu Santo." which would have been sufficient for any prudent and non-negligent man, particularly a man of his experience.

I previously asked the court to bear in mind the word carelessness. I quote from Naval Courts and Boards, section 66. There is no practical distinction between negligence and carelessness.

Now I ask the court to consider the elements of the offense under which the charge is laid in this case and to that end I quote from Section 69. The distinction between inattention and negligence is not altogether apparent, as one may be the cause of the other. Inattention means want of attention or failure to pay attention; disregard; carelessness; or culpable failure to attend. Negligence means the omission to do something which a reasonable man, guided by those considerations which ordinarily regulate the conduct of human affairs., would do, or doing something which a prudent and reasonable man would not do.

It is, I believe now pertinent to look further into this offense of negligence, and we are given a clue to that, as applicable to this case, by reading section 153 Naval Courts and Boards. The degree of care and caution to avoid mischief required to save from criminal responsibility, for instance, one who accidentally kills another, is that which a man of ordinary prudence would have exercised under like circumstances; mere slight negligence, with no intent to do harm, under such circumstances that it could not reasonably be supposed that injury would result, does not furnish a foundation for criminal responsibility for a resulting death. The degree of negligence necessary to support criminal liability must be gross and culpable.

It is not contended, gentlemen, that Captain Nelson deliberately ran the Coolidge into the mine field, not that he intended to lose the ship, the lives and the cargo. However, it is contended that this was no slight negligence under circumstances that it could not reasonably be supposed that injury would result and further it is most emphatically contended that it was, in fact gross, that it was in fact culpable and that it did therefore support criminal liability.

The words themselves are common enough and understandable enough; but it is considered pertinent to consider their legal implication. Black's law dictionary says that culpable means blameable or censurable and it says that gross means great and culpable. Surely it is beyond the realm of sane argument to contend that Captain Nelson's conduct was not blameable or not censurable.

More specifically however let us hear what this unimpeachable authority says of these adjectives when joined directly with the word negligence.

I read first under gross negligence: "The want of slight diligence. The want of that care which every man of common sense, how inattentive soever, takes of his own property. The omission of that care which even inattentive and thoughtless men never fail to take of their own property. The failure to exercise slight care. 'Gross negligence,' is substantial higher in magnitude than simple inadvertence, but falls short of intentional wrong." And I reiterate that it is not alleged or contended that the wrong of the accused was intentionable.

Under culpable negligence we find: "Failure to exercise that degree of care rendered appropriate by the particular circumstances, and which a man of ordinary prudence in the same situation and with equal experience would not have omitted." And in this definition we stress the words "particular circumstances", if same situation" and "equal experience."

The "particular circumstances" of this case are clearly and elaborately before this court. For practical purposes it may be assumed that the term "equal experience" is applicable to the members of this commission and as to the "same situation", I have only to ask the members to ask themselves what they would have done in the same situation - whether they would have blundered carelessly into an unknown passage with the odds a thousand to one that the passage was mined or whether they would have laid off and circled until the safety of the approach was proved, and this, regardless of any previous specific information as to the presence or absence of mines.

The last associated definition is that of criminal negligence which I will read: "Criminal negligence which will render killing a person manslaughter is the omission on the part of the person to do some act which an ordinarily careful and prudent man would do under like circumstances, or the doing of some act which an ordinarily careful prudent man under like circumstances would not do by reason of which another person is endangered in life or bodily safety." And please note, gentlemen, that the meat of this definition goes no further than endangering life or bodily harm, in contradistinction to the actual loss of life or the actual infliction of bodily harm, which existed in this case.

I believe that it may be conceded that some persons have misrepresented facts to this commission, possibly that perjury has been committed. The evidence as to the exchange or the sending of signals is directly contradictory. The record is replete with hair splitting questions and answers ad infinitum about the exchange and sending or alleged exchange and sending of messages by the Coolidge and the PC 479.

At its very best, from the standpoint of the defence, this testimony could be considered only as mildly mitigating, nothing more. At its worst it definitely becomes perniciously aggravating.

The point is that the PC 479 was present. It had information and it had a pilot, it was in a position to provide either or both and I don't believe that it is debatable that it would have provided both on request.

Whether the commission chooses to believe Lieutenant Davis on one hand or Ensign Weinstein and K. I. Davis on the other I do not know and it is not for me to presume to judge the veracity of the witnesses. But I do believe it pertinent to ask the court to consider who had the greatest axe to grind. A naval officer on a routine patrol or the officers of a ship which, due to somebody's negligence, went to the bottom.

However, in the very final analysis of this feature of the case, I ask "What difference does it make - what material difference does it make whether or not the PC 479 sent any signals at all. What material difference would it have made if the PC 479 had never been there or, being there, if it had swung around 1800 and run away." The answer to all these questions is "None." Neither its presence, nor its absence, neither its signals nor its lack of signals, relieved the master of the Coolidge in the slightest degree of his responsibility to proceed carefully, prudently and, under the circumstances, cautiously, to bring his ship safely into the harbor.

The time honored law of the sea and specifically article 880 of the Navy Regulations is not to be evaded. The commanding officer is always responsible for the safe conduct of the ship. There is no deviation from the law. Even in the famous Hondo disaster where the subordinate captains followed their squadron commander to disaster, the department held that they were themselves negligent and responsible.

It has further been held that even when his own subordinate officer is directly responsible, the captain is not relieved of responsibility.

The court has found the charge and specification in due form and technically correct. The prosecution has proved all the elements alleged in the specification. From this it must of necessity follow that the accused is, of the charge, guilty.

WRITTEN ARGUMENT OF THE ACCUSED.
MILITARY COMMISSION, 8-14 DECEMBER 1942.

Gentlemen:

It is not often that an officer of my rank has the opportunity to address officers of your rank. It is an extraordinary situation that would bring such about. Realizing that this is such an extraordinary situation the accused requests that full reconsideration of the evidence before the court be given before decision is made. We still wish to make it plain that we still consider that our argument of jurisdiction is still valid. Further, we wish to bring to the attention of you gentlemen that this is not a court martial but a trial before an extraordinary military commission, and that you are not acting as naval officers but as members of extraordinary commissions so that when the question of negligence on the part of the Navy is brought up that must be judged as impartial as any other question of negligence in the case.

Our argument is divided into eight divisions. First, we wish the commission to consider the duties of a merchant master and not of a naval officer. Second, an analysis of the testimony shows that the accused did not receive any special directions for approaching Segond Channel. Our third argument is that the accused was not negligent in analyzing the instructions that he had received. We will show you that he had no duty to look for missing orders and we shall show you that even though he had the duty to look for missing portions that his actions were not unreasonable. As a fourth argument we shall show you that the approach to Segond Channel was reasonable from a navigational standpoint; that it was not unreasonable to fail to anticipate mines, and that even though the probability of mines had been in the mind of the accused his actions were not unreasonable even with that possibility in mind. The fifth argument we shall show that the evidence discloses no excessive speed. Speed of the ship did not preclude taking a pilot as none was offered. The speed of the ship did not preclude acting upon timely warning. No timely warning was received. As a sixth argument we shall show the commission that even assuming negligence on the part of the accused in approaching Segond Channel, negligence on the part of the Navy intervened and was itself the cause of the loss of the ship. Seventh, we shall bring out a fatal failure of proof to establish jurisdiction over the accused. Eighth, we will summarize.

The first fact that it is desired to bring to the attention of this commission is that the Navy Regulations set down duties for the commanding officer of a naval vessel that are quite different from the duties of captain of a merchant vessel, both as to measures that are required to be taken for the safety of their ships and responsibilities for the training and efficient performance of duties of their officers and men.

In addition, the customs of the naval service has decreed duties for the commanding officer of a naval vessel that go beyond the naval regulations.

In judging the actions of Captain Nelson in regard to the negligence alleged, and considering whether he omitted to do something that a reasonable master would have done or that he did something that a reasonable and prudent master would not have done. You must remember that you are judging him as a prudent and reasonable merchant marine captain and as a prudent and reasonable naval officer.

The fundamental question of fact before the commission is whether or not the accused received a sheet of paper containing special information for entering Segond Channel. That fact, can be ascertained only from the evidence before the commission. To support the specification, proof must have been made beyond a reasonable doubt.

NCB 158: "Proof beyond reasonable doubt.-- If there is a reasonable doubt as to the guilt of the accused, he must be acquitted. If there is a reasonable doubt as to the degree of guilt, the finding must be in a lower degree on which there is no such doubt. In making its finding the court must strictly observe the rule that it must reach its conclusion solely from the evidence adduced. It is not necessary that each particular fact advanced by the prosecution should be proved beyond reasonable doubt; it is sufficient to warrant conviction if, on the whole, evidence, the court is satisfied beyond such doubt that the accused is guilty."

For the definition of reasonable doubt, the commission is respectfully referred to NCB 159.

Let the history of the instructions for the voyage of the Coolidge from Noumea to Espiritu Santo be reviewed: Yeoman Dunn typed the sheet of special information on October 24, 1942, and delivered it to Quartermaster Doyle who assembled the basic instructions and all enclosures and placed them in the drawer of a cabinet between 1030 and 1130. The cabinet remained unlocked until 1130. The papers next appeared in the hands of Lt. Comdr. Andrew and Ensign DeNovo between 1300 and 1400. At this time they were on a large chart desk in the Port Director's Office. Thereafter Ensign DeNovo brought them to the office of the accused on board the Coolidge for delivery. After delivery, the accused placed them beneath a heavy ashtray, went to the bridge, returned later, picked them up and stapled them together. The accused then took them to the chart house where they were kept in a confidential drawer and referred to from time to time by ship's officers.

The weight to be given to the testimony of the various witnesses should be considered. Dunn, Doyle and Ensign DeNovo must account for the special information sheet, otherwise they have been derelict. Particularly Ensign DeNovo, and by like token, the accused must so account. Let it not be inferred that any of these witnesses would perjure himself. But some weight must be attached to the fact that pressure of the responsibility of accounting for that sheet of paper might subconsciously affect to his own benefit the recollection of any of the four regarding it.

As to the mates, Lyon and Davis, their testimony might have been influenced by their acquaintanceship with the accused and the latter by the additional reason of his relationship by marriage to the accused. However, had either been aware of the special information, it is beyond all reason to think that either or both would suffer the Coolidge to disregard the information. Both Davis and Lyons have testified that they examined the papers on the afternoon of October 24, 1942, at the time they were brought to the charthouse by the accused. They testified that the special information sheet was not among the instruction papers at that time, nor at any time thereafter.

We must therefor analyse the history of these papers prior to the time they came to the charthouse to discover where along the line there existed possibilities for the disappearance of the special information sheet, and to discover where along the line existed the most pregnant possibilities.

Did it blow away while the accused took it from his cabin to the wheelhouse? Impossible, the papers were stapled together at that time.

After receipt of the various papers from Ensign DeNovo, the accused placed them beneath a heavy ashtray and went to the bridge. He returned sometime later, picked up and stapled the papers together, except for the Secret Identification Signal which he clipped to the stapled papers. Could the special information sheet have blown away while under the ashtray or have been extracted by persons unknown? It is possible it was there. Yet, the accused has stated that neither at the time the papers were given to him or at the time they were stapled was the special information sheet among them. The very fact that he utilized the approach that he did is the best evidence possible that Captain Nelson was never apprised by Ensign DeNovo or anyone else of the existence of directions for approaching the channel. The accused is a master mariner accustomed during his whole life time to following instructions - it must be apparent to the commission that had he any knowledge whatsoever of the existence of instructions, his actions would not have been as they were.

Could the special information sheet have been mislaid away from the other papers on the desk of the accused by the accused or by Ensign DeNovo. Yes. However, the accused has stated that he inspected his desk that night and he did not discover the sheet in question. Had he discovered it, it is submitted to the court that his statement that he would have followed any instructions that he had, must be taken as truth.

Now let the progress of the papers through the hands of persons of the Port Director's Office be examined. Bear in mind that Commander Eastern Sea Frontier Bulletin #34 was in the file as page eleven of twelve pages when Quartermaster Doyle filed it. By the testimony of both the accused and Ensign DeNovo it was not delivered to the accused. So it is definite that at least this much of the file disappeared while in the hands of the Port Director's Agents. Before 1130 Doyle placed the papers in a cabinet that remained unlocked until 1130.

The papers next appear on the chart desk in the Port Director's Office being checked by Ensign DeNovo and Lt. Comdr. Andrew. At that time the special information sheet may have been accidentally slipped beneath a chart or have been placed with other papers on the desk, or it is possible that it may not have been picked up for delivery to the Coolidge along with the rest of the papers and was subsequently lost from the desk by a person unfamiliar with its importance.

At the office of the accused on board ship, Mr. DeNovo placed the papers he brought, on the desk, sorted some to give to the accused and others to keep. He must have placed those he was to keep near those to remain in order that in picking up those papers that he was to remove from the ship that the special information sheet was accidentally removed with them, if it was in fact, ever there.

But Ensign DeNovo only states that insofar as he can be sure of his memory he did deliver a sheet that looked similar to Exhibit 3 to Captain Nelson, and here is the most important point of this trial - how much can be relied on DeNovo's memory of events occurring on 24 October. Ensign DeNovo states that he cannot remember where he was when he made the check marks on the check-off list. He does not remember whether he was in the Port Director's Office or in Captain Nelson's cabin or where he was. If DeNovo could not remember where he was when he checked off the enclosure, how can he remember where he last saw a piece of paper that was similar to Exhibit 3? It probably was when he checked it off on the check-off list. We know he did not make the check marks in Nelson's cabin.

With this in mind and added to the fact that there was no such paper on the desk when Captain Nelson picked up the instructions and stapled them together and that no such paper came to light at a later time on the Coolidge and that Bulletin 34 did disappear while in the hands of the Port Director's Agents, it goes beyond reasonable doubt that such a paper was ever delivered to Captain Nelson. It is almost a certainty that it was not delivered.

Great stress has been laid upon the paragraph found in "Exhibit 2": "Thence to Button, noting attached instructions for entering Segond Channel, Espiritu Santo."

It has been inferred that Captain Nelson should have studied these instructions before he left Noumea and by such a study determined that there were no instructions as to courses, from Point "Hypo" to the anchorage in Segond Channel and that he should have inquired at the Port Director's Office if there were any additional instructions.

The attention of the commission is called to the fact that the *President Coolidge* had received a signal to be prepared to get underway at 1400. These instructions were delivered sometime after 1330. It would have been impossible for any merchant marine captain to have thoroughly familiarized himself with these instructions in that space of time.

Radio silence was imposed on the ship after she got underway and the master could not ask for instructions by radio if he had desired to do so.

A. To consider the contention, the commission must declare as a matter of law that the accused had a duty as a merchant master not only to physically examine all instructions received from Port Director's but to interpret their phraseology the same as would a court of law and further to examine them for physical completeness with regard to that interpretation. The accused submits that such would constitute an unreasonable burden upon merchant masters. For the master to carry out such duty it would be necessary that he have knowledge of all that the instructions should contain - and he could not have this knowledge unless he had the information that the persons who prepared the instructions have. That knowledge is in the hands of the Port Directors, not the masters. The accused submits that merchant masters are entitled to a complete set of routing instructions free from omissions and ambiguities from the Port Directors and that it is the duty of the Port Directors and not the master to see that he gets them.

B. Even assuming that such an unreasonable duty be declared as a matter of law to rest upon merchant masters, let its application be examined in the case at hand:

Let us take a look at Exhibit 2 and determine how easy it would be to determine that a vital enclosure is missing, considering that the person looking at it is not a naval officer and does not know that the waters to be entered are mined. The first page of the basic letter of instructions say after reaching point "Hypo", "Thence to Button noting the attached instructions for entering Segond Channel".

Bear in mind that the instructions given the accused were not attached together but handed piecemeal to him.

Bear in mind that the word "instruction" was used -- not "courses" , "sailing directions", or even "directions" --- simply instructions. Many parts of the instructions received might very well apply for entering Segond Channel. For example: the instructions for identification signals would apply as to shore signal stations and guard vessels; the instructions regarding mine sweepers would particularly apply to the Espiritu Santo area which the enemy might mine. The signals for control of merchantmen would find application. The probable presence of aircraft would call for utilization of the aircraft action instructions.

Further the accused has testified that in checking the enclosures that he signed for, the large capital letter B on sheet 5 of Exhibit 2 indicated to him enclosure (B). Many merchant marine masters would have concluded that Exhibit 2 was a complete set of instructions. Two other merchant marine officers besides Captain Nelson have testified that they did not believe there were any missing enclosures.

Bear in mind the words "Proceed to" and "noting the attached instructions for entering" are mimeographed and are in no manner particularly emphasized.

Bear in mind that the accused was to note instructions for *entering*" Segond Channel, not instructions for "Approaching" it, and that Segond Channel does not commence until a point west of White Rock.

With these facts in mind, it must be apparent that the word "instructions", under the circumstances, even when read in connection with the following words "for entering Segond Channel, Espiritu Santo" does not bring specifically to mind *courses* to be followed in approaching but contrarily, reasonably brings to mind *instructions* as to any phase of the process of entering Segond Channel, examples of which have been given. The accused submits that the contention of the judge advocate in regards to this extract from Exhibit 2 is erroneous and the accused, as any reasonable master, finding that the extract referred to no specific instructions among his papers naming Segond Channel, assumed, he was to note portions of his instructions which would apply while entering Segond Channel.

Rather than put him on guard as existence of any dangers from the approach he might make to the channel, by exclusion the reference indicated that any approach, or the normal approach was satisfactory and that he was to watch out for other types of dangers only, while actually *entering* Segond Channel. It next must be considered if Captain Nelson acted as a reasonable and prudent merchant marine master in conning his ship from Point "Hypo" into Segond Channel. A master who does not know these waters are mined.

A. The members of the commission may readily ascertain by reference to Exhibits 5 and 6 that, except for the existence of a mine field, the approach that the accused caused to be taken was the safest approach possible from a navigational standpoint. He had general instructions saying "Thence to Button, noting the attached instructions for entering Segond Channel". There had been no instructions attached that stated anything about entering by a particular channel.

A prudent and reasonable merchant marine captain would have said that, I will take a pilot if one is available. A prudent and reasonable master would have said if there is no pilot available and there are naval vessels off the entrance I will depend on these vessels for any necessary instructions and I will depend upon the naval vessels to keep me out of danger if there is any danger not shown on the charts.

That this is a logical conclusion can be seen by the fact that Lieutenant Davis, the commanding officer of the P.C. boat stated that it was his duty to prevent friendly vessels from entering the mine field.

A prudent and reasonable master who had seen two naval vessels off the entrance and who had seen no evidence of a pilot boat and who had received no warning that there was any danger ahead of him would have said, "I will not lay off the entrance where a submarine might torpedo the ship. I will stand on into the harbor before slowing down."

Without a prior knowledge of the existence of mines in the mind of the accused, he cannot be said to have taken a "wrong" approach, nor can his causing the ship to take such approach be termed negligent, careless, wanton or reckless. Contrarily, his choice, without doubt, indicates sound judgment upon his part in view of the facts within his knowledge. He did not receive the special information for entering thus he was not advised of the possibility of mines.

B. It has been suggested that the accused should have had the possibility of mines in his mind even without specific advice. Let this contention be examined.

Remember, that the accused was not acting in the capacity of a naval officer, but that of a merchant mariner, in whose mind the instructions and tactics of war are not always paramount considerations.

Remember, that due to the absence of any special instructions or the mention of mines anywhere in the instructions he did receive, there was nothing to stimulate his mind to an inquiry of such possibility.

Remember that the commanding officer of the U.S.S. Tucker did not know that the waters at the western entrance to Segond Channel were mined and he attempted to take his ship in that entrance and he knew that there was a war in progress. Further, insofar as it is known the administrative investigation did not consider that he was negligent in his performance of duty.

Remember, that the very absence of any special instructions for entering was a factor indicating a normal approach was safe.

Remember, that upon approaching Segond Channel there were seen two naval vessels, the first of which told him she did not have anything for him, the second of which, the PC 479, never approached closer than four miles and never during the time that she was visible give indication, to the knowledge of the accused, that the approach lead to disaster.

Remember, that no pilot was proffered could but indicate to the accused that there were no dangers in making Segond Channel.

Remember, that the Navy did not deem it necessary to escort the Coolidge during this voyage, a fact tending further to obscure the dangers of war.

Remember, that upon turning into this channel witnesses have testified that various vessels were visible ahead at various anchorages - further indicative of nothing but peaceful possibilities.

Remember, that Bogacio Island passages do not present an inviting route for a vessel the size of the Coolidge, so that the possibility of using them would not be pressed upon the accused.

Remember that the accused had never been to Espiritu Santo before and that all that he knew of it was that it was an advanced base and not an established port - is it reasonable to expect him to anticipate a complete system of mines already installed?

Remember, in connection with the paragraph, "Thence to Button, etc.", that the accused had many duties and responsibilities as master of the Coolidge, that he could not reasonably have been expected, as a merchant master, to examine and interpret with judicial acumen the instructions that he received, to discover their ambiguities and to resolve their possibilities. That further, as had been explained in another portion of the argument the paragraph might well be interpreted as erasing the possibility of dangers from mines.

Remember that the accused, as master of a large and valuable vessel, with many troops and supplies aboard, had a right to expect and to assume that the military authorities would insure that every precaution would be taken to ensure the safety of his ship.

Remembering these facts, the gentlemen of the commission must but reject the inference that the possibility of mines should have been apparent to the accused without warning of any sort. With the facts in his mind and those that should have been in his mind, he took a "right" approach to Segond Channel. He did not receive the special information sheet and there has been shown no other reason why, he, as a reasonable master, under the circumstances, should have suspected a United States mine field in this area.

C. To carry the point one step further, let us assume, but not admit, that the accused should have had in mind the possibility of mines. Let us analyse what a reasonable master with or without instructions for entering this area, could be expected to do under the circumstances. Surely it would be unreasonable to expect that the merchant master to anticipate where the mines are laid. Any master could reasonable expect that the military authorities would establish methods for warning him and would in fact, warn him if his course approached the mines.

I ask you gentlemen for a moment to place yourself on the bridge of a merchant vessel as its captain. You are making an approach into Segond Channel. You have the possibility in mind that there might be mines there but you don't know where. You also have the possibility in mind that there are enemy submarines in the vicinity who may torpedo your vessel. Now you have no instructions for entering. You look at the chart. You find that there is but one real navigational safe approach to Segond Channel. What decision can you make but to take that approach as any reasonable master, you say, "They don't tell me where the mines are, surely, surely, if I start to head into the mines they will warn me away." What did Captain Nelson do? That very same thing. Gentlemen, even with the probability of mines in mind his actions were exactly those of any reasonable merchant marine master when he went into this channel.

The commission may ascertain by reference to Exhibits 5 and 6, that there is a complete absence of natural hazards, or any hazards whatsoever, except for the mines, that could make the speed used in approaching Segond Channel excessive. These facts are attested by the testimony of Lieutenant Benton. Further, the so called "excessive" speed of the Coolidge is alleged only to have precluded the accused from receiving a pilot aboard and acting upon timely warnings of danger.

A. AS TO PRECLUDING HIM FROM TAKING A PILOT: By the unanimous testimony of Lieutenant J. K. Davis., Ensign Weinstein and Mr. Robert Lyon, the *President Coolidge* and the PC 479 were within view of each other for at least 34 minutes prior to 0919 of October 26, 1942, during all of which time arrangement could have been made to take a pilot, yet the PC 479 made no intimation, whatsoever that she carried a pilot, let alone offer one. She carried no pilot flag. The entire 34 minutes were wasted making blunderous attempts to establish identification. The commission surely cannot believe it was the speed of the Coolidge that precluded taking a pilot aboard. The evidence is so clear that is if a pilot was, indeed, precluded from coming aboard, it was due to faulty communications, over which the accused had no control, and not to the speed of the Coolidge. The accused could not be expected to adjust the otherwise reasonable speed of his ship to accommodate this circumstance of which he had no knowledge.

B. AS TO PRECLUDING ACCUSED FROM ACTING UPON TIMELY WARNINGS: PC 479 flashed the warning "wrong entrance" at 0917 - a full twelve minutes before the disaster. The message was never receipted for by the Navy signalman on the Coolidge. The communications officer of the Coolidge testified that it was never received so could not have been passed on to Captain Nelson. No other warning except that at the time of striking the mines was received or passed on to Captain Nelson. The parties upon whom the responsibility to make and to convey warnings to the accused did not convey such warnings. Consequently, it could not have been the speed of the Coolidge that precluded the accused from acting upon timely warnings.

Admitting, but only for the purpose of argument, that there was negligence on the part of the accused, it is strongly contended that it was not the negligence of the accused that actually caused the loss of the ship. But, contrarily, that negligence on the part of the Navy in failing to keep the accused out of the mine field intervened and itself became the actual cause of the loss.

The commanding officer of *PC479* admits that he had a duty to keep friendly vessels away from the mine field. It would be extreme negligence on the part of the authority issuing him his orders had such duty not been included, or had such orders not included a duty to warn away from the approach that was actually taken. Yet, the Navy failed to convey such warning to Captain Nelson in the case at hand.

It was not negligence on the part of Captain

Nelson that was responsible for him failing to take a pilot. It was negligence on the part of the Navy who had a pilot boat that did not fly a pilot flag and did not send a message that a pilot was available and there was plenty of time for the pilot boat to have sent more than ten messages of this nature.

There was a warning message sent when the *President Coolidge* was still five miles from the mine field which would have been more than ample time to have turned the Coolidge or to have stopped her. It was not negligence on the part of Captain Nelson that he did not receive this message. It was due to the inefficiency of the Navy's signalmen.

The P.C. boat should have been manoeuvred so as to have been always to the west of the *President Coolidge* until it intercepted and warned her of her danger and it was the duty of this P.C. boat to keep the Coolidge out of the mine fields, according to its commanding officer's own statement. It was not negligence on the part of Captain Nelson that the PC boat did not intercept the *President Coolidge*, but the inefficiency of an inexperienced commanding officer of a PC boat.

Gentlemen, I wish to quote to you and explain to you the laws of intervening negligence. The case of Walker vs. Illinois Telephone Company, decided by Appellate Court of Illinois, Sept. 9, 1942. Citation on that case, 42 North Eastern Second, 412, Presiding Justice Stone delivered the opinion. In that opinion he states it has been repeatedly held that although an initial act of negligence may be the occasion for an intervening cause, which intervenes and produces the injury, the intervening cause will be held to be the proximate cause of the injury unless the intervening cause is within the control of the party of the initial act. Gentlemen of the commission we are now assuming that there was negligence on the part of the accused. However, there was a duty on the part of the Navy to warn him away from that mine field. The accused has stated that had he received a warning he most certainly would have acted upon it. In fact he did act immediately upon the warning that was received from the shore station but that warning came too late. Had he been warned he would have stopped or manoeuvred his ship away from the mine fields. The failure to give that warning did in fact produce a loss of the *President Coolidge*, for had that warning been given Captain Nelson could have acted upon it. There was an intervening cause, an intervening agency, the Navy. Captain Nelson had no control over the Navy. The negligence of the Navy in not giving a warning to him was the factor that was the proximate cause of the loss of the *President Coolidge*, because if that warning had been given the *President Coolidge* would be afloat today. The Navy's negligence, even though occasioned by the Negligence of the accused did intervene and itself became the cause of her loss.

In short, even assuming the accused negligently headed his ship into the mine field, it was the Navy's duty to warn him out. The Navy neglected this duty. Thus the Navy's negligence intervened and itself became the cause of the loss of the *President Coolidge*.

CLOSING STATEMENT BY THE DEFENCE
FATAL FAILURE OF PROOF
Military Commission, 8-14 December 1942.

The Prosecution has shown no jurisdiction over the accused under NCB 333:

NCB 333 ".... The officers, members of crews, and passengers on board merchant ships of the United States, although not in the naval service of the United States, are, under the laws of the United States, the decisions of the courts, and by the very necessities of the case, subject to military control while in the actual theatre of war."

The prosecution has entered no evidence that Espiritu Santo, New Hebrides was on October 26, 1942, an "actual theatre of war". Such fact is not one of judicial notice. See NCB 309. Nor, even if it were, has the prosecution requested that such notice be taken as required by NCB 309.

The judge advocate has stated that matters of geographical location are within the judicial notice of the court. But this matter of actual theatre of war is not a geographical factor. You cannot take judicial notice of the activities conducted in that area by human beings. But they have made it an actual theatre of war, the judge advocate will say, there are mines there and the captain of the Coolidge admits there was the possibility of enemy submarines there. The gentlemen of the commission will admit that there are mines in San Francisco, and there is a possibility of enemy submarines and there are mines in all the harbors of Australia, and there are submarines there. Is that going to be the indicia for actual theatre of war? Further what in an actual theatre of war? To my mind that phrase implies an area where there is combat. There was no combat in Espiritu Santo on that date.

It is maintained that the lose of the *President Coolidge* was due:

(1) To the inefficiency of the Port Director's Office at Noumea, in that, Captain Nelson was not given directions for safely approaching Segond Channel and was not informed that these waters were mined and in the haphazard way that the enclosures were attached to the basic routing instructions and

delivered to the *President Coolidge*, and

(2) To the inefficiency of an inexperienced commanding officer of a navy patrol and pilot boat, and

(3) To the inefficiency of Navy signalmen.

It is believed and it has been demonstrated that Captain Nelson should be acquitted of the charge and specification. Thankyou Gentlemen.

Chester C. Hosmer,
Lieutenant (jg) U.S.N.R.

UNITED STATES COAST GUARD
MARINE INVESTIGATION BOARD, 6 FEBRUARY 1943.

IN THE MATTER OF THE STRIKING OF MINES, THE SINKING AND SUBSEQUENT LOSS OF THE PASSENGER STEAMER '*President Coolidge*' OF 21,936 GROSS TONS, AT SECRET CODE NAME BUTTON, ON 26 OCTOBER, 1942, AT OR ABOUT 9:35 AM

FINDINGS

This 'A' Marine Investigation Board obtained information that certain members of the officers and crew of the SS *President Coolidge* were in San Francisco, also that the vessel was lost. It was established that the senior officer in San Francisco was the second. mate.

The second mate was contacted and form 924d-1 prepared and forwarded to Headquarters on 3 December 1942. Upon return of the master to San Francisco a second form 924d-l was prepared in his presence which it is believed contains more authentic information and is attached to this record.

Upon return of the master to San Francisco his initial report to this Service on 28 January 1943 inferred that the U. S. Navy had conducted an investigation, preferred a charge, conducted a trial and had acquitted the master of the charge.

The master of the vessel was called before an 'A' Marine Investigation Board at San Francisco on 6 February 1943 and based upon his initial report, it was believed an informal preliminary investigation was sufficient to be convened in order that the reports submitted be authenticated and an ex-parte statement obtained to establish res judicata in this entitled matter.

From the investigation conducted it has been established that a military commission tried and acquitted the master of the charge preferred and that

the pertinent records of the vessel have been forwarded to the Judge Advocate General, U. S. Navy, Washington. D. C.

It further appears from the investigation conducted that the vessel is a total loss with an insured coverage of $7,500,000: also that as a result of this casualty Robert Reid, employed as fireman, holding certificate of identification Z-6087, was lost; also one Army personnel was lost.

UNDISPUTED FACTS

In a document dated 9 March 1943, regarding 'matters relating to the *President Coolidge* and the findings of the Inquiry Board', the United States Coast Guard made the following report.

According to a U.S. Coast Guard documents prepared in 1963, the known and *undisputed facts* in the case of the US Navy v Henry Nelson are as follows:

(1) The SS *President Coolidge* struck two mines at about 0935 ship's time October 26, 1942.

(2) Master beached vessel at about 0938 October 26.

(3) Vessel sunk at about 1038 October 26.

(4) Master and crew of vessel remained at Espiritu Santo for about 6 or 7 days and were then transferred to Noumea.

(5) Admiral Halsey on November 29, 1942, formally charged Captain Nelson that he, "did... neglect and

fail to follow routing instructions... and did negligently, carelessly, wantonly and recklessly cause said ship to make wrong approach to Segond Channel ... and through such negligence did suffer the said *President Coolidge* to strike two mines.."
(6) The record of the proceedings and findings of the Military Commission were never made public. However, Admiral Halsey, in a letter to Captain Nelson dated December 25, 1942, briefly referred to the trial as follows: "This is to acknowledge receipt of your request for a copy of the record of proceedings of a military commission before which you were recently tried and acquitted upon the charge, 'Through Negligence Suffering a Vessel of the United States to be Lost'. "
(7) On 6 February 1943, Captain Nelson was called before the Coast Guard Marine Inspection Officer (Lt. Cmdr. Henry V. Barbieri) for an informal investigation concerning the Coolidge sinking. In view of the fact that Captain Nelson had already been tried and acquitted by a Military Commission, the Coast Guard took no further action in the matter.

CONFIDENTIAL REPORT ON U.S. FLAG PASSENGER VESSELS ATTACKED AND LOST.

UNITED STATES COAST GUARD Form N.C.G. 92461.
Report dated 6 February 1943.

SHIP: SS *President Coolidge*
DATE OF ATTACK: 26 October 1942.
COMPANY: American President Line
INFORMATION FURNISHED BY: Master

1 Year Built   1931
2 Gross Tonnage   21,936
3 Net Tonnage   12,835
4 Type of propulsion   Steam
5 Cargo on board, tons   10,000app.
6 Draft Loaded (maximum allowed)   34
7 Speed (Normal)   19 knots
8 Nature of Cargo   War material
9 Date and Time of Attack   10-26-42.
    (26 October 1942). Time: 9.35 am
10 Fire, Abandoned and Sunk. Aband.10.4?a.m.
    Sunk: 11.05 am
11 Position: Espreto Santos, New Hebrides Is. [*sic*]
12 State of Weather   Fine, clear
13 State of Sea   Smooth
14 Speed (When attacked or lost)   18-1/4knots
15 Draft (When attacked or lost) Mean draft 31-1/2',
    estimated.
16 Ship Bound For Espreto Santos [*sic*]
17 Were Routing Orders Followed   Yes
18 Any Criticism of Routing Orders   No
19 If at Night, were Navig. Lights on   No lights,
    day time.
20 Was 'SOS' Sent   Yes
21 Was Enemy Sighted (Before, during or after
    attack- give data) No

22 Was Ship Armed (Type Armament) Yes, 4-3",
    1-5", 12-20mm guns
23 Was Armament Used   No
24 Any United Nations' Craft in Vicinity   Yes
25 Nature of Attack (Give data):Struck mine
26 Number of Hits   Two
27 Location of Hits: Approx. after fire room and
    engine room
28 Did Cargo Fire (Give location, etc.) No
29 Was Deck ruptured   No
30 Did Ship Break in Two   No, turned turtle
31 Were Wood Doors or Ports Blown In
    Wood Doors: Unknown
    Ports: Unknown
32 Other Damage to Vessel   Total loss
32a No. lives saved by use of rubber suits:
    None available
33 Number of Life Boats carried   20
34 Number of life boats used & which   All
35 Number of Life Boats Lost and How: One lost
    by falls assumed due to heavy list of vessel.
36 Number of Life Rafts carried 8 rafts, 24 floats
37 Number of Life Rafts Used and Which: All
38 Number of Life Rafts Lost and How:
    When finished with left on beach.
39 Were boats or rafts attacked   No
40 If 'Yes' to #39 Any Casualties   -
41 Any casualties die Exposure: No
42 Any casualties due to lack of food   No
43 How Long in Boats or on Rafts   Minutes
44 Picked up by and where: Rowed ashore
45 Speed of ship when abandoned   Beached

46 Ship re-boarded, towed in or salvaged
  Sunk
47 If Brought in, approx, damage   Total loss
47a No. US Signal (Navy) crew carried
  Officers: 1, enlisted 5
48 No. US Navy Gun Crew carried
  Officers 1, enlisted 44.
49 No. Ship's Officers carried.
  Officers 19, Radio Ops 3
50 No. Unlicensed Crew Carried   268
51 No. US Naval Gun Crew injured   0
52 US Naval Gun Crew Lost   0
53 Ship's Officers Injured   0
54 Ship's Officers Lost   0

55 Unlicensed Crew casualties: 1 missing
56 Total casualties Officers & Men   1 missing
57 Officers and Men lost By: Unknown
58 Saved (including naval crew):
  Officers 19, unlicensed 321 Total 340
59 Officers and Men Saved By:
  All saved but one fireman by lifesaving facilities
60 No. Eng. Room Watch Below   10 approx.
61 No. Eng. Room Watch Lost   1 fireman
  believed on watch
62 No. Of Lookouts :2 in crowsnest, 1 focsle head
63 Any defective material   None
64 Any fault on Part of Personnel   None

JUST COMPENSATION

JUST COMPENSATION, STEAMSHIP "PRESIDENT COOLIDGE"

WAR SHIPPING ADMINISTRATION, Washington October 3, 1944

The purpose of this memorandum is to recommend payment in full of the claim of the American President Lines, Ltd., in the sum of $7,000,000 for the total loss of the steamship *President Coolidge* (hereinafter referred to as the *Coolidge)* while operating under bareboat charter. The facts giving rise to the claim are as follows.

The Coolidge was one of the largest combination freight and passenger vessels under the American flag. This vessel was operated in the trans-Pacific trade between the Pacific coast and the United States, in various ports in China, Japan, and the Philippine Islands. Shortly after the outbreak of war the *Coolidge* was chartered by the United States Maritime Commission under voluntary charter agreement dated as of December 31, 1941, the charter having been made under the provisions of Public Law 101, Seventy-seventh Congress. The charter provided that in the event of a total loss or constructive total loss of the vessel, the owner should be paid $7,500,000 plus interest, at the rate of 3 1/2 percent per annum commencing 120 days from date of loss. Then specific provision on this point is contained in article 13 of the charter which reads in part as follows:

"ART 13. Actual total loss liability. - In the event of total loss of the vessel, the charterer shall reimburse the owner therefor in the amount of $7,000,000, together with interest at the rate of 3 1/2 percent per annum beginning 120 days from the date of the vessel's loss, if known, otherwise beginning 120 days from the date she was last heard from".

The significant particulars of this vessel insofar as they relate to the determination of value are as follows:

Date built - October 1931.
Cost of construction (including $145,718 betterments) - $8, 017, 690.
Date chartered: December 31, 1941.

Date lost: October 26, 1942.
Dead weight: 7,200.
Gross tons: 21,986.
Speed: 20 knots.
Passenger capacity:
    First 305; Tourist 133; Steerage 402.
Refrigerated cargo capacity: 52,145 Cubic feet.
American Bureau of Shipping classification: A-1.

CONTROLLING VALUATION STANDARD FOR THE "COOLIDGE"

The *Coolidge* was chartered voluntarily pursuant to Public Law 101, Seventy-seventh Congress. It was not requisitioned for title pursuant to section 902 of the 1936 act. Section 902 contains the so-called enhancement clause which prohibits enhancement in value result in "from the causes necessitating the taking." Public Law 101 contains no such limitation. Consequently, the Advisory Board stated in rule 6 that "the enhancement clause of section 902 (a) has no application to voluntary charters or purchases under Public Law 101." However, as will be seen from the discussion, there is no prohibited enhancement in the proposed settlement; therefore the distinction between section 902 and Public Law 101 appears to be unimportant in this instance.

The $7,000,000 total loss valuation is provided for by specific agreement. A review of the agreement in the light of the rules of the Advisory Board demonstrates that the amount stipulated conforms with the requirements laid down by the Board, consisting of Hon. Learned Hand, Hon. John J. Parker. and Hon. Joseph C. Hutcheson, Jr., senior justices of the second, fourth, and fifth circuits respectively. The rules of this Board provide first for valuation on the basis of market value where a market exists. It is obvious that no market for a vessel of this class can be said to have existed in

1941 or in 1942. In the absence of a market, value is determined pursuant to rule 3, which reads as follows:

"Rule 3. Where market value cannot be determined by sufficient sales or hirings of vessels of like character, made at or about the time of taking, it is to be determined by the Administrator from a consideration of cost of construction, acquisition cost so far as relevant, improvements, replacement costs, depreciation, earnings, physical condition, appraisals for insurance, or other purposes, and any other relevant facts upon which a reasonable judgment as to value can be based. These various matters are to be given such weight by the Administrator, as in his opinion they are justly entitled to, in determining the price that would probably result from fair negotiations between an owner willing to sell and a purchaser desiring to buy."

It is also evident from the rules of the Board that the vessel is not subject to section 902 (b) and 802 of the 1936 act which Permit requisition of vessels that have received "construction differential subsidies" for book value as determined by Internal Revenue Depreciation Standards. This vessel did receive Government aid in the form of mail contracts under the Merchant Marine Act of 1928 but such aid does not constitute a construction differential subsidy. The Advisory Board so held in rule 8, reading as follows:

"Rule 8. Section 902 (b) of the Merchant Marine Act of 1936 has no application to vessels merely because they have- received mail subsidies under the act of 1928. This section has application only to vessels which have received a construction-differential subsidy under title V of the Merchant Marine Act of 1936; and a mail subsidy is not a construction-differential subsidy within the meaning of section 902 (b) of the act."
[Some text omitted here].

A. Insurance valuation history.

Since the loss of the *Coolidge* was in the nature of an insurance loss, it is especially appropriate to review the insurance valuation history on this vessel.

1. Peacetime marine insurances.

For the year 1938-39 the *Coolidge* was insured by her owners in the commercial market against marine risks in the amount of $7,570,000. From 1939 until the end of 1941 she was insured against such risks for $8,000,000. The insurance fund of the Maritime Commission had participated in this peacetime insurance to the extent of $400,000 per annum, and the premiums were allowed for operating subsidy purposes. The amount of peacetime insurance and the participation of the Commission therein has unusual significance in view of the fact that this vessel was covered by a mortgage which required the vessel to be "fully insured in amount at least equal to the full commercial value of the vessel" and further provided that "the amount of insurance shall at all times be satisfactory to the Board (Commission)."

2. 1939-41 War Risk Values.

During the period of approximately 2 years- December 19.39 to December 1941-the *Coolidge* was insured against war risks for from seven to eight million dollars; the amount was $7,000,000 for the period of 1941, and $8,000.000 for the earlier period.

[Substation legal text omitted here justifying the insurance claim, and mentioning precedents].

CONCLUSION

In view of the considerations above referred to, and particularly the history of insurance and other valuations, the analysis of the reproduction cost valuation, the consideration of values based on capitalized earnings, and a review of expert appraisal evidence. also consideration of book value insofar as pertinent, it is concluded that the liquidation of this claim by payment thereof in accordance with the terms of the charter agreement in effect at time of loss will not exceed the amounts required- to be paid under the rules of the Advisory Board on Just Compensation and is in the interests of the United States. Accordingly, it is recommended that the Administrator find and determine that $7,000,000 constitutes full compensation for all claims of the owner for the loss of the *Coolidge* under such charter, and further find that such amount conforms with the rules of the Advisory Board on Just Compensation and does not contain any enhancement value prohibited by section 902 of the Merchant Marine Act of 1936, and authorize and direct the pavement thereof, reserving for later disposition only the question of the claim for interest by reason of the delay in payment, and authorize the chief adjuster to make payment of the said $7.660.000, less payment heretofore made, upon submission of all customary claims documents.

Signed Percy Chubb, Assistant Deputy Administrator (Fiscal Affairs).

IT'S MINE!

WHO OWNS THE PRESIDENT COOLIDGE?

Burton Jaquith still legally owns the *President Coolidge* to this day. Jaquith was a stewards carpenter on the S.S. President Cleveland in 1935, doing the San Francisco-Honolulu-Yokohama-Kobe-Shanghai-Manila run, and thus had more than a passing interest in the Dollar Line. He had purchased several ships for salvage whilst working in Manila including the liberty ship *SS Russell Chittenden* in the Trobriand Islands.

In response to the authors question on the matter of ownership of the *President Coolidge*, Mr. Jaquith replied, 'I am still the legal owner of the Coolidge. International maritime law is an arcane and a very expensive pursuit. The recovery of the propellers and oil would fall under the salvage sections. I have observed that generally the right of salvage is conferred when the owner or agent is not on board or present, the division of resultant proceeds is determined by advance agreement or an admiralty court. In neither of the above instances was permission asked or granted, and while the salvers could have been prosecuted or sued, the recovery would likely not cover the costs involved. I had this happen a number of times, notably on the salvage of the *S.S. Edward Luckenbach* and the *S.S. Laertes*. We called them modern pirates. As to the ecological responsibility, again this would be up to the responsible Admiralty court, but I am advised that as the sinking was an act of war, such litigation would be inappropriate. We have never asked for nor received anything from the dive operators. Again this is something that I do not feel worth pursuing, but their acknowledgement of our permission or thanks would have been appreciated. I have never had reason to ask the government of Vanuatu whether they do or do not recognize my ownership. Again this would only be pursued by diplomatic channels or international maritime courts and I do not have the incentive to do so. I have never visited Espiritu Santos or dived the wreck myself. I purchased the ship along with the *S.S. Russell Chittenden* for commercial salvage. This was while we lived in

Manila. Our salvage boat Atlantis 11 was in New Jersey being re-engined and outfitted. We rejoined the crew of thirteen there and proceeded to Florida and the Gulf of Mexico on a salvage contract with the U.S. Maritime Administration. These efforts were less than satisfactory, so we ceased operations and have been here ever since.'

Reece Discombe offers the following record. 'I went to the then British Resident Commissioner and inquired about ownership of this and other American war asset material in New Hebrides. I was informed by the commissioner that as far as they knew, all material still came under the US government. I was told at a later date that Mr Jaquith had the salvage rights of not only the Coolidge but other ships as well in the Pacific. Fair enough. Jaquith had a time limit on his claims. Later on I was called up to the Commissioners office and was informed by him that the American Government had declared all war material in the New Hebrides open slather. Anyone could take what they wanted. Jaquith had a limited time to do something about it (salvage of the *President Coolidge*) but time ran out and there was nothing done. Colin Allen the Resident Commissioner phoned me up one day and he said that the Coolidge is all yours, do what you want with it. Thankyou very much, I said.'

That the Resident British Commissioner Sir Colin Allen informed those interested that 'all US assets, war interest, was open slather' was probably based on a prior directive from the US Government to the Condominium government that the US Army and Navy no longer had any interest in war surplus material. It would thus have been a reasonable assumption that Sir Colin Allen would have included the *President Coolidge* as war surplus, not knowing that she was a merchant ship and privately owned, even though the 'owner' was the US Department of Commerce. (The United States of America Certificate of Registry , Official Number 231 219, shows that the ownership of the *President Coolidge* was surrendered by the owners, Dollar Steamship

Lines, Inc., in favour of the United States department of Commerce on 20 July 1938.) Furthermore, a Bill of Sale dated 8 May 1953 clearly indicates a legal contract between the "United States of America, representing the Department of Commerce", and Mr Burton Jaquith, US citizen resident in Manila, transferring ownership of the *President Coolidge*. It is important to note that the President Coolidge was not owned by the US Army or Navy, and was not military property. The US Government had every right to sell the ship, but the President Coolidge could not be classed as war salvage. The question that arises is whether Burton Jaquith had only salvage rights to the ship, which generally have a defined time limit. The Bill of Sale that Jaquith received from the US Government indeed did have a time clause associated with it, which could have been interpreted as a salvage clause by those not aware that the document in question is a Bill of Sale. The Bill of Sale states *"the Buyer shall completely scrap, dismember, dismantle or destroy the hull of the vessel within two years of the date of delivery thereof, so as to prevent further use of it in any manner whatsoever"*. If this had not been complied with, the contract would have been null and void and ownership would have reverted to the US government. Two points need to be raised on this questions: (I) Jaquith received a sale contract not a salvage contract, and thus to relinquish ownership of the subject of the Bill of Sale, the Bill of Sale would need to be voided. It was not. (ii) the clause in the Bill of Sale as indicated above is not a salvage clause, and the determining factor in the clause is the statement *'to prevent further use of it in any manner'*. (Clearly, the US Government did not want the ship raised and made operable as a seagoing vessel). Now, even though Jaquith never visited the ship, and he did no work on the vessel, the subject of the clause, *'to prevent further use of it in any manner'* was clearly maintained as the ship was in no condition to be refloated. Although it may not have been noticed at the time, the ship was developing a buckle, a ripple in the hull, ever so slight, that she could not have been made seaworthy even if technology allowed her to be raised. No doubt Jaquith was not aware of this, but it is of no concern. Nature, or more specifically the way the ship was lying, with the predominant weight on the bow and the stern, allowed the ship to 'bend' in the middle. It is, perhaps, irrelevant that the Bill of Sale required Jaquith to make the ship unusable. But even if the US Government was not satisfied that Jaquith

had kept his end of the deal, the US Government did not void the contract.

It is also interesting to note that the Condominium government did not attempt to communicate with Burton Jaquith when the oil from the *President Coolidge* was causing a problem. Technically, it was Jaquith's oil and as owner of the ship, he could have been directed to remove the oil at his cost. That the Condominium government did not contact Jaquith indicates that the government thought the wreck to be their responsibility. The Condominium government appears to have been in touch with the US Government who would have, more than likely, replied that it was not their responsibility. That the US government passed on the name of the owner of the ship to the Condominium is not recorded, but it appears not to have done so. Jaquith certainly owned the oil, as the only exclusion in the Bill of Sale is in reference to 'lead and other metallic ballast'.

To reiterate, Burton Kenton Jaquith has a Bill of Sale, not a salvage agreement, and is for all intents and purposes, still the legal owner of the wreck of the *SS President Coolidge*. Furthermore, the Condominium government had no right to assume, or imply, that it had ownership of the wreck and could impart that ownership to a third party. Technically, with the support of international and maritime law, the ship is owned by Burt Jaquith, and like all property can be sold, bequeathed or otherwise disposed of in any legal manner. Ownership also implies certain responsibilities, and as previously mentioned, the Condominium government could well have requested, indeed insisted, that Jaquith remove the oil at his cost. Other legal responsibilities also involve personal liability, and under 'normal' terrestrial circumstances, a property owner can be held responsible if the property is (for example) unsafe, or if lack of due care is exercised to protect the public. A diver who drowns in the ship due to inappropriate diving practices would not result in a successful legal suit against the owner, but what would happen if the forward gun collapsed and crushed a diver? All these matters however are purely academic as it is highly unlikely that any claim could be made on the owner, given that the Condominium government had 'assumed' ownership, and *ipso facto*, the independent Republic of Vanuatu government would have 'inherited' that claim. So, technically, the ship is still owned by Burton Jaquith. The props, the oil and the engine room machinery were owned by Jaquith but he made nothing on his $10 investment.

NAVAL GUN CREW LOG

LOG

Craig Hosmer, Commander of the *President Coolidge's* naval gun crew.
(Later U.S. Senator).

SUNDAY 25 OCTOBER 1942 - AT SEA

1033	Unidentified Aircraft sighted bearing 210° Baker, Sound Battle Alarm. Set Condition 1.
1034	Tracking with all guns that can bear Zone 8, range extreme scale midpoint.
1035	Scale 700.
1037	Airplane identified as friendly.
1045	Secured General Quarters, resumed regular watches by A.G. and Army personnel.
1120	Unidentified aircraft bearing 150 o Baker. Sound Battle Alarm. Set Condition 1. Tracking commenced Zone 8, Range extreme Scale 700.
1128	Aircraft identified as friendly.
1138	Secured general qtrs. Resst regular watch. Men instructed to remain in vicinity of Battle stations when off watch during this day.
1400	Strong signal VVVV picked up on 500 K.C. Source undetermined
1547	Dusk General Qtrs. Condition 1.
1900	Instructed all hands to sleep in vicinity of battle stations --either in gun tubs or underneath. Secured Gen'l Qtrs. Reset regular watch.
	Today was very hot. I spent my time on the bridge. Passed several islands this morning.
	Night Orders
	Enroute N.C. - N.H., October 25
	All men must sleep in vicinity of Condition 1 battle Stations tonight. Maintain regular watches.
	Bright moonlight -- take special care on dark side of ship watch for torpedo wakes.
	Swing ship to parallel torpedo track if seen.
	Report all objects.
	Men as assigned to Sky. I shall keep watch on bridge lookout on dark side.
	Awaken me after relief of each watch.
0400	Reveille
	Awaken me if dawn appears to be early.

MONDAY 26 OCTOBER 1942 - AT SEA

0400	Reveille
0420	General Quarters Condition 1.
0500	Passing between two islands. Men being kept at Gen'l Qtrs in this area.
0605	1st Division sent to breakfast.
0635	2nd Division sent to breakfast.

0645	3rd Division sent to breakfast.
0720	Espirito Santos sighted.
0739	Vessel sighted bearing 345 about 10 miles, guns manned and tracking commenced. Extreme range Scale 94.
0750	Vessel ascertained to be on appro china course.
0759	Vessel challenges.
0802	Vessel ascertained to be friendly. Range 6800 Scale 90 Tracking continued for practice of pointers and trainers. Remainder of crew on lookout.
0848	Small craft sighted in cover of Island bearing about 340 guns trained on. Range extreme. Scale 496.
0858	Vessel signals a form letter group. Signal officer cannot decipher. Asks meaning.
0902	Vessel says means same as merchant ship challenge. Identification made. Vessel appears to be PC or converted destroyer. Too distant to tell. Very black smoke coming from her. Cease tracking.
0906	Standing into channel. Several ships visible. Appear to be a cruiser and several auxiliaries and merchant men. Uncock guns. Secure all ready boxes with one dog.
0925	Instruct all A.G. and Army on watch at General Quarters to stand at ease, one foot from sides of tubs, spaced evenly.
0928	Receiving challenge from cruiser.
0930	Explosion rocks this vessel. Instruct all men to remain at battle stations.
0930 1/2	Another explosion--mines! Ship shaken badly. Port list commences. Instruct Gun 1 to send men to flood forward magazine if any sign of fire and report. Instruct gun 5 to do same as regards to after magazine. Master manoeuvring ship to starboard to beach her. List increasing to port. All stations report, no casualties.
0935	Bow of vessel strikes coral at bottom about 100 yds. from shore. Nets have been lowered. Life boats lowering. Abandoning of ship by troops commence.
0936	List to port now about 8 degrees. Much oil on water. Most abandoning being done from starboard side. Some oil soaked casualties getting up on Sun Deck from engine room hatches.
0938	Secure Army officers on watch with instructions to go to their abandon ship stations if possible. Secure all Army enlisted men on gun watch with instructions to abandon ship in orderly fashion.
0940	Abandon ship continues orderly. No panic. Rescue boats can be seen proceeding up the bay from other ships and shore stations. All troops so far are getting into life boats-then taken close enough to shore to wade in and life boats returning for more. Much oil on water making things very messy. Gun 5 reports soldier struggling. in water. Order man sent to same if necessary. Rhodes is manning phones with me here on the signal bridge. Communications uninterrupted.
0945	List about 10°. It is becoming apparent that the ship will keel over and skid off the coral reef. Gun 5 reports stern going down fairly fast. Send 1st. Division to cabins to secure partial paycards and what valuables they can carry.
0950	Send 2nd Division for Paycards and valuables.
0955	Send 3rd Division for Paycards and valuables. I go to my cabin and secure various papers and publications.
1000	Order men out of sky guns to starboard side of bridge. Guns 3,4 & 5 ordered to abandon ship. List 14 o to port.
1005	Men from sky guns placed in charge of Guilmette, ordered to abandon ship in orderly fashion, and keep together on shore.
1010	Guns 1 & 2 ordered to abandon ship in orderly fashion. Signal gang except Trimbur ordered to abandon. Mr. Weinstein, Trimbur, Rhodes and myself now left upon the signal bridge. Papers and publications of Mr. Weinstein and myself entrusted to MC Call, RM2c. All A.G. and Communications personnel instructed to get together on beach and report to Naval Headquarters. I go back along sun deck and instruct remaining soldiers, etc. to abandon ship in orderly fashion. Secure some boxes of ammunition so they wont slide down and explode. Check that all sky doors are closed on starboard side so ammunition won't go out. Obtain A.G. insignia from Armoury. List about 16°. Have been checking inclinometer in chart room.

1012   Soldiers have been waiting at bottoms of nets for life boats to take them in where they can wade ashore. List increasing. Many soldiers still on deck as nets are full. I start ordering men at bottoms of nets to jump in water and swim ashore. She can't stay up too much longer. Ask Col. Alter on fwd. deck to give orders there. All soldiers have on life preservers.

1016   Am moving aft along the boat deck ordering man to jump. Water is oily. Nets about 10 feet or more above the water. Many seem afraid to jump. Keep exhorting them to kick men in face to get them off. List about 18 1/2 degree.

1045   Finish getting idea over. Am at aft end of boat deck. Footing precarious due to the extreme list. Last of soldiers now on nets and starting down. Decks apparently cleared.

1047   Reach vicinity of bridge. Mr. Weinstein tells me he sent Rhodes over side to save a drowning man-- one of the merchant marine. Weinstein, Trumbus, Ch. officer and couple more of deck and engine room officers around. Ch. Officer tells us to get over side while we can. We are all balancing ourselves in the scuppers of the boat deck. Angle of deck so steep Ch. Mate had to be pulled up here. We start down the net. They are quite slippery by now, but list is great enough that we can more or less walk down the side by using hand lines to steady. Nets stop about 15 feet from water. Go down hand over hand along undersides of ship on hand line for rest of way.

1049   Reach ship's motor boat. There has been no particular thrill or excitement so far. Everyone is calm and doing the logical things. The Captain as already aboard this boat. Am being helped aboard. Very slippery due to oil. Am in bow of the boat. The anti rolling fins are now out of the water. Some one uses them to step ashore. Mr. Weinsten about 3/4 of way down. Sees helpless Filipino man on metal ladder about 3 or 4 feet from net. Man's arm is apparently broken. Mr. Weinstein jumps to the ladder and carries man down to the boat. We help them aboard.

1050   Chief mate and all others that started down with me now in the boat. Ship gives a bad lurch to port and is now on her port side.

1051   Mr. Olson, one of the junior mates, appears on the side of the ship from somewhere. There are also visible two men trying to pull someone up out of the passenger doors about 2/3 way aft. Olson runs along sides of ship, reaches them and starts to help. Ship is slowly beginning to slide into deep water.

1052 1/2 Ship gives a great lurch. Begins to slide rapidly backward into deep water. We are now about 50 feet from her. See Olson and two others dive into water.
         Ship disappears beneath the oil and water. Tremendous waves, air bubbles, swirling- water and oil. A large self propelled barge was trying to reach those on the side of the ship. It spins around out of control; is drawn to where the men are and apparently runs some of them down. Too much happening at once for me to tell. Men visible on barge desperately clinging to its engine housing.

1054   Captain orders boat to take us to Navy headquarters up the Bay. We place most of survivors in this boat off on a raft to make their way ashore. There are now in the boat the Captain, Chief and First Mates, Chief, First and Second Asst. Engineers and an injured oil covered seaman, Mr. Weinstein, Rhodes, Trimbur and myself. Plus numerous sextants and chronometers and some Captain's papers. Many boats and rafts about us. Much confusion.

1058   Boat rapidly filling with water. We signal Navy motor launch, transfer Rhodes, Trumbur, Second Asstt. Engineer and Chief Mate. Rhodes instructed to get men together and report to Navy Headquarters. Motorboat continues on course. Injured man seems to be suffering.

1105   Condition of boat becomes more serious. Signal any invasion boat and transfer all instruments. All but First Mate and First Engineer transfer to this boat. Ship's motor boat placed in tow and continue on course.

1113   Come alongside USS Chester and disembark injured man. Nobody here seems anxious to do anything for us. Provide water upon asked. I request transportation. to search for the men.

1155   Transportation provided. We are taken as far as the Medical Centre.

1230   Find two men of Communications unit and Warner Slc pf the Armed Guard Unit here at Center. All uninjured. Hear that Rhodes has most of our men up the beach somewhere. Received instruction to wait for Captain. Hundreds of oil covered naked survivor here. Kerosene broken out. They are cleaned up. Trucks taking them to river for their washing, Injured being given medical attention.

1330	Captain of Base hasn't shown up yet so begin to search for the men. Mr. Weinstein and I obtain various rides up and down road along the beach. Many false alarms since quite a few of the soldier survivors have been given sailor uniforms to replace their oil soaked clothing. No trace of any more of my men. Continue search all afternoon.
1600	Report to Port Director. Instructed to round up my men and make report of muster.
1700	Meet up with Master and some more of ship's officers. Supper with them at C.B. Camp. Hear that my men and remainder of communications unit are at the 76th Coast Artillery Headquarters Camp.
1730	Arrive, at 76th CAHQ. Men are here.
1735	Muster men. Absentees: Wilson, Robert William Slc V-6 USNR. He has been seen off the ship, however, so am sure that he is safe. Arrange for supper for the men at one of the kitchens here at this unit (a negro outfit).
1900	Obtain two army trucks to transport men to Receiving Ship.
1830	Arrive at Receiving-Ship. They are very good to us but have very little. A few tents in a coconut grove which are already filled. They put up tarpaulins to sleep under. Get a few blankets and about ten cots. Ensign Sickerman, the torpedo officer here, arranges cots and blankets in his tent for Mr. Weinstein and myself. There is also another officer here - a survivor from a torpedoed destroyer. He was the engineering officer but managed to navigate a diesel launch here from the Solomon's area with some of his men. He is awaiting reassignment. The man, Mr. Weinstein and myself are all filthy, oil stained and tired.
1945	Muster Absentee - Wilson. Armed Guard and Communications units declared a unified command temporarily stationed at Advanced Base Button. Mr. Weinstein appointed Executive Officer.
1930	Bunked down. No one takes long to get to sleep tonight. This has been quite a day. The men are all cheerful and morale is good despite the losses they all have suffered. Little more than the clothes we wear and partial pay cards were saved in most cases. They were marvellously calm when the mines exploded. Stuck right to their posts. Some thought it was torpedoing and broke out ammunition, cocked guns, etc. This island is Espiritu Santo of the New Hebrides group. It is medium sized and French owned. All the area we have seen has been planted with coconuts. Trees evenly planted about 25 feet apart, grass in between. Coconuts now ripe and falling. You have to stay away from the trunks else you will be hit. Weather quite warm. Road very dirty. All water bad except that distilled for drinking purposes.

TUESDAY 27 OCTOBER - ESPIRITU SANTO ISLAND

0330	Tropical rain starts. Tarpaulins not quite adequate to keep men dry against such deluge.

NOTE: All of above times are approximate except those double underlined which were timed by my wrist watch, that is probably about one minute fast. [Underlining not recorded.] The events of this day were recorded by me the morning of October 27, 1942, first on paper, thereafter being copied into this log exactly as written on the paper.

C.C. Hosmer.

VANUATU
Facts and Figures

The New Hebrides has by no means enjoyed a peaceful past. Ancestral tales of early life on Vanuatu begin about 1400 B.C. The islands were first sighted in 1606 by the Portuguese explorer Pedro Fernandes de Quiros (1560?-1614), a Portuguese explorer in the service of the Spanish crown. Believing he had found a new southern continent, he christened the large island "Tierra Austrialis del Espiritu Santo". The islands were visited in 1768 by the French navigator Louis Antoine de Bougainville and in 1774 by the British navigator Captain James Cook, who named them New Hebrides, after the similarly rugged Scottish Hebrides Islands, and charted many of the islands. The islands were also visited in 1789 by La Perouse, in 1793 by D'Entrecasteaux and by other noted explorers such as William Bligh (of the *Bounty*), Dumont d'Urville, Belcher and Markham.

The commercial contact with Europeans came when Peter Dillon discovered sandalwood on Erromango in 1828. This contact was to be followed by the 'blackbirders', who often with very doubtful methods recruited labour for the sugar plantations in Queensland and Fiji. Many Ni-Vanuatu were recruited, or blackbirded, as the practice was known, to work in the sugar cane fields of Fiji and Australia or the nickel mines of New Caledonia. Many times the blackbirded islanders were promised wages that never materialized, held as indentured labourers for years past the promised termination date, or kidnapped outright. In addition, the Europeans introduced diseases hitherto unknown in our islands, decimating the population. Returning labourers to the islands did, however, bring a pidgin English they had acquired overseas, which served as a common tongue in place of the 115 indigenous dialects. Today, Bislama, as it is called, is the national language. Blackbirders from Australia and the 'ticket of leave' men from the convict settlement in New Caledonia, did little to enhance the reputation of the European in the New Hebrides. With the arrival of the first missionaries in the 1840s an attempt was made, sometimes with fatal consequences, to compensate for and repair the atrocious reputation of their fellow countrymen. The history of the European contact with the New Hebrides together with malaria, earthquakes and torrential rain, did little for the reputation of the country. Some of the first settlers to arrive had already taken part in the Crimean War (1870-71) and the Boer war in South Africa (1898-1902). Many of the descendants of these settlers are still quite-active on their original land, which has been kept in the families to this day.

The people of Vanuatu, a name which means 'Land Eternal', are predominantly Melanesian. The Ni-Vanuatu have populated these islands for centuries and with more than 115 distinctly different cultures and languages still thriving here, Vanuatu is recognised as one of the most culturally diverse countries in the world. There are small communities of French, British, Australian, New Zealand, Vietnamese, Chinese and other Pacific Islands people living in harmony with the Ni Vanuatu. Until 1980 Vanuatu, then known as the New Hebrides, was jointly administered by France and Great Britain as a 'Condominium'.

Getting There.
International Airlines: Air Vanuatu from Auckland, Brisbane, Melbourne, Sydney, Noumea and Nadi. Air Caledonie from Noumea with connections from Australia, New Zealand and Tahiti. Air Pacific from Nadi with connections from New Zealand, Japan and the USA. Solomon Airlines from Honiara and Port Moresby. The international port of entry is Bauerfield, only 10 minutes from the capital, Port Vila.
Domestic Airline: Vanair services all major islands in the country.

Banking and Finance
The introduction in 1993 of the International Companies Act made Vanuatu one of the most attractive and competitive financial centres in the world. Trading banks include ANZ, Bank of Hawaii Vanuatu, Westpac and the National Bank of Vanuatu. Vanuatu is a tax haven as there is no income tax. Foreign currency is readily transacted. The local currency unit is the Vatu.

Climate
Its climate is typically wet and tropical, moderated by southeast trade winds, with an average annual temperature of 25°C (77°F). Annual rainfall decreases from 3810 mm (150 in) in the northern part of the group to 2286 mm (90 inch) in the south. Summer is from November to March, average temperature is 28°C. Winter is from April to October, temperature average 23°C.

Economy
The economy is based primarily on subsistence farming which provides a living for about 80% of the population. Fishing and tourism are the other mainstays of the economy. Mineral deposits are negligible; the country has no known petroleum deposits. A small light industry sector caters to the local market. Tax revenues come mainly from import duties. Industries include food and fish freezing, wood processing, meat canning. Agriculture concerns export crops - coconuts, cocoa, coffee, fish; subsistence crops - taro, yams, coconuts, fruits, vegetables. The economy is based on the production of primary materials for export. These are mainly copra, fish, manganese, timber, cocoa, coffee and shell. Of late a beef industry has come into being. The Ni Vanuatu in outlying areas rely on traditional subsistence farming, clearing patches of bush or jungle to meet basic daily requirements.

Embassies/Honorary Consulates
Australian High Commission, British High Commission, French Embassy, New Zealand High Commission, and Chinese Embassy.

Entry Requirements
For stays not exceeding 30 days, bona fide visitors who are nationals of the following countries do not require a visa: Nationals of Commonwealth countries, EU countries, Fiji, Japan, Norway, Philippines, South Korea, Switzerland and the USA Check with your local travel agent or consulate for up to date details as these political requirements can vary.

Electrical Voltage:
210 volts AC, mainly three-point plugs in hotels.

Food
Dining is a highlight in Vanuatu. Fresh local fish, beef, fruit and vegetables are in plentiful supply. Top class restaurants offer Melanesian, French, Polynesian, Indian, Chinese, Thai-Vietnamese, English and Japanese specialties. Prices vary, and are generally more expensive than the equivalent in Australia. Wines are comparatively expensive, particularly Australian wines (in comparison to Australian prices), but there is also the opportunity to sample a wide range of French wines.

Health Regulations
No vaccinations are required but anti-malarial precautions are recommended for visits to outer islands.

Political
In 1887 France and England both agreed not to exercise a separate control over the group, and a Joint Naval Commission was appointed from each of the two war ships which at that time paid periodical visits to the islands. The Commission was responsible for the protection of the lives and property of both British and French citizens living in the group. In 1902 French and British Resident Commissioners were appointed. In 1906 the islands became a condominium, a jointly (British-French) administered territory, where each power was to retain jurisdiction over its own citizens. In 1914 this document was superseded by the Anglo-French Protocol, which was ratified in 1922, and which has, with some modifications, regulated the administration of the group ever since. During World War II the United States established a large naval and air base on Espiritu Santo. In June 1980, just before the islands were to receive independence, a short-lived revolt on the island of Espiritu Santo was quelled. The New Hebrides became independent as Vanuatu on July 30, 1980. Vanuatu is a self-governing Republic and a member of the Commonwealth of Nations. The President is the Head of State. The government is based on the Westminster System. The capital of the republic is Port Vila, situated on the island of Efate about mid-way within the archipelago. The country receives considerable aid from western

countries. There is no regular military force; the Vanuatu Police Force (VPF) includes the paramilitary Vanuatu Mobile Force or VMF.

Medical
Hospital facilities exist in Port Vila and at Luganville, Espiritu Santo. There are no dangerous animals or insects.

People, Population and Language
The nationality of the people is Ni-Vanuatu (both a singular and plural noun and an adjective). Population is 173,648 as of the July 1995 estimate. The people are Melanesian, called Ni-Vanuatu, with a large expatriate number from Australian, New Zealand and France. Note: Population of 112,000 in 1979 Census. Bislama, English and French. Over one hundred local 'Mother tongues' are in common use. Ethnic divisions are indigenous Melanesian 94%, French 4%, Vietnamese, Chinese, Pacific Islanders, Europeans 2%. During the British-French administration, there were two official languages, English and French, with Bislama widely spoken (a form of pidgin English).

Shopping
Foreign cash, travellers cheques and major international credit cards (Amex, Diners, JCB, Mastercard and Visa) are widely accepted. Bankcard is not normally accepted. Most shops close for 'siesta' 11.30 am to 1.30 pm. Eating places, banks, supermarkets and the Post Office do not observe siesta. Shops open on Saturday morning and some speciality shops and supermarkets open on Sunday morning. Suburban general stores open early and close late seven days a week. The colourful market in the town centre operates every day except Sundays for flowers, fruit, vegetables and handicrafts.

Tipping
No tipping or bargaining please, it goes against local tradition.

Transportation
Driving is on the right-hand side of the road. Cars, 4WDs and jeeps are available for hire. Taxis are plentiful and are all metered. Mini buses offer a frequent though not timetabled service - merely flag one down and tell the driver where you want to go, the fare is 100 vatu a trip. Inter-island travel is mainly by air, inter-island boats taking deck passengers are irregular. Cruise ships regularly call at Port Vila.

Water
The urban water supplied is safe to drink.

Acculturation.
In anthropology, acculturation is the influence of one society or ethnic group on another as a result of continuous face-to-face contact. Although acculturation involves changes in both of the societies and cultures in contact, the term generally is used to refer to changes that occur in a nonindustrial society under the influence of a complex Western society. Vanuatu is going through enormous changes as it is influenced by the western world, in trade (and hence economics), and in its social structure. The influence of tourists is minimal if one considers the full population, but on the islands of Efate, Tanna and Espiritu Santo it is significant. Most tourist operators are aware of acculturation (although are probably not aware of the term), and attempt to restrict access to the indigenous people. But there is a great demand to visit Yasur volcano for example, and to visit villages which are gradually changing with the introduction of western visitors - with their vatu. This is a problem that the government must address, and is a most difficult social issue. Tourism brings added wealth, but the argument is that introduced wealth is not the answer to the so-called development of the people. Indeed, one may well ask why 'develop' the people, who have lived comfortably for hundreds of generations without the need for western influence. It is an interesting and at times tragic dilemma but not one to be debated here. Sufficient to say that the tourist must be well aware of his or her influence on the Ni-Vanuatu, particularly those in villages and islands which do not have regular tourists. Some villages are 'primitive' according to western values, and as such attract amusement. Vanuatu is not a zoo. If visiting or meeting Ni-Vanuatu, the best way to offer the utmost appreciation is to respect their custom and learn. And be assured that there is much that the western world can learn from the Ni-Vanuatu.

Geography
The New Hebrides, including the Banks and Torres Groups, forms a Y-shaped chain of islands extending north-south for 1176 kilometres. The islands lie between latitudes 130 and 210 south and longitude 166 and 170 east There are thirteen main islands, the total group of eighty-three islands lying in a 'Y'-shape chain north of New

Caledonia and some 2500 km northeast of Sydney (Australia), 2000 km north of Auckland (New Zealand), and 800 km west of Nadi (Fiji), the geographical area designated as Melanesia. The islands are volcanic and coralline with most covered in dense tropical rainforest. The total land mass is 14,760 sq km, with a n accumulative coastline of 2,528 km.. The islands range in topography from towering volcanic cones to others covered in dense rainforest to yet others which are raised coral islands with wide beaches and deep natural harbours. Several volcanoes are accessible, the main tourist 'attraction' being Yasur on the island of Tanna - an incredible experience. The main island is Efate with the capital Port Vila at about the same latitude as Townsville. Among the principal islands are Espiritu Santo, Malekula, Efate, Erromango, and Tanna. Islands are both of coral formations and of volcanic origin, but mostly the latter and several volcanoes are active. The highest peak, Tabwemasana (1811 m/ 5942 ft), is on Espiritu Santo. Most islands are forested, and some have fertile soils.

Port of Entry

The two main ports of entry for overseas vessels are Port Vila and Luganville (Espiritu Santo).

Tourism.

Port Vila is well established with a wide range of accommodation - island resorts, international hotels, smaller business hotels and economy hotels. For short stays, or a week, most tourists remain on the main island of Efate (Port Vila). Optional side trips are available to Tanna, Pentecost, and Espiritu Santo Islands. Smaller resorts and hotels exist on these islands and cater well for tourists. Daily flights to the main islands allow day visits if time is limited. Port Vila has a number of private tourist operators who can make all arrangements.

Efate and Port Vila

Port Vila is the capital of Vanuatu and administrative centre, and lies on the south-west coast of the island of Efate. Port Vila is the entry point into the islands and the centre of government. The capital is a modern town with tall buildings and neat shops set within a magnificent natural harbour. It is a charming potpourri of cultures, blending elements of Melanesian, English, French and Chinese tastes. It is a town that you could wander around for a few days dropping in here and there into a variety of shops and boutiques, relaxing over coffee and French pastry on the terrace, checking out the wines, buying a camera , or contemplating the navel of carved figure at the Handikraf blong Vanuatu shop. Along the main street there are duty-free shops, restaurants and handicraft galleries. Design name clothing and French perfumes were once a great buy but as the French gradually leave the island so does their exquisite taste in such refinements. A pity. The French added just that little bit of class. The market is a great place to start the day. It is best at dawn to catch the mood of the people as they come into town to buy their supplies. Set between the waterfront and Bougainville Street, the market 'square' occupies some of the best land in town . I can't help feeling that as the morning leads into noon and the Ni-Vanuatu has done her shopping, the vendors stay on reluctantly to be on display for the tourist, leaving their trussed up coco-nut crabs to broil in the sun, and the bananas ripening prematurely, both wanting to crawl away with their owners and be left in peace.

NOTES

CHAPTER ONE - A DOLLAR FOR THE AMERICAN PRESIDENT

N1
Niven writes: Roosevelt had also appointed an inter-departmental committee for policy guidance on the merchant marine. Its report, made at the same time as the report from the postmaster general, was more favourable to the shipping lines. It singled out various economic factors like the decline of world trade due to the Depression, costly strikes that hampered operations, and especially the differentials in labour, construction, and ship repair costs that provided a competitive edge to foreign operators. The report recommended that the mail subsidy arrangement be discarded and that the government pay differential subsidies for trade routes that were in the national interest as defined by defence and economic needs.

N2
The preamble to the Merchant Marine Act of 1936, which has come to be known as 'The Magna Carta of American Shipping', states in effect that the merchant marine should be adequate (1) to transport all of our domestic waterborne commerce and a substantial portion (currently interpreted to mean not less than 50%) of our waterborne foreign commerce and (2) to be capable of serving as a naval and military auxiliary in time of war or national emergency. It is clear from the foregoing that the merchant marine was something more than a 'business' or an 'industry' in the generally accepted sense of such terms. Although privately owned and operated, as prescribed by the Act of 1936, and in keeping with the Free Enterprise System, the US Maritime Industry, by its very nature and necessity, become an instrument of national U.S. policy. John Niven writes: The new (Maritime) commission could build, own, and operate merchant ships directly or under charter arrangements if private interests were unable to undertake the program of modernization the act contemplated. But the clear implication was that existing shipping lines would be encouraged through subsidies, not penalized by either the threat of government ownership or outright competition from government-owned and operated lines. Throughout the debates on the Merchant Marine bill of 1936, there was an awareness that defence needs were as important in determining policy as were the economic aspects of international trade. The rise of fascism and communism in Europe and the belligerent posture of Japan in the Far East greatly concerned the Roosevelt Administration. And the strengthening of the merchant marine, especially in the Pacific, was a factor in granting such broad powers to the commission. Finally, Congress appropriated funds to finance a program that envisaged the construction of sixty-five vessels. Later, as the Sino-Japanese War broke out and the situation in Europe became more menacing, the building program was accelerated.

N3
The name 'American President Line' was chosen as a result of a contest. It was won by a Mr. and Mrs. Lloyd B. Hughes whose prize was a round trip to Hawaii.

N4
These shipping companies included: American Pioneer Line, Coastwise-Far East Line, Baltimore Mail Line, Lykes Brothers Steamship Company, Luckenbach Steamship Company, U.S. Army Transport Service, U.S. Maritime Commission (Danish Ships)

N5
Needless to say, other shipping lines also joined in the evacuation of US citizens from the Far East notably the *SS Monterey* and *SS Mariposa* of the Matson Line, and the *SS Washington* of the United States Lines, for which American President Lines acted as Far Eastern agents.

N6
A great deal of this chapter is extracted from a pamphlet written by Eugene Hoffman, Vice President Public Relations of the American President Lines in 1957. See Appendix 2, page 237.

N7
John Niven writes: 'Davies merged APL Associates, the holding company that controlled the shipping lines, into a gold-dredging firm called Natomas Company. In the early sixties, Natomas became increasingly involved in the exploration and production of oil and gas, particularly in Indonesia. Its interest in Pacific Far East Line was sold in 1967. But until Natomas was acquired in 1983 by Diamond Shamrock, a large Texas-based oil company, it maintained its control of American President Lines. In 1974 American Mail was merged into American President Lines. In 1983 the line regained independent status under the newly created American President Companies, Ltd. APL's former parent organization, Natomas, had been acquired by Diamond Shamrock and American President Lines was spun off, becoming a separate corporate entity again.'

N8
The following message was sent by Captain Yardley of the President Hoover to his head office after the stranding: Aboard Hoover: Stranded north-west point Hoisho Island resting rotten coral heading 104 degrees with 7 1/2 degree list to port. Present weather strong northeast monsoon. Pounding slightly. Soundings forward average 3 1/2 fathoms both inshore offshore to

break forward house; about 3 fathoms inshore 4 offshore to after part midship deck; from there aft 3 to 5 inshore, 4 to 5Y2 offshore. No divers have been down yet. Seawater rising falling with tide in all cargo holds, deep tanks. Vessel set up in no. 3. Forward boiler room bulkhead leaking. Port motor strained. Engine and boiler rooms kept dry by vessel's pumps. Estimate 60% cargo damaged oil and seawater. Salvage depends largely upon condition weather.

CHAPTER TWO - BIRTH OF A PRESIDENT

N1
The President Hoover established another unusual precedent during her sea trials. For the first time in the history of the shipyard, ladies were aboard overnight to 'lend their charm and dignity to a man-infested ship'. They were Mrs. J. Harold Dollar, Mrs. K. Ferguson, Miss Mary Lett and Miss Clarissa Keller who 'seemed to bring good luck to the voyage'.

N2
Calvin Coolidge was inaugurated as the thirtieth president of the United States of America on 3 August 1923. Born in Plymouth, Vermont on 4 July 1872, Coolidge was the son of a village storekeeper. He was a popular president but known for his character rather than any forceful policies. It was suggested that perhaps his greatest talent was the ability to effectively do nothing, not a derogatory remark as it was further noted that business America just wanted to be left alone. He was both the most negative and remote of Presidents, and yet the most accessible, a willing subject for the camera in perhaps the most absurd of situations, and a genial host to any White House delegation. A man of wit and yet few words, the story is well known of a young lady seated next to the President at a dinner party. She confided in the President that she had taken a bet that she could get at least three words of conversation from him. Without even a sideways glance, the President quietly replied, 'You lose'. He died in January 1933, just two years after the launch of the ship bearing his name. It is not recorded whether he took a voyage in her, but it is likely that he did not.

N3
Note: An official 'Launching booklet' issued to commemorate the launching indicates a date of Saturday, 28 February 1931. This does not agree with all other records, and it is presumed that the launching booklet was printed prior to a change of date. [R21] A 'sponsor' in this context refers to the people who christen the ship, ie the Coolidges.

N4
The Presidents Hoover and Coolidge were fitted to carry passengers in four classes: first class, special class (a euphemism for what was generally known as tourist class), third class, and steerage for Orientals. Several records put the accommodation of the ships at 330 first class passengers, 140 tourist class and 800 "oriental steerage". Such racist designation would certainly not be tolerated today, but in these pre-war years, orientals were seen as only fit to travel in the lowest (and cheapest) class on board. Even a wealthy 'Oriental' was not permitted passage in the upper classes.

N5
Despite these incidents, the President Coolidge was presented with an 'award of merit' by the accident prevention bureau of the Pacific American Steamship Association, as the winner of the safety flag for Class A passenger liners.

N6
It was at this time also, October 1938, that six Japanese aircraft bombed the British gunboat Sandpiper anchored at Changsha, about 200 miles south-west of Hankow.

N7
There is some confusion as to the actual passage dates, and the position of the President Coolidge when Pearl Harbour was bombed by the Japanese on 7 December 1941. Appendix 1 places her at berth, or within a day of leaving her berth, at Honolulu. Another record shows he outward bound from Manila to Honolulu, between Santa Cruz and Ellis Islands when Pearl Harbour was bombed. This doesn't seem right as the President Coolidge would have to travel south, off course, to be between Santa Cruz and the Ellis Group. It would be better not so much to consider the dates indicated, but rather the route and ports of call which seem to be accurate.

N8
There is a suggestion that some of in the crew of in the President Coolidge walked off in Suva in the belief that Captain Henry Nelson was a German-American and that he would deliberately run his ship into mines in order to destroy the ship. The crew were apparently taken into custody, and a 'scratch' crew was recruited to get the ship back to San Francisco. This 'incident' was apparently reported in Life magazine; the 'incident' could have resulted from journalistic license. The Army was particularly concerned about security, and the log of the President Coolidge for the date 30 June 1942 includes: 'Guards at gangway and about vessel. Watchman on regular rounds. Semi-blackout. Carl Swinding, 3rd Pantryman caused a beef in sailors mess room, while intoxicated, suffering an injured lip from A. Domergue, AB, who injured his hand. Both received medical attention from ship's surgeon. Witness S. Wright, AB. Few clouds. Quartermaster and military personnel at gangway. Every precaution taken for in the safety of in the vessel. Watchmen making regular rounds.'

CHAPTER THREE - STATEROOMS
No notes.

CHAPTER FOUR - PEKOA, PALIKULO & PALMS

N1
The actual date is in question - 27 or 28 May. References sources differ. Reference 31 has both dates within the same document, lending some doubt to its overall credibility.

N2

Efforts to bolster other islands of the South Pacific were intensified in 1942. In May the 37th Infantry Division, then being readied for shipment to New Zealand, was ordered to Fiji instead. The unit, which included the 17th Engineer Combat Battalion, reached its destination in June. Later that month steps were taken to enlarge an old French runway at Koumac, near the northern tip of New Caledonia, to enable it to take heavy bombers. The 810th engineers, assisted by Australian workmen, had the field operational by the end of the month. Construction of the alternate ferry route got under way when natives began clearing runway sites on Atutaki and Tongatabu in June and Penrhyn in July.

N3

Many types of aircraft used Pekoa field. Take for example the month of November 1943 when a total of two thousand five hundred fifty two planes of twenty different types landed. About one-half of these were C-47s, indicating the great number of passengers and cargo carried. Also high in the figures were the nine hundred fifteen (915) B-24s.

N4

LSTs - Landing Ship, Tank - were also used to bring in equipment. These 'cargo' ships were on average about 4,000 tons (later 6,000 tonners were built) and were used in all aspects of transport, including tanks. They were not honoured with a 'personal' name, and designated by LST and a number. Like the prolific Liberty ships, they were the workhorse of the sea.

N5

This 'quotation' of services available at the base in Santo appears to have put into print initially by author James Michener in his excellent 1951 'factual novel' Return to Paradise, and has since been unceremoniously quoted by virtually all and sundry, including, unashamedly, the incumbent author. James A. Michener was based for some time in Santo during the war, and the island is a feature in his books, "Tales of the South Pacific" and "Return to Paradise". It is said that it was whilst on Espiritu Santo that Michener was inspired to create his mystical and mythical island of Bali Hai.

N6

The term 'snafu' is well known in military circles and ungraciously refers to 'situation normal, all fouled up'. The second last word is often substituted for a profane term used to describe the act of creation and recreation.

N7

The five airfields were as follows:
Bomber 1: Situated near Palikulo Bay, and used by the US Navy Fighter Squadrons and Navy Field Overhaul. Also used by the Royal New Zealand Air Force for fighter planes.
Bomber 2: Between three and four miles west of Bomber 1, and used by the Thirteenth Air force and SCAT.
Bomber 3: Inland from bend in the Segond Channel (between the Sarakata and Renee rivers). The field is built on high ground and was used by Navy planes, mostly reconnaissance and bombers.
Fighter 1: Situated in the vicinity of Turtle Bay and used by Marine Fighter Squadrons. Most new pilots coming into the area did their advanced training from this field.
Sandburg Field: Three miles west of the Renee river, used for light aircraft.

N8

There were six major piers on Espiritu Santo. Numbers 1a to 4 were to the east of the Sarakata River, with Number 5 about half a mile west of the Sarakata. Their uses were as follows: 1a: Fleet Post Office Pier. 1b: Personnel landing pier. Mainly a landing pier for boats from the various ships in the Channel. Also a small patrol launch depot. 2: Unloading pier for lighters from ships in the channel. 3: Ship Repair Pier. This pier would take a Liberty ship without difficulty, and was generally used for minor repairs. 4: Main loading and unloading pier. This is near the main storehouses, about three quarters of a mile east of the Sarakata River. There was ample space for two Liberty ships to berth alongside the pier. 5: Loading and unloading pier, with the capacity for one Liberty ship. All piers had ample depth, with 35ft at piers 4 and 5. The sixth pier, although not numbered as such, was probably the one at the Q.M. Warehousing Area #1, just north of Pier 5 between the Renee and Sarakata Rivers.

N9

Destroyer *Gamble* was launched 11 May 1918 by the Newport News Shipbuilding and Dry Dock Company and commissioned at Norfolk on 29 November 1918. She was decommissioned at San Diego 17 June 1922, recommissioned 24 May 1930, and reclassified as a light minelayer (DM-15) on 13 June 1930. In April 1941 she proceeded to Pearl Harbour for war readiness patrol in Hawaiian waters as a unit of Mine Division 2. On 7 December 1941 Gamble had returned from offshore patrol when her peaceful Sunday morning routine was broken by the first of the Japanese carrier-based planes. Gamble's gunners joined the fire of other warships and saw one enemy plane fall into the sea on her port beam. In mid-February 1942 she headed south in the escort for a convoy to Pago Pago, Samoa. She returned to Pearl Harbour for heavier armament, and helped safeguard convoys to Midway during the time of the historic battle. On 27 August 1942 Gamble joined a task unit headed to Guadalcanal. On the morning of 29 August 1942, when her lookouts spotted a large enemy submarine, she immediately went into action. After several depth charge attacks, Gamble ran through large oil slicks. Later her victim was identified as Japanese submarine I-123. On 30 June 1943, during the invasion of New Georgia, Gamble laid a string of mines off the beachhead. In July 1943 she returned to the US for overhaul. She returned to the Pacific theatre on 20 September 1943, and operated in Empress Augusta Bay, Bougainville Strait, and New Hebrides, before returning to San Francisco 12 October 1944. Gamble departed San

Diego 7 January 1945, to assist at Iwo Jima, lending fire support and to explode floating mines. On 18 February 1945 Gamble was hit just above the waterline by two 250-pound bombs. Five men were killed, one missing in action, and eight wounded. As marines stormed the shores of Iwo Jima the next day, Gamble was taken in tow by Dorsey who turned her over to LSM-126 for passage to Saipan. She was decommissioned on 1 June 1945 and on 16 July was towed outside Apra Harbour, Guam, and sunk. Gamble received seven battle stars for service in World War 2. Commanding officer at the time of laying the mines was Cdr. S.N. Tachney, who received the Navy Crossfor the sinking of a Japanese submarine off Guadalcanal in August 1942. Gamble was capable of carrying eighty-four Mark IV mines, but on operation to New Hebrides carried only fifty-seven. USS Tracy and USS Breese probably did likewise. It is suggested that a total of 171 mines were laid in the two minefields protecting the west and east entrances to Segond Channel. Richard 'Pete' Peterson later became the last Commanding Officer of USS Gamble.

N10

With say twenty mines dropped over a six hundred yard distance, the mines would be spaced 30 yards apart if dropped every 5 seconds whilst travelling at 12 knots. This is approximately the situation of the mines laid at Espiritu Santo. A typical minelaying operation (as described in an operation by USS Gamble across Blankett Strait, was - making fifteen knots, each (of three) ships dropped a mine every twelve seconds, planting 250 mines in 17 minutes.

N11

Destroyer USS Breese (DD-122) was launched 11 May 1918 by Newport News Shipbuilding and Dry Dock Company, the same company which built the S.S. President Coolidge, and was commissioned on 23 October 1918. She was attached to the Atlantic Fleet and then the Pacific Fleet and was decommissioned on 17 June 1922. Breese was redesignated a light mine-layer (DM-18) on 5 January 1931, and recommissioned 1 June 1931 following overhaul and conversion at Mare Island Navy Yard. She returned to San Diego for trials before being stationed at Pearl Harbour. She was out of commission in reserve from 12 November 1937 to 25 September 1939 when she joined Mine Division 5, battle Force. On 7 December, Breese was anchored at pearl Harbour and by 0757 she opened fire with her machine guns at close range on the attacking Japanese planes. Although she received no material damage from the Japanese attack, she aided in the sinking of one midget submarine and damaged numerous enemy planes. Breese operated in the Central pacific from 7 December 1941 to 10 October 1944, before travelling north to the Marianas-Philippines zone, and later at the Leyte landings, Iwo Jima and Okinawa. She was decommissioned 15 January 1946 and sold 16 May 1946. During her World War 2 service she received ten battle stars.

CHAPTER FIVE - NO TUCKER FOR TERRELL

N1

Official reports indicate that at 0810 Tucker's main battery opened up on high flying planes, firing for half an hour. Fifteen minutes after the order to cease fire, another wave of aircraft came over, followed at 0905 by several dive bombers coming in low from all sides. During this time Tucker registered hits on three planes, two of which crashed on a hill in flames. The other disappeared over a low ridge, smoking and flaming badly. The last group approached from the north at 0917 and two minutes later the attack was over.

Tucker's first escort duty in April 1942 was escorting Kaskaskia and Wright to Suva, Fiji Islands. She then escorted Wright to New Caledonia, Sydney, Melbourne and Fremantle, Australia and returned via the same route to Suva, arriving on 4 June 1942. Getting underway again the same day, Tucker rendezvoused with a convoy on 7 June, escorting two transports to Suva and from there to Auckland, New Zealand. The group then returned to Suva, and Tucker sailed back to Auckland arriving on 6 July. After acting as ocean escort for a Melbourne-bound convoy, she returned to Auckland to escort Monowai to the Fiji Islands. The two ships rendezvoused with an amphibious force north of Koro island, Fiji Islands, and Monowai transferred troops and materials to the ships of the force. The ships arrived in Suva on 29 July and on 1 August Tucker was ordered out on her last mission, escorting SS Nira Luckenbach to Espiritu Santo. And a special note for non-Australian readers. 'Tucker' means 'food' in Australian outback language.

N2

Lieutenant Commander Arnold Lott, USN, states in his book Most Dangerous Sea. "A 'Q message' began wending its way out to the fleet. The Q-message system was fine when it worked, but radio channels were so crowded that Q messages sometimes arrived a month late.

N3

Abnetare Mission on Aore Island is documented in some reports as Avunatari.

N4

Official communication from the Commander South Pacific Area and South Pacific Force, Robert L. Ghormley, to the Secretary of the Navy, indicated: 'At 2145 GCT on August 3rd, Tucker struck a mine, one of the field laid by MINDIV TWO on the previous day. [Actually, on the same day]. No blame can be attached to the commanding officer USS Tucker. The Tucker had not been informed of prospective mining operations at Espiritu Santo. Approach data had not been promulgated. The conduct of officers and men in the emergency was apparently in keeping with the highest traditions of the service.'

N5

The initial report suggested that the 'gap' between the bow and stern sections was only twenty feet. It may well have been at the time, but more likely it was a greater distance, as the gap is now as indicated.

Although underwater visibility on the wreck site is generally excellent, it is a rare day that one section can be seen from the other. The initial report R93 suggests that the stern was sitting on an even keel - it now has a slight list to starboard.

N6

Local politics however have, on occasions, prevented divers from visiting the wreck site. As she lies close to Abnetare village on Malo Island, the villagers have at times shown displeasure with divers on 'their' wreck. Such squabbles can usually be overcome with gentle diplomacy, and for he past few years there has been no problem in gaining legitimate access to the site.

CHAPTER SIX - FOR WANT OF A STAPLE

N1

Civilian officers in command of the *SS President Coolidge*.

Commanding Officer Henry Nelson
Chief Officer Milton McManus
First Officer Kilton Davis
Second Officer Charles D. Hammel
Third Officer Robert A. Lyon
Junior Officer Frank Gannon

N2

Chief Officer on the *President Coolidge*, Milton McManus was aware of the contents of the various holds in the ship, and at the Military Commission in Noumea on 8 December 1942, gave evidence in that regard: 'Well, in number one trunk we had airplane propeller impedimenta, airplane propellers, then we had barracks bags also. In the C deck we had vegetables, potatoes, onions, etc. Then in B deck we had jeeps, 6 boxed jeeps and machinery, more ammunition. In F deck we had cases of ammunition, we had ammunition in all those holds. Then in the lower holds we had more heavy ammunition and mats. The trunk in number two hatch of B deck we had two trucks, heavy lifts, and barracks bags. Two C deck was troop quarters. Two D deck we had more trucks, that is 6-wheel trucks, we had a howitzer in there. We had a tractor, machinery and we had alcohol. Two C deck we had 15 millimetre guns and 14 trailers with machine guns on them. Had more trucks. Down in F deck we had trucks and ammunition. In the lower hold we had airplane mats, mats for landing fields, on top of that we had ammunition and machinery. Number three D deck you had a lot of stores, supplies, and general impedimenta. Three E deck you had more rations and stuff, same in the three F deck. The refrigerator hatches, three starboard aft box had ammunition, small gun ammunition that was reloaded in this port. The rest of the ice boxes was ship's stores except the ship's ammunition. Number 4 D deck we had some ambulances, all the rest of the stores came out here. Number four E deck more trucks and equipment, that's all. Number 5 trunk of the hatches we had two cases of heavy lifts, I don't know what was in them, and barracks bags. Number 5 D deck was quarters, troop quarters. Five E deck we had stevedore equipment, slings, you had canned goods, just general stores.

That's all, that finishes it up.' It was the responsibility of the Army Transport Service to load and position all the cargo.

N3

Canton Island is one of the Phoenix Islands group, to the east of the Gilbert and Ellis Islands - about two-thirds of the journey from San Francisco to Noumea. There appears to have been a small advance base stationed here.

N4

There were two three-inch guns on A-Deck toward the stern, and two on the bow. The stern gun on B-Deck was a five-inch gun.

N5

Positions as indicated on the Routing Instructions, issued by the Port Director's Office, Noumea, New Caledonia:
Queen Lat. 23° 15' S Long. 167° 00' E
Roger Lat. 23° 15' S Long. 168° 00' E
Sail Lat. 22° 00' S Long. 168° 30' E
Tare Lat. 19° 00' S Long. 170° 00' E
Unit Lat. 16° 20' S Long. 169° 00' E
Victor Lat. 16° 00' S Long. 168° 00' E
Hypo Lat. 15° 34' S Long. 167° 22' E

N6

Destroyer Sterett (DD-407) was the second by that name, and was laid down on 2 December 1936 at the Charlestown navy yard; launched 27 October 1938, and commissioned 15 August 1939. On 1 July 1942, Sterett steamed out of San Diego as part of TF18 to the Fiji Islands. She was assimilated into Rear Admiral Richmond K. Turner's Pacific Amphibious Expeditionary Force. She spent the rest of 1942 and all of 1943 supporting the Allied forces as they struggled up the island staircase formed by the Solomon Islands and the Bismarck Archipelago. She later saw action in the Solomons. She was decommissioned on 2 November 1945, and sold 10 August 1947 to the Northern Metal Company of Philadelphia for scrapping. Sterett earned twelve battle stars for World War 2 service.

N7

Several reports indicate that the first explosion occured *during* the transmission of the message. Be that as it may, the explosion certainly occurred before any action could be taken.

N8

The final entry in the Deck Log of the *President Coolidge* , voyage #65 commencing October 21, 1942, is as follows. The entry is made by First Officer Kilton Davis.
26 October 1942
0000-0400
Blackout. Continue Zig Zag course 0306 c/c 289° gyro. Watchmen on regular rounds and reports. Sharp lookouts maintained. Soldiers, Gun crew, Signalman. Mod E x N breeze, sea & swell.
0400-0800
Blackout. Gun crews, lookouts, guards on duty. Watchman on regular rounds. 0450 ceased ZZ, resumed course 290o increased to 122 RPMs

approaching Selwyn Stit. 0525 e/c 291°G. 0619 South Point Pentecost Island 021° 3 mile distant up'd 20.0K 0653 e/c 305°G. 284psc 283 wHc. Slik[?] e'ly sea and low confused swell. Part cloudy.

N9

Author Wolfert also states that the first mine hit amidships and the second forward of amidships. This is incorrect - should be the other way round. He also indicates that the ship turned turtle, a reasonable observation from those on shore (or in the air), but in fact she slide down on her port side.

N10

Robert Reid was born in the Philippines of American parents. He was thirty years of age. His brother was also on board the *President Coolidge* as a bell hop.

N11

As would be expected under the circumstances, there are various written reports on exactly what did happen to Captain Elwood Euart, but the first hand account by Warrant Officer Robert Moshimer is no doubt the most authoritative of contemporary reports. In fact it is so recent (September 1997) that another week and the material would not have been able to be included in the book. No matter what the source of the report, there is no doubt that the actions of Captain Euart, and indeed all the officers mentioned, were heroic.

Another report mentions a P.C. Olsen who is reported to have been a 'junior officer' on board, presumably a civilian merchant marine officer. It is well to include mention of Olson, as Robert Moshimer does recall a third man involved in the rescue drama - but that could have been Lt. Ward MacDonald.

Commander Craig Hosmer, in charge of the naval gun crews, recalls in his log, '(10.51 am) Mr. Olson appears at the side of the ship from somewhere. Men are trying to pull someone up out of the passenger doors about two-thirds way aft. Olson runs along side of ship, reaches them and starts to help. Ship is slowly beginning to slide into deep water.' The report mentions that Olson tried to get a line down to Euart below decks "...but escaping air kept blowing the line away. When finally the line reached Euart, he was simply too weak from exhaustion to tie it around his waist and hang on to the line to be pulled to safety. Had the ship remained stable for another five minutes, he may have made it." This same report mentions Captain Covill and 'a Warrant Officer', obviously Moshimer.

As the ship began to slide back and down, Hosmer '...saw Olson and two companions dive into the water. Olson also went down with the ship but was blasted to the surface by a tremendous discharge of air and was picked up by a lifeboat. Trapped within the vessel and unable to be hauled to safety, Captain Elwood Euart went down with the ship. Captain Covill too went down with the ship. "I knew I was going to be sucked down by the ship and all I could think of was to get it over fast as possible". Covill was fortunate. An air bubble blasted him back to the surface where he was picked up by a boat'.

Indeed, was Olson attempting to rescue Euart, or was it someone else 'two-thirds way aft'. Euart's door is about 2/3 *from* the stern, ie 'one third way aft'. There is another door two thirds way aft - the entry for Tourist Class passengers, which is clearly seen in several photographs.

No matter which rescue Olson was involved in, it is apparent that his deeds are worthy of mention.

Needless to say, rumours were rife when the loss of Euart became known to the survivors on shore. The men had a hero to admire in their temporary discomfort on a crowded shore. One story that did the rounds however suggests that Captain Euart had successfully cleared the listing ship, but swam back to rescue the wedding photograph of his wife whom he had married just before sailing to the South Pacific. Not so. Euart was not married. He was a well respected and responsible officer and his prime concern was his men. He was a mess officer on board and he was trying to enter at the most accessible point to check the galley, aft of the dining rooms. There was always the thought amongst the men that the ship had beached and they would be able to return to unload the following day, and to retrieve personal effects. This was soon dispelled when the list of the ship gradually increased. There is no doubt that Euart's intentions were to save his men, and in doing so, he paid the ultimate price.

Captain Warren Covill was a great friend of Captain Euart, and was a member of the same Artillery Unit of the Rhode Island National Guard that was inducted into service on 24 February 1941. They served and trained together and were good friends training together for shipment overseas with the 43rd Infantry Division, Army National Guard from Rhode Island.

Elwood Euart was second eldest of a family of seven, four girls Rita, Monica, Eleanor and Ruth, and three boys Elwood, John and Len. His home town was Pawtucket, Rhode Island, USA.

Finally - in a tribute to Captain Euart, Dr. Harold W. Browning, Vice President, Rhode Island State College, said, 'It is in the hour of tragedy that the character of man receives its severest test. It is what a man does then that expresses his true worth and tells what he really is. In moments of sudden crisis the primal instincts of all men is self-preservation. Captain Euart loved life, but, in that final hour of strife on the ill-fated *President Coolidge*, neither the repeated warnings nor insistent urging of his friends, nor his love of life, did he permit to over-shadow his love for his fellow man. Many a man lives today because a devoted islander, with gallant heart, directed and physically assisted his men to safety.'

N12

Various documents and popular magazine articles differ in the number of lives lost as a result of the *President Coolidge* hitting the mines. The fact of the matter is that two men died - the fireman Robert Reid, and the Army captain Elwood Euart. This is made quite clear at both the Court of Inquiry in November 1942, and the Military Commission in Noumea in December. And yet, even the highly creditable *National Geographic* states, 'Amazingly only five lives were lost - fireman Reid and four soldiers - 5,435 were saved'. (National Geographic Society, Vol 173, No. 4, April 1988). 'Today' Magazine, (Spring 1984), states, 'Two were APL crew members, killed by explosions. The third was an Army captain.'. The 'official' *Navy History of Espiritu Santo*' by Lieutenant D.W. Kralovec states, 'The casualties were one officer and three men definitely known lost. One fireman, Robert Reed was lost.'

N13
The only recorded references to Espiritu Santo in official navy Communiques between December 1941 and March 1943 was as follows:
Oct. 15th 1942: During the night of Oct. 14 & 15 our positions on Espiritu Santo Is. in the New Hebrides group were shelled by an enemy ship believed to have been a submarine.
Oct. 22 & 23; Exactly the same occurred.
Jan 22 1943: A Japanese plane dropped several bombs on Espiritu Santo Is. in the New Hebrides group. There were no casualties to personnel. Our installations were not damaged.
Feb, 24 1943: During the morning Japanese planes carried out a light raid on U.S. positions on E. S. in the N.H. R58

N14
Dean Jackson was speaking at a meeting of a Kiwanis Club in California. The Kiwanis are a service club along the lines of Rotary, Lions and Apex. Jackson went on to say that when the ship reached the entrance to the harbour two US destroyers were outside the harbour. "Her captain asked if the harbor was all clear. He was told there was nothing to worry about - his ship ploughed into the harbour and struck two American mines". This was not strictly true, but the public got the message.

N15
The newspapers reported that Captain Nelson had been acquitted by a Navy 'court-martial'. It was actually a Military Commission as Captain Nelson was a civilian.

CHAPTER SEVEN - PICTORIAL   No notes.

CHAPTER EIGHT - CHAOS RULED SUPREME
N1
Quinine is a substance derived from the bark of the cinchona tree, and was vital in the treatment and suppression of malaria. Atabrine was a manufactured chemical also used as a malaria prophylactic.

N2
The Commanding Officer, General William Rose, ordered the immediate issuing of clothing to survivors of the marine tragedy by way of a letter to the Disbursing and Supply Officer of the 7th. United States Naval Construction Battalion. 'You are hereby appointed and directed to make such gratuitous issues of clothing as may be necessary to care for the basic needs of the survivors of a marine disaster occurring 26 October 1942. These issues are to be made to any and all survivors under your care, regardless of the

branch of service in which enlisted, various detachments involved. The total value of the gratuitous issue will be reported to this command for final approval.'

N3
In these early days of the war, the United States forces experienced severe setbacks, both militarily on sea and land and in their supply lines to the fighting forces. During the first thirteen months of the war, up to New Year 1943, 333 merchant ships were lost. Among them were several large transports - such as the *Normandie*, *Manhattan* and the *President Tyler* - either lost or damaged to such an extent that they were useless for months. The 15,000-ton *President Harrison* was deliberately run aground in the China Sea on December 8, 1941, to prevent her capture by the Japanese. 'Now, here was the *President Coolidge* sunk by our own mines because of what I believe to be one of the great blunders of the war,' wrote Edward Oliver in Sea Classics. 'A month after the Coolidge was lost sister ship *President Cleveland* was lost off the coast of Morocco. Two vitally needed transports had been lost at a time when they were most needed. With them went the end of a short-lived gallant era when American flag liners almost recaptured dominance of the world's vast sea routes.'

CHAPTER NINE - NELSON'S BLOOD
N1
Captain Nelson speaks of two destroyers. In actual fact, one ship was a patrol craft, *PC479* under command of Lieutenant John Davis, whilst the other was destroyer *USS Sterett* (DD407).

N2
USS Whitney was a Fleet Auxiliary ship, 8325 tons. Auxiliary ships were equipped to serve as depot ships, repair ships and hospital ships, generally serving a fleet of destroyers. They were also fitted out as flagships, ie had the facilities to accommodate the admiral of the fleet or the commander of a particular operation.

N3
It is interesting to note the tone of other reports that purport to officially document the loss of the *President Coolidge*. In Lieutenant D.W. Kralovec's 'A Naval History of Espiritu Santo', it is clear to see where the author places the blame for the loss of the ship, even though he makes no actual accusation. 'At about 0020 on 26 October 1942, the *SS President Coolidge* was sighted off the East entrance to Segond Channel headings approximately north at high speed. In spite of efforts of the patrol vessel, which had a pilot on board, to communicate with her she continued on her way north seaward of Tutuba Island, rounded that Island and entered the mined channel between Tutuba and Santo Islands. The shore signal station finally succeeded in warning her that she was in danger and the master attempted to stop the ship. Before headway could be killed the Coolidge hit two mines at about 0930.' Note the use of the terms 'in spite of', and 'finally succeeded' giving clear indication of the

author's emotions; besides, the patrol vessel did not succeed in warning the ship of impending danger.

CHAPTER TEN - FUTILITY OF WAR

N1

Ray Jenkins lived with a local lady and died many years ago in Luganville where he is now buried. He is one of the few Americans to have returned to the New Hebrides after the war. Reece Discombe helped Jenkins set up the local cinema for Tom Harris, and Jenkins ran the cinema for Harris.

N2

Ambae was also, in the past, known by a number of names - Oba, Aoba, Omba, and Opa.

N3

The original hotel was owned by Fung Kwan Chee, who sold out to the Rossi family. Antoine Rossi had the now well-known hotel in Port Vila. Brother Francois Rossi was a gendarme (policeman). After the fire, the Rossi sold what was left to Dinh Van Tho and his wife Mary Jane. The Hotel Santo, built after the fire, has since been added to. Dinh Van Tho died in 1993. Mary Jane retains ownership.

N4

Also found at the army base were 'thousands and thousands' of boxes of condoms, a gross in each box. Many friends of Andre Naturel and Reece Discombe received a rather unusual, but eminently useful gift, for Christmas. Although it would appear that troops in these remote Pacific islands would have little use for such personal items, they did come in very handle in jungle warfare. It is not know if any condoms were sent to Guadalcanal, but it is well documented that troops landing at Cape Gloucester in New Britain kept their valuables, and matches, dry in a condom tied in a knot, and stretched them over their gun barrels to keep the rain and mud out.

N5

Coral pits dot the near-shore landscape although most have been disguised with time, tropical vegetation unhesitatingly springing to life in any apparently barren place. There is a huge coral pit to the right when travelling on what used to be US Highway 2 heading inland past the post office. Another pit lies to the left of the road leading to Bomber 3 airstrip, and the clearing where divers kit up to visit the President Coolidge is another.

N6

It is rather simplistic to suggest that the Pacific War was not of a concern to the island natives of countries such as New Guinea, Solomons and New Hebrides. True, these countries were not at war with Japan, but had the Japanese not been stopped in their move across the Pacific, the people of these very countries would have now been saluting the flag of the rising sun.

N7

Tobin bronze is a mixture of brass and copper - and time. Brass is an alloy of copper and zinc, so tobin bronze looks like brass, but has more copper in it. (Actual bronze is an allow of copper and tin). Non-

ferrous metals were at a premium after the war. All the US shell cases were made of brass. Some Japanese shell cases were made of steel and brass coated.

N8

The *El Retiro* probably did not settle on a bull-dozer blade as the dozers in shallow water had been removed by Reece Discombe - but the ship did certainly puncture her bottom plates on some equipment which then put her on the bottom. The *Dedelle* was scraped by Dinh Van Tho and Allan Power on Sunday, 13 May 1990. I took my recently wedded wife and brother-in-law for a snorkel at Million Dollar Point, and the *El Retiro* and *Dedelle*, in 1995 whilst on my honeymoon. (What was my brother-in-law doing on my honeymoon? Don't ask!). They are not divers, so they had no opportunity to see the *President Coolidge*. Hardly a substitute, the *El Retiro* is at least a wreck and as we came upon it, my wife expressed the same apprehension as do most divers when a wreck emerges from the gloom. She was both fascinating and apprehensive, and thoroughly enjoyed the experience, describing it simply as 'weird'. Million Dollar Point could well be developed further for tourism as it is a fascinating place to snorkel.

N9

The biblical saying is, I believe, 'Lest thou not lead to temptation' - thus it is wise not to leave equipment, clothing and especially money and valuables lying around unguarded on the beach whilst diving Million Dollar Point. The usual arrangement is to have a taxi drop off a party of divers and return an hour or so later. Try and have someone remain on the beach at all times.

CHAPTER ELEVEN - BLASTING FOR BRASS

N1

Reece Discombe was perhaps the first person in the southern hemisphere, maybe even outside Europe, who had used the new demand regulator developed by Emile Gagnan and Jacques Cousteau - the 'aqualung', or SCUBA (self contained underwater breathing apparatus). Gagnan and Cousteau sent a traveller to the Pacific French territory of New Caledonia in 1947. Reece recalls, 'He had bottles, and we had the boats. I bought an outfit from him and used it extensively in New Caledonia before taking it over to New Hebrides. Meanwhile the 'aqualung' had not hit Australia as yet, and probably not the US.' Commander Pat Williams, in charge of the diving at the Australian Naval base at Rushcutters Bay, was a friend of Reece Discombe. On a visit to Sydney, Reece went to Rushcutters Bay with the new 'aqualung'. Reece recalls, 'The Navy boys, the engineers, tore this valve apart, got out their micrometers and what have you and measured it all up. They were using rebreathers at the time - and they had killed a lot of people. They were called 'Salvus' I think, made for submarine escape apparatus. Anyone could buy them at a surplus place in Parramatta Road [Sydney]. The Aussies were buying them up and going spearfishing - but they exceeded the depth of thirty feet - as you know oxygen and depth don't agree and a lot never came back. No knowledge of underwater breathing in those days, unless you were a Navy bloke. The foul air was scrubbed through a canister of Berry Lime. However there was also a small oxygen bottle attached to the front of the apparatus to replenish the [air] system. If by chance seawater mixed with the Berry Lime it formed a caustic soda. No need to tell you the results. Hans Hass used a similar outfit but he used mixed gases and not pure oxygen. There was a valve on the mouthpiece to close so that when taken out, no seawater could enter. Meanwhile the Aqualung hadn't hit America - late 1947 early 1948 - in Australia it was 1948 before it arrived.' Pat Williams left the navy and worked for Tom Massey (of Massey Battery fame), diving and recovering materials from wrecks in Darwin harbour. Reece believes the Navy engineers were interested in the demand valve for their own personal use, and the Australian Navy did not construct a demand regulator based on the measurements they took.

N2

For those unfamiliar with underwater breathing equipment, perhaps a brief explanation is in order. 'Hard hat' diving, also refereed to as Standard Dress, is the old 'traditional' way of working under water, with the diver wearing a solid brass or bronze helmet with ports or windows in which to observe the underwater world. He (as they invariably were) would be dressed in a waterproof canvas-base suit completely covering the body, to which the helmet was screwed or bolted. Air was supplied from the surface, pumped down manually from aboard a diving platform or boat above the diver. The diver was therefore always 'attached' to the surface, and a distinct advantage of this was the provision of a telephone line so that communication between diver and surface tender was possible. As air filled the helmet and the body suit, it was necessary for the diver to wear heavy boots so that he would remain upright. The diver was always in great danger of falling and thus increasing the water pressure on his body at a rate greater than that being supplied and at which he could control, and thus a fall could result in the diver being crushed. The severance of the air-line was an obvious cause of concern, and could occur if the diver penetrated a shipwreck and the line became tangled or severed on sharp metal. This severely disadvantaged the hard-hat diver as he was not able to manoeuvre easily and had to literally plod around on the bottom or on a wreck in an upright position. Although penetration of a wreck was possible, the lay of the airline was always of prime concern. With the invention of the 'aqualung' by Emile Gagnan of Air Liquide Societe, (manufacturers of oxygen, gases and gas-regulating and flow apparatus) and Jacques Cousteau, and its further development and availability after the war, the diver was able to take his, (and her), air supply with him. The relatively low cost of the 'aqualung', which centres on a 'demand valve' that allows the diver to draw in the required amount of air from a tank (bottle) irrespective of surrounding water pressure, opened up the underwater world to amateur and professional

divers alike. The 'aqualung' or SCUBA (self contained underwater breathing apparatus) consists of an air tank (one or more) strapped to the divers back. The air is under pressure in the tank and is provided 'on demand' by the 'regulator' attached by a mouthpiece to the diver. The diver needs no helmet or suit, but wears a mask to enable him or her to see underwater. What the diver gains in manoeuvrability is lost in communication, as there is no connection with the surface. Scuba diving is the most common form of recreational underwater diving, and gives the diver about an hour underwater within sixty feet with minimum exertion. Increased depth means less time underwater (with the same amount of air in the tank), but additional air tanks can be strapped on. This however can then lead to the diver being susceptible to decompression sickness, or 'the bends' if ascent is not controlled. A 'decompression stop' of several minutes may be required at various 'stages' to allow the body gases to equalize and not 'bubble' into the body. For longer times, a 'hookah' unit is often used, and is favoured by abalone divers, for example, who may 'stay down' for several hours at a time. In principle, this is similar to the equipment used for the scuba diver except that the air supply remains on the surface. The hookah diver uses a demand regulator to obtain air just as the scuba diver does, but a hose connects the hookah diver to the air supply on the surface boat. The hookah diver does not have the same manoeuvrability as the scuba diver because of the airhose, but he can penetrate a shipwreck so long as the airhose is well cared for. A development of the hookah and the hard-hat concept has been established over the past twenty years with the use of what is commonly called a Kirby-Morgan rig (after the inventors and manufacturers) which consists of a small, light 'hard-hat' but where the air is received again on demand from the surface. The helmet allows the diver to communicate by telephone with the surface. This is the system favoured by professional divers, particularly those working on oil-rigs. It is important to stress that the air supplies is just that - air, not oxygen. Occasionally one will read in the popular press of divers wearing 'oxygen tanks' on their backs. This is not so. Recent developments in SCUBA include the use of 'mixed-gas' equipment where a combination of helium, nitrogen and oxygen is used, generally for deeper divers, but that is a subject in itself, and the cost of the 'mixed-gas' limits its use - at the moment. Another form of SCUBA, considering the true use of the acronym, is the 're-breather', which was used by frogmen during the war. This equipment had the advantage of not releasing exhaust bubbles which would have given away the location of a diver, certainly not desirable in a military situation. The rebreather recycles the air and 'scrubs' or absorbs CO_2 from the exhausted air. Apart from early US Navy divers who used the 'standard dress' hard-hat system, all amateur and professional (salvage) divers on the President Coolidge have used standard single air tank SCUBA equipment.

N3

The *Pacific Seal* was later owned by the late Dinh Van Tho who owned the Hotel Santo. It has been renamed *Kili*. Allan Power mentioned that only a few French expatriates had dived the President Coolidge up to the time he arrived in Luganville in 1969. And of course Reece Discombe, who was living in Port Vila.

N4

Allan Power still lives in Luganville on Espiritu Santo within five minutes drive of the *President Coolidge.* Keith Beverley remained in New Hebrides also, based in Port Vila, and ran scuba diving tours. Reg Thomas remained on the team till he went to the Solomon Islands. He obviously took a liking to the place and still lives in Honiara. Others on the Prop. Project with Barry May include his partner Des Woodley, Peter Cole, John Vui (a Ni-Vanuatu), Ron Hutchinson, Ray Abbott, and Bob (Skippy) Delander.

N5

U.S. Navy Decompression times for 240ft for 15 minutes , is 3 minutes at 30-ft, 6 minutes at 20 ft, and 18 minutes at 10 ft.

N6

Propeller lugs are located on the stern of a ship above the location of the props, and assist in removing and fitting the propellers when the ship is in dry dock - and on an even keel. The *President Coolidge* however was lying on her port side, so the lugs were not directly above the props. Hence, when the prop came off the shaft, it would have swung down and inward (to the left facing the stern) causing additional strain on the slings.

N7

After salvaging the props off *the Coolidge,* Peter Cole did several small jobs which included dives on Million Dollar Point, then travelled to Vanikoro in the eastern Solomons to salvage cartridges. This was a two-day trip from Santo, and the salvage group usually spent three to four weeks working there. In July 1971, returning from the fifth trip, the *Onewa,* a wooden boat with no copper sheathing underneath, struck heavy weather and, fully loaded with a cargo of scrap metal, sprang a leak and began taking water. They had sailed without a replacement auxiliary bilge pump, and after fifteen hours of manual pumping, she eventually sank about 25 kilometres off Vanikoro. The *Onewa* had been bought in Noumea by Australian Bill Martin, who wanted to get into the salvage business and joined up with Barry May. Cole and his fellow salvagers took to an aluminium workboat, and with a life raft in tow, and motored to Vanikoro. They were picked up from Vanikoro four days later by the *Konanda,* a local trading ship, and were taken back to Santo, 'none the worse for our experience - but considerably poorer'. Chris Turner, the British District Agent in the Solomons is reported as having quipped, 'One could say the arse has fallen out of the scrap business'.

N8 - Removed. See N9.

N9

Peter Cole bought the *Pacific Seal* in 1972 when Barry

May returned to Australia, and continued to use the vessel for salvage work. On July 14, 1972, he had an accident on the boat which put him out of action for a couple of months. He returned to Santo for several months, but the price of scrap had fallen, operating costs had doubled, and the lack of sophisticated modern equipment led him to fold up the operation and take the boat to Port Vila to lay it up.

From the New Hebrides, Barry May and his team moved on to Bougainville where they worked on the Japanese destroyer *Hatsuyuki* in 80 ft. off Buon. Then on to the Solomon Islands where the Japanese transport *Toa Maru* near Gizo was left minus her prop and a hole in the engine room hull plates. She was a wartime-built ship and therefore had much less in the way of alloy metal fittings. In 1972 Barry returned to Sydney after a slump in world metal prices made it unprofitable to continue salvage. He devoted more time to the business he established in 1958 with Ron Harding. Barry was the silent partner in Ron Harding Sports Store, a retailing, manufacturing (wet suits) and importing business. He commenced building the 50 ft. *Auriga Bay* in Sydney in 1976 and has since completely remodernised the boat, as Auriga Bay 2, running dive charters to the far north Great Barrier Reef. His major project at the time off writing was the construction of a semi- submarine for the tourist industry.

N10

The British District Agent at the time was Mr Richard Baker. In recent correspondence he writes, 'I do remember one thing though which reinforces the thought that the U.S. Government must have been involved and that was the fact that somewhere in the documentation was a clause reserving to the U.S. Govt. the rights to all drugs and medical supplies that were on board. I well remember we all wondered at the time what that was all about and concluded that perhaps there were large consignments of morphine and similar powerful (and valuable) drugs destined for the battle zone in Guadalcanal. Presumably the Americans were worried about such material falling into the wrong hands. Whether or not any such supplies were actually on board the vessel I never learnt but presumably Ian would have had a good look, if only out of curiosity.'

N11

Salvage Pacific Limited's submersible decompression chamber (SDC) was designed by Ian Lockley, with steel work by Bish Limited, of Suva, Fiji. It was designed for a maximum capacity for four people and could operate from ten to sixty feet. Divers are familiar with land-based decompression chambers where the air is pressurised by mechanical means. The submersible chamber uses the pressure of the surrounding water to provide the appropriate air pressure within the chamber, and by lowering or lifting the device, the air within the bell-shaped chamber alters pressure accordingly. For example at 33ft (10m) the air pressure is twice that of atmospheric pressure. Depth control was maintained from within the chamber by manually raising and lowering by a diver operating a wire puller tirfor on a counter balance system. (The tirfor system is similar to that manually used by 4-wheel drive enthusiasts, a ratchet and lever system that applies a grip to a line). The air supply was maintained from the surface, supplying purified air and/or oxygen. A self-contained emergency supply system was incorporated, comprising three 220 cubic-ft. cylinders of purified air and three 220 cubic-ft. cylinders of medical oxygen. These could be used either on demand (using a regulator) or free flow. The chamber was also fitted with an alarm system, and submersible/surface telephone communications. Piped music provided comfort, or otherwise, according to the whim of the surface operator.

N12

The U.S. Navy Diver's Handbook gives the following decompression times for a dive of 180 ft for sixty minutes (it has no listing for seventy minutes): 5 minutes at 50-ft, 16 minutes at 40-ft, 19 minutes at 30-ft, 44 minutes at 20-ft, 81 minutes at 10-ft. Total time in chamber 171 minutes - thats a lot of *Playboys* to read.

N13

The *Tui Tawate* was bought by the Fijian company Narain Construction, who had bought the tug three years previously in New Zealand and brought it to Walu Bay, where it apparently was never used and never left its berth. The *Tui Tawate* was later bought by Reece Discombe for $850. The New Zealand press reported that it was going to be recovered and taken to Auckland to be turned into a restaurant. The ship was in a bad state of disrepair as could be imagined, and would not have made the long sea voyage. The *Tui Tawate* has some historic significance as it was used in the rescue of survivors from the *Wahine* disaster. After lying derelict at Luganville for many years, the old tug was towed out into the Segond Channel and sunk. Reece kept the compass, steering wheel and engine binnacle.

N14

The full New Hebrides News report questioning the profit made from the oil sale to the *Arcadia* is worth reading. It was published in April 1977.

"A British Residency spokesman commented last week an a letter about the wrecked *President Coolidge* received by the Resident Commissioner from the Santo political parties, MANH and NA-GRIAMEL. The letter, dated April 21, asks two questions: first, who got the profit from the sale of the fuel oil taken from the wreck? The letter said it seemed the money had not gone to the Condominium treasury nor to any Santo organisation. The second question dealing with scrap metal being extracted from the wreck, said the population of Santo, and the two parties, thought the total value of the scrap should go to the Municipality of Luganville. Finally, the letter, signed by Aime Malara for MANH, and Jimmy Stephens, asked that pending a ruling on their complaint any metal should be stopped from leaving Santo.

"Far from there being a profit from the sale of the oil, it had cost a great deal to extract the oil, and recalled that there had been demands from the Santo population for a long time to remove the oil to prevent pollution. The gross cost of the operation was in the region of $92,000. The sum received from the sale of the oil was around $17,000, so the removal of the oil cost $75,000. The original survey indicated that there might be up to 4,000 tons of oil in the wreck, but the salvage operation showed there were only 550 tons. In view of the age of the oil, a reduced price per ton was negotiated with P & 0, whose liner "Arcadia" took the oil in Santo. With regards to the scrap metal, under the terms of the contract, the salvage company has the right to extract salvageable metal from the wreck. However, it appears that from the 33,000 tons gross weight of the sunken liner, no more then 50 tons can be economically salvaged. The revenue from the sale of this scrap metal goes to the company, as part of the contract, with which they would not have undertaken the difficult and dangerous operation. The spokesman added that any scrap metal which may be recovered from the wreck will be subject on export to the normal rates of duty, this money going to Condominium revenue.

"The letter requests that the entire revenue from the salvaged metal should be credited to the Santo Municipal Council. However, the revenue from possible re-sale of this metal will only just cover the cost of its salvage, as profit levels in diving operations at this level are extremely low. Moreover, the wreck itself is outside the boundaries of the Municipal Council.

"To sum up, the original estimate of 4,000 tons of oil in the wreck was proved wrong, as long ago as 1974, when it was decided there was only about 650 tons. The revenue helped to pay for the cost of getting the oil out but there was a loss, not a profit. Finally, the Condominium will benefit by duties payable to it when any of the scrap metal, such as copper alloys from the condensers and feed pipes is exported."

CHAPTER TWELVE - A LADY IN WAITING

N1

The dive site is just to the west of the flight path, so is visible from the port (left) side of the aircraft, which generally lands coming in from the south-east. Million Dollar point is virtually directly under the flight path. When I first travelled to Espiritu Santo the domestic airline was Air Melanesie. At the time of writing, the domestic airline is Vanair, running Twin Otter, and Islander aircraft throughout the islands of Vanuatu.

N2

Underwater visibility is one of those chances that divers must take. It is frustrating to come half-way round the world to find only 40 ft on the wreck, but it is equally exciting to be fortunate enough to get over 100ft. Such visibility gives a much better appreciation of the size of the ship, although a lesser visibility does not greatly diminish the enjoyment of the dive. The main problem is the rainy season early in the year, when the two main rivers, the Sarakata and the Renee empty the rainwaters down from the inland mountains into the Segond Channel. These soil laden fresh waters then flow to the extremities of the channel, south toward Malo or east toward Scorff Passage and the site of the President Coolidge. Invariably, the worse visibility is on the surface, and as you descend, the visibility clears appreciably. The flow of the tide will also influence the visibility during the rainy season as an incoming tide will bring in 'cleaner' waters from the ocean. It is all a matter of chance, and one that must be accepted by the diver.

N3

The pistol is a Colt M1911A1, with a .45 ball cartridge, and was the standard US Army service pistol for some seventy years, which says something of its durable and effective design. It was said that the Colt 45 could stop a man dead in his tracks, but required training to use to its full capability. It had a 7-round box magazine and an effective range of seventy-five yards.

N4

There is some confusion in the nationality of Oskar Schwitter as some information has have him as a Swiss. Allan Power believes he was Dutch, and his yacht was registered in Switzerland. Considering his name, and the fact that Switzerland does not have the greatest fleet of pleasure yachts, it could well be the other way around. Whatever his nationality, it does not lessen the tragedy. His grave is in the Luganville cemetery, which Allan recently described as a depressing place as so many graves were neglected. The full reading on the gravestone is 'Oskar Schwitter, Died 5-11-80. In Loving Memory of a Good Sailor and Wonderful Companion'. [R146]

N5

Alan Power advised the *Vanuatu Trading Post* that both divers had already been diving the *President Coolidge* during the week on guided tours but on the Friday morning had specifically requested to go on an unaccompanied dive of the wreck. Both were known to be experienced divers and had dived the *President Coolidge* a number of times. It should be noted at this point that no dive operator or any individual person has the right to prevent anyone from diving the *President Coolidge*. Allan Power told the newspaper, 'We could not stop them', and advised that prior to diving the ship, divers see a promotional video called *The Grave of the President* which advises on the danger of unaccompanied dives of the wreck. Interestingly, the release of the *Grave of the President* caused a few long term problems for Allan. Local land owners saw the value of the wreck and charged Allan for use of the small clearing where the divers kit up. And he was encouraged to obtain a local business licence to continue operating.

N6

The police and ambulance transported the bodies to Vila via Vanair. From Vila they were transported out of the country back to their families for burial.

N7

This dramatic description (Jane Hutchinson, The Age Travel Supplement, 5 April 1997), is probably close to the mark, and is included here with some hope that it may deter anyone anticipating a dive that involves the risks that these two most unfortunate men took. They made a mistake, but the penalty was far too severe. It proves the point that experience is not the only criteria for a safe dive. It would appear that the divers succumbed to a combination of narcosis, disorientation and heavy silting to the extent of blackout conditions, resulting in an inability to find their way out of the interior of the ship. As a result, they drowned when their air supply ran out. The penetration of wreck requires intimate knowledge of its layout, but even so, guide lines should be adopted if the penetration is greater than 'one blind turn'. The 'one blind turn' principle suggests that the diver can enter a wreck and make one turn only into a darkened, blind or unknown area. In doing so, the experienced diver should have little difficulty returning to the exit point of the ship, providing of course siltation has been avoided. Any further turns can and will cause disorientation in even the most experienced diver, and hence guide lines should be constructed to ensure a safe return, even in fully silted conditions. These are simple rules to follow, but are sometimes neglected due to narcosis. For this reason, a deep, penetrating dive into an unknown or difficult area should be planned on the surface, and the guidelines strung as per the plan. It is not acceptable to make the decision as to whether or not to string guidelines whilst actually down on the wreck, assuming that guidelines are taken down in the first place, as judgement under even mild narcosis can be affected. The decision must be made as part of the dive plan.

N8

The Vanuatu government takes a dim view of souveniring from the wrecks site, which has been declared a Marine Park. Don't be surprised if luggage is checked prior to leaving the country. It doesn't happen often, but it can happen.

N9

The diver who took the measurements of The Lady was John Read, a commercial diver and PADI instructor.

N10

An examination of engineering plans of the President Coolidge show that the fitting of large guns was already planned, even if not implemented. Considering the ship was launched in 1931, there was obviously some concern that the luxury liner would one day be used in a military fashion. The initial plans showed provision for a large bow gun (probably 5-inch like the stern gun), and two smaller guns (3-inch) on each side of A-deck just behind the larger bow gun, but in conversion to military use the 5-inch bow gun was dispensed with and the two 3-inch guns moved forward slightly.

N11

Scooters used by Santo Dive Tours staff are made by Apollo. In general, two deep dives are possible on one battery charge. The particular units at Luganville have been down to 72m.

N12

Was it Lynton Diggle who introduced bungee jumping to New Zealanders where the 'sport' was 'invented'. Not likely, but ten years later crazy Caucasians would amaze the rest of the world by emulating the Pentecost islanders. At least on Pentecost there was a male ritualistic reason for jumping off a tall structure with nothing to stop your fall but a vine attached to your ankle. But why do it by choice - and pay for the privilege. Come to think of it, perhaps it is a continuation of the male ritual. The only thing in common between bungee jumping and scuba diving is that you don't wear a toupee. Lynton Diggle and wife Edith prepared a local newsheet to keep the salvage crew amused. Called *The Coolidge Chronicle*, this fun sheet of several pages was produced 'weakly', with snippets of information about the crew, all with fictitious names of course.

N13

Don't for a moment think Lynton Diggle a klutz of a diver. On the contrary, he is one of New Zealand's finest, and a superb underwater cameraman.

N14

There is a report, unconfirmed, that the mail was actually recovered and that the letters were dried on a flat field near Santo, the covered area measuring one square mile.

N15

For Want of a Staple was the title of an unpublished manuscript by Colonel Arthur G. King, MD, U.S. Retd. and refers to the fact that had the Special Instructions been stapled to the rest of the sailing documents given to Captain Nelson, perhaps the ship would not have gone to the bottom. It is a great title, one I would have liked to have used for this book. It has been used on a number of articles published by Dr. King.

N16

The 155mm 'Long Tom' long range artillery gun was the mainstay of the US military. Its eight-wheeled (four tandem) carriage was designed for rugged cross-country haulage which other comparable power equipment could not cover. It had a maximum range of 25,715 yards (14.6 miles, 23.5 kilometres) and a rate of fire of forty rounds per hour. The weight of the gun is 15.1 tons, with a barrel length of 23 ft, and it required a crew of fifteen including two drivers.

N17

Nitrox is a mixture of nitrogen and oxygen in various proportions, typically $68\%N_2$ and $32\%O_2$, but various combinations are possible depending on the dive plan. Trimix is a mixture of helium, nitrogen and oxygen (HeN_2O_2). The advantage of the use of a mixed-gas breathing medium in scuba diving is the significant reduction in narcosis, and the ability to reach greater depths without oxygen poisoning, through control of the various gas components and proportions. Mixed gas diving is not new and was used pre-war by the military. It availability to the general public is only recent, and special dive courses are conducted in the use of mixed gases. The restriction to amateur use is predominantly availability and cost, particularly in remote regions. Specialist dive training is required.

N18

The scooter is a battery operated 'torpedo-like' submersible vehicle which the diver holds and is dragged toward the destination. Steering is by pointing the scooter in the required direction. Propulsion is by a propeller at the stern of the scooter, suitably protected of course. The scooter is neutrally buoyant and 'dies' if the diver releases hand contact. Apollo (brand) scooters have been used to reach the stern of the *President Coolidge*. A further comment from dive instructor Rodney Sales on the use of scooters: If you take off on your own, it is likely your buddy can not catch you, so stay together with good buddy communications and contact, an important ingredient for deep diving. Allow for the swim back if scooter breaks down or the battery goes flat. Watch your gauges, depth, time, air and assent alarms; it is easy to do a fast ascent. You need to make sure you have no dangles like a gauge or octopus regulator that could get caught in the prop of the scooter. Also watch for regulator free flows, as second regulators and octopuses have a tendency to free flow while motoring.

N19

Allan Power: By now he was diving on scuba, and had a compressor sent over to Lord Howe by boat. A dive boat was supplied by Pinetrees Lodge owner Gerald Kirby. Allan would catch fish for the hotel. The airfare at the time was thirty pounds return from Sydney. Tariff at Pinetrees was eleven pounds per week full board. Edward Du Cros was living on Lord Howe island at the time. Wally Gibbons came over to Lord Howe - as did other diving partners Billy White and Brian Larkin. (Du Cros was the author of *Skindiving in Australia*, published in 1960, the first book on the subject in Australia).

It took him four years to receive his actual prize from the Lenanto organisers - one hundred pounds.

Allan's Great Barrier Reef was first published in 1969 and over 150,000 copies have been sold. It is now in its 9th printing. This is Allan's one and only book. *The Great Barrier Reef* by Allan Power was only the second book published by the Hamlyn Group in Australia, now a very large publishing company. (The first Hamlyn book was the Margaret Fulton Cookbook).

The author was a partner in Aquarius/Dive Travel Australia, and, as a photographer and travel writer, assisted the promotion of Espiritu Santo with several articles on the *President Coolidge* in skindiving and travel magazines.

CHAPTER THIRTEEN - CHAMPAGNE AFFAIR

N1

Bokissa (Bogacio) Island lies between Aore and Tutuba islands, and it was past here that the 'safe' entrance to the Segond Channel was located during the war. It is a delightful island and the resort is comfortable, with a large lounge dining area opening out onto a huge sea-water pool. It was commenced in 1976 and completed in 1978 as a private club by Bill and Ruth Duffy from Victoria, Australia, at an enormous cost of some $760,000. Dewar Goode took it over in 1978. A syndicate turned it into a public resort in 1979, and it was managed by Willem Nyholt (ex Naiviti in Fiji) from August of that year. He left the following year. Then came Santo Rebellion in 1980 and the tourists were not forthcoming. Nyholt was not paid and the resort went into bankruptcy. Alan Power came over as caretaker for five months in 1981 just to make sure it didn't fall into ruin, after which the custom owner of the land, one Ben, took over as caretaker for four years. It then went through a number of owners and managers, and has emerged as a popular destination for scuba divers, and others wanting a quiet island resort. Bokissa is 165 acres (60 hectare), nearly circular, with a diameter approx 800 metres. The resort takes up five acres (two hectares). Eight fares (four finished in 1985), provide accommodation. The earlier units have marbel from Italy. Transfers from Luganville to the island, and between the wreck of the President Coolidge and the island, take about thirty minutes depending on the boat used. The original name of the island was Bogacio, but is now referred to as Bokissa since the Duffys established their private resort in 1976.

N2

Stan Combs came to Vanuatu initially as a member of CUSO, a Canadian quasi-government overseas volunteer organisation. From 1989 to 1992 he was the first Regional Development Planning Adviser for the central Government's National Planning and Statistics Office under the Prime Minister's Office. 'My function was to inject some rural influence into the development planning process, which was and continued to be dominated by the interests of the urban minority and aid donors. It was a useful position, as the NPSO had previously been run by expats who had little knowledge of Vanuatu outside of Vila'. For an interesting and thought provoking observation of Vanuatu and its people, see Stan Comb's website at

http://members.home.net/scombs/vanuatu.html

CHAPTER FOURTEEN - IN MEMORIAM

N1

Sergeant Parisi was wounded three times while an enlisted man, but not serious enough for evacuation during the Solomon Islands campaign. As a platoon sergeant during most of the campaign, he led the second platoon without an officer. The eighty three combat and/or reconnaissance patrols were led by Parisi without a single man killed. On 24 December, 1943, while on Arundel Island, Parisi was summoned back to regimental headquarters to receive a battlefield commission as 2nd Lieutenant, and transferred to B company in the First Battalion where he took command of the second platoon there also. Shortly after while on New Guinea he was assigned to organize and train his men as an assault platoon, proficient with flame thrower, rocket launchers, and demolitions. The team included a demolition man, Browning automatic men, and riflemen for the purpose of destroying tunnels, and gun emplacements. This was in preparation for the invasion of the Philippines. Parisi was wounded for the fourth time on 4 April, 1945 in Dagupan Province, Philippine islands, by a Japanese sniper. This time the wound was more serious, and he spent the next year and a half in and out of military hospitals in Manila and the USA. He was discharged from the service with the rank of Captain on 9 September 1946, having earned two Bronze stars and four Purple Hearts. At the time of writing, Parisi was in retirement, his waterproofing and restoration business in the hands of his four sons. He has one final ambition as far as the Pacific War is concerned - to dive the *President Coolidge*. At 80 years of age, he is fit and agile and completing a scuba course in anticipation of a return visit to Luganville. But it may not be that easy, as it takes some talking to convince a dive operator to take a novice 80 year old down to beyond 100 ft.

Note - he made it - see page 232.

REFERENCES & BIBLIOGRAPHY

PUBLISHED WORKS - BOOKS

Barker, General Harold R. *History of the 43rd Division Artillery*. Barker was commander of the 43rd Division, which included the 103rd Field Artillery, from 1937 to the end of the Pacific war.
Bevan, Denys. *United States Forces in New Zealand 1942-1945*.
Bowdrey, Bob, Judy Beaty & Brian Ansell. *Diving and Snorkelling Guide to Vanuatu*. Pisces Books, Houston, Texas. 1995.
Charles, Roland W. *Troopships of World War II*. The Army Transportation Association, Washington, D.C.
Coggins, Jack. *The Campaign for Guadalcanal*. Doubleday & Company, New York, 1972.
Dod, Karl C. *United States Army in World War Ii. The Corps of Engineers: the War Against Japan*. Office of the Chief of Military History, U.S. Army, Washington, DC 1966.
Gibbs, Jim. *Disaster Log of Ships*. Bonanza books, 1978.
Grant, Neil. *Chronicles of 20th Century Conflict*. Reed International Books, 1993.
Harcombe, David et al. *Vanuatu - Travel Survival Kit*. Lonely Planet Publications Pty Ltd. Melbourne.
Hocking, Charles. *Dictionary of Disasters At Sea*. Two volumes. Lloyd's. 1969.
Kludas, Arnold. *Great Passengers Ships of the World. Vol 3: 1924 - 1935*. Patrick Stephens, Cambridge.
Lott, Arnold S. Lieutenant Commander. USN *Most Dangerous Sea*. Naval Institute, Annapolis, MD.
Lucas, Alan. *Cruising Vanuatu and New Caledonia*.
Michener, James A. *Return to Paradise*. Secker and Warburg Edition 1951, Corgi Edition 1967.
Niven, John. *The American President Lines and its Forebears 1848-1984*. University of Delaware Press, 1987.
Sawyer, L.A. & W.H. Mitchell. *From America to United States. The History of the Merchant Ship Types Built in the USA under the Long-Range Programme of the Maritime Commission*. World Ship Society, 1984.
Stone, Peter. *Hostages to Freedom - the Fall of Rabaul*. Oceans Enterprises. Yarram, Australia. 1994.
Wolfert, Ira. *Battle for the Solomons*. Chapter 11, The Sinking of the President Coolidge.
(Unknown author) . *Building the Navy's Bases in World War II*. History of the Bureau of Yards and Docks and the Civil Engineering Corps. 1940- 1946. Volume 2. US Government Printing Office, Washington. 1947.

PUBLISHED WORKS - MAGAZINE & JOURNAL ARTICLES

A Story of American Courage, Sergeant Mack Morris. Yank Magazine. No date.
A Visit to the President's Lady. Peter Stone. Boat Directory magazine. 1987.
Barry May. Peter Stone. Skindiving in Australia magazine. Vol 13. #1. 1983.
Cruise of the "Whai". Peter Spurdle. New Zealand Dive magazine. Circa 1970.
Diving the President Coolidge - the World's Largest Accessible Shipwreck. Peter Stone. Skindiving in Australia and the South Pacific. Volume 12, #2. 1982.
Diving the USS Tucker. Sandra Middleton and Peter Whitelaw. Skindiving in Australia magazine. August/September 1985.
Dollar Liner President Coolidge. Marine Engineering and Shipping Age. H.C. Coleman, Manager, Marine Engineering, Westinghouse Electric and Manufacturing Company, East Pittsburg, PA. Date unknown. (Probably August 1931).
For Want of A Staple. Arthur G. King, MD, Colonel, A.U.S. Retd. (Published in a number of magazines).
Ghosts of War. National Geographic Society. Vol. 173, No. 4, April 1988.
Interior Architecture. Marine Engineering and Shipping Age. August 1931.
President Coolidge. Army & Navy Magazine. US publication. No date.
President Coolidge - Underwater Adventure. Peter Stone. Club Marine Magazine.
Propelling Machinery. Marine Engineering and Shipping Age. August 1931.
Reece Discombe, OBE. Pacific Islands Monthly People. Malcolm Salmon feature. September 1980.
Santo. Peter Stone. Club Marine Magazine.
Secrets of the Lady. Mike Scotland. Sportdiving magazine.
Steamers of the Past - Dollar Liner "President Coolidge" of 1931. J.H. Isherwood. Sea Breezes. May 1975.
Sunken World War Ii Troopships Surveyed for Oil Salvage. Oil Industry Journal. August 1976.
Ten Years Ago in Santo. Peter Cole. Pacific Islands Monthly, December 1981.

PUBLISHED WORKS - MAGAZINE & JOURNAL ARTICLES (continued)

The Bizarre Death of the President Coolidge. Martin Grish, based on a report from Edward F. Oliver. Sea
Classics magazine (date unknown).
The Death of Th President Coolidge. Ships and The Sea magazine, June 1953. Edward F. Oliver.
The Dollar Lines. Only Yard-built Sister Ships to Be Christened by U.S. President Wives. Unknown author,
unknown publication, possibly a journal of the dockyard which build the ships, Newport News
Shipbuilding and Drydock Company.
The Grave of the President Coolidge. Paul Callaghan and Debra Collins. Skindiving in Australia magazine.
Vol 14, No. 4. 1984.
The Last Minutes of the President Coolidge. The Mast Magazine, May 1946. Author: Frank Cameron.
The President and the Lady. Peter Stone. Club Marine magazine. April/May 1986.
The President Coolidge Launched. Shipyard Bulletin. Published Bi-Monthly by Newport News Shipbuilding
and Drydock Company. Vol IV, Number 1. February-March 1931.
The President Coolidge Revisited. Today Magazine, Spring 1984. Author unknown.
The President Coolidge Launched. Extract. No date, no identification of journal.
Trial Trip. Marine Engineering and Shipping Age.. Date unknown. (Probably August 1931).
Vanuatu - Diving Vila and Santo. Peter Stone. Skindiving in Australia. Volume 12, #2.
Vanuatu - Rim of Fire. Jett Britall. Fisheye View Scuba Magazine. Vol 4, Num 2. Oct/Nov 1990.
Wreck of the President Coolidge. Bulletin of the Sunbelt Chapter of the 43rd Infantry Division Veterans
Association. Bulletin 1996-4. December 1996.
Wreck of the "President Coolidge". Lynton Diggle. Skindiving in Australia. Volume 5 # 4. 1974.

PUBLISHED WORKS - NEWSPAPER FEATURES

Nabanga. Translation of French article in Nabanga, Port Vila, New Hebrides, 21 August 1976. Michel
Charleux. *La Carburant Du "Coolidge" Est Pompe*.
New York Times. Sunday, 13 December, 1942. *Troop Ship is Sunk in Pacific But Only 4 of 4,000 Are Lost*.
New York Times. Extracts. 16 December 1942. et al.
New Hebrides News. Extract. No date. Post April 1977. Kindly provided by Mr Ian Perrott , Perrott Salvage and
Construction Pty Ltd, Cairns Queensland.
North American Newspaper Alliance. 1942. Extract. Author Ira Wolfert. *Sinking of President Coolidge*.
San Francisco Call-bulletin. Clipping file of many articles on the SS President Coolidge, period 1931-1958.
Compiled and edited for the National Maritime Museum by Herbert H. Beckwith, San Francisco National
Maritime Museum, 1981.
San Diego Dispatch. 28 October 1966. *The Sinking of the Ss President*
The Age Travel Supplement. 5 April 1997. *Legends of the Deep*. Jane Hutchinson.
Vanuatu Trading Post, #195. 13 November 1996. *Two Divers Die in President Coolidge*.
Various newspaper extracts. From an album kindly loaned by Mr Ian Perrott , Perrott Salvage and
Construction Pty Ltd, Cairns Queensland.

PUBLISHED WORKS - PAMPHLETS

Booklet. *Launching Booklet*. Issued at the launching of the S.S. President Coolidge, at the works of the
Newport News Shipbuilding and Dry Dock Company, Newport News, Virginia. 28 February 1931.
Brochure. *Drift Travel*. Espiritu Santo Tours.
Brochure. *Cabin Plans. S.S. President Coolidge*. American President Lines. Brochure listing agents; photos.
Brochure. *Dive Vanuatu*. Prepared by Aquarius/Dive Travel Australia, and reproduced in Skindiving in
Australia and the South Pacific.
Document. *A Tribute to One of Rhode Island's Great Heroes of World War Ii. Captain Elwood Joseph Euart,
D.S.C., R.I.C. 103rd Field Artillery, 43rd Division, A.U.S*. Published by Narragansett Council, Boy
Scouts of America.
Marketing flyer for film, President Coolidge, made by Film New Zealand; notes from producer Lynton Diggle.
Pamphlet. *American President Lines' Role in World War 2*. American President Lines, prepared by Eugene F.
Hoffman, Vice President Public Relations. June 15 1957.
Promotional notes. *Bokissa Isle Dive*.
Promotional notes. *Santo Dive Tours*. Diving and Geography. Kindly provided by Allan Power.

GENERAL DOCUMENTS

Bill of Sale of Formerly Registered Vessel.
History of USS Tucker. Division of Naval History, Ships Histories Section, Navy Dept. Compiled March 1953.
History - SS President Coolidge. Seaweed's Ships Histories, USA.
History of USS. Tucker (DD-374). Seaweeds Ships Histories, USA.
History of USS Breese (DM-18). Seaweeds Ships Histories, USA.
History of USS Gamble (DM-15). Seaweeds Ships Histories, USA.
History of USS. Sterett (DD-407). Seaweeds Ships Histories, USA.
Log of the President Coolidge. Ship's Log. Extract. San Francisco Maritime National Historic Park
Report of Marine Casualty Or Accident. Department of Commerce, Bureau of Marine Inspection and
    Navigation. 27 January 1943.
SS President Coolidge. Museum Reference Cards. National Maritime Museum, San Francisco.
Vanuatu Agents File. Travel Agents guide.

UNPUBLISHED WORKS

Discombe, Reece. *War in New Hebrides..*
Moshimer, Mr. Robert H. *Odyssey.* Military autobiography. Includes sinking of *President Coolidge* and
    attempted rescue of Captain Elwood Euart.
Nisley, Elmer. Private Notes. Nisley was on board President Coolidge.
Parisi, Stephen. Memoirs. Was on board *President Coolidge*.
Renton, James A. Untitled. Was on board *President Coolidge*.
Schumacher, Henry. Untitled notes. Schumacher was on board the *SS President Coolidge* when she hit mines
Stone, Peter. *Revolution - Or Revelation ?* Notes on theSanto Rebellion.

INTERNET DATA

AMERICAN PRESIDENT LINES LTD. Brief chronological history of the company.
    http://www.apl.com
GUADALCANAL AIR WAR Series of articles posted to the World War II mailing list.
    http://www. netstuff/military/airpac
INFORMATION ON PRESIDENT CALVIN COOLIDGE.
    http://www2.whitehouse.gov//WH/glimpse/presidents/html/cc30.htm
NEWPORT NEWS SHIPBUILDING. 110 YEARS OF SHIPBUILDING HISTORY.
    http://www.nns.com/
STAN COMBS
    http://www.silk.net/personal/scombs/vanuatu.html
THE MEMOIRS OF WILLIAM TREWHELLA PAULL.
    http://www.sihope.com/~tipi/marine.html.

MILITARY DOCUMENTS

A History of Espiritu Santo Prepared At the Close of War. Department of the Navy, Office of the Chief of
    Naval Operations, to Rear Admiral Dale E. Collins USN (Ret), American President Lines. 20 November
    1963. (Extract)
A Naval History of Espiritu Santo. Command File World War 2. Data complied by Lt. D.W. Kralovec USNR,
    Base Historian, and submitted by Captain N.M.Pigman USN, Island Commander, Espiritu Santo, New
    Hebrides. 4 November 1946.
Action Report: Espiritu Santo, New Hebrides. Sinking of USS Tucker. W.R. Terrell, Commanding Officer, to
    Secretary of the Navy. August 12, 1942.
Additional Material on Just Compensation, Steamship "President Coolidge". War Shipping Administration.
    Washington October 3, 1944.U.S. Government Report. No. 20-E.
Attack on Submarine. 31 May 1943. F. Gibbs. U.S.U. SC-669. Declassified document
*Department of the Navy, Office of the Judge Advocate General, Washington Dc, 23 December 1963 to
    Honorable Wayne Moss, United States Senate.*
*Destruction of the SS President Coolidge in Allied Mine Field, October 26, 1942, Espiritu Santo, New
    Hebrides, South Pacific, World War 11.* U.S. Coast Guard. 27 November 1963.
Finding of F4U-1 Crash Site. Report from the Department of the Army, United States Central Identification
    Laboratory, Hawaii.
Finding of Facts. The findings, opinions and recommendations of the Court of Inquiry. W.F. Halsey. Admiral,
    US Navy, Commander South Pacific Area and South Pacific Forces.

MILITARY DOCUMENTS (continued)

General Orders 22 December 1942. James A. Lewis, Colonel, Infantry Commanding.
Henry Nelson, Master, SS President Coolidge, to Captain Roberts, Commanding Officer, Naval Forces Base Button. Subject: Loss of S.S. President Coolidge. Date: 28 October, 1942. Base Button. (Base Button is Luganville).
Log. Congressman Craig Hosmer, previously Commander of naval gun crew, *President Coolidge.*
Military Installations At Espiritu Santo. Military Report by Lieutenant A.E. Gordon. Australian Military Force. Navy Dept. Communiques. Period December 1941 - March 1943. Various extracts.
Record of Procedure of A Court of Inquiry on Board the USS Whitney.
Record of Procedure of A Court of Inquiry Convened on Board the USS Whitney. 12 November 1942. Also Memorandum on file. *Navy Department, Office of the Chief of Naval Operations, Washington. January 19, 1943.*
Record of Proceedings of A Military Commission Convened At College La Perouse, Noumea, New Caledonia. Case of Henry Nelson, Civilian, 8 December 1942.
Ship's Log - USS Gamble. Various dates. August and September 1942.
Sinking of USS Tucker. Commander South Pacific Area and South Pacific Force, Robert L. Ghormley, to Secretary of the Navy. Now declassified.
South Pacific Force of the United States Pacific Fleet, Headquarters of the Commander. From The Commander South Pacific Area and South Pacific Force. W.F. Halsey, Admiral, U.S. Navy. To Captain Richard Fagan, Jr. U.S. Marine Corps, retired, Judge Advocate, Military Commission, Headquarters, First Marine Amphibious Corps. 29 November 1942. (Confidential Memo).
United States Coast Guard Form N.C.G. 92461. Confidential Report on U.S. Flag Passenger Vessels Attacked and Lost.
United States Coast Guard. 9 March 1943. Matters relating to the President Coolidge and the findings of the Inquiry Board.

CORRESPONDENCE WITH THE AUTHOR

Ruth M. Allard, on behalf of Arthur Allard, Infantry, 43rd Division. USA.
Howard F. Brown, Colonel, 43rd Infantry Division Association, Rhode Island, USA.
William L. Chilcott, Oregon, USA.
Stan Combs, Canada. Several email communications, 1997.
Bob Cox, The American Legion Library and Museum, USA.
Reece Discombe, Port Vila, Vanuatu. Numerous faxes and letters during 1995-1997.
John Eley, Ohio, USA
Len Euart. Massachussets, USA September 1997.
Bud Feuer, Roanoke, USA.
Carl Fritts, USA.
Fred L. Fuge, Oregon, USA. September 1996.
Charles W. George, New Hampshire, USA. October 1995.
Richard Hansen, Oregon, USA. October 1996 and later.
Stephen Harding, Virginia, USA.
Fred E. Harris, Kentuckey, USA. October 1995.
Don R. Hoffman, California, USA. October 1995 and later.
Burt Jaquith, Florida, USA. 28 May 1997 and later.
Arthur G. King. (Colonel, Ret). Cincinnati, USA. August 1996 and later.
Ian Lockley, Borroloola, N.T. Australia. 1996.
Ken MacGowan, Port Vila, Vanuatu. 1996-1997
Barry May, Sydney, Australia. 25 June 1997 and later.
Frank Montcalvo, Renton, WA, USA
Robert Moshimer, Kennebunkport, USA. July 1997.
William Murray, Pawtucket, USA. September 1997.
Stephen Parisi, USA. October 1996 and later.
William T. Paull, USA. September 1997.
Ian Perrott, Cairns, Australia. July 1997.
Richard J. Peterson. Ensign, *USS Gamble.* Childersburg, USA. Several 1996-1997.
Allan Power, Espiritu Santo, Vanuatu. Numerous faxes during 1996/1997.
Rodney Sales. Dive 2000, Sydney. July 1997.
Charles H. Schubert. (US Capt. Retd), New Zealand. September 1997.
Terry Thompson, Virginia, USA. September 1996.

CORRESPONDENCE BETWEEN OTHER PARTIES

Dick Baker, British District Agent at Santo after the Pacific war, to Reece Discombe, 4 July 1997.
Reece Discombe, Port Vila, to J. Kalo Nial, Luganville, re Million Dollar Point. Undated.
George Killion to D.E. Collins, 7 January 1964.
Arthur G.H. King to Reece Discombe, 8 August 1991.
E. M. Wieseke, Commander, Department of the Navy, Bureau of Supplies and Accounts, Washington, DC,
      USA, to Reece Discombe, Port Vila. 29 November 1957.
Ivan Peterson to Captain F. Kent Loomis. 19 April 1961.
Robert Singhaus to US Coast Guard Headquarters. Undated.
Telegram (copy) re collision of *President Coolidge* with *Frank H. Buck*. 6 March 1937
Tom Wheeler, American President Lines, to Reece Discombe, Port Vila. 8 September 1965.

INTERVIEWS AND AUTHOR'S NOTES

Author's notes. *First Visit to Vanuatu, February/March 1982.*
Interview notes. *Allan Power. October, 1985. Luganville.*
Interview notes. *Allan Power. 15-16 July 1996. Luganville.*
Author's notes. *Reece Discombe. July 1996.*
Recorded notes. *Reece Discombe.* Recollections Recorded tape, Anzac Day, 1997, Port Vila, Vanuatu.
Author's notes and observation, taken over fifteen years visiting Vanuatu.
Author's notes. *President Coolidge and Espiritu Santo.*

MISCELLANEOUS MATERIAL

Report, extract. *Nets and Lifelines.* Inspector Kennedy. Source and date unknown.
Specifications Sheet. *Submersible Decompression Chamber.*
Specifications sheet (general). *Ss President Coolidge - General Characteristics.*
News sheet. *The Coolidge Chronicle.* Monday, 26 July 1976. Lynton and Edith Diggle. Humorous.
Original Menu. *Captain's Farewell Dinner Monday, 16 November 1936. President Coolidge.*
Deck Log of the President Coolidge. 26 October 1942. San Francisco Maritime National Historic Park.
Ships Departure Log. *President Coolidge.* Section only. December 1941 - October 1942.
Archives extract. *The 1930's: A Decade of Grand Passenger Travel in the Pacific.* APL Archives. Sept.1981.

CHARTS, MAPS, PLANS

Admiralty Chart. Number 176, Espiritu Santo Island. The south coast and off-lying islands from a survey by
      Lieutenant Commander H.E.Purey-Cust, R.N., H.M. Surveying Ship Dart, 1892. The remainder from a
      United States Government Chart of 1949. Published 7 November 1952.
Deck Plans of the *President Coolidge*. American President Lines
Drawing, plans, diagrams from Allan Power, showing location of various items on the wreck.
Engineering drawings of the *President Coolidge*, published in an edition of Marine Engineering and Shipping
      Age, date unknown. (Possibly 1930, 1931)

ACKNOWLEDGEMENTS

This book would not have been possible without the dedicated co-operation of Reece Discombe and Allan Power. Toward the end of preparing the manuscript, over a hundred faxes went back and forth to clarify even minor points. As Allan said, 'We have to get it right'. I have dived the *President Coolidge* many times but now that I think back and try to remember each dive in detail, I find it impossible to recall the dive plan with any resemblance of accuracy. That is where Allan comes in. Reece provided most of the information regarding the military occupation of Espiritu Santo, and the early days of diving the ship, and Million Dollar Point. Allan also assisted with the chapter on salvage. It was also their leads that allowed me to gather further information, and no less than 180 separate references are used in the compilation of the manuscript. Allan and Reece also supplied many of the photographs, some in original form, and others that I copied. Where quality was not sufficient, I managed to track down the original source of the photographs. So to Allan Power and Reece Discombe, I, and anyone enjoying this book, owe them a wealth of gratitude.

Of course there are many others whose assistance has been invaluable, some who have provided first-hand information, and others who have assisted in the gathering of information and in the production of the book. I mention these in no particular order of importance and contribution as all have given their time and knowledge with courtesy and competence.

My research started over ten years ago, in 1986, with the Australian President Lines Archives in Oakland, California. From their archivist Colette Carey I obtained a few photos for personal use, and general information. When I commenced serious research for the book, the APL Archives were no longer and Colette had moved on to pastures unknown. Through the Internet I tracked down the American President Lines, and contacted Lisa Hernandez in Marketing Communications, who was most helpful, but advised (as did the APL page) that their archives were now with the National Maritime Museum in San Francisco. This led to a communication with William Kooiman at the National Maritime Museum Library, and resulted in further excellent material and photographs. The problem Bill had was that they had received a wealth of information from APL and not all had been catalogued. However, with the assistance of Roberto Landazuri who is in charge of the APL collection, Bill managed to forward all the material that I requested - and more. To Bill, a fine maritime historian and author and in his own right (*The Grace Ships 1869-1969*, Komar Publishing, 1991), I offer my most sincere appreciation for his dedication and courtesy; and to Roberto also for allowing me to disrupt his procedures. Appreciation is also extended to the National Maritime Museum Association who control the sale of photographs, and to Lynn Cullivan, Public Affairs at the San Francisco Maritime National Historic Park.

It was also through Lisa Hernandez that I tracked down a copy of John Niven's excellent book *The American President Lines and Its Forebears 1848-1984*. This gave me the background needed to understand the operations of the Dollar Line and the American President Line, the material suitably complementing what I had obtained from other sources. To Mr Niven, to whom I had no communication, I offer my appreciation for an excellent and valuable work of research. And to Renee Lukaszek of the publishers Osterman API where I obtained the copy, thankyou for your courtesy and prompt despatch. Thankyou also to Jean-Louis Boglio of Currumbin, Queensland for chasing up a copy of the book before I had a chance to obtain one for myself - and to Dallas Hogan, a former shipwright with ANL for its loan.

The National Archives Still Picture Branch in Maryland was a valuable source of photographic material as usual. Thankyou to Lynda L. Mouchyn of User Services, and to Holly Reed who kindly followed up with a few questions on specific prints. The National Archives and Record Administration (NARA) no longer provides photographs direct. Their reproduction services have been privatised, and NARA provide a list of companies that provide reproduction services. I chose Visual Image Presentation for no other reason that their prices seemed reasonable; their service was excellent, so I have no complaints. Contact VIP direct with the image number of the photograph as shown in the Photo Credits if you want a 10 x 8 inch print.

To Bernard Cavalcante at the Operational Archives Branch of the Naval Historical Centre in Washington I once again express my appreciation for advice, and guidance for further research. This is the third time that Bernard has assisted with one of my publications. His leads to several military associations gave rise to most of the first-hand accounts of the sinking of the *President Coolidge*. Through Bernard's advice I contacted as many military associations as I could seeking assistance from anyone connected with the *President Coolidge*, particularly those on board at the time. This resulted in a number of notices placed in the associations' newsletters, and in turn solicited a number of interesting letters. I do not know of all the associations who responded with a notice, as suddenly a letter would arrive out of the blue with further details but no indication as to how they came to know of the book project. I also had a page on the Internet which may have resulted in further contacts.

My appreciation is extended to Colonel Howard F. Brown, Secretary/Treasurer/Editor of the 43d Infantry Division Veterans Association, Rhode Island, USA, whose notice solicited a number of excellent contacts. Of course, once one contact is made, several others usually follow as a result of leads provided. Appreciation is also extended to The Retired Officer Association, and the Veterans of Foreign Wars Association for likewise including a notice in their journals. Bob Cox at the American Legion Library and Museum provided a number of service contacts which were most appreciated, and led to further information. There may be others, and for their omission in this acknowledgement, I sincerely apologise.

Thanks to old-days diving colleague Paul Sheaffe for tracking down Clarrie Lawler. It was Clarrie who did the drawing of the ship used on each chapter title page. Thankyou Clarrie for permission to use this.

I find the Internet to be fascinating, and have gathered a wealth of information for a number of projects I and my wife have been involved in. But one of the greatest benefits I have found is the excellent contacts that can be made with people of similar interests. One such person is Stan Combs in Canada. Stan has a marvellous website covering his days working in Vanuatu. I corresponded with Stan on a number of issues, and respect his knowledge and concern for the people of Vanuatu. Stan has provided information and inspiration, and kindly obtained an original copy of a menu from the *President Coolidge* when she was travelling the Pacific as a luxury liner. Thankyou Stan for all you have done - I hope we may keep in touch, and eventually meet one day.

The Internet also provided the excellent memoirs of William T. Paull, extracts of which I have used in Chapter Six and Eight. For this I am most grateful to Mr Paull, in Montana, and to his daughter Michelle (Tipi) in Minnesota. It was Michelle who created the excellent web site for her father's memoirs.

Although I did not use the services of Australian Archives (Melbourne) as much for this publication as I have in the past, I am however once again indebted to Esther Carey for her kind assistance, and in one instance saving me a five hundred kilometre round trip to Melbourne. The courtesy extended by AA staff is always appreciated.

Many thanks to Burt Jaquith, Florida, USA for prompt replies to my questions, and discussions on ownership of the vessel.

Arthur G. King, Col. (Retd) MD of Cincinnati, Ohio was chief medical officer on Espiritu Santo and provided a wealth of information, initially through colleague Reece Discombe, and then in direct correspondence. The title for Chapter Six, *For Want of a Staple*, is that used by Dr. King in several of his published features.

The much decorated and respected Colonel (Retd) Stephen Parisi, of Massachusetts, USA was one of the first of the "Coolidge men" to respond to a notice in an associations newsletter. Stephen was a Lieutenant on board the *President Coolidge* and provided excellent first hand material for which I am most grateful. Last I heard, Stephen was doing a diving course so that he could visit the *President Coolidge* once again. I do hope you get the opportunity Stephen. (He did - see page 232).

James Renton, from Oregon, USA was also aboard the *President Coolidge* and provided an excellent first hand account. Thankyou. Mrs Ruth M. Allard of Vermont kindly wrote on behalf of her husband and contributed further details for which I am most grateful. Fred E. Harris of Madisonville, Kentucky; and Fred L. Fuge of Haines, Oregon also contributed. Many thanks. And to William Perleth whom I could not reply to as I did not have a return address. Also to Charles Fritts also whose father-in-law Don Meredith was on the *President Coolidge* - the manuscript was completed by the time we made contact but thankyou anyway.

Richard J. Peterson, of Alabama was Ensign on board *USS Gamble* when she laid the mines that sank the *President Coolidge* (and later was commander of the ship). Mr Peterson contributed greatly with his recollections of events, recorded in Chapter Six. Richard Hansen, from Oregon USA was also on board minelayer *USS Gamble*, and provided material for which I am most grateful. Also to Don R. Hoffman, of Rohnert Park, California who provided further information and charts. Thankyou.

A most sincere and somewhat belated appreciation for two gentlemen who were on the *President Coolidge* when she was mortally wounded, and assisted tremendously with the manuscript in the later stages of its compilation - Robert Moshimer and Charles Schubert. Bob Moshimer assisted in the attempted rescue of Captain Euart, and it is he at the door in the lower photograph on page 117. Appreciation is also extended to several people who corresponded with the author whilst the book was in for printing, and after its release: William Murray of Pawtucket, Rhode Island, USA; Mr Leonard Euart, brother of Captain Euart, and Mrs Helen Euart; Ted Blahnik, Director, Guadalcanal Campaign Veterans.

Salvage Pacific (Fiji) directors Ian Lockley in Northern Territory and Ian Perrott, Cairns, Queensland, both assisted with details of their salvage of the oil from the *President Coolidge*, used in Chapter Eleven. I met Lynton Diggle in New Zealand back in the 1970s. He shot the film of the oil recovery from the *President Coolidge*. Thankyou for permission to use his excellent description of diving the shipwreck. I attempted to find more details on the oil transfer to the *Arcadia* from P. &. O Australia, but they had no information. I am nevertheless grateful to Mr Ric North, of P&O Australia for seeking information, and further contacts.

Kevin Deacon from Dive 2000, in Sydney was one of the cameramen with David Doubilet when he shot the National Geographic feature on the *Wreck of The Coolidge* (Vol 173, No.4, April 1988). Kevin's work is always superb and although I have not used any in this publication, I am always grateful for his friendship, courtesy and willingness to assist in any project. Also from Dive 2000, I met Rodney Sales in Luganville in 1996 after having spoken to him on the phone for a number of years. Rodney was involved in the recovery of the unfortunate divers lost in the engine room. I am grateful for his advice on this incident, and for his description of diving the stern

298

which, I am sure, I will never see. Thankyou also to Barry May for excellent memories of days diving the Great Barrier Reef from the *Auriga Bay*, and for assisting with details on the lifting of the propellers from the *President Coolidge*. It would be appropriate to show gratitude at this stage also to Barry Andrewartha, editor of the then *Skindiving in Australia* magazine (now *Sportdiving*) for introducing me to Barry May and giving me so many opportunities that literally changing my life. I will always be most grateful. Thankyou to dive photo/journalist Mike Scotland of Kirrawee, NSW for his observations, and excellent regular contributions to dive magazines.

Ken MacGowan was a major player in my *Hostages to Freedom - The Fall of Rabaul*, and by some coincidence, is involved also in this production. Apart from his business interests in Australia and Vanuatu, Ken is a keen adventurer and has been involved in the discovery of aircraft on Espirito Santo. He contributed to sections in Chapter Fourteen.

I am grateful to several people and organisations who have assisted with allowing me to research and prepare the publication over a number of years. To Jean-Paul Virelala, Managing Director, Air Vanuatu, and to Willie Wilson, Managing Director, Vanair, I am most grateful. Likewise, for assistance in 1992, appreciation is extended to Ian Carew-Reid, Manager, Air Vanuatu, Melbourne, and to Shaun Holland, Vanair, Port Vila.

To my diving buddy and good friend Phil Cherici who has joined me on so many adventures, thankyou once again for your companionship particularly on our last visit to Vanuatu in 1992. And a special thankyou to my ex-wife and business partner Jan whose shared in many of the adventures on Espiritu Santo and assisted so many divers to visit the *President Coolidge*.

Apart from the inimitable Allan Power, I am also grateful to a number of dive operators at Espiritu Santo over the years: Kevin and Mayumi Green at Bokissa, now in Luganville with Aquamarine; and Nigel and Louise Hill, and Paul Hill of Exploration Diving, previously in Luganville who gave me the opportunity to visit the destroyer *USS Tucker*.

Of those who assisted in some respect with accommodation, be it in kind or courtesy, I will always be grateful to Mary-Jane Dinh for her friendship and courtesy at Hotel Santo over many years. To Eddie and Pauline Beljars at Bokissa in the early 1980s, thankyou and I hope we meet again; and to Elaine and Yvan Charles at the Bougainville Resort where I was extended the most courteous service. Thankyou Charles for the visit to Bomber Three and the tour.

And thank heaven for Leslie Conklin at Natangora Cafe in Luganville for preventing CWS - 'cappuccino withdrawal symptom', with her excellent coffee and cakes, and marvellous breakfasts. To Fred Kleckham of Drift Travel also in Luganville, and to Joyce Graham at the Hotel Santo for photocopying.

Also to Loyalty Rovu and Jimmy Tapasei of Tour Vanuatu; and to my faithful drivers Timmy Rovu in 1992 and Kenneth in 1996.

My sincere appreciation to the late, charismatic Jimmy Stevens, and his son Franki, for welcoming my small party to their compound near Vanafo village. I will always remember this visit as a highlight of my life, and although the mal-mal doesn't get much use nowadays, it is a treasured possession.

I could not forget the charming Selena Layden of Melbourne who was assisting Allan Power in 1992 and took me on yet another visit to The Lady. It is she that is in the colour photograph of The Lady. Thankyou Selena, and I trust your studies went well.

There are many others that have made my visits to Vanuatu so memorable: Merrell and Denny Smith of Nautilus Scuba Port Vila, and Warwick Davidson and David Roe at Nautilus Scuba ; perennial friend Alex Bodian; Bob Bowdey and Judy Beatty of *Coriolis*; Peter Whitelaw and Sandra Middleton; the McGeough brothers of Tanna Beach Resort, Jim, Brefni and Rory; Reg and Margaret Gibson of Scuba Holidays in Port Vila; Rick Hogg at the Waterfront Restaurant, Port Vila; Paul D'Arcy, Manager, Radisson Royal Palms Resort & Casino; Rick Graham, Manager, Iririkki Island Resort; Chief Gowya at Yekel Village, Tanna; Lyn and Eddie Cooper at Erakor Island. Thankyou to all for your kindness and courtesy.

And of course to the Deputy Mayor Mr Meralilui Moffet who performed our wedding ceremony for Wendy and I on the balcony of the home of Reece and Jean Discombe in Port Vila in 1996.

Ross Campbell has been my guiding light at Australian Print Group in Maryborough for several publications. Knowledgeable and always courteous, Ross epitomises the attitude of APG in providing top customer service and a quality product. Oceans Enterprises is but a very small fish in the large pond of publishing, and yet I am always treated with the utmost respect. Darren Mitchell took over from Ross during the preparation of this title, and I look forward to working with him. To Ross, and Managing Director Trevor Lea, I extend my sincerest appreciation.

To Carole Jones, my first wife and mother of my wonderful daughter Catherine, who by some coincidence is now living in Luganville, the wife of the ANZ bank manager, Peter Jones. Carole is doing a tremendous amount of work for the Northern District Hospital in Luganville, as a volunteer. Her dedication to the people of Espiritu Santo is most encouraging, and I, for one, thank her for a magnificent effort.

On the home front I must once again express my love and appreciation to my three constant partners, wife Wendy, Gracie our beautiful boxer/kelpie cross and the delightful Lulu the cat, for I could not have survived the long hours at the computer without their continued love and affection. And for this second printing, may I say, welcome Sam, my wonderful young boy who joined us on 22 February 1999. You have now fulfilled my life.

USEFUL ADDRESSES

ON ESPIRITU SANTO

Bougainville Resort, P.O.Box 116, Luganville, Espiritu Santo, Vanuatu. Ph: (678) 36257, Fax: (678) 36647
Hotel Santo, P.O.Box 178, Luganville, Espiritu Santo, Vanuatu. Phone: (678) 36250. Fax: (678) 36749
Aore Resort, P.O.Box 306, Luganville, Espiritu Santo, Vanuatu. Phone: (678) 36705. Fax: (678) 36703
     Email: aore@vanuatu.com.vu
Bokissa Island Resort, P.O.Box 261, Luganville, Espiritu Santo, Vanuatu. Phone & fax: (678) 36855.
Deco Stop Lodge. Luganville, Espiritu Santo. Phone: (678) 36175. Fax: (678) 36101.
Santo Dive Tours, P.O.Box 233, Luganville, Espiritu Santo, Vanuatu. Phone and fax: (678) 36822.
     Email: apower@mail.vanuatu.com.vu
Aquamarine, P.O.Box 395, Luganville, Espiritu Santo, Vanuatu. Phone & fax: (678) 36196.
     Email: aquamrne@vanuatu.com.vu

GENERAL

New Steamship Consultants (World's Largest Dealer of Original Ocean Liner Memorabilia)
Post Office Box 30088, Mesa, Arizona 85275, USA. Telephone: (602) 924-4334; Fax: (602) 807-3624
Email: ships@pobox.com   Website: http://www.pobox.com/~ships

Visual Image Presentations
4321 Baltimore Avenue, Bladensburg, Maryland 20710-1036, USA. Fax: (301) 927 5013
For National Archives photographs.

Seaweed's Ships Histories. A private company. They were most useful.
P.O.Box 154, Sistersville, West Virginia 26175, USA. Fax: 0015 1 304 652 1557

Real War Photos
P.O.Box 728, Hammond, Indiana 46325, USA.
They have been a good source of photographs for many years.

Osterman API, publishers of *The American President Lines and its Forebears, 1848-1984.*
Contact Renee Lukaszek in the USA on fax: (419) 893 3696;
or Jean Louis Boglio, Marine Books, Queensland, Australia on ph (07) 5534 9349, fax (07) 5534 9949

Oceans Enterprises, publishers and distributors
303 Commercial Road, Yarram, Vic 3971, Australia. Phone (03) 5182 5105. Fax: (03) 5182 5823
email: oceans@netspace.net.au or peter@oceans.com.au   http://www.oceans.com.au
For a wide range of diving and marine books including this publication. Ask for their catalogue.

WEB SITES

Information relating to the *President Coolidge*, and Vanuatu may be found on the following web sites.
An entry of "vanuatu" using a search engine such as AltaVista will provide over 7700 links. Entering "espiritu santo" and "vanuatu" will give nearly a hundred links.

http://www.oceans.com.au/pc.html
    This is the web site for this book and links to other useful sites.
http://www.allan-power-santo.com
    Homesite of Allan Power's Santo Dive Tours - dive operator on Espiritu Santo
http://www.aquamarine-santo.com
    Homesite of Aquamarine, Ltd - dive operator on Espiritu Santo.
http://www.vanuatu.net.vu
    Vanuatu Online - a most useful site for a range of information.
http://members.home.net/scombs/vanuatu.html
    For a most informative and personal view on Vanuatu, the islands and the people.
http://www.sihope.com/~tipi/marine.html
    Memoirs of a marine on *President Jackson*, William T. Paull. An excellent site.

PHOTO CREDITS

Page

3	Dollar. SF, rd, #P77-007.0015	54	Dry dock. NARA 80-G-314220.
6	Petersen. SFMNHP, apl, #P96-007 B47, F2	56t	Airstrip. RDc.
9	Docks. NARA, #80 G 410012	56b	Airstrip. RDc. Also NARA # 339-AO-124-23.
12	Hoover. SF, cb, # P82-019a.1317	57t	Airstrip. RDc. Also NARA 80-G-224013
18	Launching. SF,apl, # HDC 279, APL Subgroup III, Series 7, Folder 18, #44.	57b	Flying boat. RDc
		59	Santo road. PSc, rwp.
22	Launching party. SF, apl, # HDC 279, APL Subgroup III, Series 7, Folder 18, #30.	60t	Santo road. PSc, rwp.
		60b	Santo tents. RDc.
23	PC. UBL, nn. #1045.	63.	Bob Hope. RDc.
26	PC. RDc.	64.	Artie Shaw. RDc.
27	PC. PSc.	67	Catalina. RDc.
28	PC. RDc.	71	Gamble. PSc, sw.
32	Bathers. SF, apl. # P96-007, B47, F3	75	Tucker. NARA, #80-G-465928.
34	PC library. RDc.	77	Tucker aerial. RDc.
35	PC lounge. RDc.	79	Tucker uw. PSp.
37	PC dining room. SF, atp, apl, # P96-007, B3, F1.	80	Tucker uw. PSp.
		81	Tucker uw. PSp.
39	PC childrens. SF, apl, #P96-007, B47, F2.	95	PC sink. RDc.
40	PC engine. SF, apl, #p96-007, B47, F5.	90	Sterett. PSc, rwp.
43	PC bed. RDc.	96tl	PC sink bow. RDc.
49t	Aerial. RDc.	96tr	PC sink. RDc.
49b	Aerial. PSc.	96bl	PC sink. RDc.
51	Aerial. NARA. #339-AO-124-16.	96br	PC sink. RDc.
52	Aerial. RDc.	99	PC men. PSc, rwp. Also US Navy N-24502B; and NARA 80-G-35927.
53.	Docks. RDc.		

100   PC sink. NARA 80-G-36983.
103   Ross. San Francisco Call-Bulletin, nd.
104t Euart. RDc
104b PC sink. PSc. Also NARA 80-G-36957.
106   PC sink. PSc. Also NARA 80-G-35929.
107   PC sink. PSc. Also NARA 80-G-37000.
109   PC from air. Photo bu unknown navigator of
      B-17 bomber. Courtesy of Robert Moshimer.
110   PC sink. RDc.
111   PC sink. PSc.
113   PC sink. PSc.
115   PC sink. PSc. Also NARA 80-G-36973.
116t PC sink. NARA 80-G-35925.
116b PC sink. NARA 80-G-36869.
117t PC sink. PSc, rwp MM-24501.
117b PC sink. PSc. Also NARA 80-G-36958.
118t PC sink. PSc. Also NARA 80-G-36974.
118b PC sink. PSc.
119t PC sink stern. PSc.
      NARA 80-G-36870 is similar.
119b PC sink stern. PSc.
120t PC sink. PSc.
120b PC sink. PSc. Also NARA 80-G-36884.
121t PC sink. PSc. Also NARA 80-G-36881.
121b PC sink. NARA 80-G-37010.
122   PC shore. NARA 80-G-35930.
125   Oil soaked. PSc.
132   Nelson. SF, apl, atp, #P96-007.
142   Segond Channel. PSc.
144   PC sitee. PSc. Also NARA 339-AO-124-9.
145   Million Dollar Point. PSp.
146   Discombe. PSp.
148   Bulldozer uw. PSp.
149   Ship uw. PSp.
151   Steering wheel. PSp.
157   Bell. PSp.
159   Barry May. PSp.
163   PC props. RDc.
166   Chamber. Courtesy Ian Perrott.
168   Tui Tuwate. Courtesy Ian Perrott.
169   PC site. Courtesy Ian Perrott.
170   Diver. Courtesy Ian Perrott.

171   Valve. Courtesy Ian Perrott.
173   Arcadia. Courtesy Ian Perrott.
176   Divers on shore. PSp.
177   PC bow uw. PSp.
181   PC uw Power with gun. PSp.
182   PC uw. Prom-deck. Allan Power photo.
183   PC uw, The Lady. PSp.
184   PC smoking rm. APLA.
185   PC uw The Lady. PSp.
185   PC uw, fireplace. PSp.
186   PC uw, lantern. PSp.
187   PC uw, toilets. PSp.
189   PC uw, mast. PSp
190   PC uw, shark cage. PSp.
192   Alan Power. PSp.
194   PC uw, rifle. PSp.
195   PC uw, anchor. PSp.
202   PC sink. PSc. Also NARA 80-G-36984.
203   PC sink. PSc. Also NARA 80-G-36950.
205   PC uw, helmets. PSp.
207t PC uw, fountain. PSp.
207b PC stairwell. APc.
208   PC uw, jeep. PSp.
211t PC uw, controls. PSp.
211b PC control room. SF, apl, atp, # 96-007,
      B47, F45.
212   PC uw electric board. PSp.
215   PC gun on stern. PSc.
217   Luganville. PSp.
218   Jimmy Stevens. PSp.
219   Vanafo. PSp.
221   Blue Holes. PSp.
222   Fighter One. PSp.
223   Champagne Beach. PSp.
224   Euart's Memorial. PSp.
225   Bomber Three. PSp.
226   Quonset huts.PSp.
228   Parisi. Courtesy Stephen Parisi.
229   Corsair. RDc.
231   Catalina. Courtesy Ken MacGowan.
232   Catalina. Courtesy Ken MacGowan.

Colour Section.
Photographs numbered sequentially.
#s 1-6, *President Coolidge*. Courtesy APLA.   #s 7-16, Peter Stone.

Front Cover.
The Lady. Drawing courtesy Shirts North, Cairns, Australia. Artist: Angela Stark.
PC abandon ship. NARA 80-G-36966

Endpapers.
Front. *President Coolidge*. Courtesy APLA.
Back. PC abandon ship. PSc. NARA.

Chapter Headings drawing. Clarrie Lawler.

Maps, deck plans, diagrams. Peter Stone

Author & Allan Power. Photo Jan Stone. PSc.

INDEX

Peter Stone (left) with Allan Power on the author's first dive on the *President Coolidge* in 1982. Peter Stone is a writer, photographer, publisher and book dealer with an interest in the sea, Pacific war history, local history, genetics and human behaviour. His articles and photographs have been featured in many general, travel, sporting, marine and airline magazines, and he has contributed with text and photographs to a number of travel and sporting books. He has been a scuba diver for over twenty-five years and has travelled the Pacific in his role as a photo/journalist, and as co-proprietor of a travel agency specialising in adventure travel holidays. He has dived the *President Coolidge* on many occasions since 1982, and when the ship went down in October 1942 was no more than a glint in his father's eye. Published books include the acclaimed *Hostages to Freedom - The Fall of Rabaul, Dive Australia, Rabaul's Forgotten Fleet* (co-authored with Monica Foster), *Australia's Island Shipwrecks* (with Jack Loney), *High and Dry* (with Jack Loney), *Diving Guide to Australia: Southeast Coast & Tasmania,* and *Splendid Isolation - A History of the Yarram and District Health Service.* In 1990 the author moved from Melbourne with the intention of settling in Queensland but only made it as far as Yarram, 290 kilometres east of Melbourne in the rich dairying country of Gippsland. Here he resides in one of the town's historic 19th century buildings which he is gradually restoring, when time permits, with wife Wendy. He drives a very old car, takes little interest in sartorial elegance, loves his daughter, wife and boxer-kelpie cross, the affable Gracie, misses his bull terrier Baxter, enjoys country life and the people, and gets involved in local community matters as a proud member of Rotary, and as an occasionally outspoken individual.